Collected Columns

Michael Frayn was born in London in 1933 and began his writing career as a journalist. He quickly established himself as one of the funniest writers of his generation with columns which appeared in the *Guardian* and the *Observer* throughout the 1960s. His novels include *Towards the End of the Morning*, *The Trick of It*, *A Landing on the Sun*, *Headlong*, which was shortlisted for the 1999 Booker Prize, and *Spies*, which won the Whitbread Novel Prize in 2002. His fifteen plays range from *Noises Off* to *Copenhagen*, and most recently *Democracy*. His most recent book, *The Human Touch*, was published in 2006.

D1290662

Michael Frayn

Collected Columns

Methuen

Published by Methuen 2007

2

This collection first published in 2007 by
Methuen Publishing Ltd
8 Artillery Row,
London SW1P 1RZ

www.methuen.co.uk

A CIP catalogue record for this book
is available from the British Library

ISBN 9 780 413 77648 8

Typeset by MATS, Southend-on-Sea, Essex
Printed and bound in Great Britain by
Creative Print and Design Wales, Blaina

Author's note

Most of the pieces in this book originally appeared in a newspaper column I used to write, first three times a week in the *Guardian*, from 1959 until 1962, and then once a week, from 1962 to 1968, in the *Observer*. Although I've entitled them 'collected' they are in fact a rather discreet selection from the 636 columns I originally wrote (359 for the *Guardian*, 277 for the *Observer*). I have added a further 32 that I wrote for the *Guardian* much later, in 1994, together with another four pieces of varied provenance. They have all appeared in book form before, in various permutations under various titles, and selections of them have also been recorded, by Martin Jarvis, and broadcast. My thanks, once again to the editors of the publications concerned for permission to reprint. This is the first time, though, that they have been assembled in a single volume. They are arranged in alphabetical order because ... because I couldn't think of any more rational system.

Michael Frayn

Contents

Welcome aboard!

Hi! My name's Mike, and I'm your author today. Welcome aboard, and thank you for choosing to read me. It's a pleasure for me to write for you, and I shall be doing my best to make your trip with this article a happy one.

I have twenty paragraphs of in-article entertainment for you today, and I shall be starting the service of meaningful sentences just as soon as I've finished with all these introductory announcements. Thank you.

We've a slight delay, I'm afraid, in getting Paragraph 1 under way. This is because we missed our place in the queue at the beginning of the article, due to essential announcements. I'm now expecting Paragraph 1 to run immediately after Paragraph 6. I apologise to readers for any inconvenience this may cause. Please bear with me. Thank you.

Just to keep you up to date: Paragraph 5 has been cancelled, due to the non-arrival of Paragraph 4. Rest assured that I'm doing everything in my power to rectify the situation. Thank you.

No, hold on. That *was* Paragraph 4. With any luck we should be getting away round about Paragraph 7. We shall be routing through Paragraph 8, with onward connections to Paragraphs 9 to 24, just as soon as we've found Paragraph 6.

In the meantime you might like to have advance warning of delays between Paragraphs 14 and 19, due to major grammatical works which are expected to last until the summer of 1997.

This is a call for readers of delayed Paragraph 6. This paragraph is not now expected to depart until after Paragraph 18.

Still waiting for clearance on Paragraph 7. I think we all need a bit of a break here, so I'm going to come round serving free asterisks.

* * *

I know how frustrating all these delays and cancellations are, but bear with me. What I'm trying to do is to bring Paragraph 9 forward, and see if we can make a start with that. There are an awful lot of words here that have got to be organised into paragraphs, and an awful lot of paragraphs all trying to go somewhere. They can't all get there at once! So bear with me. Thank you.

This is a staff announcement. Will whoever has the words for Paragraph 9 please go to Paragraph 8 immediately.

Just to keep you in the picture: Paragraph 10 has been withdrawn after complaints by religious leaders. Last-minute talks are going on between management and staff to save Paragraph 11. Paragraph 12 is covered by the thirty-year rule. Paragraph 13 has failed to meet the standards laid down by the European Commission.

Still having trouble with Paragraph 9, I'm afraid. I've been badly let down by my suppliers. Bear with me. Please accept another round of complimentary asterisks.

* * *

Right, Paragraph 9! Here it is at last, and this is what it says: 'Paragraph 27 . . .' What? I don't believe this! They've given me the wrong paragraph! Bear with me just a little longer, will you?

Will readers of delayed Paragraph 6 please go immediately to Paragraph 13, and extinguish all hope, ready for immediate disappointment.

Yes, I know you've been waiting a long time! You think *I'm* enjoying this? Look, I'm on my own here – I've no staff!

I'm trying to write this entire article single-handed! All right? Just bear with me, will you!

Correction to my previous announcement: Paragraph 3 *is* running. Paragraph 3 has come in! I've got Paragraph 3 right here! Anyone here still waiting for Paragraph 3 . . . ? No? No one interested in Paragraph 3 . . . ? Is there any wonder I can't get staff? Is it surprising that morale in the industry is so low?

Look, I've had cutbacks, just like everybody else! I've no paper to write on! I'm struggling with a lot of obsolete equipment! Sitting on a broken chair – writing at a desk with three legs . . . !

Hold on . . . Right – we're ready to go at long last!

I've now used up my maximum permitted space, however, so I shall be leaving you at this point. It only remains for me to say thank you for bearing with me today. I hope that next time you're bearing with anyone, you'll bear with me.

(1989)

Almost too utterly common entrance

'A most unusual seminar,' says the heading on an advertisement which has been appearing in undergraduate magazines recently. The advertisement is issued by a firm who describe themselves as 'the most brilliant of all the advertising agencies,' looking for 'the most brilliant of all this year's graduands.'

'They propose to invite up to twenty of you,' it continues, 'after a long interrogation in London, to spend a weekend with them during the Easter vacation. The hospitality at this weekend will be almost vulgarly profuse. Continual distraction will be offered. But there will also be one written paper of the most taxing kind. It will need great stamina to endure it all.'

It certainly will if this is anything like the weekend which Harris-Harris, the brighter than brightest agency, hold each year at Wosby Hall, the ancestral home of the Selection-Board family. Here the daiquiris flow like water, served by top models in fishnet stockings, while fashionable dance bands play softly among the Picassos.

'The ambience here,' says Garth Peacock, one of the agency men assigned to the job, waving an odoriferous Balkan cigarette at the time-hallowed setting, 'is almost, *comment dit-on*, vulgarly profuse, don't you think?'

'Er, yes,' mumbles R. Slodge, former President of the Oxford Union. Garth Peacock presses a tiny pocket transmitter key which registers at headquarters the damning comment *'This man considers himself superior to popular cultural values.'*

'Have another cigar, Nubbs,' says Peacock to the former Cambridge stroke. 'Er, no thanks,' replies Nubbs, and Peacock signals ruthlessly *'Deficient in phallic motivation'.*

Nubbs passes the solid gold humidor on to Cropper, once editor of the *Isis*, but Cropper, who has smoked five cigars already, shakes his head queasily. Peacock adds another comment to the Nubbs report: *'Complete failure to persuade in face of difficult market conditions.'*

'I hope,' says Peacock, 'you're not all finding the weekend too utterly boring?'

'Not me,' replies Potkin, the noted Oxford actor, gesturing for another bottle of champagne. 'Can't soak the stuff up fast enough.' (*'A certain lack of moral fibre'*, signals Peacock.)

'Oh, far from it,' adds Mark Smoothe, undergraduate son of the Minister of Chance and Speculation, also ordering another bottle. 'I think the amenities we are enjoying here are a fitting background to the sort of seminar which, today more than ever, plays an absolutely vital part in the progressive development of the free world.' (*'A brilliant creative mind'*, transmits Peacock.)

'Where's the lavatory?' demands Cropper urgently. (*'A poor ability to choose language that brings out the most attractive aspects of a subject'*, notes Peacock.)

By the time Cropper has hacked his way back through the almost vulgarly deep pile of the carpet, bowing footmen have ushered the whole party on to the luxuriously appointed assault course, where Roscoe is waiting to put them through an almost disgustingly elegant initiative test.

'What we should like you to do,' he explains, 'if it's not too almost utterly tedious, is to imagine that this ditch is full of synthetic raspberry jam. You have to get the synthetic raspberry jam over this wall of consumer resistance without touching the real raspberry jam made by the same firm. To do it you've got nothing but four feet of tarred twine, two empty oil drums, one model in black lace underwear, and £100,000 . . .'

When the fleet of Rolls-Royces takes them back to the almost sickeningly exquisite house, they face the most testing moment of all. One by one they are shown into the presence of J. B., the head of the agency himself, as he sits in the Sheraton Room surrounded by Cellini champagne-coolers and Fabergé foot-warmers.

'Sit down, Mr Nubbs,' he murmurs in an almost insupportably aristocratic tone. 'Tell me, Mr Nubbs, do you believe in God?'

'Er, well, I, er . . .'

'Of course you do. Take a cigar and then sell me the idea in fifty punchy, easy-to-read words.'

Yes, it certainly demands stamina. And remember, stamina demands Fub, for only new wonder Fub has magic Zub!

(1962)

Among the funny bones

The evolution of man has not ceased. By the inscrutable processes of natural selection there is evolving from *homo sapiens* a new and more complex species of anthropoid: *homo jocans*, or Joky Man.

Homo sapiens has been defined as a tool-making animal. *Homo jocans* is a gag-making machine. Just as *homo sapiens* became ashamed of his urge to copulate and sublimated it into a culture of solid complexity, so Joky Man has become ashamed of his urge to communicate and is sublimating it into a culture of elaborate facetiousness.

I think Joky Man will prove to be the dominant form. Pre-Joky Man will be made to feel smaller and smaller by Joky Man for failing to see the joke, until he becomes entirely extinct. By the end of the Uranium Age, Joky Man will cover the whole of the Western Hemisphere. The archaeologists will find his tumuli everywhere, and the remains of Joky Man inside will be instantly identifiable; the skulls will all be trying to keep a straight face.

Our literature does not do justice to the subtlety of our culture. In books people say what they mean, in the *sapiens* style. ('Don't you see, Lisbet, that my feeling for Paul is only a desperate counterpoise to Mark's instinctive rejection of Anna?') In life Joky Man speaks almost entirely in irony, sarcasm, understatement, hyperbole, and parody, and I am going to have a fresco painted inside my tomb that will bring home to archaeologists something of the staggering intricacy of life in Joky times.

It will show Joky Man at work, sitting for hours rubbing gag against gag in the hope of producing a spark. It will show Joky Man at leisure, still chipping one gag against another. A frieze round the margin will display the huge variety of gags a man might have at his disposal – cutting gags, gags that grind the nerves, gags that scrape the bottom of the barrel, gags for falling in love, gags for ending marriages, gags for dying – as well as how a man of small resources might make one or two durable basic gags do for everything.

A further series of panels will show Joky Man speaking in funny voices – joke adenoidal voices, joke television commentator's voices, joke Prime Minister voices, joke Queen voices.

In one of them he will be seen speaking in what he takes to be a joke working-class voice, to show his rejection of bourgeois values and his solidarity with the masses. The panel will include a representative selection of the masses, showing their touching gratitude for this compliment by talking in what they take to be a joke Joky Man's voice.

In a big tableau, Joky Man will be shown speaking in his most important funny voice – what he conceives to be the voice of a low-class theatrical agent. A frieze running round the edge of this scene will make it clear that since he has never actually met a low-class theatrical agent, but only a man whose elder brother's friend does a very amusing imitation of Peter Sellers impersonating Sidney James playing the part of a low-class theatrical agent, this causes no offence to low-class theatrical agents.

The funny-voice series will be surmounted by a tablet depicting Joky Man's larynx, showing typical enlargement and inflammation caused by the strain of speaking with all the voices of men and of angels except one's own. Elsewhere in the fresco there will be scenes from Joky Man's everyday life, with balloons coming out of his mouth reading 'Don't call us, we'll call you,' 'What we in the trwade call a nice bit of crwumpet,' 'How very different from the home life of our own dear Queen!' 'And now – a big hand for someone we all know and love,' 'My husband and I . . .', 'What we in the trwade call one of our own dear queens,' 'Don't call us, my husband and I will call you . . .'

One whole wall of the tomb will be occupied by a scene representing the spiritual core of Joky Man's life. On one half of the wall – Joky Man appearing on television, saying satirical things in his theatrical agent voice, his Prime Minister voice, and his commentator voice. On the other half of wall – joky Man watching the television, mimicking the performers and maintaining a stream of witty observations about them in no less funny voices. The balloons will make it clear that it is the less joky specimens of Joky Man who appear on the screen, and the more joky specimens who watch. Or that at any rate the ones who appear never seem to manage to answer any of those devasting sallies back.

In one corner of the tomb there will be a small picture illustrating a rather sad aspect of Joky Man's life. It will show him trying to say something straight, in his own voice. He is red in the face and glassy-eyed with the effort, but, as the archaeologists will see, the balloon that is emerging from his mouth is completely empty. In the last picture Joky Man is being carried off, deceased from an excess of humours. As the headstone movingly records:

'Here lies what we in the trwade call dead funny.'

(1963)

And Home's son's father is
Hume's father's son

What a dynamic start! In the first six days of his ministry Sir Alec Douglas-Home has got rid of an earldom, three lordships, and two baronies; and the new Chancellor of the Duchy of Lancaster and the New Minister of State at the Board of Trade have acquired a viscountcy and a barony respectively.

Meanwhile, at the Conservative Central Office Lord Spoon is trying to drop the Barony of Spoon and pick up the Barony of Bosworth, to complete a set of 'Battle' class titles he is collecting. 'If I can send in the full set, together with the backs of three old Burke's "Peerages", I shall win an electric blanket,' he told a Press conference late last night.

This vigorous programme cannot, of course, be carried through without some hard rethinking of fundamentals.

At the request of the Garter King-of-Arms, according to the *Daily Telegraph,* the Queen's advisers have been 'urgently' considering the question of style and precedence of the former Lord Home's family. A spokesman for the College of Arms told the *Telegraph*: 'The question is, for the purpose of precedence, whether the children of peers who have disclaimed are still children of peers.'

How the College of Arms faced the problem I don't know, but its rather more venerable rival, the College of Arms and Legges (the name is a corruption of *armorum leges,* the laws of arms), responded with great promptitude. As soon as the urgency and gravity of the question was fully understood, an emergency meeting was called. Members of the College were rushed to London with police escorts, and a jet airliner was specially diverted to bring the Dexter Lord of Legges back from Southern Rhodesia, where he was inspecting pre-war baronetcies for signs of wear.

'Gentlemen,' said the Dexter Lord of Legges, 'the

question is this: Are the children of disclaiming peers still children of peers; and, if not, whose children are they? Would you like to kick off, Rouge Garter Extraordinary?'

Rouge Garter Extraordinary: Well, let's put this question another way. Can commoners whose children are peers' children be in any meaningful sense fathers?

Morte Puissance: *Ex nihilo nihil fit.* Vide Tollemache v. Tollemache on the strong presumption of non-paternity in the case of an ox that was cited as putative sire of a pig.

Swart Beast: Could not the difficulty be very easily surmounted by requiring peers renouncing their peerages to disclaim the paternity of their children?

Twicester Herald: Then the wife could apply to the courts for a paternity order made out in the name of the extinguished title.

Rouge Garter Extraordinary: The important thing is that these unfortunate children should not be take away from their homes and put in orphanages unnecessarily.

Morte Puissance: What we must establish here and now, surely, is whether the son of Lord Home (as he then was) is Lord Dunglass (as he now is) or Mr Douglas-Home junior (as he may well be).

Vray Halidom: Or indeed whether *either* of them is the son of Sir Alec Douglas-Home, or the Earl of Home, or Lord Home, or Lord Hume of Berwick, or Baron Hume of Berwick, or Lord Dunglass, or Baron Douglas of Douglas. As he then was. Or as they then were.

Dexter Lord of Legges: Douglas spelt 'Douglas' of Douglas spelt 'Douglas'?

Vray Halidom: Precisely so, Legges.

Dexter Lord of Legges: Dashed funny way for a fellow to spell his name.

Swart Beast: Anyway, the permutations are endless.

Rouge Garter Extraordinary: There must be some way of telling. There must be some birthmark or other one of them could produce.

Dexter Lord of Legges: What we must ensure above all is that this unhappy young man is not deprived of someone to call 'Father.' Or 'Lord Father,' or 'Lord Father of Father,' or 'Baron Father of Berwick,' as the case may be.

Twicester Herald: But my dear Legges, surely Sir Alec (as he now is) could register the titles as a public company – Home, Home, Hume, Hume Douglas and Dunglass Ltd. – and appoint himself and his son co-directors of it?

Morte Puissance: Would it not be an equally satisfactory solution if the young man's name was spelt 'Mr Douglas-Home' and pronounced 'Lord Dunglass'?

Rouge Garter Extraordinary: How about a new title altogether? After all, we must move with the times. I suggest 'Lord Dunglass-Home.'

Vray Halidom: I like the note of freshness it strikes. And it's obviously an immensely practical little title for running around in. But – well, frankly, it doesn't *speak* to me.

Dexter of Legges: Beast?

Swart Beast: Well, for my money I don't think you can beat 'Lord Douglas-Dunglass.' There's a tremendously rugged integrity about that title. It's a valid response – a nexus of creative outgoingness – what I might call an essentially dynamic act of awareness. Also the hyphen takes out for cleaning.

Morte Puissance: I'm prepared to go some way with Beast. But when it comes to sheer, solid craftsmanship, give me a good old-fashioned title like 'Lord Douglas, or, As You Like It.'

Rouge Garter Extraordinary: Preferably pronounced 'Lord Dunglass, or, What You Will.'

Vray Halidom: Well, I think, you'd have to go a long way to beat Lord Home Number Fifteen, in B Flat Minor.

Swart Beast: Or the sheer sensual awareness of 'The Rokeby Douglas.'

Morte Puissance: May I put in a word for 'On Hearing the First Dunglass of Spring?'

Dexter Lord of Legges: Well, there we were, then. The team can't make up its mind whether former peers' children are peers' children or not. But we're all agreed that a rose by any other name smells just like a rose, a ruse, a rouglas, or a runglass, as the case may be.

(1963)

Another little job for the cleaners

We're not asking for much (*said Miss Modula MacPlastic, secretary of the 'Clean Up the Bible' campaign*). We simply want the ecclesiastical authorities to agree that an advisory body composed of ordinary young agnostics-in-the-street like myself should have some say in the planning of new scriptures, so that we can help them to avoid giving unnecessary offence.

Believe me, we have solid backing from the ordinary mass of decent young people in this country, such as the Bishop of Twicester, who writes: 'I am absolutely horrified and disgusted to discover exactly how much unnecessary and gratuitous sex does go on in the Bible.'

It's not even as if readings from the Bible could be confined to Religious Knowledge classes in school. Extracts are deliberately and knowingly read out at church services when there is a strong likelihood that impressionable adults are present. Copies of the Bible are sold openly in back street bookshops, with nothing to prevent highly suggestible men and women of 50 and even 60 from buying them.

One can only shudder at the effect it must have on them. I know of one case where an ordinary middle-aged man read Leviticus, and next year went out and committed a serious traffic offence. I am absolutely certain that if research were done among middle-aged people convicted of crimes of violence it would be found that a very high proportion of them had at one time or another in their lives been exposed to the influence of the Bible.

As soon as our advisory council started reading the book we came across scenes involving nudity in the first few pages. We protested about these to the Archbishop of Canterbury, but he refused to see us. Since then we have come across descriptions of every possible form of sex, including homosexuality, bestiality, incest, and self-abuse. On each occasion we have tried to take them up with the ecclesiastical authorities. But each time the result has been the same; the little men in the Church did not have the courage to meet us and listen to the voice of decency.

Some people try to argue that this continual harping upon sex is not corrupting. What rubbish! Our whole sexual ethos has been affected by the Old Testament: if Sodom and Onan had never been mentioned, for example, should we ever have heard of sodomy or onanism?

One cannot but be sickened, too, by the endless violence. With monotonous regularity the characters smite and are smitten, slay and are slain. In one particularly unsavoury incident, a woman is turned into a pillar of salt. Whole cities are wiped out. Violence is made to seem a commonplace part of life.

And scarcely a page goes by without some mention of sin. Sin, sin, sin – it's dragged in obsessively. Anybody reading the Bible naturally gets the idea that an obsession with sin is a smart thing to have. Is it a coincidence that the middle-aged generation has got sin on the brain? Or is there nothing less than a gigantic conspiracy at work all over the world to make us sin-conscious?

Some silly people argue that writers must have 'freedom' to express themselves. But could anyone honestly maintain that disgusting incidents such as the mass rape of the concubine by the Gibeonites are artistically necessary? Great storytellers like Agatha Christie and Denise Robins are able to entertain and delight a middle-aged audience without descending to such cheap forms of titillation. Are the faceless men behind the Old Testament frightened of being beaten in the bestseller lists?

We shall be asking our members to monitor the lessons read in their local churches, and to complete a questionnaire about what they heard. One of the questions will be 'Was womanhood respected, or was it degraded?' I think it's pretty plain what the answer will be for episodes like the presentation of the concubine to the Gibeonites, or the one in which Lot offers his daughters to the Sodomites.

Another of the questions will be 'Was authority represented as something worthy of respect, or as something to be feared and hated?' It seems to be the fashion in many parts of the Bible to make people sneer at divine authority by showing it always as capricious, cruel and unjust. A particularly horrifying instance of this is the episode at Nachon's threshing floor, when David is bringing back the Ark of the Covenant on an ox-cart. The Ark wobbles, and one of the cart-drivers, Uzzah, puts out his hand to steady it – whereupon God instantly strikes him dead.

We pointed out to the ecclesiastical authorities that this could only encourage lorry-drivers to break the law regarding the proper securing of loads, and we suggested that the text should be amended to show Uzzah receiving some small award for his contribution to road safety. Again, our views were not taken into account.

We feel that in general the Bible concentrates far too much on the sordid side of life. Plagues, famines, oppression – all right, we know they happen, but is it really necessary to dwell upon them so insistently? The picture of life that is presented in the Bible is simply not typical of this country today. The great majority of middle-aged people in Britain are not bearded, unkempt tribesmen who go round living with concubines and strumming psalms on the harp. They're soberly-dressed men and women living in decent two- and three-bedroomed houses, who believe in

proper sanitation and life insurance. They should be represented as such in their religious literature.

Honestly, we're not asking for much. Just that the
scriptures shouldn't fall too far below the ordinary standards of decency maintained in public life by bodies such as
the BBC.

(1965)

At bay in Gear Street

It's been hardly possible to get up and down Carnaby
Street recently for the great crush of American journalists
observing the swinging London scene. I was practically
knocked down by a stampede of perspiring correspondents
as I stepped out of Galt's toyshop the other day holding a
doll I'd bought for the children.

'Holy heaven, it's Actor Terry Stamp, 26, in mini-wig and
PVC spectacles!' screamed the reporter from *Time* magazine. 'And he's squiring diminutive dolly Cathy McGowan,
22, in an eight-inches-above-the-knee, Campari-red skirt-
let, spectre-pale make-up, and kinky wobble-as-you-walk
celluloid eyelids! I love you, Terry!'

'Are you crazy?' shouted the representative of *Status*
magazine. 'That's Jean Shrimpton in a trouser-suit, carrying Vidal Sassoon in newly groovy Now-We-Are-Six gear!
Swinging, Shrimp, swinging!'

'No, listen!' cried the *Esquire* man, reading the label
round the dolly's neck. 'This is some new couple altogether
called Non Toxic and Fully Washable! Hey, these are two
totally unknown faces making the scene, boys!'

At this they all came crowding round, gazing at me and
the doll as if they were going to eat us.

'Look at his trousers!' breathed the *Chicago Tribune*.
'Two and a half inches above the shoe!'

'Two and three-quarter inches,' said Associated Press, getting down on his hands and knees with a pocket rule.

'But only on the right leg!' pointed out NBC excitedly. 'The left trouser leg's practically trailing on the ground! Boys, this is the newest thing since yesterday, if not this morning!'

'And how about this – bags under the knees!' cried the *Daily News*. 'Zowie! Back in New York they're still wearing their bags under the eyes! I tell you, these kids'll drive us into the sea!'

'Central button of jacket hanging on three-inch thread!' noted someone else.

'Two inches of shirt-tail worn outside bellyband of trousers!'

Well, they all started shouting questions and trying to photograph me up the leg of my trousers. I gazed at them, stupefied.

'The guy can't understand,' cried the *Wall Street Journal*. 'Where the hell's the interpreter? Where's Jonathan Miller?'

'Leave it to me!' shouted *Time* magazine. 'I know these people's patois.'

He turned to me and the doll.

'Greetings, British bird and British Beatle!' he said very slowly, waving his hands about. 'You – with it, yes? You – making scene, no?'

'*I'm* not making a scene,' I replied nervously. 'I was just suddenly set on by all you lot.'

'He says he's set-on,' reported *Time* magazine to the others. 'That's the now-now-now phrase for switched-on,'

'"Set" spelt S-E-T and "on" spelt O-N, Henry?' they asked him, writing it all carefully down.

'Hey, listen, boys! The dolly's saying something! What's she saying, Henry?'

'She's saying "Mama."'

'"Mama" spelt M-A-M-A, Henry?'

'Right. What she's trying to get across is that today she is able to lead a deeply fulfilled life, thanks to the ready availability of artificial eyelashes and the policy of successive British Governments in granting independence to the country's overseas possessions.'

They wrote it all down. I took advantage of the pause to explain that unfortunately I had to go.

'"Go", is short for "go, go, go," of course,' explained *Time* magazine. 'I think what he's trying to say is that in this swinging new meritocratic young Britain the handsome young son of a peer can breeze up to the chemmy tables and lose a cool four or five hundred thousand dollars in a night as easily and naturally as the humblest mill-girl in Bolton.'

'Where's he go-go-going to, Henry?' asked the *St Louis Post-Dispatch*. 'Annabel's? The Scotch?'

'British Beatle,' translated *Time* magazine to me, 'Where you make the scene along towards?'

I said I was on my way to Oxford Circus Tube Station. They all looked it up on the map of The Scene in *Time*.

'It's not marked, Henry!' they cried.

'Don't worry, fellers – I know all about it. It'll be on the next edition of the map.

'What is it, Henry – a boutique or a discotheque?'

'It's a Tube station, men – "Tube" meaning "groove", of course. It's a sort of groovotheque.'

'What kind of set does he meet down there, Henry? Gamine Leslie Caron, 34? Ace Photographer David Bailey, 27? Or daughter of former Ambassador to the US Lady Jane Ormsby-Gore, 23?'

I explained that the circle I moved in (though on the whole not in Oxford Circus Underground Station) consisted of Christopher and Lavinia Crumble, Horace and Doris Morris, and people like that. There were gasps of astonishment from the Press corps.

'Suffering saints!' they cried. 'This is clearly some inner scene not as yet made by US newsmen, which opens up entirely fresh dimensions of fabness, and brings within the reach of long-suffering mankind the hope of a whole gear universe of prime-quality grooviness!'

But just at that moment they saw Peter O'Toole coming by in bell-bottomed lederhosen and aluminium Boy Scout hat, and my fashionable career was over.

The dolly's been right off her food ever since.

(1966)

At the sign of the rupture belt

There's the shop with the rupture belt outside! (*said Nicolette*). Now we've driven halfway to Granny's, haven't we, Daddy?

Father: Halfway exactly.

Nicolette: I always remember we're halfway when we get to the shop with the rupture belt outside, don't I, Daddy?

Dominic: And I always remember we're three-quarters way when we get to Acme Motors, don't I, Daddy?

Mother: I wish you two would stop your silly pestering. I don't know why we bring you out in the car to Granny's.

Father: It's good for them to travel, Eileen. They see new things. They get something fresh to talk about.

Dominic: There's the factory with the rusty bike on the roof!

Nicolette: There's the advertisement for Viriloids Rejuvenating Pills!

Dominic: There's the Tigers!

Mother: The *what*?

Dominic: The Tigers! That's what we always call the Lyons there, don't we, Daddy?

Father: We certainly do, son. And there's the brewery where they brew the Adam's ale.

Nicolette: Daddy always says that now when we pass the Wemblemore waterworks, doesn't he, Dominic? He never used to, did he?

Father: What's this place on the right, children?

Dominic: I know! I know! It's the site for the new eye hospital.

Nicolette: Say your joke, Daddy, say your joke!

Father: It's a proper site for sore eyes.

Nicolette: Did you hear Daddy say his joke, Mummy?

Mother: Are we in Sudstow yet, John?

Dominic: Mummy, you *never* know where this is. You always ask Daddy if we're in Sudstow when we get to the site for sore eyes.

Father: Where are we then, Mr Knowall?

Dominic: We're just coming to the place where we saw the drunk men fighting –

Nicolette: – where Daddy always says: 'Can you imagine a more godforsaken hole than this?'

Dominic: And Mummy says she can't.

Father: We're just coming into Surley, Eileen.

Dominic: And you're not sure, are you, Daddy, but you think Wemblemore ends and Surley begins just after Wile-U-Wate Footwear Repairs, don't you?

Father: Look at it, Eileen. Scruffy people, cheapjack stores, rundown cinemas. I wonder how many pubs there are in this street alone?

Dominic: There are nine, Daddy.

Nicolette: We always count them for you.

Father: Can you imagine a more godforsaken hole?

Nicolette: Daddy said it, Dominic.

Dominic: Now say you can't, Mummy.

Mother: Oh, do stop pestering. Can't you think of some game to play as we go along?

Dominic: We *are* playing a game, Mummy. But you're not playing it properly.

Nicolette: You haven't said you can't imagine such a godforsaken hole, has she, Dominic?

Mother: Those children! They're enough to try the patience of a saint!

Father: There's Acme Motors, anyway – we're three-quarters of the way there now.

Dominic: *Daddy*! That's what *I* say! *I'm* the one who sees Acme Motors and says we're three-quarters of the way there!

Nicolette: Yes, Daddy, that's *Dominic's* thing to say!

Father: Well, I've said it now.

Nicolette: But that's not fair, Daddy! You say: 'I hope to God there's not going to be a holdup in Sudstow High Street.'

Dominic: You've *spoilt* it, Daddy, you've *spoilt* it! You've said my thing!

Nicolette: Now you've made Dominic cry.

Father: Calm down, Dominic. Be your age.

Dominic: How would you like it if I said your things? How would you like it if I said 'A site for sore eyes'?

Mother: Don't be disrespectful to your father, Dominic.

Dominic: I don't care! *A site for sore eyes! A site for sore eyes! A site for sore eyes!*

Mother: If you don't stop this instant, Dominic, I'm going to . . .

Nicolette: Daddy, Daddy! We've gone past Cook and Cook (Wholesale Tobacconists) and you haven't said your joke about spoiling the breath!

Father: Oh, dry up.

Mother: Now they're both howling. It's all your fault, John. They just copy you.

Father: That's what you always say.

Mother: And that's what you always say!

Father: Well, all I can say is, I hope to God there's not going to be a holdup in Sudstow High Street.

(1963)

The bar sinister

According to usually reliable gossip columns, considerable efforts are being made to clean up the Hotel Petersberg, outside Bonn, where the Queen will stay on her visit to Germany. Apparently they're taking down 'all the usual hotel signs, such as *bar* and *toilet*'.

Experts have long known about the suggestiveness of the word 'toilet', of course. Which of us, indeed, has not crept past the sign in some lewd five-star hotel, his eyes averted, a crimson blush mantling his cheek for very shame?

The obscene connotations of the word 'bar' for the moment elude me, I must admit. *Bar* . . . BAR . . . No, I don't quite get the full lascivious frisson. I see the objections to 'public bar', of course; the L might drop out of 'public' just as the Queen walked by. There's something vaguely indecent about 'saloon bar', too – I think it's the combination of the *sal* of 'salacious' with the *oon* of 'spittoon'.

I'm sure there's no need to mention what the 'private' parts of 'private bar' call to mind for a person of sensitivity. As for 'c-cktail bar', I'm astonished that it has ever been allowed, even in places where only commoners would see it. How many perfectly common folk must have staggered back in astonishment and disgust from the 'c-tktail bar' sign, only to find themselves among the tasteless liberties of the Off Licence?

I've just seen what's wrong with 'BAR'. Heh, heh, heh! Hnuh, hnuh, hnuh! Got it? No? Boys, there's a feller here who can't see anything dirty in the word 'BAR'! Shnuh, shnuh, shnuh!

No? All right, I'll take pity on your simplicity. Stand well back from the page. Close one eye, and screw up the other until everything begins to look fuzzy. Now, look at the word

'BAR'. Got it? The A and the R appear to change places, so that the word seems to read 'BRA'! If that's not an indecent announcement I don't know what is. Some member of the royal party, returning after a hard day's hand-shaking, screwing up their eyes in the sudden twinkle of lights behind the Campari bottles, might easily get it smack across their consciousness.

Did I say C-mpari bottles? Correction; all the alleged C-mpari bottles will have been hidden in the cellars. On display in the bar there'll be nothing but a lot of Bols. Sorry – a lot of B-ls is just what there won't be. I mean brandy. What? Brandy spelt b. randy? Curaçao and curaçao! They'll be shouting for large highballs next.

Now, wait a moment. You may think it doesn't matter all that much what the Queen sees or doesn't see. Do you know the story about the Labouchère Amendment, which first made male homosexual behaviour a criminal offence? According to the reforming journals I read, it was originally drafted to include female homosexuality as well. But when they showed it to Queen Victoria she objected on the grounds that female homosexuality was impossible, and since no one had the courage to enlighten her, the amendment became only half as brutal as had been intended.

Now had the Queen enjoyed a *really* pure upbringing, and not been allowed to catch glimpses of signs saying 'Public Conveniences' as she forayed forth among her people, she wouldn't have known that male homosexuality was on the cards, either, and the whole amendment would have been frustrated.

But back to the Hotel Petersberg. Did I tell you that the word 'service' is being deleted from the Queen's bill, in view of its connotation in the field of animal husbandry?

They're taking all the numbers off the doors, too. They started with the sixes, since 'six' in German is *sechs* (they're much more outspoken about these things on the Continent). Afterwards the Palace said they weren't too happy about *elf*, *zwölf*, or *zwanzig*, either. Just a feeling that there might be something a bit off-colour here if they'd known more German.

Then they admitted frankly that they weren't entirely easy in their minds about *fünf*, *acht* and *neun*. And then they thought, hell, in for a penny, in for a pound – why have naked figures prancing about the corridors at all? By the time the royal party arrives the whole hotel will be in a very decent state. All through the livelong night gentlemen will be stealing along the passages trying the anonymous doors, searching for the t--l-t, and bursting instead by mistake into the rooms of unchaperoned single ladies.

The unchaperoned single ladies, I trust, will scream in discreet tones about their h-n--r, and flee in their delectable diaphanous nightgowns to seek sanctuary in the M-n-g-r's Office. By a pardonable error in the circumstances, they will almost certainly rush headlong into the G-ntl-m-n's L-v-t-ry, where a merry party will be in occupation already, leaning their elbows on the wash-basins and knocking back glass after glass of water, shouting 'Set 'em up again, b-rm-n!' and selling each other potash concessions in Eastern Bohemia.

Meanwhile, sitting round the extraordinary vast green table with six pockets in what they erroneously take to be the R-st--r-nt, the royal party waits patiently for dinner to appear . . .

(1965)

The battle of the books

The literary quiz game on BBC2 'Take It or Leave It,' is driving me into the depressives' ward.

They read extracts from well-known books to a panel of four, some of them apparently ordinary people much like you and me, who try to identify the extracts and then discuss them. So far, since I've been watching, it's turned out that almost all the panel have read almost every book which has come up, not to mention all the author's other works as well.

But I haven't read a single one of them. Not a solitary book that's been mentioned on the programme since I've been watching have I read.

I sit in front of the darkened set long after the programme has finished, sunk into a melancholic trance, waiting for my wife to talk me back to a state of reason.

'You may not have read the books,' she says, 'but you guessed some of them. Or at any rate, you almost guessed some of them. Now that really *is* an achievement, almost guessing a book you haven't read.'

I groan faintly.

'That bit of Kafka that none of them knew – as soon as the word "Kafka" came up on the screen you shouted "Christ! I was going to say Capek! I got the right country!"'

'I shouted that, did I?'

'Certainly you did, I'm sure you'd have got a lot more right if you hadn't had to jump up and shout it out so hurriedly before the title came up on the screen.'

'What about the time I shouted "Charlotte Brontë" and it turned out to be Rider Haggard?'

'Everyone makes mistakes. But what about the time you shouted *1984* and it turned out to be *Brave New World*? That was very close.'

'I meant to shout "Brave New World," as a matter of fact.'

'So you kept shouting afterwards.'

'I got over-excited. Shouted the wrong word.'

'Exactly. You were terribly good. And even if you hadn't read any of the books, you'd read reviews of some of them.'

'Oh, I'd read *reviews* of some of them.'

'Anyway, there's reading and reading. I expect this lot just skim through books at great speed, without really taking them in at all. Now when you read you really *read*. You frown. You breathe hard. You take an extremely long time to get through a page.'

'Don't tell me.'

'It took you nine months to read *War and Peace*,'

'I was an old man by the time I'd finished.'

'And six months of travelling back and forth between London and Manchester, with sleepless nights on the sleeper and interminable hours waiting for delayed planes, to get through *Ulysses*. Now that's what I *call* reading.'

'Have I read *Ulysses*?'

'Certainly you have.'

'Ah. That's one that might well come up on the programme.'

'Exactly.'

'About a man in Dublin, is it? Kind of stream of consciousness?'

'That's right – with a green cover. That's what I mean. All that lot tore through *Ulysses* one wet games afternoon in the fourth form. But when you read a book it really gets right down into your subconscious like some infantile trauma. You can't remember a word of it.'

'That's true.'

'Anyway, you know all about all sorts of things they don't. You know about Wittgenstein, and – well – Wittgenstein . . .'

'Oh God, so do they!'

'That lot? Know about Wittgenstein? Don't make me laugh.'

'You really think they don't?'

'They don't know the first thing about him.'

'Seriously?'

'Seriously.'

'No, they know about Wittgenstein all right. You can't get away from it – I simply don't read enough books.'

'You've read at least four this year.'

'They were only paperback.'

'They were the paperbacks of the hardbacks everyone said were the best books of the year.'

'Yes – of the year before last.'

'You're only two years behind.'

'I'm slipping further back all the time. At this rate I won't be reading this year's books until 1970.'

'Why don't you miss out a year or two? Otherwise you're only going to be getting round to books just as everyone realises how bad they are after all. You know how that depresses you.'

'But what about the backlog from earlier years?'

'You mean Defoe and Smollett and Richardson?'

'Exactly.'

'And Johnson's Lives of the Poets, and Boswell's Life of Johnson and Carlyle's essay on Boswell, and Froude's Life of Carlyle . . . ?'

'That's enough. Don't run on about it.'

'Couldn't you skip, like everybody else?'

'Skip? Me? With my completion neurosis?'

'Well, couldn't you possibly start reading now, instead of just talking about it?'

'What? With my depression syndrome?'

'Oh well, never mind. One of these days they'll do a book you've read.'

(1964)

Black whimsy

The Fabulous
£EARN-TO-RITE
Postal Course
£earn now, then earn £s!

Lesson 7 – £EARN-TO-RITE
BLACK COMEDY!

So-called 'black' comedy is much in demand these days, and anyone who has the knowhow to provide the right sort of goods has a first-rate chance of hitting the jackpot. Of course, as any seasoned writer will tell you, there's nothing new under the sun. For many, many years now West End comedies have touched humorously upon such subjects as death, senility, insanity, prostitution, and sexual assault. But in the old days plays of this sort were known as 'saucy comedies,' 'whimsical comedies,' and 'comedy-thrillers.' To serve these subjects up in their modern guise as 'black' comedy a few simple rules must be learned.

But first – a word of warning. We are on dangerous ground here. One wrong step, and we shall find ourselves guilty of the sort of tasteless work which could appeal only to a perverted sense of humour, and which could be put on only at private theatre clubs of the less desirable sort.

Be daring, yes. Be shocking, by all means. But never, never, never be disgusting. The line is a fine one. Your job is to get as close to it as you can, without once crossing it. Be naughty – but don't be nasty!

Remember what we learnt in Lesson 4, £EARN-TO-RITE COLOUR NUDIES!, and Lesson 5, £EARN-TO-RITE GOLDEN-HEARTED WHORE PLAYS! The audience are paying to be teased, not to be shown anything indecent, or to be read a lecture on the sociology of prostitution. Remember, teasing demands a £IGHT TOUCH!

All right? All right, then. The key to black comedy is our old friend

PARADOX!

Remember PARADOX? We came across it in Lesson 3, £EARN-TO-RITE A SHAFTESBURY AVENUE PLAY! We decided that once you'd got the knack, there was no easier way of filling three acts than a generous supply of paradoxes. We used them in comedies ('You can't imagine how hard it is to be a woman of easy virtue!' 'Oh, this life will be the death of me!'). We used them in Shaftesbury Avenue serious plays (*Paul*: But don't you see! Only by living in the world can we withdraw from the world! Only by rising above ourselves can we truly be ourselves! Only by stating the self-evidently false can we tell the truth! *Leonie*: Oh, Paul, we belong to each other, utterly! Now I shall go and tell Xavier I will marry him).

But in modern black comedy verbal paradox is unfortunately more or less ruled out. Among the lower and lower-middle classes, where black comedy takes place, people do not, alas, have the education to talk in paradoxes. Instead we use *character paradox* and *action paradox*. At first sight these may seem strange and difficult. But as we look at some examples, you will see that they are knacks which anyone can quickly pick up. The trick is to think of the stereotype – to think of the cliché character, the cliché action – and then

WRITE EXACTLY THE OPPOSITE!

You have a father and son in the play? All right, then, how do stereotype sons behave? They respect their fathers, right? So you make your son *devastatingly* rude to his father! The father's a widower? Stereotype widowers speak tenderly of their dead wives, so make yours refer to his as a bitch! Got used to the idea of his calling her a bitch? Make him start calling her an angel!

Get the idea? Try this one.

Favourite son returns home after six years in America to introduce his charming young wife to his old father. What's the father's reaction? Obviously, tears of joy, speeches of welcome. So put a minus sign in front of it! Have Dad launch into a blistering tirade, telling his son to get himself and his filthy whore out of the house!

Easy enough for you? There's easier to come.

Suppose one of the characters suddenly, without warning, drops dead (and why not?). Do the other characters show astonishment or concern? They do not. Do they show relief or malicious pleasure, then? Certainly not – this is black comedy, not 'The Curse of the Vampire.' Their reaction is the £EARN-TO-RITE Black Comedy Special –

NONE!

It's as simple as that! Everyone just goes on talking as if nothing had happened. Perhaps they have a brief, desultory discussion as to whether the corpse is still breathing or not. Otherwise –

NOTHING!

The audience will gasp!

Another example. Someone starts making love to a woman whose husband is present. How does the husband react? Does he hit the intruder, become embarrassed, storm out of the room? All these reactions are tired and obvious. We want something brand-new, the £EARN-TO-RITE Special –

NO REACTION!

Let's take it further. The wife (mother of three; husband a university professor) is invited by her father-in-law and two brothers-in-law to set up as their joint mistress, and to keep them all by becoming a prostitute. Gasp, gasp – titter, titter. But wait! How does she respond? With horror? Embarrassment? Prurient curiosity? Not if she's done the *£EARN-TO-RITE* Black Comedy Course! She responds with NOTHING, apart from insisting that as a prostitute she'll need a flat with at least three rooms!

Fantastic, you say? Fantastically simple! This is nothing less than BUILT-IN ORIGINALITY! Now work through these exercises on your own:

1. Fred, a foreman welder, stumbles and drops his father's coffin on top of his bedridden mother. Does he (a) make desperate attempts to free her, or (b) begin to apply rust-remover to the lavatory cistern?

2. René, a middle-aged pessimist, comes downstairs to fill her hot-water battle and finds her slow-witted sister Lou helping herself to one of the family's Rich Tea biscuits. Does she (a) go on into the kitchen, muttering, or (b) beat Lou's epicene husband to death with the hot-water bottle?

(1965)

Bodbury: the nation waits

Any moment now (*said Brian Bright, the well-known television personality*), any moment now the candidates and the returning officer will be appearing on that small balcony there on the front of the Town Hall, and we shall hear the result, we shall hear the result of the Bodbury byelection. There's been a series of delays – the announcement was expected much earlier than this – but I think, we think, we've had word that the result of the Bodbury byelection, the result, here, in Bodbury, of the byelection, the Bodbury byelection, should be coming through very shortly.

When it does, the returning officer will come through that door, at the back of the balcony. With him will be the three candidates. All three of them, with the returning officer, will come on to the balcony, through the door at the back. And it'll be on that balcony, the one you can see there, on the front of the Town Hall, that he, that the returning officer, will announce the result, the result of the Bodbury byelection.

I think there must be another delay. There's no sign of them. We heard, we learnt a few minutes ago that the returning officer would be coming out very shortly, but there's still no sign of him, so I think we must conclude – because we did hear he was on his way and he hasn't come – I think we must conclude that there's some delay.

I'll take the opportunity to remind you that we're in front of the Town Hall at Bodbury, waiting for the result of the byelection, the Bodbury byelection. There's great speculation here about the result among the very large and cheerful crowd in the square – or there was, until they all went home to bed. It could be a Conservative victory, if the Liberal and Labour candidates haven't done as well as they might. It could be a win for Labour, with the Conservatives at the bottom of the poll – depending on how well the Liberals have done. Or, of course, the Liberal swing could have put the Liberal in, if it was strong enough, if it was strong enough to put the Liberal in.

Well, here we are, then, still waiting for the result, for the result of the Bodbury byelection. If the swing to Labour is more marked than the trend to Liberal, or vice versa, then there's a chance, I think there's a fair chance, that he, whichever one it is, may profit from it – that's to say, from the swing. Or the trend, of course. If not, then, of course, not. And if the inevitable midterm dissatisfaction with the Government means, as it may, that the Conservative gets *fewer* votes than other candidates, then I think there's a pretty strong possibility he won't get in.

We spoke to a Conservative voter earlier in the evening, here in the main square, and asked him which way he had voted, and he said Conservative. I think that may be a pointer, it may be some sort of indication. I think it may go to show that if the trend shown at Bodbury is followed throughout the rest of the country, then the result here may be a guide to the way the trend is going. But if the result here is not going to be repeated in other constituencies, then it's no use, no use at all, taking it as any sort of guide.

We shall know, of course, when the results are brought out, in the traditional way, through that door at the back of the balcony, by the returning officer, who will open the door at the back of the balcony, and come out with the candidates, through the door, to read the results, from the balcony.

Still no sign. If the absence of swing, either to the left or to the right, shown by the door at the back of the balcony, is any pointer at all, it points, it points to a natural mid-term dissatisfaction among returning officers with bringing the result through the door at the back of the balcony, and indicates a growing trend, a fast-growing trend, to the sort of situation where all three of the candidates are left to swing from the front of the balcony, there, on the Town Hall, and we can all go home and have breakfast, have breakfast in a beautiful totalitarian silence . . .

(1962)

Bodbury speaks out!

BODBURY BYELECTION RESULT

F. Muncher (Lab.)	14,931
J. P. R. Cramshaw-Bollington (C)	8,101
S. W. Dearfellow (L)	7,123

Labour majority 6,830
(General election:
Lab. 23,987; C 16,021; L 9,980. Lab. maj. – 7,966)

F. Muncher: It's a wonderful result. Not only have we held the seat, but we have increased our share of the poll –

a real smack in the eye for the Government. The voters of Bodbury have told Mr Macmillan and his friends in no uncertain terms what they think of the Government's record on such things as the Common Market (or will have done, as soon as we have actually decided which policy on this question it was that our supporters were voting for). And if you take our vote in conjunction with the Liberal vote, it's evident that there is a definite anti-Tory majority in Bodbury.

J. P. R. Cramshaw-Bollington: I'm absolutely delighted with the result. At a time when the pendulum traditionally swings against the party in office, we've slashed the Labour majority in this Labour stronghold. I take this as a most encouraging vote of confidence in the Government – a message from the people of Bodbury to Mr Macmillan, urging him to carry on with the good work, whatever it may be. And taking the increased Liberal vote into account, its evident that there is a definite anti-Socialist majority in Bodbury.

S. W. Dearfellow: The result couldn't be better. Our share of the vote is up sharply, while the numbers of votes polled by both the Labour and Conservative candidates have slumped heavily. This is Bodbury's way of saying 'A plague on both your houses – we want to have it both ways with the Liberals.' And if you take the Liberal vote in conjunction with either the Labour or the Conservative vote, you can see that either way we've got a clear anti-extremist majority.

Sprout: Thank you, gentlemen. Now, what do the commentators think about the national significance of the Bodbury result? Haddock?

Haddock: Well, it should give real encouragement to the Liberals. But then again, it might be said that though they have gained, they have gained much less than might have been expected. And since anyway the gain will almost certainly disappear again at a general election, I feel they should temper their encouragement with a feeling of disappointment.

Trouncer: I interpret the quite noticeable fall in the Labour majority as a clear endorsement of the Government's position on manganese quotas. However, this fall was accompanied by an increase in Labour's share of the vote, which suggests to me a movement of Conservative supporters who have become disillusioned by the Government's record on departmental procedure reform.

Pinn: Though since the actual *size* of the Labour vote fell, this movement may have been accompanied by the abstention of Labour voters disillusioned with the Opposition's record on the same question. Or perhaps with Harold Wilson's personality. Or George Brown's face.

Sprout: To me, I must say, the real meaning of Bodbury lies in the reduction of the Conservative vote, which spells out in words of one syllable comprehensible to even the dullest back-bencher that there is no support in the country for the Government's lukewarm attitude to Chile.

Haddock: Possibly. The permutations are endless. And when one considers the local factors . . .

Trouncer: . . . the possibility that Fred Muncher's local reputation as deputy chairman of the Bodbury Amateur Weight-Lifters' Association was cancelled out by xenophobic suspicion of his living a quarter of a mile outside the constituency boundary . . .

Pinn: . . . and whether the Liberal gain from middle-class resentment against credit restrictions stopping the building of a new cricket pavilion was balanced by the propaganda effect of the Cramshaw-Bollington Dogs' Home founded by the Conservative candidate's father . . .

Haddock: . . . and whether the rain in the morning hindered the Tories more than the fog in the evening deterred the Socialists . . .

Sprout: . . . one realises that there is plenty of scope yet for imaginative conjecture about what the voters thought they were voting for, provided no unspeakable blackleg actually goes and finds out by asking them.

(1962)

Brought to book

The literary life, which I have largely managed to avoid for my forty years as a professional writer, finally caught up on me with a rush last Tuesday afternoon. At about two o'clock my publishers rang to tell me that my novel *Headlong* was on the Booker shortlist. At about three o'clock someone announcing himself as the Arts Corre- spondent of the *Guardian* rang to tell me that I had been accused of plagiarism.

I was shaken, I have to admit. But not entirely displeased. This is what happens to writers in serious departments of the literary world, such as the Booker shortlist. They get accused of things. They hurl the accusations back in their accusers' teeth. There are rows and fights, and people don't speak to each other. No one had ever bothered to accuse me of plagiarism before. I had got somewhere in life at last.

And it was all happening with such breathtaking speed. I had been elevated to the literary peerage at two, and disgraced at three. This really was life in the fast lane.

Even more astonishing was that the accusation appar- ently came from one of the Booker judges themselves. The Arts Correspondent of the *Guardian* said he had been talk- ing to John Sutherland, he said, who had told him that my novel bore suspicious similarities to a story by Roald Dahl.

'In your novel,' he said, 'there is a picture being used as a soot-guard in a fireplace. Yes?' I couldn't deny it. 'Well,' he said, 'in this story by Dahl there is apparently a piece of Chippendale up a chimney.'

Soot-guard in a fireplace – Chippendale up a chimney. It

looked black, I had to admit – and not just the picture or the Chippendale, but the whole case against me. I did indeed recall a story by Dahl which featured a furniture-dealer buying some valuable piece of furniture, possibly by Chippendale, off an ignorant yokel, though I couldn't recall the item in question being up a chimney at any point.

'But the *soot*?' I queried keenly. 'Was the Chippendale stopping the *soot* coming down the chimney?' Because if I could show that this crucial element in my version was original, it occurred to me – if it turned out that Dahl's Chippendale was stopping, say, Father Christmas rather than soot from coming down the chimney – then I had a complete answer to the charge.

The Arts Correspondent of the *Guardian* said he would find out and call me back. When he did he reported that he had misunderstood what John Sutherland had told him. There was no Chippendale up a chimney. The Chippendale-up-the-chimney charge had been totally withdrawn by the prosecution. What was now alleged was some general similarity between my plot and Dahl's.

This was even more baffling than the Chippendale up the chimney. I could remember the outlines of Dahl's plot, even if not the exact location of the furniture. Dealer cunningly persuades yokel that the Chippendale is valueless except as firewood – yokel obligingly chops it up while the dealer fetches his van. In my novel dealer and yokel are replaced by art historian and landowner. Art historian keeps his identification of landowner's picture as a missing Bruegel to himself; same story so far, I have to confess. Landowner, however, far from chopping it up, either literally or figuratively, becomes interested in it, in spite of art his-torian's dissembling, and tries to work out its correct identification for himself.

I explained this to the Arts Correspondent of the *Guardian*. 'This is the Booker,' he said apologetically. 'You have to expect this kind of thing.' He went off to take further instruction. Half-an-hour later he was back on the line. 'Martin!' he greeted me, in what sounded like some excitement. *Martin*? We seemed to be getting into very deep water indeed. Martin is the art historian in my novel. The Arts Correspondent of the *Guardian* was trying to phone my *character* to ask him whether he had been plagiarised! But this is exactly the kind of thing that happens in the higher reaches of the literary life! Fact and fiction turn out to be in some profound sense inextricably intertwined!

And I thought, 'This Arts Correspondent is no fool. He knows that Martin is the narrator of the story. He has information suggesting that it was *Martin* with his fingers in the till!'

I explained that he had got the wrong number, and that I was not Martin but Michael – Martin's author, certainly, but not responsible for his torts, surely, since Martin was of age and of sound mind. I urged him to ring Martin direct.

But when I open the *Guardian* next morning, there are our pictures. Not Dahl's and Martin's, but Dahl's and mine. Our names, as they say, have now been linked in the press. You can see from the reflective expression on Dahl's face that he is busy thinking up an original plot. You can see from the sly expression on mine that I am busy stealing it.

The pictures are illustrating John Sutherland's column. In the text Sutherland retails the accusation as an example of the kind of ridiculous nonsense that is probably going to be confected about the Booker finalists. 'Perhaps,' he says, as if he might actually believe it himself, 'the story lodged forgotten, like some old Bruegel, in the attic of the novelist's mind.' Though it's just as likely, he agrees, that the resemblance is 'purely accidental'.

So there the case rests. It may be plagiarism; on the other hand it may not be. What John Sutherland is too modest to mention is my much clearer and even more blatant plagiarism of *him*. There are glaring similarities between my book and his own excellent biography of Mrs Humphry Ward. Mrs Ward lives in a large house; so does the landowner in my story. Mrs Ward's house is in the country; so is my landowner's! Mrs Ward had difficult relations with her son; *so does my landowner!* In fact he has difficult relations with *two* sons, which by my calculation makes him twice as plagiarised as if he'd only had one.

Martin has obviously been up to his tricks again.

As the headline on John Sutherland's column says, You Couldn't Make It Up.

(1999)

Business worries

Children and animals are always reckoned to be the great scene-stealers against whom actors are reluctant to compete. But to my mind the greatest scene-stealer of all in films is a corpse.

Whatever the other attractions on the screen, if there's a corpse about I gaze at it fixedly. I have a nagging ambition to catch the actor who plays the corpse breathing when he thinks everyone's forgotten about him. A small ambition for a grown man, I dare say, but it gives me a hobby.

No luck so far, though I may have blinked just at the crucial moment. I suppose those bodies *are* actors holding their breath? It's not all faked up somehow with corpses rented out from the mortuary and just made up to look like actors holding their breath? I must write in and ask the fan magazines.

Anyway, it shows you how relaxed and secure one can be in the cinema, knowing nothing can really go wrong except the projector or the air-conditioning. It's a very different matter in the theatre. One wouldn't dare so much as glance at a corpse on the stage. After that great sword-fight all the way up the set and back one knows the poor man's bosom must be heaving up and down like a piledriver. One wouldn't dream of embarrassing him by looking. Anyway, he might feel one's eye on him and start to cough. No doubt, for that matter, he's fallen with one leg agonisingly doubled up – on his keys – with his ruff tickling his nose. His whole situation doesn't really bear thinking about too much.

All the time in the theatre one is waiting aghast for some embarrassing disaster to occur. Whenever there's a pause, one starts praying they're not going to forget their lines, or be taken ill on the stage. It's like walking through a minefield. Every day in the papers one reads about actors having heart attacks in the middle of their performance, breaking their legs, getting their heads split open in the fights, knocking themselves out against the scenery, and generally making a spectacle of themselves. At any moment, one feels there might be some sort of scene.

Audience anxiety reaches a peak, as all sado-masochistic directors know, whenever the cast indulge in one of those little bits of business which depend on physical dexterity, or the workings of some notoriously fallible machine. My heart leaps into my mouth every time somebody offers to light somebodys else's cigarette with a lighter. Flick – it fails to light! Flick – and again it doesn't light! Flick – look intently at ceiling, think about something else.

Flick – there's no logical reason why we shouldn't be stuck here all night, not daring to breathe, while he grinds away at the thing. Flick – will he give up after ten flameless flicks? After a hundred? Flick – praise heaven, there's a flame!

But *now* they're both shaking so much they can't get the flame and the cigarette to meet! Yes! No! Yes – they've done it! 'Ah, that's better,' she sighs contentedly, blowing out a thoughtful column of smoke. But, crumbling sanity, there *is* no smoke! The cigarette's gone out again!

One's palms sweat. Of course, one keeps telling oneself

that it doesn't really matter, because no one nowadays expects a naïvely literal realism in the theatre. One wants to see the figures on the stage both as the actors acting and the characters acted. In a sense, of course, one's consciousness of this valuable duality is if anything heightened when one or two little things go slightly . . .

Oh God, he's not going to throw her the revolver! Of course, they rehearse these things for weeks . . . She's dropped it. Now she's picked it up – she's carrying bravely on. Don't feel you need to be brave on my account, dear. Honestly, it didn't embarrass me a bit. No, I had my eyes shut. I mean, I know I caught my breath when he threw it, but . . . I suppose you can't possibly have *heard* me catching my breath, can you? I mean, it wasn't my catching my breath that made you . . . ? Oh, *God!*

I have a haunting fear that one night when I'm present some piece of business is going to go so completely wrong that the play as written cannot proceed at all, and the actors will be reduced to improvising some new line of development entirely. Take the famous Locket scene at the end of 'Error for Error,' when young Ferdinand shows Duke Oregano and the assembled court the locket which proves he is the Duke's son, carried off at birth by a waterspout. Suppose that after the lines –

> *A locket sav'd I from that spoutsome day,*
> *Most curiously incrib'd. I have it here.*

Ferdinand tosses the vital instrument to the Duke, and the Duke fumbles it and drops it out of sight. What can they do, except make the rest of the scene up as they go along?

DUKE: Alas! Methinks I have misfinger'd it!
FERDINAND: Sire, bend thou down thine aged frame
    And do thou smartly pluck it up again.
DUKE: Bend as I might, I cannot see the thing.
    My lords, do you explore your cloggy beards.

No sign? Ah me, I fear it must have roll'd
Amid this mazy grove of cardboard trees.
FERDINAND: Was not one glance as it came winging by
Enough to grasp the general sense of it?
– That here before thee stands thy long-lost son?
DUKE: A fig for *your* problems – what worrieth me
Is how I speak my major speech, which starts:
'Come, locket, let me kiss thee for thy pains,
And taste the savour of fidelity,'
Without the bloody locket. Come, let's shift
This forest. Take the yonder end and heave.
FERDINAND: Is this meet welcome for a long-lost son?
DUKE: Meet welcome for a long-lost son, forsooth!
What kind of long-lost son is this, that chucks
Essential props outside my senile reach,
And cuts his long-lost father's longest speech?
Lose thee again, son, till thou learnst at last
The art of throwing props and not the cast.

(1964)

Can you hear me, mother?

I enjoy the woman's page of the *Guardian*. Unlike the men's pages of newspapers, where Interdepartmental Committees are Set Up, Machine Tool Prospects Look Brighter, and Proposals Deserve Careful Consideration, it seems to be concerned with individual human beings.

One has an impression of particular women, struggling with children and consciences and loose doorhandles; wondering gloomily whether it's God or madness tapping on their skulls: getting some strange illogical pleasure out of misconceived holiday ordeals with family, van, and tent through Wester Ross . . .

The other day the page made an even more striking excursion into the world of the personal and the particular; and I must say, the knife seemed to me to be getting a little near the bone.

It was an article by one Mair Thompson about mothers-in-law. Or, rather, about her own mother-in-law. One of the kindest and most generous people she knows, apparently, and she *loves* her.

'Yet she drives me crazy. Her mannerisms irritate me, her elderliness irritates me. I don't like her face, and her feet are silly-looking. Her conversation infuriates me. I let off steam by mimicking and muttering silently when she talks to me from another room. When she tells the same story for the umpteenth time it is with great difficulty that I restrain myself from either giggling or saying it along with her, word for word; I am amazed at my husband's ability to look interested and ask prompting questions.'

I must admit, I felt the beads of nervous sweat start forth when I read this. I'm all for the unvarnished truth; I'm all for delivery by candour from inhibition and frustration.

All the same – poor old mother-in-law! I take it that 'Mair Thompson' is a pen-name . . . I take it that mother-in-law never reads the *Guardian* . . . But, all the same . . . !

Of course, once you've got the problem into the open like this, everyone wants to help. Barbara Nuttall, of Leeds, writes to the *Guardian* to say that Mair Thompson's mother-in-law 'ought gently to be told to come less often to her children's home.' (Mrs Nuttall's own mother-in-law 'has never failed to help when needed,' but at the same time 'has never forced her attention' on the family.) But it's all the fault of the *husband,* according to Mrs E. M. Selby, of Loughborough, who writes to say that 'the weakness in the family structure mentioned lies more in the mother–son relationship . . . The fact that the husband can sit patiently and listen to repetitive stories of his mother shows a childish dependence on her approval.'

So poor old husband, too! It really is group therapy on the heroic scale, this candid assessment of one's relations' shortcomings in the public prints. Perhaps the impersonal abstractions of the men's pages have something to be said for them after all. I should certainly hate to pick up the paper one morning when my children are grown up and find some son-in-law of mine holding forth about me in the middle of the business news.

'A finer man than my father-in-law never drew breath,' I can imagine the young puppy declaring sententiously, 'when it comes to washing-up, carrying messages, waiting at our dinner-parties, and looking after our pet ocelots while we go on holiday.

'But ye gods, the price one pays for these small services! Take one's eye off him for an instant and he's poured himself a generous measure of one's best Scotch, and sprawled himself out at his ease in one's favourite arm-chair with the evening paper.

'Like as not he's also taken his shoes off to aerate his feet. Moreover, he hums to himself endlessly, with a strange, infuriating *shushing* noise, which I believe is supposed to represent the sound of a symphony orchestra. We all make fun of him behind his back, of course. But somehow that no longer seems enough.'

After a lead like this, I should think, the floodgates would open, and the Letters to the Editor column would be full of brutally candid letters from everyone in the family.

'Sir, – May we say how heartily many of us ordinary aunts and uncles agree with your correspondent's remarks about our nephew? It is high time that the conspiracy of silence about his personal habits was broken. – Yours, etc., Arthur Wroxby, Millicent Wroxby, Clara Frayn Steadfast.'

'Sir, – I regret to add to the melancholy tale of my cousin's shortcomings, but I have been present on at least two occasions when he has told deliberate untruths. Indeed, I have often been struck by his inability to look one straight in the eye. I wonder if this is an experience which has been shared by any other of your readers? J. N. G. Portly-Walker, Godalming.'

'Sir, – Your readers may be interested to know that Michael's indifferent social behaviour was the despair of his parents from an early age. But many of us in the family felt that they had only themselves to blame. They should have been much stricter with the boy, as I myself told them on more than one occasion, though small thanks I got for it. If only they could have foreseen what their thoughtless indulgence would lead to! – I am, &c., (Mrs) Louisa Ironmaster, Southsea.'

'Sir, – When he comes to our house, our granfather wissles through his teeth and makes boreing jokes which bore me and my brothers and sisteres. He is a tall man, but boreing to have as a granfather. – (Miss) Phillida Frayn (aged 4).'

'Sir, – I was interested to see Mr Portly-Walker's reference to my cousin's dishonesty. I am myself only a second cousin once removed, but on the few occasions we have met, Mr Frayn has invariably breathed into my face and attempted to borrow money, saying that he has left his change in his other trousers, or got to the bank too late. It is high time that this man was hounded out of private life. – Yours faithfully, T. Wesley Topples, Stroud.'

I don't like it, men – I don't like it one little bit. Let's stick with those grand old Interdepartmental Committees after all.

(1967)

Chez crumble

One of the principal benefits that matrimony confers on the young professional class is that it enables us to give up that tiresome pretence of being interested in spiritual and cultural matters – forced on us by our education and our courtship rituals – and lets us settle down to a frank and total absorption in our financial and material circumstances.

When, for instance, you call on the newly married Crumbles – formerly socially conscious Christopher Crumble and sensitive, musical Lavinia Knudge – do you talk about the problems of secondary education, or English choral music of the sixteenth century, as you would have done back in the good old days of Crumble and Knudge? You do not. Because Lavinia says . . .

Lavinia: Before you do anything else, you must come and look over the flat!

Christopher: . . . that's right, just take your coat off – I'll hang it on this automatic coat-rack . . .

Lavinia: . . . which Christopher made himself, didn't you, darling?

Christopher: Got a kit from Rackkitz of Wembley – costs

about half the price of an ordinary automatic coat-rack . . .

Lavinia: . . . and it's fire-resistant, too . . .

Christopher: . . . now this is the hall, of course . . .

Lavinia: . . . which we made ourselves by partitioning off part of the bedroom . . .

Christopher: . . . with half-inch Doncaster boarding, at a shilling a foot, if you know the right place . . .

Lavinia: . . . Christopher got it from the brother of an old school-friend of his, didn't you, darling? Now – mind your head on that steel brace – this is the bedroom . . .

Christopher: . . . we picked up the bed for a song in a little shop I know in Edmonton . . .

Lavinia: . . . and fitted it out with a Dormofoam matt-ress. They're so much the best, of course. In fact there's a waiting-list for Dormofoams, but we had tremendous luck and got one ordered for someone who died . . .

Christopher: . . . and this is the kitchen opening off in the corner here. It was really the handiness of having the kitchen opening directly into the bedroom that made us take the flat . . .

Lavinia: . . . you should have seen it when we first moved in! But Christopher had the brilliant idea of covering up the holes in the floor with some special asbestos his uncle makes . . .

Christopher: . . . so we got a discount on it. We're frightfully proud of that stainless steel bootrack, by the way. I don't know whether you saw it recommended in *Which?* last month . . . ?

Lavinia: . . . it's so much more practical than all those silver-plated ones you see in the shops. According to *Which?* they pounded it with 140 average boot-impacts an hour for 17 days before it collapsed . . .

Christopher: . . . I'd take you out to show you the lava-tory, but it is raining hard. Remind us you haven't seen it next time you come, won't you, and we'll make a point of it . . .

Lavinia: . . . and here we are in the living-room . . .

Christopher: . . . have you seen this Plushco plastic carpeting before? We think it's awfully good, don't we, darling? Half the price of ordinary carpet, and terrifically hard-wearing. We've had it down, what, two weeks now? Not a sign of wear on it . . .

Lavinia: . . . I see you're looking at all those old books on music and education. You won't believe it, but we had those shelves built for five pounds, timber and all . . .

Christopher: . . . by a marvellous little man we found by sheerest chance in Muswell Hill. Remind me to give you his address . . .

Lavinia: . . . though I think he did it specially cheaply for us just because he happened to take to us . . .

Christopher: . . . by the way, would you like a glass of Sardinian sherry?

Lavinia: . . . we've developed rather a thing about Sardinian sherry, haven't we darling?

Christopher: . . . we get it by the gallon from a little shop in Sydenham. Found the place by sheer chance . . .

Lavinia: . . . tremendously practical, and it works out at six-and-four a bottle . . .

Christopher: . . . incidentally, what do you think we pay for the flat? No, go on, have a guess . . . Well, I'll tell you – five pounds a week . . .

Lavinia: . . . it's an absolute bargain, of course. We only found it through a friend of my mother's, who just by sheerest chance happened to be . . .

Christopher: I say, you're looking rather groggy. Lavinia darling, run and fetch him some Asprilux. I don't know whether you've tried Asprilux, but we think it's much better than any of the other brands of aspirin . . . No, sit in this chair – it's got a rather ingenious reclining back – we just got the last one to be made. Comfortable, isn't it? What do you think of Lavinia, by the way? Such practical, easy-to-clean hands and feet. You won't believe it, but I picked

her up by the sheerest chance at a little bookshop I know
down in Wimbledon . . .

(1962)

Child and superchild

It's terrible to think of the manpower the world has wasted
up to now by failing to commence the education of the young
in earnest infancy. Children have been allowed just to throw
away the first five years of their lives; when all the time they
could – as researchers, journalists and anxious parents all
over the world are now coming to realise – have been learning
to get ahead and lay the foundations of successful careers.

Now all that's a thing of the past. These days, the mother
who has her child's future at heart sets to work before it's
even born, and spends part of each day during pregnancy
inside a decompression suit to increase the supply of
oxygen to its brain, with the result that it subsequently
learns to crawl and walk (and presumably also to graduate
and get a peerage) earlier than less fortunate children from
underdecompressed homes.

The privileged infant has not long opened its eyes upon
the world, of course, before its loving mother is holding up
Teach Your Baby to Read cards in front of it, and develop-
ing its 'need for achievement' (the *n* Ach rating, as identified
by Professor McClelland of Harvard) by setting 'moderately
high achievement goals' and helping the child to reach them
in a 'warm encouraging and non-authoritarian' way.

And now, I see from the series of articles on 'Success
before Six' in the *Sunday Times,* it's been discovered that
parents have 'a potent chance to accelerate the intellectual
development of their children' by the way they talk to
them. The helpful parent should speak to his child in a
rich vocabulary, using 'modelled' conversation techniques

rather than 'systematic expansion,' and an 'elaborated code' rather than a 'restricted' one.

According to a book called 'Educating Your Baby' which is quoted in the series, 'a parent can help the child by repeating consonant and vowel sounds, slowly and deliberately ... by letting the baby see lip movements, and pausing to let him imitate them. One compresses the lips into a thin line and parts them with the sound, "ba". Smiling at the baby may induce him to smile in return; lips parting then produces the syllable and mother and child laugh gleefully. The syllable can be made repeatedly; "ba-ba-ba" until the child is ready for something else.'

The next part of the training course, according to the article, is the Naming of Parts. 'If this is started early enough then by the time he is 12 months old he will be able to point to parts of his body when asked. "Can you touch your mouth? Touch your mouth." Show him how. "Good boy. You're touching your mouth." *Not*: "You are doing it."'

Certainly not! With that kind of teaching he could fail his one-plus! Anyway, from the age of 18 months the object is to get the child to repeat after his mother or father the names of familiar objects. Then we get on to the more severe disciplines involved in advanced studies.

'Once the child can talk,' says the article, 'it is best to ask for complete responses to questions. "How many days are there in a week, Alice?" "Seven." "Good. But it could be better. The correct answer is 'There are seven days in a week.' Say for me, 'There are seven days in a week.'"'

It sounds to me as if they're having trouble with this Alice child. Isn't this casual, slipshod approach to academic work, this lackadaisical mumble of 'Seven,' only too typical of youth today? I bet Alice has a sugar cigarette hanging out of the corner of her mouth during lectures – I bet she tries to cut compulsory hopscotch! The next thing you know, she'll be sprawling on the floor with a banner outside her father's study, demanding another threepence a week pocket money and a bigger say in planning her syllabus.

Where did Alice's parents go wrong? Was the pressure in her mother's decompression suit not low enough? Did her father hurry her on to 'dad-dad-dad' before she'd fully mastered 'ba-ba-ba'? In any case, she's sadly retarded in her development compared with Algernon, a child of my acquaintance whose intellectual life was accelerated in accordance with *really* modern methods.

In the first place, Algernon's parents took care to conceive him during the first hour of his mother's fertile period, in accordance with a survey by Progel and Hergstrom which showed that early-fertilised ova have the highest chance of A/B class membership in later life.

Next, his parents began talking formatively to him by the use of deep-penetration sonic waves while he was still in the womb. By the time he was born he could recite the subjunctive of most irregular French verbs reasonably reliably, and his parents felt free to address him thenceforth, as they croodled encouragingly over his cot, entirely in mathematical equations, to which the delighted infant would reply by gurgling the solution, with many a gleeful laugh.

He spent a year travelling to broaden his horizons after leaving school, and therefore did not go up to Cambridge until he was nearly four. He took his PhD at six, after two very fruitful months at MIT, and entered the Mashmaestro Corporation on the research side, where he enjoyed a brilliant career, rising to become head of his department at the age of seven, and joining the Board in the following year.

And there he will remain for the next 57 years. His hobbies are conkers and marbles, and he is writing what is likely to be the standard work on the after-effects of precocity, entitled 'The Problems of Teenage Senility.'

Get older younger, that's the aim, and come fresh and unspoiled to second childhood.

(1968)

Childholders

What my wife and I have now got more of than anything else, it occurred to me the other day, as I staggered through the front door with another armful of the stuff, is child-handling equipment.

I mean devices for holding small children up, holding them down, moving them along, and keeping them in one place. We must have got a hundredweight of the stuff. The only thing we're a bit short of is the children for all this wealth of plastic and bent tinplate to be used upon. I keep counting up incredulously, and we've only got two.

We're thinking of opening our home and making the collection public. I've been compiling a catalogue. What I've tried to do is to provide the visitor – and indeed myself – with some sort of *catalogue raisonné*; a coherent, step-by-step account of exactly how we came to build our great collection up.

The first exhibit is

1 THE PRAM. Naturally there must be a pram. All children have prams. Where we were rather shrewd, I think, was in choosing a special patent collapsible model which at the turn of a nut lifts off the wheels to become a cot, or subsides into a push-chair. In which case, why do we need

2 THE CARRY-COT? Well, you see, the patent collapsible pram's downstairs and the bedroom's upstairs. And in any case, without the wheels the top of the patent collapsible pram would have to stand among the draughts on the floor. Whereas the carry-cot can stand on

3 THE CARRY-COT STAND. A great economy, a carry-cot

and stand, because we didn't need a crib. All we needed was

4 THE DROP-SIDED COT. Now why the devil did we need a drop-side cot when we had a carry-cot? Because the baby had grown too big for the carry-cot. Then why didn't we skip the carry-cot and get a drop-side cot in the first place? Well, have you ever walked through the streets carrying a baby in a drop-side cot?

5 THE FOLDING WEEKEND BED. Why, you ask patiently, didn't we take the drop-side cot away for weekends? Because we'd have needed a larger car. A folding weekend bed was cheaper than a larger car.

All right so far? Now,

6 THE PUSH-CHAIR. We must have forgotten, you laugh, about that patent collapsible pram we started with which turned into a push-chair at the turn of a nut, the wrench of a bolt, the heave of the chassis, and the couple of thumps with the starting-handle. By no means. The fact is, the patent collapsible pram is now occupied by the second baby, while the original infant sits on top in

7 THE CLAMP-ON SEAT FOR ELDER CHILD. What? – you scream – why isn't the elder child sitting in the brand-new push-chair? Now, come, come. My wife could scarcely walk to the shops pushing the pram *and* the push-chair. Good God, man, you cry, make the elder child *walk*! Certainly. But this the elder child would consent to do only if bought

8 THE TOY PUSH-CHAIR to push. Unfortunately, the toy push-chair turned out to be large enough for the elder child to sit in and wait to *be* pushed. So we had to get her

9 THE DOLL'S PRAM, of a type so small that there was

no room for the elder child. Indeed, there was only just enough room for the elder child to cram the younger child in. So the younger child had to be placed in protective custody inside

10 THE PLAY-PEN, from which it was released only to be sat up for meals in

11 THE PATENT ADJUSTABLE ALL-PURPOSE BABY CHAIR. Now why on earth couldn't we sit the child up in the clamp-on pram seat? Because the only thing the clamp-on pram seat clamped on was the pram, and the pram was downstairs. The patent adjustable all-purpose baby chair, however – strongly recommended by a liberal-radical woman's page – proved to have one small drawback; it turned upside-down if the child moved. The child did move. The answer, we felt, was not a high chair, but – much more economical –

12 THE CAR-SEAT, because it could be used both in the car and on the back of an ordinary chair at table. Then

13 ANOTHER CAR-SEAT, because the baby could lever the first one right off the chair. Then

14 THE HIGH CHAIR, because the baby could lever the second car-seat right off the chair, too. Then

15 THE SMALL CHAIR for the elder child, to stop it jealously insisting on sitting in the younger child's high chair.

16 THE CARRYING SLING, for taking younger child on health-giving nature rambles (don't tell me we should have pushed the patent collapsible pram over all those stiles and up all those mountains). Unfortunately the sling – strongly recommended by the liberal-radical woman's page –

exerted intolerable pressure on the top of my spinal cord, and the agony was relieved only by the child falling out. Replaced by

17 THE RUCKSACK SEAT, a rugged structure of solid welded steel, recommended by the same damned liberal-radical woman's page. We hadn't got very far up the first mountain when it struck me that steel and child together, presumably, had the same effect on the heart as being three stone over-weight. Came down the mountain hastily, and haven't tested the equipment since.

That's as far as the collection goes at present. Just the 17 items. No doubt we shall add to it in time.

The only other point of interest, I think, is that between them (if I have counted correctly) the 17 exhibits are decorated with 43 frogs, 47 rabbits, 51 fairies, 108 pussy-cats (60 with bows), 46 pigs, 96 ducks, 48 dwarfs, 103 mice, 204 doggies (40 of them stark naked), and one rat.

And I may say that every one of them, except the rat, is grinning fit to bust.

(1965)

Cleveland Suede Accuses

Good evening (*smiled Cleveland Suede, the well-known young Bow Labour MP and television personality*). Welcome once again to 'Cleveland Suede Accuses,' our weekly series in which well-known personalities come along to the studio here and try to offer me some sort of explanation for themselves. This week, by a remarkable technological achievement on the part of Eurovision, we have managed to set up a direct link with Leonardo da Vinci, the well-known painter and inventor, in our Renaissance Studios. To many millions of people throughout the world, Mr da

Vinci is known as one of the greatest geniuses of all time. Mr da Vinci, may I ask you, how have you managed to sell this line to so many people?

L da V: Well, I . . .

Suede: I take it you'd agree that you're fairly overrated?

L da V: I suppose . . .

Suede: After all, your pictures are pretty dull, aren't they, compared with Veronese's, say, or Van Gogh's?

L da V: Yes, well, they're different . . .

Suede: I suppose it's just a personal thing, but I don't like all those dark colours. Look at the brightness in a Dufy, for example. Have you made any serious attempt to catch up with him?

L da V: Well, I'm not really trying . . .

Suede: I suppose you're going to say the varnish changed colour. Did you always use cheap varnish?

L da V: Now, look, there are several technical questions involved here . . .

Suede: I see it's a sore point – I won't labour it. What about the way you draw people, Mr da Vinci? Is that deliberate misrepresentation or simply lack of skill?

L da V: I try to draw people as I see them. I can't help it if . . .

Suede: Everyone's out of step but our Leonardo, eh? A lot of people complain about the quality of your exports. Someone was telling me only the other day that he'd just seen a picture of yours which you sent over here without any paint on it at all. What have you got to say about that?

L da V: If you mean the cartoon . . .

Suede: The same story as the varnish, I suppose. Mr da Vinci, we've heard a great deal about the flying machines you've designed. If it's not a rude question, when are we going to see one actually in service?

L da V: Well, I simply sketched . . .

Suede: Or have they been refused an airworthiness certificate? Incidentally, what qualifications have you got as an aircraft designer? Do you feel any responsibility at all for the lives of the ordinary men and women who may one day travel in your machines? Wouldn't it be better if you stuck to painting?

L da V: Which question do you want me to answer first?

Suede: None of them if it would be embarrassing. Do you get any satisfaction from painting and designing and so forth?

L da V: Yes, of course.

Suede: Then do you ever worry about the moral point of doing absolutely nothing with your life but amuse yourself? Perhaps that's a rather loaded question. What else do you do besides painting and inventing and so on? Any hobbies?

L da V: Hobbies?

Suede: Isn't it rather a narrow life? Wouldn't it be healthier if you got out of the rut occasionally and played the odd game of golf? I mean, there must be something unhealthy somewhere if you agree to appear on a programme like this. Are you conscious of having some streak of masochistic exhibitionism? Never mind, now you're here perhaps you'd like to say something about art as it appears to you, Leonardo da Vinci?

L da V: Well, it's not easy to make any brief general statement. But there is one thing I should like to say.

Suede: And so we come to the end of another 'Cleveland Suede Accuses'. Next week – a simultaneous exhibition match in which I shall try to cut all the Twelve Apostles down to size at one go. Good night.

(1962)

The cogitations of the Earl of Each

Sometimes, as I sit beside the little electric fire in the morning-room, with *The Times* sports pages open beside me, and Henry muttering quietly to himself in his sleep at my feet, I fall into what I call my *cogitational* mood. At these moments it begins to seem to me a matter of some wonder that things are as they are and not otherwise.

Everything! Just thus and so! When it could have been not thus and so at all! Indeed, it could have been not thus and so in various different ways. In a thousand different ways, when you think about it – while there is only the one single way in which things could have been thus and so in the way that they are.

The horse has come in at a thousand to one!

*

And every time I begin to think like this it seems to me that the most surprising thing of all is that I am the Earl of Each.

I. Not my brother Charles or my cousin Shandon. Not some complete stranger. Not some Chinese fellow – and there are a great many more Chinese fellows in the world than there are cousins of mine. Not to mention brothers, of whom there are only three.

None of these people is the Earl of Each. I am. And of me

there are even fewer than there are of brothers, let alone cousins or Chinese. Of me there is only one.

Good God.

*

And here's another thing which is almost as remarkable.

Not only am I the Earl of Each, but the Earl of Each is what I am.

I am not, for example, Sir Alfred Upward. Nor the Marquess of Hight. I am not my brother Charles, nor my cousin Shandon, nor the estimable Wun Hung Lo, nor yet the redoutable Hoo Flung Dung. I am the Earl of Each. No less. No more.

And this astonishing fact is something that everyone takes absolutely for granted. Never has my cousin Shandon said to me: 'Good heavens, Pot, you are the Earl of Each!'

Most of the time I take it pretty much for granted myself.

The Earl of Each. Goodness. I am. My word. The twelfth earl, moreover. Not the eleventh or the thirteenth. The twelfth. Just so. Just exactly so.

*

How has this surprising state of affairs come about?

It is because my father, in his day, could say much the same.

So now we must think what it was like for him. And if it is cause for wonder that *I* am the Earl of Each, then it was no less cause for wonder that *he* was the Earl of Each before me. So look here, this isn't a matter of a single horse coming in at a thousand to one! This is the Spring Double!

Another question comes knocking at my brain immediately: how was it that my father was the Earl of Each? It was because *his* father was the Earl of Each before him!

And back we go in time to the beginning of the line, wonder before wonder, each as astonishing as the one before it. A tower of improbability twelve floors high!

What we are discussing is not simply the Spring Double. It is nothing less than a twelve-horse accumulator!

*

I sometimes even wonder if we can stop at the first earl. Would Sir George Shy, as he then was, have been created earl if he had not been Sir George? Evidently not, since it was indeed Sir George and no one else who was so created!

Now, would Sir George have been Sir George if his father had not been the father he happened to be? No, plainly, he would have been someone else altogether!

Back we plunge through the centuries to Adam, or the apes!

Yes, and which do I find it easier to believe? That my being the Earl of Each is the final product of God's purpose for the world, or that it results from the blind interaction of chance and natural selection?

I have to confess that I find both hypotheses a little difficult to accept.

*

Another thing: my earldom is a perfect *fit*. At least as good a fit as my shirts and shoes, and a rather better one than my suits, because that fool Stubbs insists on cutting the bellyband of all my trousers too wide – to allow, as he says, for natural development, while never making accommodation for any other natural development – for example, the settling of the head forwards and away from the collar that occurs as the years go by, so that I look like a tortoise in its shell.

I wasn't absolutely sure about the earldom when I first

came into it, I have to confess, any more than I was with the Oxford brogues that Tapsell made me at about the same time. It took a little while for those shoes to settle to my feet, I recall, but settle they did, just as Tapsell said they would, closer and closer, and it's the same with the earldom. The Earl of Each has become more exactly who I am with every passing day. The bellyband of my earldom, unlike the bellyband of my suits, neither sags nor presses, the collar stays close to my shirt.

And yet it fitted my father before me, who was of a very different temperament from me. In the first place he was not, so far as I know, given to these cogitational moods of mine. It made no difference, though. Earl of Each he was, no less than me.

It fitted his father before him, and his father's father before that.

An amazing garment!

Unless – a new and most striking thought – unless it is not the earldom that ever more closely fits me, but I who ever more closely fit the earldom!

I believe the truth is this – that we have both changed. Just as Henry and I have both changed and accommodated ourselves to each other's ways. He has learnt not to disturb me in my pensive moods; he opens one eye and glances up from the toecap of my shoe, and knows at once that the toecap of my shoe is where he must remain while the mood is upon me, that he must not think of aspiring to rest his head upon my knee. While I, for my part, have learnt not to disturb *his* thoughtful moments by any sudden withdrawal of my foot from beneath his head.

But now a different question arises: am I master or am I dog? I mean, figuratively speaking, in the relationship between me and the earldom. Am I the one sitting by the electric fire with the earldom drowsing on my brogues, or am I down upon the floor, with my chin supported by the tolerance and patience of the earldom above me?

*

Henry's looking up at me now. I believe he's a little anxious on my behalf. Yes! Deep waters we're getting into here, Henry!

Or is he thinking: 'What surprises me is that I am Henry and he is the twelfth earl'?

Back to sleep, Henry!

*

Today, at the fresh fish counter in Tesco's, I met Wiggy Hight, buying prawns for those cats of his. 'Hello, Pot,' he said. It occurred to me that had the world been a slightly different place I should have been the one who was saying 'Hello, Pot'. Then I should have been returning to that dreadful old ruin of his at Godforth and sitting in front of the fire thinking: 'Goodness me, I'm the Marquess of Hight!'

I was very struck by this, but kept my counsel. 'Hello, Wiggy,' I said. I was struck, though, very struck.

*

Well, let us imagine that things *were* arranged differently!

I am imagining as an experiment that I am not an earl at all. Not even a marquess. I am . . . Who am I? Yes, I am Fred Upward! Now, here's a laugh.

Let's see . . . I'm all skin and bone. I look down at my shoes. Are they Oxford brogues? Not at all, they're mildewed carpet slippers. All right so far. The telephone rings. 'Upward here,' I say. Good. I'm doing rather well so far! Master of disguise!

Hold on, though. Not so fast. Is this still me or isn't it? Is this the Earl of Each telling the world he's Sir Alfred Upward? No, no, everything's changed – I'm old Fred himself in this arrangement of things! This is Sir Alfred Upward saying he's Sir Alfred Upward.

In which case ... In which case where do we stand? Where do *I* stand? Nowhere, evidently! I seem to have dropped out of the picture completely. In any case Fred's always answering the phone as things are and saying 'Upward here'. So nothing's changed at all!

Who's on the other end of the phone, anyway? Me, in all probability!

By which, of course, I mean the Earl of Each.

*

I realise that these reflections will be of little interest to others. I raised the matter once with Nippy. We were sitting quietly on the terrace after dinner one warm summer evening, enjoying the scent of the tobacco plants. I felt an unusual sense of quiet understanding between us. 'My love,' I said, 'has it ever occurred to you that if things were not as they are, and I were not who I am, then you in your turn would not be who you are?' She didn't reply. I had the impression that she was thinking about it, though. She is not greatly given to abstract thought, so I tried to put the matter in more concrete terms. 'Suppose, for the sake of argument,' I said, 'that I were Alfred Upward. Then you, my love, would be Lady Upward instead of Lady Each.' Another silence ensued. But all she said at the end of it was: 'I think Henry needs worming.'

I tried to discuss it once with Shandon. We were in the butts at Wiggy's, and the birds were remarkably sparse. I put it very simply, in terms of which gun was in whose hands. 'Well, Pot,' said Shandon, 'you always were the brains of the family So I don't think you can be *this* gun, because I'm pretty sure there's not much in the way of brains lurking about over here.'

Curious that it doesn't strike other people, too. After all, the consequences of my being the Earl of Each are almost as considerable for Nippy and Shandon as they are for me. They reach out to our children, and our children's children. They go on down the generations, for ever and ever.

*

I am the *Earl of Each*. And then again, *I* am the Earl of Each. But every now and then, when my thoughts run very deep, I find yet another cause for wonder – that I *am* the Earl of Each.

Is this less surprising than the first two things, or even more so? But this deep I cannot think for long without fear of never coming to the surface again.

*

Another plunge into deep waters!

If it is against long odds that I am the Earl of Each, how much longer are the odds against the Earl of Each being me.

I'm not making a muddle here, am I? I'm not simply recogitating the same cogitation that I've cogitated before?

I don't believe so. After all, there would have been an Earl of Each sitting here in front of the fire in the morning-room now whenever my dear mother and father had seen fit to begin their eldest son. He might have been a month older than me, or a month younger. He might been a completely different age altogether, and an inch shorter, with darker hair and a less ruddy complexion. He would still have been the Earl of Each, if he was my father's son.

But he wouldn't have been me.

For the Earl of Each to be *me*, the actual fellow who as it happens is indeed sitting here now and cogitating these particular cogitations, then there was only one night in all the years that my parents were married that would serve. I believe this lengthens the odds by another five or six thousand times.

Good God, once again.

Supposing my father had gone up to the House that day, as he sometimes did when some measure relating to land drainage or bloodstock was under discussion, and had stayed overnight at his club! The fellow sitting in this chair now, the present Earl of Each, would have been another fellow altogether!

I feel decidedly peculiar at the thought.

Yes, Henry, well may you look at me like that! Well may you speculate!

Enough!

Come on, dog – a turn around the lake before lunch.

Let us hold on to one absolute and unfailing certainty, Henry, amidst all the dark seas of speculation and conjecture. Let us plant our colours in this one thought and never strike them: that I, old dog of mine, that I, I, am the Earl of Each.

(2000)

Comedy of viewers

Thank you, BBC Television! (*runs a letter which Mrs Ada Vacancy has asked me to use my influence to get published in* Radio Times.) What a grand job you're doing bringing culture to people like me! (Perhaps I should explain that though my father was a Featherhead, I am connected on my mother's side with the Easeleigh-Boreables of Bournemouth.)

Your production of *A Comedy of Errors* this week was 'just the ticket!' It ran for six-and-a-half minutes by my clock before a single word of Shakespeare was spoken, and my husband and I enjoyed every second.

Of course, all good things must come to an end, and eventually we had to face up to it and suffer 'the slings and arrows of outrageous Shakespeare', to coin a phrase! But a word of praise to the actors. Some of their amusing antics between the bouts of literature that followed were highly diverting. They quite 'saved' the evening, and as I said to my husband, 'They may be "classical" actors, but some of them are almost good enough for the pantomime in Newcastle!' Which coming from me is praise indeed! (I mean of course Newcastle-under-Lyme, where my mother was born.)

But my 'first prize' I reserve for the 'back-room boys' who allowed us to see the audience from time to time when things got too bad. There must be many people like myself who now switch on all the cultural programmes on BBC Television in the hope of a glimpse of the audience. I acquired a taste for 'audience-viewing' during the lessons which Mr H. Trevor-Roper gave recently on the subject of (I think) 'History,' and I must confess I have become something of an addict!

Of course, addiction to anything can be carried too far! I don't agree with some people who complain bitterly that the 'natural breaks' between one picture of the audience and the next are too long. I think these breaks give one a chance to get back to one's ironing!

Perhaps your readers would be interested to know how we arrange our viewing in this house. First we turn the set on in good time for it to warm up before the cultural programme begins. We watch the preliminary antics or trumpet voluntaries – which we love! – and then we turn the sound down. I go out into the kitchen while my husband sits watching the set and listening to the wireless.

As soon as anything of note occurs, he calls me. 'Quick!' he says. 'Breakdown!' Or it might be someone forgetting his 'lines,' or even occasionally someone who has had 'one over the eight!'

We enjoy all these diversions. But we like the pictures of the audience best of all. They seem such nice, ordinary people – nothing 'stuck up' or 'special' about them at all. What I particularly appreciate is that they're not fussing about doing something all the time, like the majority of the people one sees on the television! Most of the time they're just sitting there quietly, so that one has a chance to take them in and see them as they really are.

Of course, I'm always looking out to see if I can see anyone I know! In one of Mr H. Trevor-Roper's lessons I saw a young woman who looked exactly like a housemaid I had for a time after the First World War called Susan Hargreaves. I was so surprised that I called out 'Well! Susan Hargreaves!' My husband dryly pointed out that Susan would be over 60 now!

'It's all right, she couldn't hear me,' I said. 'The sound's turned down.'

How we laughed over that!

Seriously, though, 'audience-viewing' does give one chance to see how ordinary folk can 'keep smiling' in the most difficult conditions. A dreary lecture seems to bring out the best in people, just as the war did, and I often hope that some of our national Jeremiahs are looking in and seeing these wonderful young people doing their best keep their chins up. It always brings a lump to my throat.

Alas, there are sometimes one or two 'black sheep' in the audience who 'let the side down.' In that scene in *The Comedy of Errors* in which seven people were sitting in the stalls smiling slightly, with a gentleman on the extreme left who looked exactly like the late Duke of Kent, there was a man in a spotted bow tie who kept laughing in rather a suggestive way. It gave the unfortunate impression that some of Shakespeare's poetry was not so much 'immortal' as 'immoral'!

I wonder if I might ask your advice in a personal matter? I should like to 'break into' television audiences! I am 76, but still young and adventurous in outlook. I realise it is a career which would call for great dedication and a lot of hard work, but I am not quite a beginner – I have nearly 50 years' experience of working in the audiences of various provincial 'reps' behind me. I know enough not to expect to star in something like *The Comedy of Errors* overnight!

I should add that my husband has given his blessing to the project.

Yours truly, Ada Vacancy (Mrs)

(1964)

Composition for ten hands

The admiration and respect which I feel for Kingsley Amis, John Braine, Robert Conquest, Edmund Crispin, Iain Hamilton, Anthony Hartley, Bernard Levin, Simon Raven, David Rees and Peregrine Worsthorne severally is as nothing to the awe in which I hold their corporate talent. They know whose side they are on in Vietnam, and have written in a body to *The Times* twice now to announce their verdict to the world.

I wish I knew which side I was on. But I don't; and the more I read about Vietnam, the less able I am to pick a team. No such indecision hinders Amis, Braine, Conquest, Crispin, Hamilton, Hartley, Levin, Raven, Rees and Worsthorne. 'When all the lesser issues are cleared away,' they asked themselves, 'whose side are we on?' And at once they replied: 'Our answer must be that we unequivocally support America and her allies . . .'

There was heartfelt relief in Washington, naturally, when the State Department found they had the unequivocal support of ten English men of letters. Weary troops in Vietnam took heart to learn that Amis, Braine, Conquest and Crispin were right there, but a short 7,000 miles behind them, not to mention Hamilton, Hartley and Levin, or Raven, Rees and Worsthorne.

But then another letter appeared in *The Times*, penned by Brigid Brophy, Peter Buckman, Anthony Burgess, Ivy Compton-Burnett, Len Deighton, Gillian Freeman, B. S. Johnson, Julian Mitchell, John Mortimer, Alan Sillitoe and William Trevor, deploring the idea of unequivocal support for American policy in Vietnam.

'. . . Considering the available information on this atrocious war,' argued Brophy, Buckman, Burgess, Compton-Burnett, Deighton, Freeman, Johnson, Mitchell, Mortimer, Sillitoe and Trevor, 'we do not believe that the policies of America and her allies are likely to bring about the peace which is earnestly desired by all.'

The mood of elation in Washington slumped when this copy of *The Times* arrived. As the State Department's statistical experts can scarcely have failed to notice, they have ten writers for them, and eleven against. And I have the impression that the writers who are opposed to American policy have on average written more books than the writers who are in favour of it. Which must count for something in Washington and Hanoi. Mustn't it?

But there are other teams of writers who have yet to speak – as I discovered at a little literary soirée the other night when I was introduced to K. D. Haddock, Walter Pinn, Pennington Pownall, O. J. Sprout, and Thorsten Trouncer.

'What?' I cried. 'Not *the* K. D. Haddock, Walter Pinn, Pennington Pownall, O. J. Sprout and Thorsten Trouncer? The authors of that marvellous little letter on decimal coinage, and that very stylish missive against racial provocation in Fiji?'

They blushed.

'The same,' they murmured.

Well, I told them what a terrific admirer I was of their stuff – what a deeply personal style and individual view of the world I thought they had.

'Whenever I come up against some rather tricky subject,' I told them, 'such as the wage-structure of the Bolivian tin industry, I always think to myself: "I wonder what Haddock, Pinn, Pownall, Sprout and Trouncer would say about that." '

They were very bucked.

'We think we speak for all of us,' they said, 'when we say that we're as pleased as a dog with two tails. If not five dogs with ten tails.'

I asked them if they were working on another letter.

'No,' they said. 'At the moment we're working on a critical edition of the love-letters of Drossel, Gudney, Lidless and Nane, to Adbrow, Bantling, Cold-Brightman and Zimmer. It's one of the great literary romances – in the end they married, and had twenty-three children.'

Anyway, when they found out that I was Frayn, of Barnold, Brevis, Frayn, Frowder and Straithwaite, they were kind enough to say that they rather admired some of our work, too – particularly our Middlesex dialect stories, and our relentless opposition to the entry of Ireland into the Common Market.

After a bit, of course, we got round to the problems facing writers today.

'You can't get over it,' sighed Haddock, Pinn, Pownall, Sprout and Trouncer, 'the days of the old one-man-band type of writer are pretty well over.'

Barnold, Brevis, Frowder, Straithwaite and I agreed.

'We mean,' said Haddock, Pinn, Pownall, Sprout, and Trouncer, 'we'd never have been able to make up our minds about decimal coinage in the way we did if there hadn't been five of us.'

'What we personally feel,' said Barnold, Brevis, Frowder, Straithwaite and I, 'is that if there were ten or eleven of us, as in the Amis outfit, or the Brophy concern, we might be able to stand back far enough from the details to come down clearly and unambiguously on one side or the other in Vietnam.'

Because the truth is, of course, that today writers have got to merge and amalgamate to survive, just like everybody else. Big issues demand big thoughts; and big thoughts require big teams of thinkers.

Anyway, we're all going to write to *The Times* about it.

(1967)

Cottage industry

The wonderful thing about having a country cottage, say our good friends Christopher and Lavinia Crumble, is that they can have their good friends (such as us) down for the weekend.

'And the wonderful thing about having our friends down for the weekend,' explains Lavinia, as they take our bags and show us our room, 'is that we really have the chance to *talk* to them down here, away from all the mad rush of town life. Don't we darling?'

'We like to feel we've created a setting for the sort of relaxed house-party thing that used to be such an important part of the civilised way of life in the past,' says Christopher. 'Plain living and high thinking – that kind of thing. We find ourselves talking like *mad* down here. Don't we, darling?'

Apparently the place was absolutely derelict when they found it. All their friends thought they were *crazy*. But of course they got it for a song, and they did it all up themselves.

'We really have put a tremendous amount of work into it. Haven't we, darling?'

'People think we've been spending our weekends idling about in the countryside. But we've scarcely had time to sit down! You really can't imagine how much we've had to do. Can they, darling?'

Apparently *all* the beams we can now see were covered with plaster and wallpaper when they moved in! The

doorway we've just come through didn't *exist!* The floor
we're now standing on was *completely* rotten! The whole
house *reeked* of mildew! We can't really appreciate its
present condition, of course, not having seen it in its original state.

'I mean, Christopher did have a tiny worry when we
bought it that we might be doing local people out of a house.
You know what Christopher's like! But it was absolutely
derelict . . .'

'And of course what these people want is really some neat
little two-up-and-two-down semi. Isn't it, darling?'

'And if we hadn't done it up somebody else would have.
Wouldn't they, darling?'

'They're not all as tender-hearted as we are. And we have
put the most tremendous amount of work into the place.'

Have we admired their view, they ask? Oh, God, the view
– no, we haven't. Admire, admire. Only six miles or so
beyond that electricity sub-station, apparendy, is the Vale
of Relpham, which Walter Bridmore mentions in one of his
novels! The window-frame itself, it appears, is treated with
Osterman's 'Windowjoy' polyester window-frame sealer.

They expect we'd like a wash etcetera after our journey.
It seems terrible to interrupt our discussion of architecture
and literature for anything so mundane as a wash etcetera.
But there's plenty for us to admire and meditate upon in
the bathroom. Apparently Christopher did most of the
plumbing himself, and is rather proud of his handiwork.
And we're to help ourselves to hot water as lavishly as we
like, because they've installed a Supa-Heata, the literature
about which we must remind them to give us before we go.

Over lunch the conversation turns to the world of art.

'Did you admire that old Agricultural Show poster in the
loo?' inquires Christopher. 'We're frightfully proud of it.
Lavinia got it from a little man over in Market Strayborough. Didn't you, darling?'

'Of course, the loo's our great triumph altogether. I found

a little man in Morton Winchevers who built us the septic tank for about half what we'd have had to pay a big firm.'

'And she found another little man practically next door to the little man in Market Strayborough who got hold of that Victorian pedestal and cistern for us. Lavinia's got an absolute genius for getting hold of little men. Haven't you, darling?'

In the afternoon we go for a stroll, so that our hosts can point out various features of the locality of which they're particularly proud, and introduce us to one or two *marvellous* locals we absolutely must meet, now that the Crumbles have succeeded by dint of hard work and perseverance in penetrating their natural rural reserve. The long grass in the meadows and the summery smell of the cow-parsley along the lanes put everyone in a gently reflective mood.

'You can get down here in 4½ hours, you know,' says Christopher, 'if you avoid Snaith, and take that little road through Chocking which comes out just this side of Griever . . .'

'Or 4¼, if you don't get held up by all that terrible weekend traffic to the coast where you cross the main road at Westchamps Peverel . . .'

'Which is awfully good, you know, when you think about it. It means that we can leave here at half-past four on a Monday morning, and be in our respective offices by nine . . .'

Tea on the lawn, of course, sparks off an earnest debate on the nature of lawns in general, and of Christopher's efforts upon this one in particular, which we gather are beyond all praise, given the patch of thistles and nettles he had to start with.

Night comes down, obscuring the lawn wrested with such difficulty from the weeds, and the much-discussed patch of earth which Lavinia hasn't yet decided whether to fill with orodigia or flowering pangloss, and the blue paintwork on the doors and windows (Luxibrite's Melanesian Blue, which they think – and we definitely agree – is a much more subtle colour than Housallure's Gulfstream or Goyamel's Stratosphere); making the peripatetic conversationalists on the terrace only shadowy shapes as they murmur on into the dusk.

'I'll put the terrace light on. No, no – no trouble at all. We're rather proud of our electric lighting, as a matter of fact. Aren't we, darling?'

'Honestly, you'd never believe the struggle we had to get this place on the supply. It seems a pity not to use it, now we've got it. Doesn't it, darling?'

Yes, it's wonderful, as the Crumbles say, to get away from the dreadful rat-race in town for a day or two, and take a look at the one in the country for a change.

(1966)

D.Op.

Some previously indeterminate figure on the fringes of the middle-men's society, I see, was recently described as 'a man of opinion.' Now there's a great new rank to aspire to – a high new destiny for all those arts graduates without vocational training who would in the past have ended up as mere men of letters.

I think I might start studying for it. I should soon be indispensable. Theatre managers would cry 'Is there a man of opinion in the house?' and I should stroll nonchalantly up to the stage, only too accustomed to have my evenings off sacrificed to the desperate public need for my professional services.

'Thank God you're here,' the theatre manager would say, leading me backstage. 'We're in a spot, I can tell you. The stagehands have come out on strike, the juvenile lead's run off with the backer's wife, the backer's withdrawn his money, the Lord Chamberlain's banned the whole of Act Two, and the theatre's on fire.'

'It certainly sounds as though you need some frank and stimulating opinions expressed pretty urgently,' I should say, settling comfortably into a convenient armchair and sucking on a property pipe. 'Let's take the question of striking for a start. It perpetually amazes me that responsible trade union leaders apparently cannot understand that full co-operation with the Government's economic policy is absolutely essential if this country is to be able to afford to keep men of opinion like myself in the style to which we are accustomed. Not that I don't blame the managements as well. In fact I always make a point of blaming both sides in any dispute.

'And that reminds me, in the queer way that we men of

opinion are reminded, of another thorny subject – censorship. Now this is a question I have pretty controversial views on. I believe – quite passionately – that we ought to ask ourselves – all of us, you, me, the chap next door – to what extent plays, for example, should be subject to censorship. I know – in my heart – that there are a great many things to be said both for and against it. I'm not going to make any bones about saying frankly that I feel very careful consideration should be given to both sides of the question before we jump to any hasty conclusions.

'You may think that's pretty outspoken. But we have to realise what sort of world we live in – and it's a world where nowadays a juvenile lead doesn't think twice about running off with the backer's wife. I don't know what other people think about this sort of thing, but I can tell you this – whatever they think, I think the opposite. I mean, I could scarcely expect to be paid for my opinions if they were the same as everybody else's, could I?'

By the time I got on to the question of theatrical finance and the human problems behind the enforcement of fire regulations, the crisis would be practically solved, for everyone – deliquent juvenile lead, the enraged backer, his errant wife, and the Lord Chamberlain's stool-pigeons – would all be standing round bewitched by the Orphean flow of melodious opinion.

'What do you think of William Gerhardi as a novelist?' they would demand dreamily. 'Do you believe in telepathy?' 'Do you agree with Macleod's assessment of Chamberlain?' 'Is the dodecaphonic scale an argument for duodecimal arithmetic?'

'Well,' I should reply comfortably, 'I think a reappraisal of Chamberlain was long overdue. And I'm sure there is some sort of affinity between music and mathematics, though whether the duodecimal system would prove to be more popular than ... Is the universe expanding? I'm inclined to support the school of thought that holds ...

What is truth . . . ? Wasn't it jesting Pilate who was asked this one, and who . . . ? Do I prefer belt or braces? Well, I think the sensible man . . . By the way, is it getting suffocatingly hot in here, or do I really think that by appeasing Chamberlain the duodecimal system could be averted, while the braces are so immensely readable that I incline to the old-fashioned biblical view of the Common Market as being unfair to the older woman, with a crime rate expanding all the time through the baroque splendour of the Soviet leadership into a universe which is, in my view at any rate, just one huge, spongy, gaseous, ecto-plasmic mass of stewed opinion . . . ?'

(1962)

Destroy before reading

I wrote a piece a few weeks back in which I expressed some scepticism about a mnemonic that one of my daughters used to have for remembering her personal identity number at work. I subsequently got letters from one or two people who accused me of destroying my daughter's confidence and losing her her job.

Ridiculous, of course. But then I realised that my daughter hadn't said anything about the article herself . . . I began to worry. My children have all been amazingly supportive over the years about my professional activities – as scrupulously encouraging as the most devoted parents indulging the most insufferable child. Maybe I *had* been a little heavy-handed, I thought, perhaps even a little insensitive about mentioning the matter at all.

So I rang her to check, and she said she hadn't read the article yet. She'd put it aside to read, she said, but what with work and the children she'd been extremely busy, and they'd got the builders everywhere, and somehow the paper must have got thrown away. To my horror I realised that she had a rather defensive tone in her voice. She had understood my query not as an expression of tender regard for her feelings, but as a reproach for failing in her filial obligations. Not only had I destroyed her confidence and lost her her job – I'd somehow transferred my parental anxieties to her.

This was, needless to say, the last thing I wanted – particularly since I know she scarcely has time to breathe, let alone read newspapers – and since I am in a permanent fever of guilt myself about not having read all the things that people I know have written. I can't! There are too many people writing things, and only me to read them all!

So of course I felt more anxious than ever. To set her mind at rest I made a copy of the article and sent it to her, then forgot the whole matter. I rang her a week later about something else – and before I could speak she said quickly: 'I'm afraid I still haven't read the article yet.'

I said I didn't know what article she was talking about. She said she'd put it carefully away to read as soon as she had the leisure, only what with work . . . Yes, yes, I said . . . And the children, she said . . . Please, I cried . . . And the house being rebuilt . . .

I said she didn't have to read it. She said she was longing to read it. I forbade her to read it. She said she knew what it was like if you wrote things and people didn't read them. I said I knew what it was like if people wrote things and you felt you had to read them. Etcetera.

By this time I was feeling terrible. I thought of the burden I'd imposed upon all my children. Scribble scribble scribble. Articles, scripts, and advance copies of books piling up accusingly on their plates, like more and more helpings of nightmare strained spinach.

Another week went by. I didn't dare ring my daughter. And when at last I did – on some totally unconnected topic, I most solemnly swear – she confessed that she had now also lost the copy I had sent her. She had filed it carefully away in her kitchen, treasuring it up until she really had time to enjoy it to the full – and the builders had demolished the kitchen!

It seemed to me that this thing was getting entirely out of hand. She'd had to destroy a substantial part of her house to find an excuse! Confidence – job – peace of mind – and now her kitchen – all gone! I ran to the copier to rush her another copy, if not another kitchen.

Whereupon the copier ceased to function. A small enough punishment for destroying one child's home and livelihood, but it relieved my feelings a little. I called the service engineer. (£45 call-out fee, which relieved them a little further.) He said that according to the meter inside the machine I had made 98,000 copies in the couple of years I had owned it. He implied that I had worked the wretched machine to death. So now I began to feel bad about the copier as well. Not to mention my children. 98,000? Had I forced *that* many copies of articles on them? No wonder they were being driven to such desperate measures!

As soon as he had gone I rushed to the machine again to copy the article, and ease my daughter's burden of guilt, if not mine. And immediately it died again. A curse had fallen upon our entire house! Or what was left of it.

A second engineer came, and operated on the machine for most of the morning. When he emerged from the sickroom he told me that according to the meter I had produced only 1,900 copies in all the time I had owned it. I hadn't used it enough, he said reproachfully. As a result the grease inside had gone cold.

Since then the fax has jammed, the phone has gone on the blink, and the television has packed up. Either I've used them too much, or else I haven't used them enough. I should have given them a proper balance of exercise and rest each day, like dogs, or a string of racehorses. A little light copying, a little light faxing, three times a day, so that they didn't become bored and demoralised and start having breakdowns. Then a blanket over them and a brisk rub-down to stop them getting their grease chilled. And I shouldn't have kept making the fax and the copier read things I'd written.

Then I began to think of all the little machines I have with *batteries* in them. Some of them were lying forgotten in various drawers, their batteries never renewed, so that by now the acid would be corroding their little insides. I thought of all the machines with rechargeable batteries that I had failed to recharge – no, worse! – failed to *dis*charge regularly, so that by now their capacity for holding a charge would be wrecked beyond recall.

And now of course, I'm starting to worry about my daughter reading *this* article, and feeling that it's somehow her fault that the copier jammed, and the miniature vacuum cleaner for getting dust out of electronic machinery has got corroded, and the laptop won't charge. I'll have to keep it from her somehow.

Blow up the rest of her house, perhaps, just as this morning's paper is delivered. I suppose it's a fairly standard family saga. You start off with a passing remark and you end up with *Götterdämmerung*.

(1994)

Dig my dogma

'If you don't "dig" dogma,' said an advertisement for a religious magazine in *The Times* this week, 'you should certainly "get with" the current issue of *Prism*. The first five contributions concern themselves with John Robinson's "Honest to God," and concern themselves with it very deeply. To the agnostic who wrote this advertisement they were intensely stimulating and revealing reading . . .'

The agnostic whose services were retained by *Prism* to testify to the stimulating qualities of their theology does not reveal his identity. A pity. The astigmatic who wrote this article (his name can be inspected on request at our Erith works) has gone into the advertisement pretty deeply and would have liked to congratulate him on a stimulating and intensely revealing piece of work.

Not to mince words, I thought it was a unique combination of getwithery and godwottery. Or to put it another way, an exquisite blend of dogma and digma. In fact I thought it was the most stimulating and revealing bit of devotional prose published on the subject of John Robinson, aka the Bishop of Woolwich – known to millions of ordinary religion-lovers as Jack Woolwich – since Mike Canterbury said he was 'specially grieved' because Jack had published his views in a newspaper article which was, among other things, 'crystal clear in its arguments.'

Most stimulating and revealing of all was the advertiser's basic idea of getting an agnostic to write the testimonial. It amazes me that Christians didn't think of this earlier. ('To the agnostic who wrote this gospel, the events narrated seem verily "far out" – but wondrously "swinging" none the less.') I hope they will appoint a panel of neutral agnostic advisers to go right through the Thirty-Nine Articles from beginning to end and sort out the stimulating from the unstimulating.

It would certainly be in line with the most enlightened modern practice as I have come to know it. Almost every single article I have ever written on the subject of religious belief has subsequently been either commended or reprinted by some religious publication. I'm not entirely sure with what motive the other cheek is not only turned but so relentlessly hammered against one's fist. But I have an uneasy mental picture of a procession, like the terrible band of medieval flagellants in 'The Seventh Seal,' crawling across modern England on their knees, grinning with horrible pleasure as they scourge one another with anti-religious satire and blasphemous jokes, bearing aloft images of broad minds, and crying 'Like us. Please like us!'

'May I say how much I'm enjoying this article?' writes the Bishop of Twicester. 'I shall certainly take your tip and reprint it, if I may, in my *Diocesan News,* in a session we have entitled "The Other Chap's Point of View."

'There's nothing I enjoy more than having my leg pulled – the harder the better! I'm sure God enjoys it, too – though of course the question of whether His Leg exists to be pulled is one which, as you have shown in in your amusing articles, we musn't take for granted too complacently!

'You're absolutely right of course. We are, alas, sometimes tempted to curry public favour. But it is also true that the best way to protect one's most cherished convictions is not always to stand rigid against the enemy and be cut down, but to smile and co-operate with him. I think some of us are discovering that the Vicar of Bray was not as "square" as he has sometimes been painted!

'After all, if we go some way to meet you chaps, you can scarcely help but come some way to meet us! Such is human nature. I saw in the paper the other day David Frost saying that after one of his little religious skits which had offended some people he went to church – and the sidesman told him how much he had enjoyed the programme. One concession calls forth another, you see. I myself had an interesting chat with Ken Nocker after that delightful take-off he did of the Crucifixion, and he told me that it was only the commercial aspects of it he was against really.

'It used to be rock-and-roll singers we found ourselves entirely in agreement with, and then it was teenage satirists. Now it's agnostic copy-writers. Of course, it's a good thing for all of us – it helps to keep our minds open and flexible.

'One of the most encouraging things about the age we

live in is this ability not to take ourselves too seriously. There's no harm in behaving like men of the world, after all, and I like to think that we can all enjoy a joke and a prayer together, whichever side of the fence we are on.

'I dare say you'll satirise this letter! It might deserve it, too, for all I know. More power to your elbow – I thoroughly enjoy having any complacency shattered!'

(1963)

Divine news, darlings!

Among the aristocracy, reports a man at Glasgow University who has been studying their ways, one marriage in every four now ends in divorce. In other words, the aristocracy have reached the status of a Problem, and the Bishop of Twicester and I are deeply concerned about it.

'I am convinced,' he writes in a helpful little booklet entitled *The Aristocracy Today: a Challenge and an Opportunity,* 'that there is nothing fundamentally wrong with modern aristocrats. We hear a lot about the bad ones, but at heart most of them are perfectly decent and uncommonly high-spirited folk.

'The trouble is, they lack leadership. They have plenty of money to spend' and they're subjected to all sorts of unscrupulous commercial pressures. A regular barrage of suggestive advertising screams class, class, class at them seven days a week. Do we wonder they sometimes take the wrong turning?

'Those of us who go among them to any extent know how resentful they are of ill-informed criticism, and how lost and bewildered they feel in a world which seems to be run entirely for the benefit of their inferiors. My work takes me into a large club for lords and ladies in the parish of Westminster, and I know from personal experience how very likeable and human some of them can be. In a club like this, where they are given proper facilities for self-expression, there is very little hooliganism or other delinquency.'

The Bishop and I believe that the Church isn't getting through to the aristocracy because it doesn't really speak their language. All this 'thou' and 'thee' and 'yeah, yeah, yeah,' mean nothing at all to the average lord. And many of the teachings of the Church – particularly those that lay stress on poverty and humility – seem to have little relevance to life as they know it.

We feel that the only reason so many lords hang about racecources and grouse moors is that they have nowhere else to go. They drink and gamble and inflict suffering on animals because they're bored. We want to see more clubs set up for them along the lines of the one at Westminster. It doesn't take much – some red leather upholstery and a begged or borrowed woolsack – to turn the average church crypt into a very gay and inviting little House of Lords, where the local nobility can enjoy soft drinks together and take part in constructive activities such as debating.

These clubs should be places where lords and ladies can feel at home in the sort of clothes they like to wear – which may mean anything from baggy tweeds to the full traditional 'gear' of robes and coronets! Sober citizens may sniff, but very smart some of them can look, believe me, when they're 'dressed to kill' at the local meet!

Above all, we want to encourage the lords and ladies to do their divorcing in a healthy, open atmosphere of camaraderie and good fellowship, and get right away from the old hole-and-corner approach. Let all the questions and worries be thrashed out fully and frankly. 'Can pre-marital divorce ever be right?' 'Will I lose my husband if I refuse to divorce him?' You'll be amazed at the things that worry these high-spirited old families.

But this by itself is not enough – we must try to attract

them into the churches. The Bishop made a remarkable start last Sunday by holding a Lord and Lady Day Service. He decorated the Cathedral with sporting prints, and replaced the choir and organist with Debrett Dansant and his Debs Delights, who rendered a number of hymns which the Bishop had translated into straightforward upper-class English, such as 'Too super, too dishy, too marvellous Chap!'

His Lordship himself galloped in on horseback, wearing hunting pink and plus-fours. Crying 'View halloo!' he threw a gun into his shoulder, gave the angels in the roof a right and left, and brought down a cock and a hen. Pausing only to set the port circulating among the congregation, he got the Rural Dean to give him a leg up into the pulpit, where all the known tongues of dukes and of barons descended on him simultaneously, and he preached thus: 'My text today is from Ecclesiastes chapter 5 verse 12: "The sleep of a labouring man is sweet." Or as we say, "The sleep of a labourin' man is puddin'."'

'How true that is, what? I mean to say, sometimes we draw a covert for the meanin' of life, and it seems to double back and go to earth. I know I do, what? But when you go forth from here today I want you to bear in your hearts the knowledge that whenever things get too utterly ghastly, too absolutely filthington, you can always drop in on God for a quick spiritual snifter.

'You see, I like to think of prayer as a kind of spiritual grouse shootin' – a chance to get shot of the odd brace of grumbles. Yes, as I said in the Teenagers' Service last week, goin' out after the birds is as much part of religion as toddlin' along to Vespers or Holy Communers. And doin' a ton in the Rolls is just about as religious as you can get short of actually goin' in for Holy Orders kit. I mean to say, what?

'To him who hearkeneth not to the voice of righteousness the consequences could be dashed desperate, not to say hellish. But the man who doth the best he can in the jolly old circs is likely to have a heavenly time, doncher know, what?

'Shall we Johann Sebastian kneelers-peelers?'

And the whole congregation – Mrs Thrumley, Mrs Arthur Upstreet, and the Lord Bishop's old mother – fell upon their knees and repented bitterly of the way of life that had brought them into that place.

(1963)

East of Suez

An extract from the signal log of HMS Ubiquitous, on passage in the Indian Ocean.

C-in-C Singapore to Ubiquitous: Urgent amendment sailing orders. Courtesy call South African ports cancelled. Re-embark all coloured personnel and Chinese cooks debarked in anticipation SA visit and alter course forthwith for Aden. Render all necessary assistance required by local civil and military authorities to maintain order during disturbances.

Report position and estimated time of arrival Aden.

Ubiquitous to C-in-C Singapore: Your signal received and understood. Wilco. My position 3.15N 79.44E. Estimated time of arrival Aden – early June.

C-in-C Singapore to Ubiquitous: Cancel my last signal. Re-debark Chinese cooks and proceed with all possible speed Hong Kong make show of strength during civil disturbances. Equip shore patrols with anti-riot weapons. Stand by to take over Hong-Kong-Kowloon ferry service from strikers.

Report position and ETA Hong Kong.

Ubiquitous to C-in-C Singapore: Wilco. Have fetched round to take up easterly course and my position is once again 3.15N 79.44E. ETA Hong Kong – Tuesday week.

C-in-C Singapore to Ubiquitous: Most urgent. Abandon course Hong Kong and make all possible speed Gulf of Aqaba. Stand by southern approaches to Strait of Tiran outside territorial waters establishing British presence but in view delicate situation in area establish it with maximum circumspection.

Report position and ETA Tiran.

Ubiquitous to C-in-C Singapore: Wilco. Have come round on to westerly course again and am back at 3.15N 79.44E. ETA Tiran – mid-June.

C-in-C Singapore to Ubiquitous: Note amendment previous signal. In view local customs and feelings debark Jewish personnel before proceeding Tiran.

Ubiquitous to C-in-C Singapore: Wilco. In view of possible Papal pronouncement on situation advise whether should keep RCs below decks.

C-in-C Singapore to Ubiquitous: Urgent amendment previous signals. Re-embark forthwith all Jewish personnel debark coloured personnel and proceed with maximum dispatch Macao. Establish British presence outside territorial waters in support British consul. Report ETA Macao.

Ubiquitous to C-in-C Singapore: Wilco. ETA Macao uncertain but expect to be back at 3.15N 79.44E in approximately 10 minutes.

C-in-C Singapore to Ubiquitous: Urgent re-amendment to amended orders. Political situation United Nations re Aqaba question makes immediate courtesy call African port essential. Debark all white personnel and proceed forthwith Mombasa.

Ubiquitous to C-in-C Singapore: Wilco. Advise whether Chinese cooks classified white or coloured in Mombasa.

C-in-C Singapore to Ubiquitous: Correction. Proceed Shanghai establish discreet British presence in support two British diplomats being glued by crowd. In view local sensibilities re defectors re-debark Chinese cooks again.

Ubiquitous to C-in-C Singapore: Wilco.

C-in-C Singapore to Ubiquitous: Cancel last signal.

Proceed at once Gibraltar make discreet show of strength outside territorial waters off Algeciras.

Ubiquitous to C-in-C Singapore: Show of strength impossible without full complement of Chinese cooks.

C-in-C Singapore to Ubiquitous: Re-re-embark Chinese cooks forthwith. Astonished not re-embarked already.

Ubiquitous to C-in-C Singapore: Wilco. Advise whether should circumnavigate world eastabout or westabout.

C-in-C Singapore to Ubiquitous: Westabout calling at Malta for major refit. Imperative you reassure local population HM Government still using base.

Ubiquitous to C-in-C Singapore: Wilco. Have kept helm hard over and am almost back at 3.15N 79.44E again.

C-in-C Singapore to Ubiquitous: Correction. Proceed eastabout via North-West Passage so as to pass Iceland protect British trawlers suffering harassment Icelandic gunboats.

Ubiquitous to C-in-C Singapore: Wilco.

C-in-C Singapore to Ubiquitous: Your signal very faint.

Ubiquitous to C-in-C Singapore: My signalman very dizzy. But British presence at 3.15N 79.44E almost over-powering. Situation here entirely under control.

C-in-C Singapore to Ubiquitous: Well done Ubiquitous. But in view of general world feeling debark all personnel with British nationality before proceeding further.

(1967)

Eating for others

The beggars you meet in the street these days don't seem to know anything about modern fundraising.

They ask you for money. This is a very naïve and counter-productive approach. You know they propose to spend the money entirely on themselves, and no one finds blatant self-interest very appealing. They haven't grasped the essential point of all commercial enterprise, that to make a profit you must first invest. They don't understand that the most effective way to solicit a gift is to offer a gift.

But, you protest, the old man outside Marks and Spencer who keeps asking you for the price of a cup of tea – how can he offer you a gift? He hasn't anything to give! No, but then nor has the Royal National Metropolitan Centre of Cultural Excellence. According to their last published accounts they have about £4 million *less* than the old man outside Marks and Spencer. Has that ever stopped them sending you free glossy brochures, which you put by to read at the weekend, but which then get covered up by the week's newspapers, so that you never even discover there's a quid pro quo in the shape of a banker's order form inside the back cover?

It's not *their* money that they're spending, this is the point. It's *your* money. It's the money you will give them out of the sense of obligation imposed by their giving something to you. Or would have given them, if you hadn't taken their little offering round to the recycling depot first. And *you* have plenty of money. I hope. Because once I've explained these basic principles to the old man outside Marks and Spencer you're going to need it.

I'm preparing a business pack on the subject, which I shall be giving him instead of money the next time he approaches me. So the next time he approaches you, after he has digested my advice, and raised the appropriate venture capital from his merchant banker contacts in the City, he won't ask you for anything.

Instead he will thrust a very large invitation card into your hand, printed in raised italic script, with his family coat of arms at the top embossed in gold. Even before you read it you will feel a simple pride at the thought of being able to prop this thing up casually on your mantlepiece, where its sheer size, and the glitter of its gold embossing, will arouse the envy of every visitor who walks into the room.

When you do read it you will discover that, far from being asked for the price of a cup of tea, you are being offered refreshment yourself. Not only you, but your partner as well. Not on the pavement outside the Kwality Liquor Mart, where this man usually consumes any cups of tea he has been able to raise finance for, but in the banqueting suite of some more central hostelry, such as the Royal Imperial Intercontinental Hotel. Not in the company of him and his fellow tea-drinkers, but in the presence of a Royal Highness.

You talk it over sensibly with your partner and you decide to invest 25p in a stamp to put on your acceptance, which is probably already 5p more than you would have advanced towards the cup of tea. You take your dinner jacket and evening dress to the cleaners (another £15 or so, but they need cleaning anyway). When you look at the results you make a joint reasoned decision to invest a further £200 in a new evening dress, because you are after all going to be hobnobbing with royalty, and perhaps, if you seem presentable enough, getting invited to some delightful little intimate party they are giving themselves. Then, when the day comes, you spend another £15 on a taxi to get to the Royal Imperial Intercontinental Hotel, because you can't really travel on public transport in your amazing new evening dress, and you don't want to risk driving home still intoxicated by the delightfulness of the royal presence.

You know that at some point, sooner or later, you will be writing a cheque for some not too gracelessly mean amount in return for all this. But what you'll be getting for your money! No question of a cup of tea. You'll be getting champagne and canapes, followed by four courses of food specially rich in health-giving cholesterol, washed down by several different sorts of wine, followed by brandy or liqueurs. You will be entertained by delightful speeches, which various public relations consultants and equerries have given up whole highly-paid days to writing.

The Royal Highness will turn out not to be sitting at your table, sadly, but you will have the pleasure of being among people who seem to be as wealthy as you hope you look yourself. If a gentleman, you will find yourself sitting with a lovely wealthy lady in a new evening dress on either side of you; if a lady, with a distinguished wealthy gentleman in a newly-cleaned dinner jacket. Your head whirls with the possibilities of moneyed romance. Which of your two partners to exchange delicious gallantries with first? You turn gracefully to the one on your left, say, and you talk about . . .

You talk about . . .

About . . . well . . . where he or she lives. You talk about where *you* live. You talk about where you are both going on holiday, the precise numbers of your respective children, their educational arrangements and professional prospects.

Enchanting as this conversation is, you will remember halfway through the *sole avec son coulis de kiwi* that you haven't said anything to your charming and well-heeled companion on the right, so you will turn to him or her. Your tongue loosened now by wine, you will find no more difficulty in finding conversational topics. You will talk about . . . where you both live . . . where going/gone on holiday . . . numbers of children . . . children's outstanding charms and achievements . . .

By the time you have got on to the *kiwis dans un parfait de chèvre* it will come to you that there is something suspiciously familiar about this person's entire life. Slowly you will realise that you sat next to him or her at some similar occasion last year, and went through precisely the same conversation. In the ensuing silence you will find time to eat three *petits fours* instead of one, and have a brandy, which you never normally do. You may go so far as to take the cigar you are offered, even though you don't smoke, and put another one in your breast pocket or handbag, something you'd noticed other people doing but had never thought you would be bold enough to do yourself.

So you go home with a feeling in your chest which is either heartburn or heart disease, or possibly just the cockles of your heart being warmed by all the good you have done. You pay another £15 for a taxi, or £20 in parking fees, because you couldn't in fact find a taxi when you set out and had to bring the car after all, or £100 to release the car from the car-pound, because you couldn't find a parking-space, plus a £1,000 fine for driving with more than the permitted limit of royal highness in your blood, all of which, together with the loss of your licence and consequently your job, at say £50,000 a year for the next ten years, brings the bill for the evening up to somewhere around half a million pounds.

Not to mention your generous contribution to the organisers of all this, which will at last provide the old man outside Marks and Spencer with his cup of tea, unless all his 20p share of the proceeds has gone in administration.

And you have the pleasant prospect of doing the same thing again the following week, to finance a cup of coffee for the man who usually stands outside Sainsbury's.

(1994)

Eternity in a tube of toothpaste

The lotos-eaters, in Tennyson's poem, live in a land where it seems always afternoon. Tennyson reports no complaints from them about this arrangement, and Odysseus's men, as soon as they have eaten a little of the fruit themselves, decide they are perfectly happy to settle down here as well, and give up all prospect of morning, evening, or night.

Permanent afternoon would have its drawbacks, of course. It would be sad if one never got to teatime, tragic if dinner remained forever beyond the horizon. But at least it's better getting stuck in the afternoon than where all the rest of us are stuck – in the morning. And in one particular bit of the morning, at that. Not breakfast-time, or coffee-break, or the approaches to lunch. In the land of the Gala apple-eaters, where you and I live, it's always getting-up time.

Have you noticed this? I mean that whenever you become conscious of the time, that's when it is. Whenever you think about what you are actually doing at this particular moment in time, what you're doing is cleaning your teeth. You're looking at yourself in the mirror and you're thinking, Here I am again, cleaning my teeth. And you're thinking that this is a pretty dreary thing to be doing. You're also thinking that the last thing before this that you can remember being actually conscious of doing was looking at yourself in the mirror as you cleaned your teeth the previous morning.

You remember what you were thinking as you did it, too. You were thinking, Here I am again, cleaning my teeth. And you were thinking that this was a pretty dreary thing to be doing. You were also thinking that the last thing before this that you could remember being actually conscious of doing was looking at yourself in the mirror as you cleaned your teeth the *previous* morning. Etcetera. It's as if there were another mirror behind you as well, and you could see your life stretching away in both directions into glass-green infinity. And what are you doing in each increasingly remote green moment of this infinity? You're cleaning your teeth.

No, there is some variation. For men, at any rate, it's sometimes a slightly different time. It's a few minutes later, when they're shaving, and things are even drearier than they were when they were cleaning their teeth. Or, worse, in my case – it's a few minutes earlier, when I'm lying in bed trying to decide whether I should get up and *start* brushing my teeth and shaving. I'm trying to decide whether to get up precisely *now*, or whether I could safely leave it an instant longer, and get up say . . . now. Or . . . now . . . Then worrying that if I don't get up *now*, which is where it's got to now . . . or even *now* . . . then it's difficult to see how I'm ever going to get up at all, so that the dreary prospect of looking in the mirror and all the rest of it is always going to be in front of me, which is even worse than its actually happening.

You're vaguely aware at these moments that other things have somehow been going on in your life as well as getting up, though it's difficult to know when you managed to fit them in. Some of these things, you dimly recall, were more agreeable than this, others were even less. But they were notably agreeable or disagreeable enough – notably *notable* enough – for you to be conscious only of the things themselves, and not of yourself experiencing them.

A lot of perfectly ordinary things have happened, for that matter. You had lunch the previous day, you walked down the street, you felt a cold coming on. But they were so ordinary that you were scarcely conscious of them at all. You weren't looking in the mirror at the time, of course. This probably helped.

But the last time you were actually thinking about what you were doing, you were getting up. So your life, as something that you are actually conscious of, rather than something that's just rushing past without your quite being able to take it in, has closed up into one long, continuous, extremely dreary moment of getting up. It's Wednesday, and it's time to get up. It's Monday, and it's time to get up. It's November 13th, 1959, and it's time to get up. It's January 19th, 1995, and it's time to get up . . .

One day somebody is doing to be writing your biography. Is it going to appeal to a wide readership, this biography of yours? I believe it's not. I believe your biography is headed straight for the remainders table.

This is obviously what eternity is going to be like. Today, and time to get up . . . Still today, and time to get up . . .

I understand this kind of thing happens to space travellers in science-fiction stories – they get stuck in time-warps. They presumably manage to extract themselves and struggle back to earth with the help of various pieces of implausible science and fictitious mathematics. How are we ever going to get out of ours, with nothing but a tooth-brush and a razor strangely encrusted with solidified shaving cream?

Actually it's not just space-travellers who get trapped in time-warps. It's always happening, in the most respectable kind of books. But they're stuck in the past in some kind of way, which might be more interesting. They've reverted to their childhood, or they're still living in some rather memorable moment of triumph or disaster. It wouldn't be much fun to spend your entire life watching the rats running over the cobwebbed ruins of your wedding-cake, I see that. But it would surely be more interesting than spending it cleaning your teeth, or shaving the lefthand side of your face.

People are always recommending living in the present, it's true. But couldn't it at least be a different present? Couldn't it be breakfast time? Yes, why doesn't one get stuck in breakfast time, which comes round just as often as shaving? Why couldn't it happen that every time one notices what one's doing it turns out to be drinking delicious fresh orange juice, with the morning paper propped up against the coffeepot, full of appetising fresh catastrophes? Perhaps if one fixed up a mirror on the breakfast table . . . ?

After all, the lotos-eaters never seemed to have cleaned their teeth at all. Maybe their teeth fell out before they were thirty. Are they worrying about this? Apparently not.

How *do* you get out of the warp? You never discover. One moment you've been cleaning your teeth since the beginning of time, and you're going to go on cleaning them until the end of time, at which point, if Stephen Hawking is right, you'll start cleaning them backwards, and go on cleaning them backwards until you get back to the Big Bang, when you'll start cleaning them forwards again . . . Then somehow, miraculously, you've broken through to breakfast time, and orange juice and economic crises are going on around you.

But scarcely have you got on to your second cup of coffee when out of nowhere it's tomorrow, and it's time to get up.

(1994)

Every day in every way

If there's one thing I enjoy it's curling up with a good book entitled *Release Your Hidden Personality – and Find God!* or *How to Sell Friends and Merchandise People.* At the moment I am curled up with the latest of these treasure chests of wisdom, *Word Power – Life Power,* by one Vernon Howard.

Sooner or later, I am sure, *Reader's Digest* will regurgitate the quintessential cud of Mr Howard's argument, but for readers who would prefer it in tablet form here and now it is roughly 'Say beautiful things, and you will be a beautiful person.'

What I enjoy are the anecdotes these books abound in, about nerve-racked, unsuccessful salesmen who go groaning to their doctor, a chuckling, genial old bird who gives them a simple mnemonic to remember, equipped with which they swiftly become president of the company, turning up under a thin disguise one or two anecdotes later to chuckle genially and show the reporter who is asking them for the secret of their success the letters 'C.G.' carved on their wall (standing for 'Chuckle Genially').

Apart from chuckling, the basic technique for self-improvement is usually a programme of exercises and mnemonics with which the reader is urged to keep pounding away at himself all the time. Mr Howard, for example, suggests repeating phrases like 'My words are daily dynamite,' 'I rest in the best!' and 'A smile is my style!' He would also like you to 'create vitalising verbal visions – don't just day-dream,' 'build your dream castles with constructive word-nails,' 'try the "tomato technique",' 'bake a say-cake!' (which consists of a cupful of cheery remarks, a generous amount of enthusiasm, a full quart of prayer, and a pint of humour), and 'make every adverb a gladverb.'

A devotee of these pep books (particularly if he is trying to put more than one of them into practice at the same time) must maintain inside his head an interior monologue unsurpassed in richness since James Joyce ceased creating his vitalising verbal visions. Take the case of Walter, for instance. Walter, an elastic-hosiery salesman, is driving back to his head office in Walsall after being tossed out into the street by a chuckling cheesemonger in Rugeley. He has a hangover, an overdraft, and good reason to believe he is just about to be declared redundant.

'I'm feeling fine,' he is saying to himself as he drives along. 'Things fine are mine. I rest in the best. I bask in the task. I wash in the slosh. Uh-huh, wrong one there. Try the tomato technique, instead. Just a moment – which is the tomato technique? Forgotten. Oh, well, all I need to do is use the cucumber technique for remembering things. How does that go? H'm, seem to have forgotten that one, too.

'Never mind, keep smiling. A smile is my style. Check smile in driving mirror. Look out! Damn' fool of a woman stepping off the kerb then! They ought to flog jay-walkers! Calm down. Make every adjective a gladjective. That's wrong. What the hell is it? Every noun a gloun? God, I feel shaky. Nonsense. Never felt better. Things mine are fine. Every verb a glerb.

'Headache. Pain in back. Quick, some constructive word-nails. Create a verbalised, visual vitamin . . . a virtualised verbal victual . . . skip it. Try baking a say-cake. A cupful of word-nails, a quart of gladverbs . . . gladverbs! That's the word! Slow down for this roundabout, now. Watch for the posting to Gladverb.

'I'm fine. Things fine are mine. I roast on toast. The toast floating down the Rhine, and the Rhine coasting down my spine. Now steady. Get a grip. Try laughing. Can't. Say "ha." Now say "ha" again. Ha-ha. That's laughing. I laugh in the bath. I bath in the laugh.

'Funny. Been going round this roundabout for a long time, but still no posting to Gladsall. Ah, policeman waving on the paving. Stop and ask him. Wind down window. Now, big, big smile, friendly slap on back for copper, never felt better. Officer, there's no posting boasting Gladby. I mean Gladsall. No, no, Gladverb. What? Get out and walk along that white line? Why, certainly. Big smile, feeling fine. Both feet upon the line, like a bug upon a vine, feeling fine, fine, fine . . .'

(1960)

Facing the music

In theory, television ought to be bringing the arts within reach (as they say) of millions who would not otherwise etc. etc. It seems reasonable enough. You've got sound, you've got vision. What more do you want to communicate every known art form, except perhaps gastronomy?

But in practice it doesn't work out too well. The sight of a great painting reproduced a foot high, in monochrome and in low definition, isn't a very compelling aesthetic experience. Nor is watching someone read poetry off the teleprompter – even a teleprompter with hand-tooled calf binding.

You'd think that the performing arts at least would be naturals. And, indeed, stage plays and opera are; but ballet is hopeless, and music is very tricky.

Most of the older arts have to be communicated on television, if at all, by suggestion and association. Details from paintings can be very poignant, glimpsed as the raw material for some quiz programme. Poetry can be highly effective, read as the background to film shots which are evocative in their own right. It's a sort of titillation, like the suggestion of sexual feeling by glimpses of suspenders; it's not really art itself which is being communicated, but a kind of nostalgia for art experiences with which one is already familiar.

Music is the most tantalising of all. It's odd; surely the performers (the perfect monochrome subject in their black tail-coats and white ties) are no smaller or less distinct on a television screen than they would be from the back of a concert hall?

But there's something about the sight of them which unsettles television producers, at any rate, and makes them feel the medium's being misused. They tried to get round it first of all by creative cross-cutting. They'd cut to the oboes to show them playing five particularly significant notes. Dissolve to horns, for a telling tootle from them. Then they'd show you the piano keyboard superimposed over the clarinets, so you'd know that the piano and the clarinets were playing significant bits simultaneously. If only they'd put up sub-titles, too, saying 'coda,' or 'modulation into E flat,' or 'attribution of this passage doubtful,' we'd really have known where we stood.

Evidently the producers still weren't happy, though, because the tendency is increasingly to show music only in some secondary role, as the by-product of its performers' personalities, or as the raw material of more telegenic processes.

Instead of actual performances we are shown rehearsals. A little music occurs – then some celebrated and well-loved character in the musical world waves his arms despairingly and stops everyone. 'No, no, no, no!' he cries in compellingly broken English. 'Not *so* – la, la-la, la – like from leetle mouses who are frighten of cat. Beeg, beeg! LA, LA-LA, LA . . . !'

And again music breaks out; but of course by this time we are all turning to each other at home and saying, 'My God, what a tyrant! But they all *love* him, you know – he's such a character!' Or they show the musicians in question on tour. We see them starting Opus 59 No. 1 at a concert in Denver, but after a few bars they leave the music playing of its own accord on the soundtrack, slip into sports shirts and drive by a scenic route through the Rockies to some millionaire's ranch, where the cellist falls amusingly into the swimming-pool. By the time he's out, and had a drink, and complications have set in on the Beethoven, they've abandoned it anyway, and started playing the second Bartok quartet in Salt Lake City.

The latest and most fruitful technique is to show the

music being recorded for stereo, a complex process which gives scope for every conceivable sort of human and technical diversion – and even offers a legitimate excuse for superimposing more entertaining sounds over the music while it's actually being played, in the form of the 'talkback' between the recording engineers.

'Stand by for the drum roll . . . Fade up Don Ottavio and stand by to kill Miss Nielsen as soon as she's finished her A . . . We're getting a bit of resonance off Siegfried's glasses, aren't we, George . . . ?'

Fascinating, certainly. In fact when you come to think about it, a lot of television itself isn't all that televisual; it might be greatly improved by the application of the same sort of techniques. A man sitting reading the news out, for instance – wouldn't it be much more exciting, much more real, to have the *rehearsal* of it, with all the talk-back between control room and studio floor audible?

'. . . five, four, three, two, one – cue Bob.' *'The Prime Minister told the House of Commons today that . . .'* 'Hold it there! Something's wrong with Bob's microphone . . . Well, get him to sit a bit closer, then . . . All right? All right – from the top, everyone . . . five, four, three, two, one – cue Bob.' *'The Prime Minister told the House of Commons today that . . .'* 'Hold it, everyone! The lines on Bob's forehead are strobing.'

And if a programme about the enginers recording the music is better than just the music, surely it's logical to suppose that a programme about the cameramen filming the engineers recording the music would be better still, and that even better than *that* would be a programme about the cameramen filming the cameramen filming etc. etc. Lord, think of the richness of the talkback!

'Go right in tight, two!' 'Back a bit, one! No, my God, Ken's two's right behind you!' 'Get that blasted mike up out of the picture!' 'Come back down with Miss Sutherland's mike, damn you!' 'Up a bit, three!' 'Down a shade, three!' 'Track round on to Ken's one, two!' 'In on to Dick's two, one . . . !'

It may be slightly spoiled by interference from various hooligans singing and otherwise creating a disturbance in the background. But it should prove once and for all that it's possible to get television across on television.

(1967)

The faith of a snout baron

It must have been a moving moment when Lord Sinclair of Cleeve, the tobacco baron, stood up in the House of Lords during the debate on smoking and said he wanted to 'refute conclusively some of the baser allegations made against the reputation of an industry which I have been proud to serve.'

I wonder how many people had realised before that the tobacco industry was an institution which men were proud to serve, and which had a reputation they were prepared to stand up and defend against dishonour? I'm not sure that the industry shouldn't make the facts more widely known – perhaps commission a film about life in the tobacco industry which brought out something of its essential nobility. But why should I be modest? Gentlemen, I have the scenario you want right here:

Handsome, dashing young Simon Ricepaper, scion of one of the oldest and proudest tobacco families in the land, who has passed out of the Royal Tobacco Academy top in smoke-ring blowing and winner of the Cigarette-holder of Honour, joins a crack Kingsizer company.

As the youngest member of the boardroom here he has to undergo all the time-honoured initiation pranks and rituals of the Company, and in these his chief tormentor is the boardroom madcap, Freddie Twenty. Simon despairs of ever being accepted by his fellow directors. But one day, when Freddie and Simon are leading a detachment sent out to bring a tribe of blackamoors in a remote colony under the cigarette, Freddie gets cut off and surrounded by dangerous anti-smoking killjoys. Simon goes to help him, fearlessly bombarding the killjoys with any arguments that come to hand. 'Fwightfully decent of you to wescue me like that,' drawls Freddie as together they manage to evade the issue. From then on Simon and Freddie are fast friends.

But at the next boardroom dining-in night, Simon is in trouble again. Colonel Flake, the Chairman, is holding forth about the Great Sales Drive of '53, when the Company massacred over a thousand smokers in one campaign. Simon, exhausted after advertising practice, falls asleep. One of his fellow-directors, dark, saturnine Rupert de Luxe, draws Colonel Flake's attention to it, and Simon is given an extra two weeks as duty director.

Instead of enjoying himself at the annual Company ball the following week, therefore, Simon has to be at his post, ready to deal promptly with any outbreak of non-smoking in the Company's distribution area. It is here that lovely Virginia Flake, the Chairman's daughter and the toast of the boardroom, finds him when, filled with a strange melancholy, she slips away from the brilliant throng within. All his chivalry aroused, Simon offers her a cigarette, and she tells him she is engaged to Rupert de Luxe. But when their eyes meet, they both know that the curling blue ribbons of smoke from their cigarettes are hopelessly entwined.

But Simon's trials are still not over. The very next day, as Simon offers Colonel Flake his cigarette-case in the ante-room, the monocle slips from the Chairman's eye. 'Cork-tipped!' he exclaims, going white with anger. 'This is an insult which I should never have expected to see bandied about between Kingsizers, Ricepaper. Kindly have your papers in my hands by the morning.'

Simon accepts the sentence stoically, although he knows it was not he who filled his case with the cowardly cork tips. As soon as they are safely outside, Freddie cries: 'It's that cad Wupert de Luxe! I saw him at your cigawette-case while you were out last night!'

Simon accuses de Luxe, who challenges him to a duel. Simon chooses to fight with cigarettes, and they slog it out behind the fives court, swapping puff for puff for twelve hours before de Luxe, wheezing and gasping, cries: 'I give in! I don't want to die! I confess everything. I planted the cork tips on you because I didn't want a rival for Virginia – and her father's money! And you may as well know that I'm a deserter from the Woodbine Corps.'

'I just did what I had to do,' says Simon modestly, one arm round Virginia, the other being fervently shaken by Colonel Flake, 'for the honour of the Company and the good name of tobacco.'

'Bwavo!' cries loyal Freddie, 'and here's a telegwam to say that thwee of the customers you were wesponsible for have died of lung cancer. Blooded at last, Simon – now you're weally one of us!'

(1962)

A farewell to arms

I'm glad the Pope's against war. Because so am I, and so is Horace Morris, and so are quite a number of other people I know.

The Pope and I don't always see eye to eye, but I'm bound to admit that on this one I think he's got hold of the right end of the stick. 'No more war, war never again . . .' as he told the assembled delegates at the UN. 'If you wish to be brothers, let the arms fall from your hands.' It touched a chord. In fact, judging by the headlines and the discussions on television, it seems to have evoked widespread acknowledgement and admiration, and no disagreement at all.

All the same, I think it is only fair to point out that the Pope was not the first to declare himself in favour of peace. The previous week very similar views were expressed by Mr Patrick McGoohan, described as Britain's highest-paid television actor, in an interview in *TV Times*.

Mr McGoohan was being interviewed by Iain Sproat (who, the *TV Times* was careful to point out, was educated at Winchester and Oxford, so you can be pretty sure he got it down right). 'We were once talking,' writes Mr Sproat, 'about the totally hypothetical question of what he would do were he Prime Minister. I remember he said nothing for a moment, and then:

'"I would be overwhelmed with fear, but if I were, I would try to get everyone to cease combat just for one minute. Just peace on earth for one minute! It's a fairy tale but you never know. It would feel so good that they might not start again."'

Harold Wilson must be kicking himself. Not once does it seem to have occurred to him to arrange a trial run of peace on earth! That's why they pay Mr McGoohan so much as an actor – to keep him out of politics.

Now I'm not for a moment accusing the Pope of lifting Mr McGoohan's ideas. I don't suppose he even set eyes on a copy of last week's *TV Times*. By some fluke Mr McGoohan missed the headlines – 'MCGOOHAN CALLS FOR PEACE ON EARTH,' 'CEASE COMBAT, URGES HIGHEST-PAID TV ACTOR' – and the Pope collected all the glory for much the same idea. Like Darwin and Wallace discovering evolution. Just one of those coincidences.

'Hasn't this peace business been around before?' asked my friend Horace Morris, as we sat discussing the history of ideas, in the way we often do. 'Weren't there some rather scruffy people you and I knocked around with in our youth who used to walk about the roads every Easter saying roughly, in effect, let the arms fall from your hands?'

'You mean the Aldermaston marchers?'

'That's right. Very statesmanlike of them, one realises now. Tremendous sense of moral leadership they were showing.'

'Good heavens, Horace, that was a different matter altogether! They were just a bunch of vague, muddleheaded idealists!'

'Not statesmanlike at all?'

'Certainly not. They weren't making a broad appeal to the hearts and minds of mankind – they were trying to get our own Government to disarm! That's politics, Horace. We'd have weakened our strategic posture against Communist intimidation.'

'But haven't the Communists been coming out for peace themselves recently, in a rather broad, statesmanlike way?'

'Broadish, I suppose, Horace. But what the Communists mean by peace is peace in circumstances favourable to the spread of Communist ideas and influence.'

'Whereas the Pope means peace in circumstances favourable to the spread of anti-Communist ideas and influence?'

'I should think that's what he means, Horace. He doesn't specify, of course – he's had the sense not to get bogged down in particularities and details. But I don't suppose he means "Let the arms fall from your hands, and let the Communists peacefully take over South-East Asia." There's peace and peace, as I'm sure the Pope would be the first to recognise.'

'What he's telling us is "Let the arms fall from your hands, but go on defending freedom against tyranny and the rule of law against lawlessness"?'

'As it were.'

'By virtue as it were of the tyrants and outlaws responding to this broad supranational appeal too?'

'Exactly, as it were.'

'He sees both sides of the question?'

'I think seeing both sides of the question is his strong point, Horace. For instance, you remember he said he was against birth control?'

'I was a little worried by that, I must admit.'

'Ah, yes, but at the same time, Horace, he came out very strongly against people going hungry.'

'I see what you mean. The broad view? The bipartisan approach?'

'Quite. In fact, he advised people to make new efforts to increase the world's food supply. Rather a bright idea, don't you think?'

'I see what you mean. Really, short of doing anything it lies in his power to do, like changing his mind about birth control, he's doing everything he can.'

(1965)

51 to Blangy

Another kilometre stone coming up . . . 51 to Blangy-le-Duc. Superb views on either side of the road, any of which we could stop and look at if we chose. Delightful sensation of being captain of one's own destiny. Muse on therapeutic effect car has on human ego. One's choice potential is extended, and . . . Become conscious of wife asking question. Stop musing. Listen.

'. . . *just thinking why don't we stop along here somewhere and look at the view?*'

Stop? Of course. Could easily, anywhere. With so many superb views, only difficulty to know where. Not *there*, obviously – right next to electric pylon. And not *there*, clearly – two cars there already. Now a very narrow bit with nowhere to pull off the road. Just get this stretch over and look again.

Now, slow. That spot would have been all right anywhere

else, but not quite as good as some of the places we passed a mile or two back. What's that hooting behind? Good God, lorry I overtook five minutes ago trying to overtake me! Damned liberty! If I go back to my normal speed, like this, you'll realise what a big mistake you're making, my friend.

'*That looked quite a good place.*'

'What? Oh, I didn't see it. Not worth going back, is it?'

Rather dull stretch here. Kilometre post coming up. Still 48 kilometres to Blangy-le-Duc. Hm. Now 11.30, so must have been averaging scarcely 60 kilometres an hour since St-Sévère. If it's the same sort of road ahead, that means we shan't be at Blangy until about 12.15. Then it's about, say, 70 kilometres from Blangy to Le Hoquet – say, 1.30. Then, say, half an hour for . . .

'*Aren't you going to stop, then?*'

'Um? Stop?'

. . . half an hour for lunch. Say two o'clock. Then round about 100 kilometres from Le Hoquet to Pisaller. Say . . .

'*To look at the view.*'

'What view? Rather seedy bit here.'

. . . say four o 'clock, allowing a bit of time in hand, which will give us about two hours to get down to Uze . . .

'*Perhaps we ought to stop in Blangy instead, then.*'

'Is there something we ought to see there?'

'*Fifteenth-century castle, Romanesque cathedral, musée gastronomique, and traditional slipper-weaving industry.*'

Just a moment, what does that kilometre stone say? Blangy 45. Must stop looking at kilometre stones. Tedious obsession. Still, done those three kilometres in just under three minutes. If we kept that up we'd make Blangy at say 12.05, and Le Hoquet at . . .

'*What do you think?*'

'What? Oh, yes. Yes.'

. . . Le Hoquet at, say, 1.15. Though not if we're stopping at Blangy, of course. Forgotten that. Throws the whole calculation right out.

'We don't want to stop very long at Blangy, do we?'

'We ought to look at it for a bit, oughtn't we?'

Let's see. Say 10 minutes for the Romanesque cathedral, 10 minutes for the museum, five minutes for the castle – oh, say about 30 minutes altogether. Here's another kilometre stone coming up. Won't look this time. Well, perhaps just this once. Forty-three! Two kilometres in two and a half minutes! That means we shan't be at Blangy until about 12.20, and if we stop for half an hour, that means 2.10, no, 2.20 at Le Hoquet and . . . Must explain all this carefully to wife.

'I was just thinking, we don't really want to look round a museum in this heat, do we? What do you think?'

'What do you think?'

Cut the museum, then. After all, we've got 170 solid kilometres to do between Blangy and Pisaller. What's that in miles? Multiply by eight and divide by five: 270 miles. 270 miles! God, it can't be! Can it?

'I was thinking, perhaps we ought to give the traditional bedsock factory a miss. After all, we did spend at least half an hour looking round Cahiers yesterday. No one could accuse us of – well, I don't know, whatever anyone might start accusing us of. What do you think?'

'I don't know. What do you think?'

Cut the bedsock works, then. That saves us, what, 15 minutes? So we should reach Le Hoquet at . . . Did I say 270 miles? I must have meant 170 miles, or 270 kilometres. Mustn't I? Still, either way . . .

'We saw a Romanesque cathedral yesterday at Cahiers, didn't we?'

'Did we? I thought it was a Gothic bell-tower we saw at Cahiers.'

Gothic bell-tower . . . ? Watch out, another kilometre stone coming up. No, no! Must stop looking at the damn things!

'Perhaps you'd rather not stop at Blangy at all?'

'Of course we must stop there. We don't want to go charging across the country without ever seeing anything, do we? We're not in a charabanc. It's just that I don't want to spend the whole damned holiday looking at Romanesque cathedrals, that's all . . .'

'Two in ten days is scarcely . . .'

'Two? What was that thing we drove past in the rain at Grince? Wasn't that a Romanesque cathedral?'

Have to stop at Blangy for petrol, anyway. Will it see us through the 270 kilometres to Pisaller if we get 20 litres, plus the gallon and a half in the tank now, less the 40 kilometres from here to Blangy at 38 miles per gallon? Let's see, 20 divided by about 42.5, plus or minus 40 times 5 divided by 8 multiplied by 38. No, no . . .

'Look out!'

'All right, all right. I could see him perfectly well, I assure you.'

I suppose if it's a fifteenth-century castle . . . Perhaps we could just find a petrol station where we could see the castle without getting out of the car. Now, say we stopped for 10 minutes. In English minutes, that's 10 times 5 over 8, say 61 minutes. Or do I mean 16 kilominutes? If I could just work that out in cathedrals per litre . . .

(1962)

57 types of ambiguity

To the Pope and his advisers, the subject of contraception seems to be what power politics were to Shakespeare, or Nature was to the Romantics – an inexhaustible inspiration to the most profound and astonishing literary utterance.

Again and again, reading the works of the Papal school on the subject, one is struck by their universality, their fertile ambiguity, their articulation of feelings and experiences for which one has never before found words.

Take just for a start the minority report of the Pope's advisory commission. The Church's traditional position on contraception *must* be right, the four dissenting members are said to have argued, 'because the Catholic Church . . . could not have so wrongly erred during all these centuries of its history.'

Heavens, but that touches a chord! I feel they've seen into my soul! In one sentence those good and holy men have captured the inmost logic of my attitude to politics, religion – indeed, contraception itself. They've cut through all the specious tangle of particular argument I might have used, and located the unacknowledged real one – that I've thought what I've thought about these subjects since the age of 16 or 17, and I just *can't* have been wrong for all those years.

Of course, a process does sometimes occur which, seen from the outside, might be described as changing one's mind. But somehow it doesn't feel like that inside. Indeed, what it does feel like was beyond the range of language until the Vatican Press officer got to work on it.

He was asked, according to George Armstrong, the Rome correspondent of the *Guardian,* to elucidate the Pope's statement last October – that while he needed more time to study the question of contraception, this didn't mean that the Church's teachings on the subject were in a state of doubt.

'The teaching of the Church,' explained the Press officer, 'is now in a state of certainty. After the Pope completes his study of the matter, the Church will move from one state of certainty to another state of certainty.'

Yes! That's how it is – that's exactly how it is! You're going along in a complete state of certainty about something – the ludicrousness of Victorian architecture, say, or the moral inferiority of television – and everyone you know thinks the same.

Then various public crackpots start saying the opposite. Victorian architecture ought to be preserved, they bleat; television culture involves the whole man in a way that the print culture does not. You enjoy a good laugh at their antics. Then some of the people you know start falling for the same nonsense themselves! It doesn't bring one's own views into any state of doubt, of course. But then one day one hears oneself talking about the subject – and one realises that somehow, quite unconsciously, one has completed one's study of the matter and moved without a break to another and indeed opposite state of certainty!

So multi-levelled and many-faceted does the Pope himself wax on the subject that no one can tell whether he is still in the first state of certainty, or whether he has already moved on to the second. All that's certain is that *something* is certain – 'It is certain that,' he wrote in his encyclical 'On the development of peoples.' But what? 'It is certain the public authorities can intervene, within the limit of their competence, by favouring the availability of appropriate information and by adopting suitable measures . . .

Many people, including apparently the director-general of the United Nations Food and Agriculture Organisation, believe this means that the Governments of the over-populated countries should start actually handing out the suitable means (though whether in this case the suitable means are the sort which are digested through the proper channels, or the sort which are inserted in the appropriate place, is another rich field for speculation).

But according to an unsigned article in the Vatican newspaper, *L'Osservatore Romano*, described by the paper as 'authoritative,' this understanding of the encyclical is entirely wrong. When the Pope talks of 'suitable measures,' the article argues, he means growing more food; when he says that the authorities should 'favour the availability of appropriate information,' he means that they 'must inform the country of its population problem.'

My personal interpretation – and here I follow Sprout and Trouncer – is that the encyclical is so rich in meaning that it means *both* these things. And yet . . . neither. Only somehow . . . more, much more.

For isn't what the Pope is stating here really the general and unalterable moral rules governing suitable measures of *every* sort, and the availability of appropriate information *whatever* its subject? However many states of certainty we move through, two great moral beacons will guide us: if ever the question arises of what one should do about the availability of appropriate information, the answer is plain – favour it! And if ever a suitable measure crosses one's path – adopt it!

If only the gentlemen who wrote the Bible had been able to rise to this level of universality, how much less open to carping criticism it would be today! Really, it would be worth re-writing it from page one:

'In the beginning the Competent Authority took certain steps.

'And the resultant state of affairs was without form, and void; and an unavailability of the appropriate information was upon the face of the steps. And the Competent Authority studied the question.

'And the Competent Authority said, Let further measures be adopted: and further measures were adopted.

'And the Competent Authority saw the further measures, that they were suitable: and the Competent Authority divided the measures from the steps.

'And the Competent Authority called the measures one thing, and the steps he called another. And what with one thing and another it was the first move in the right direction . . .'

(1967)

Firm friends of ours

We've just had another of our regular visits from Christopher and Lavinia Crumble, our private consumer research, marriage guidance, home heating, and child welfare advisory service.

They come in about once a month and straighten us out. What I admire about them is their tremendous firmness in dealing with us. It's no good just offering vague suggestions to feckless problem families like us. You've got to tell us exactly what to do, and then you've to damn well stand over us and make sure we do it.

With their great sense of social responsibility and their unbounded moral energy, the Crumbles usually set to work even before they are through the front door.

'I see you've still got one of these old-fashioned locks,' says Christopher. 'You realise that any half-wit burglar could pick this with a bent pin and a nail-file in about five seconds flat? Couldn't he, darling?'

'Christopher will give you the addsess of the firm that imports those new draught-proof Swiss micro-precision locks,' says Lavinia. 'Won't you, darling?'

'Oh, I'll give their local office a ring tomorrow and get them to send you a fitter round right away. No, no – no trouble at all. Is it, darling?'

Christopher has scarcely had time to make a note in his diary before Lavinia has stepped back in amazement. Oh God, the doormat! We've forgotten about the doormat!

'You *said* you were going to get one of those hand-knitted Vietnamese ones like ours,' says Lavinia. 'Didn't they, darling? What happened? I mean, goodness knows, it's your home – it's up to you to decide what sort of doormat you want in it. But when it's been scientifically *proved* by independent experts that the hand-knitted ones have by far the highest mat-sole abrasion co-efficient . . . !'

By the time we sit down to dinner the Crumbles have already put our domestic economy right on a number of points, and it's the turn of wife's cooking for a helping hand. But the tact they do it with!

'This apple-pie is absolutely marvellous, isn't it darling?'

'Marvellous!'

'*Marvellous!* Of course, we've rather gone off having heavy pastry dishes on top of great, greasy meals – haven't we, darling? – and I've got a wonderful new recipe for mango sorbet that you absolutely *must* try.'

'We think it's the *only* pudding in the world, don't we, darling?'

'Though, of course, we *adore* apple-pie, too.'

It also turns out in the course of conversation – and this we had not known or suspected before – that we are absolutely obliged to read Ned Ogham's new novel (which Lavinia will send us) about a Midlands couple who keep a chicken grill, and who barbecue a passing encyclopaedia salesman in the Rotisso-mat as a sacrifice to the sun-god. We are under a further categorical imperative to see Fred Umble's new play (Christopher will get us the tickets) about a group of workers in an expanded polystyrene factory who ritually beat the tea-girl to death with plastic spoons, and eat her for lunch in a Dionysiac frenzy in the works canteen.

And what about the floor? Do we like the way it is? inquires Christopher with all the old tact. Or shall he bring over the five-gallon drum of Simpson's 'Florscraypa' they happen to have left from doing their lavatory, so we can really get down on our hands and knees this weeked and start all over again?

'Of course,' says Lavinia, 'it would make all the difference to the room if the *ceiling* were brightened up a bit, wouldn't it, darling?'

'They'd be far better off with *something* on the ceiling, certainly. How about *wallpaper*!'

'*Yes!* One of those rather William Morrissy ones!'

'That's a tremendously exciting idea, darling. We'll pop

along to that little man of ours in Muswell Hill tomorrow and see what he's got.'

'Then we could throw out that ghastly old sofa and get a chaise-longue. We could cover it with one of those rather art-nouveauish prints, couldn't we, darling?'

They're also going to get our children into a marvellous pre-nursery school that all our friends use, with a very high pass rate into the top nursery schools in the district, though whether to send them now or after the Christmas exam season they haven't quite decided yet. They don't think there's any need to worry too much about the children's development, we're relieved to hear, provided we treat them as rational human beings, on a man-to-man basis, the way the Crumbles would treat their own children, if they had any.

'Of course, what children need most,' explains Lavinia, 'as psychiatrists now agree, is a constructively disturbed home background.'

'As I expect you know,' smiles Christopher, 'the really well-adjusted couples aren't the ones who are so suspiciously polite and loving to one another all the time. Are they, darling?'

'No – the really well-adjusted couples are the ones who fight like cat and dog at every opportunity. We have the most tremendously helpful fights, don't we, darling?'

'Oh, all the time. We were just thinking the other day – weren't we, darling? – that whenever we see you two you scarcely so much as say a word to each other. It's very bad to bottle it all up, you know. If you want to have a bit of a scrap, you go ahead. We don't mind. Do we, darling?'

Heavens, we're grateful for all they've done for us. About the only service left unperformed is to tell us that of course our breath smells *marvellous,* but we absolutely *must* try a wonderful little deodorant toothpaste they know about . . .

How about it, darlings?

(1964)

Fog-like sensations

(According to some sympathisers, the reason why drivers on the motorways failed to slow down in thick fog recently, and so crashed into each other in multiple collisions of up to thirty vehicles, was simply because the authorities had failed to provide illuminated signs explaining that the fog was fog. This is a situation on which Wittgenstein made one or two helpful remarks in a previously unpublished section of 'Philosophical Investigations'.)

694. Someone says, with every sign of bewilderment (wrinkled forehead, widened eyes, an anxious set to the mouth): 'I do not know there is fog on the road unless it is accompanied by an illuminated sign saying "fog".'

When we hear this, we feel dizzy. We experience the sort of sensations that go with meeting an old friend one believed was dead. I want to say: 'But *this* is the man philosophers are always telling us about! This is the man who does not understand – the man who goes on asking for explanations after everything has been explained!'

(A sort of Socratic Oliver Twist. Compare the feelings one would have on meeting Oliver Twist in the flesh. 'And now I want you to meet Oliver Twist.' – 'But . . . !')

695. Now I feel a different sort of excitement. I see in a flash a thought forming as it were before my mind's eye – 'This is at last the sort of situation which philosophers have always waited for – the sort of situation in which one as a philosopher can offer practical help!'

696. Imagine that the motorist said: 'The trouble is, I can't see the fog for the fog.' We might understand this as a request for *practical* information, and try to answer it by showing him the definition of 'fog' in the dictionary. To this he might reply: 'I can't see "fog" for the fog.' We respond by

putting the dictionary an inch in front of his eyes. Now he says: 'I can't see the fog for "fog".'

697. At this point a philosopher might want to say: 'He sees the fog but he does not perceive its fogginess.' Ask yourself what could possibly be the object of saying this.

698. Now the man says: 'I can see the fog perfectly well, but I don't know that it's fog.' I feel an urge to say: 'Yet you know it's fog that you don't know to be fog!' (The deceptively normal air of paradoxes.) One can imagine his replying: 'Naturally – it looks like fog.' Or, if he is familiar with philosophical language: 'Of course – I know that I am having fog-like sensations.' And if one asked him what he meant by *that,* perhaps he would say: 'It looks like what I see in places where I should know what I was seeing if it were labelled "fog".'

699. *Now* the feeling of dizziness vanishes. We feel we want to say: 'Now it seems more like a dull throbbing behind the eyes.'

700. Of course, one is familiar with the experience of seeing something ambiguous. 'Now it is the Taj Mahal – now it is fog.' And one can imagine having a procedural rule that anything ambiguous should be treated as the Taj Mahal unless we see that it is labelled 'fog'.

701. The motorist replies: 'What sort of rule is this? Surely the best guarantee I can have that the fog is fog is if I fail to see the sign saying "fog" because of the fog.' – One can imagine uses for the rule. For example, to lure people to their deaths.

702. Still the man seems uneasy. 'To be sure that the fog is fog because it is labelled "fog", I must first be sure that "fog" is "fog". Now, supposing, without its being perceptible to the naked eye, the top of the "o" were slightly open. How am I to be certain that it could be accepted as a "u", so that the word was not "fog" at all but "fug"? Or how can I be certain that the first letter is really "f" and not a grossly deformed but still meaningful "b"?'

So now we have to have a label for 'fog'! And another label for the label of 'fog'!

703. But we are not yet out of the wood! (Or, as one might say, out of the fog.) The motorist might object: 'I *still* cannot understand. I see that the fog is labelled "fog", and that "fog" is labelled '"fog"', and so forth. But how am I to know that "fog" *means* fog, or that '"fog"' *means* "fog"?'

So we must qualify still further. We must expand 'fog' to read '"fog", where "fog" means fog.'

704. Now imagine the motorist's face. Imagine that the doubtful expression remains. Imagine that he says: 'But how do I know that the expression " 'fog', where 'fog' means fog" means " 'fog', where 'fog' means fog"?'

705. What sort of game are we playing here? What sort language are we using? I am tempted to ask, what sort of man am I being used by? I have a certain feeling that goes with grating teeth, a frown, flushed cheeks. I want to say: 'My offer of help is being abused.'

706. One might try to provide the man with a mental picture, a working model of his position – as it were a map to enable him to get his bearings. I might say: 'You are in a complete mental fog about the whole business.' He seizes on this eagerly. He goes through the motions of assenting – nodding his head, pursing his lips, saying: 'Yes, yes, that's it exactly. I am in a complete mental fog.'

Now one asks: 'But how do you *know* it's a mental fog you're in?'

707. At once he cries: 'NOW I see! I see that I don't know I'm in a mental fog at all! I need an illuminated mental sign saying "mental fog".'

708. If a lion could speak, it would not understand itself.

(1964)

From the Improved Version

The news that the statue of Nkrumah in Accra, which was damaged by an explosion, bore on its side the inscription, 'Seek ye first the political kingdom and all the rest shall be added unto you,' has touched off a great deal of speculation. Where does the quotation come from? I have heard both the Book of Amazing Free Offers and the Second Book of Unsolicited Testimonials suggested – even the Book of Fub.

In fact, it comes from the Book of Usually Reliable Sources, and was reprinted in that very handy little devotional work for these troubled times, 'Selected Wisdom from the Improved Version.' In case you are unacquainted with the range and usefulness of this book, or are looking for an inscription of your own, here are a few more extracts:

Out of the mouths of babes shall come statements of opinion; out of the mouths of princes and counsellors, maid-servants and players of the lute and tabor; and each shall be harkened unto according to his purchasing power. (*Majorities xii 15.*)

The wise king holdeth his tongue before his people, and maketh his servant to speak on his behalf unto the multitude. For if the multitude find fault with his servant's words, then shall the king make public sacrifice of him. And the king shall gain great credit thereby. (*Parliamentarians vii 6.*)

And there was heard the voice of one crying in the metropolis: Come ye to have a drink and meet Rock Richmond, who maketh glad the people with his lute. And this same prophet had a coat of camel's hair, and his meat was oysters and champagne. For he that goeth before must be as empty as the oyster-shell, and his tongue must be soft with wine, that he may become a vessel of smooth and vacant speech. (*Fub. ii* 18.)

If a prince seeketh to increase his army, he summoneth not the servant from his master nor the husband from his wife, lest he maketh them wroth. Rather shall he grind the faces of those warriors he hath imprest before, causing them to toil by night even as by day. For these are already wroth, and their labours will not increase the number of the wrathful, nor doth the law permit them to make known their burden in epistles to the press. (*Majorities v* 20.)

Seek not to share misfortune evenly among the people; but let it bear heavily upon the few. For howsoever sore afflicted they may be, if they cry out thou mayst rebuke them, saying: Ten thousand thousand are them that praise me; what are ye few against this mighty host? The voice that crieth out in you is the voice of devils, yea, and chastisement shall be added to your afflictions. (*Majorities v* 23.)

And he that had mocked the king was brought before him. And the king saith: Mock me again, that I may enjoy that which even the humblest of my subjects hath enjoyed. And the man did as he was bid, and mocked the king, and they that stood about him were sore afraid. But the king betook himself to laughter, and they that were about him did likewise. Then saith the king: Thou shalt have riches, and stay with me, and mock me all the days of my life, that I and no other may have the enjoyment of it. And I shall taste the sweets both of power and of the mockery of power. But when he heard these words, the man was troubled in his soul, and went aside and hanged himself. (*Jokers xiv* 2.)

What shall it avail a man, if he keepeth his own soul but loseth his ministry? (*Parliamentarians ix* 3.)

Sweet is music, and sweet the playing thereof, yet not so sweet, as to be honoured in its playing. To be virtuous is worth more than gold; but to be known is more precious than rubies. For all the goings in and the goings out of such a man shall be reported. And his wife shall partake of his glory; yea, and his concubine and his dog. And their opinions shall be sought and prized above the judgements of Solomon. (*Celebrities iii 9.*)

He that findeth old words for new teachings: he is the friend of merchants and the comforter of princes. (*Adverbs i 1.*)

(1962)

Frox 'n' sox

Theologians now believe that the wide variety of beliefs and practices observable among the different Christian churches must have derived originally from some common source – perhaps from some kind of gospel preached by an itinerant religious leader in the Middle East about two thousand years ago.

What exactly was in this gospel it's very hard to reconstruct. Not all churches, for example, seem to accept central tenets such as a belief in organised violence and the preservation of wealth and privilege. But scholars think they have located the one profound and passionate conviction that they almost all share – a horror of loud ties.

They point to the remarkable unanimity with which the priests of almost every known Christian sect have avoided the wearing of ties of any sort – not only ones with a motif of lightly-clad women or favourite cartoon characters, but even simple stripes signifying membership of the Garrick Club or the Old Haileyburians. Indeed, in their efforts to avoid any temptation to wear unsuitable ties, priests of all denominations have tended to eschew even suits or jackets, at any rate on formal occasions. With striking singleness of mind they have elected to wear frocks.

Scholars are insistent that at no point in the history of the church were frocks ever worn to show off the figure of the wearer, or to titillate in any way whatsoever. The original doctrine, they believe, must have made it clear that the frocks were to be full-length evening gowns, with no hint of décolletage, and no leg showing. Any suggestion of tightness over the hips or around the bosom was to be most sedulously avoided. Black seems to have been thought the safest colour, though brown, grey, and dark blue were evidently regarded as acceptable. Various shades of green have sometimes been tried by the adventurous, but considerable caution must have been recommended with lilac and puce. Red and purple, yes, possibly – but you had to be the kind of person who could carry it off.

The choice of material was another area where discretion had to be exercised. Silk for a really special occasion could be lovely, perhaps with a tasteful embroidered stole thrown around the shoulders. But definitely no sequins, no lamé, no lurex, and nothing diaphanous. Jewellery – yes, certainly, why not, provided it was reasonably discreet. A nice gold chain, perhaps, with something dangly at the breast. A few chunky rings. Not earrings, though, and nothing in the nostril. A hat could be a definite plus – a little pill-box worn at a slightly cheeky angle was always thought to look smart, and you can't really go wrong with a low crown and a broad brim. But no feathers and no veils!

Up to this point the doctrine seems very straight-forward and commonsensical. There was another side to it, though, scholars have established, which is more mystical, and which has to be pieced together with great delicacy and sensitivity to metaphysical nuance. This is the question of what was to be worn underneath the frocks.

It was understood that some priests would wish to wear trousers under their skirts and that others would prefer not to. The choice was left entirely to the dress-sense of the individual priest, and his sensitivity to the climate in which he found himself. The crucial question related to socks. It was made plain that socks, if worn, should be thick, woollen, and reasonably short. They should be worn either sagging around the ankles, or supported by strongly-made brass and elastic suspenders somewhere about the mid-calf. They might be obtained from Marks and Spencer, or home-knitted by devoted relatives and parishioners. They were to be, in a word, *male socks*.

Now it was always recognised by Christian doctrine that priests are not the only people in the world who wear frocks. There are others, superficially indistinguishable from priests, who can be told apart only because they wear not male socks under their frocks, but much longer, more exiguous pieces of hosiery often smooth and diaphanous in texture, and held up not by forthright brass and scarlet elastic around the calf, but by flimsy contraptions of straps and frills emanating from mysterious recesses of under-wear which need not concern us here. People with arrange-ments of this sort under their frocks have therefore often been known as *the weaker socks*.

The reference is purely to the lower tensile strength of the materials, and it must be stressed that the weaker socks have always been recognised as absolutely equal in the sight of God, who has no personal interest at all in people's under-garments. Christians have never been encouraged to go round peering under other people's frocks to see what they are wearing beneath. In fact the various churches have always tended to discourage any very close interest in this whole question. They have never been able to understand why people seem to think of nothing but socks, socks, socks.

Indeed their chief concern has been to keep the two different kinds of socks apart. Those ordained by God to wear thick socks under their frocks, they have felt, should not experiment with silk stockings and high heels. Those born to silk stockings and high heels should not start throwing their frocks off, and going round wearing pin-stripe suits and Brigade ties. Trousers, possibly – though preferably short enough to be entirely concealed beneath their frocks. The exact form of these concealed trousers has never been of direct concern to the church, but normal good sense suggests that they should be made not of thick materials like tweed or corduroy, but of silk or cotton, trimmed perhaps with a little lace ... However, this is straying from the central theological issue.

Which is at all costs to stop the weaker socks wearing the same kind of frocks as the male socks!

This is of vital importance, because otherwise the two different sorts of frocks might get mixed up in church, and it has always been an essential belief that the frocks with the rough woollen socks under them should be kept up one end of the building, and the frocks with the long translucent silk socks under them should be down the other end, with some kind of fence or rail separating them.

This is so that the thick socks can be clearly seen and heard while they explain that anyone having problems about frocks and socks can take heart, because things will be much easier to understand when they are dead. In the next world everyone will be wearing long white frocks and no socks at all, so there will be a very relaxed atmosphere, and a very jolly time will be had by all.

Apart, that is, from those people who have got confused about questions of frocks and socks in this life. If they have, then they *won't* have white frocks when they're dead – they won't have frocks at all – they'll just get flogged and tortured in the nude.

Though if that's what they *like*, if they've been taking, their frocks off and getting themselves flogged and tortured in the nude in *this* life, then very probably they won't get flogged and tortured in the nude when they're dead after all. They'll find themselves *forced* to wear frocks as a punishment, for all eternity.

And horrible tickly socks, with huge holes in them.

(1994)

Fun with numbers

I'm on my way to the cash-dispenser, and I'm feeling rather pleased with myself, because for once I've remembered to do it before I go into a shop or get into a taxi and find I've no money to pay with.

What I'm also doing as I walk along the street is rehearsing my personal number inside my head, to make sure I can still remember it. 4273 . . . 4273 . . . Yes, OK, got it. I'm being a little over-anxious, perhaps, but I don't want any embarrassments of the sort I've had in the past, when I've put the card in the machine in front of a long queue of people, and got 'Incorrect personal number entered', and had to take it out again smartly before I also got 'Your card has been retained', then walk round the block for ten minutes while I calmed down and sorted out the digits in my mind. Not to mention the time when I put in the right number but the wrong card . . .

I won't think about that just now; though. I'll simply concentrate on the number. 4237 . . . 4237 . . . Right. Firmly in place. Everything's going to be all right.

It's just that it sounds a bit funny, somehow. 4327 . . . These machines are so pedantic – you not only have to have the right four digits, which you'd think would be enough to win you something reasonably substantial in the lottery, let alone get a few miserable pounds out of your own account, but you have to have them in the right order. Four digits in the right order! That must be worth at least ten thousand pounds of someone else's money!

But it's all right, because I have a mnemonic. One of my daughters, who is a little shaky on numbers, taught me this trick. At one stage in her career she had to remember a four-digit number to get past security into her job every morning. She explained to me that, since literature was more her kind of thing than mathematics, she had turned the number into a story, about a young woman of 27 who was having an affair with a man of 54. I said I couldn't see how she remembered that it wasn't a woman of 24 having an affair with a man of 57, or for that matter a man of 31 and a woman of 62, and she said, no, nor could she, now I mentioned it. And a terrible uncertainty came into her voice.

My daughter is now self-employed. In any case I was never very convinced by this love affair. I find it difficult to remember my own age, let alone the ages of fictitious characters, because ages keep changing. My mnemonic is purely mathematical – a much more solid basis. Three of the digits in my number; as you can see, are an anagram of three naturally sequential digits, and the fourth digit is the sum of the last two digits in the sequence.

Actually this is a fictitious version of my mnemonic, because, needless to say, we're talking about a fictitious version of my personal number. If I published the real one, not only might you be tempted to hack into my account, but, much worse, the bank would insist on changing the number, as they did once before, when the cards and the numbers got themselves crossed, and then I should have to start remembering a new mnemonic.

Which would be a pity, because the real mnemonic I've got is so elegant. Let me just say, without giving too much away, that the *first* digit is *two* larger than the *third*, so I just remember one, two, three. Yes? Then the *fourth* digit is the sum of the *third* and the *second* – easy, because four is one more than three, and then we're simply going back down the scale again: four; three, two . . . Hold on . . . What's the second digit? Yes, right, sorry – I'm getting confused – the *second* digit is two more than the first . . . Or twice as much as the first. . . . Or rather . . .

Anyway, I don't need to remember the mnemonic – I can always work out the mnemonic from the number. Except that while I was trying to remember the mnemonic the number's gone out of my head.

You'll notice how calm I'm keeping about this. No blind panic, as you might have expected, even though I've already walked past the machine while all this has been going on, and I'm going to have to go on and walk all the way round the block again while I get it sorted out. In fact it doesn't actually matter at all that I can't remember the number – just so long as I remember I can't remember it – because I've got it written down in this little electronic organiser thing I keep in my pocket here for exactly this kind of eventuality.

I'm not giving any secrets away here. The number isn't written in some place where you could find it even if you came round and stole my little organiser thing – or worse, my God, if someone checking up from the bank stole it! – but in a special bit you can't get into without entering a secret number. And yes, don't worry; I can remember this number; because with simple cunning it's my bank machine number written backwards . . .

Which of course in this particular case presents a problem. Or *would* present a problem, if I hadn't taken the precaution of writing down the secret number in the non-secret part of the organiser. And that's perfectly secure, because it's disguised as a telephone number. You don't know which of the thousand telephone numbers in the list it is, but I know it's the one that belongs to a fictitious character . . .

Well, the name will come back to me in a minute . . . And if it doesn't, never mind, bit of a nuisance, but I've got this thing covered every way – I took the name out of a book lying on the third shelf up from the bottom in my office. I'll just have to go back to my office first. And don't think I'm not going to be able to get into my office – that in my rising panic I have forgotten the code to punch into the keypad on the door; because the code is very simply the date of one of the major battles in European history, with two of the digits transposed, and I may be able to forget a mnemonic, but I'm not likely to forget the name of a *battle* . . .

Except that I have.

No! This is not possible! This is pure self-sabotage! I'm talking myself into this!

Calm down. Think . . . Right, here's what I do. I jump into a cab and I go to a reference library and I look through some standard work on European history from, say, 1300 to 1900. Won't take all that long if I can just find a . . . and yes, there *is* one, my luck's changed! . . . ! *Taxi* . . . ! Take me to the local library, will you . . . ?

No, sorry, hold on. Of course – I've no money on me. Take me to a cash machine . . . Oh, we're next to it . . . Wait I'll be two minutes . . . As long as I can remember my number . . .

Ah. Yes. Right. Problem. And now there's a pound on the taxi meter. This is going to be embarrassing.

No, it's not. Let's go right back to the beginning. Back to the moment when I was walking towards the cash-dispenser; and I was remembering my personal number. Because I can remember remembering it. So it must be in my head somewhere.

Right, then, clear everything else out. Never mind remembering – concentrate on forgetting. Forget the taxi standing there. Forget the meter ticking away Forget the traffic, forget the world. Forget the little organiser thing, forget the mnemonics. Just go down through the veils of consciousness into the deep, dark caverns of memory . . . down to the lost golden hoard of codes and numbers . . .

And I've got there!

Battle of Lepanto, 1571!

Right, here we go. One . . . five . . . seven . . . one . . . What's this? 'Incorrect personal number entered.' Of course – I didn't transpose the digits! Try again. One . . . seven . . . five . . . one . . . No, no, no! Five . . . seven . . . one . . . one . . . Seven . . . one . . . one . . . five . . .

What? 'Your card has been retained . . .' No! Stop! Come back! I made a mistake – that was the battle – that was the

door! Listen – I've remembered the fictitious character!
He's 84! He's having an affair with a woman called
Rosemary . . . !

(1994)

Gagg speaks

'How,' I have sometimes heard people gasp admiringly as they looked at the work of this country's cartoonists, 'do these chaps manage to make their stuff so true to life? How do they discover the situations which mirror the human predicament and the world as it is today with such accuracy and originality?'

I put these razor-sharp questions to one of our leading cartoonists, Gagg, at his semi-detached residence in the cartoonist belt. 'It's easy,' he replied. 'I simply draw the world around me and life as I see it lived in my own family circle from day to day.'

Q: *Perhaps you would describe a typical day, Mr Gagg.*

A: Certainly. First of all I take a bath, in the middle of which I am always called to the door or the telephone with a towel round my waist. At breakfast, of course, I find myself completely hidden behind the morning paper, a situation which gives my wife (not a comely woman, I am afraid, and a head taller than me) the opportunity for some highly risible remark. Then off to the office. I still sometimes leave without my trousers – very amusing! – though less frequently than in the past. Trousers or no trousers, on the Tube I invariably look over my neighbour's shoulder at his paper.

Q: *And when you get to the office?*

A: The first task is to indulge in some humorous badinage or repartee with The Boss, as he is called, over my lateness. Then my secretary sits down in my lap and we start the day's work.

Q: *Why does your secretary sit in your lap?*

A: It seems to be a tradition of the firm. I believe it dates from the years of austerity, when chairs were difficult to come by, and has been kept on as an uplifting mortification of the flesh for both parties.

Q: *Does she remain there all* day?

A: No. Occasionally I have to go and ask The Boss for a rise. He can never afford to give me one, of course: the line on the sales graph slumps so sharply it has to be continued down the wall, and men with masks and horizontally striped vests keep robbing the safe. The police who chase them, incidentally, are for some reason usually American.

Q: *And when you get home at the end of a hard day?*

A: I find that the Little Woman, as she is called, has crashed the car while trying to get it in the garage. I am further enraged to discover that she has bought a new spring hat. Nor is this all. The supper she has cooked turns out to be burnt to a cinder, and when I make some humorous reproach about it she packs a bag and returns to her mother. I try to console myself with a little Indian snake-charming, but it's no use. There is nothing for it but to go out to a public-house and drown my sorrows.

Q: *Are you successful?*

A: Entirely. As the evening wears on my collar becomes loosened, my hair gets dishevelled, and my shpeech grows shlurred. On my way home I shtop to shupport a shtreet-lamp under a creshent moon and find that I am wearing a battered top-hat and a somewhat dis-harrayed evening dresh.

Q: *The scene* you *have depicted a hundred times.*

A: Yes, indeed. Like the ensuing scene, when I reach home and find that my wife is waiting for me with a rolling-pin. A poignant moment.

Q: *And then to sleep?*

A: Far from it. I lie tossing and turning on my bed of nails for a long time, counting sheep which get up to the most amusing antics inside their balloons. But I have to go down to throw out my daughter's young man, who has still not left, and who is kneeling in front of her with some ludicrous proposal of marriage. Then I am called away to the local maternity hospital, where my wife is now confined. The nurses hold a highly rib-tickling assortment of monkeys and other animals up to the glass of the waiting-room before my quadruplets arrive.

Q: *Quadruplets, Mr Gagg?*

A: I'm afraid so. A truly phenomenal output of children has to be maintained to be eaten by wild animals at the zoo.

Q: *Do you get any time at all in the comfort of your bed of nails?*

A: A little. I usually spend it dreaming about a holiday I should like to take one day, shipwrecked on a very small desert island with one palm tree. Oh, it's a full and satisfying life, you know. We don't aspire to the sort of society where you find ladies labelled 'Peace,' or piebald horses inscribed 'Arab resentment over British Middle East policy.' But for ordinary folk who like familiar things spiced with a bit of sub-human interest, you can't beat it.

(1961)

Gentle reader

Chapter One

The old man's head tolled helplessly from side to side like a rag-doll's as Zack heaved him up off the bed. 'What are you doing?' cried Precious. 'He needs some air,' grunted Zack, as he half-carried, half-dragged the inert fat body across to the open window. He propped it in the window-frame for a moment and looked out. They were ten floors up. It was difficult to estimate how big an area the old man would spread over . . .

I know what you're doing, incidentally. You. Yes, *you*! I, the author, know what you, the reader, are doing. You think I have the imagination and insight to understand what's going on inside the dark, twisted souls of Zack and Precious, and I don't know what some simple citizen like *you* is up to?

You're standing in the bookshop, and you're flicking through the first page or two of this novel, trying to decide whether to buy it or not. You're worried that a whole paragraph has gone by already, and so far not a sign of anyone having even the most mundane form of sexual intercourse. Look, be reasonable. One thing at a time. How can they have intercourse when he's trying to push her old father out of the window?

If they gave him a really good shove, thought Zack, he might fall slightly wide of the building, and hit one or two of the winos lying stretched out on the pavement . . .

Also, you're trying to remember whether you read anything in the paper about my getting some huge advance. It would help you to believe that this novel was worth £14.99 if you knew that the publishers had laid out a little more than £14.99 on it themselves.

In fact you're starting to worry about the whole level of the publishers' commitment to this enterprise. You're very suspicious because the book wasn't in a dump-bin, stacked fifty copies high. There was no showcard in the window. You're not even sure there's an author tour, with readings and signings in selected bookshops, and wide media coverage.

Look, come on. We're not discussing your life's savings. We're talking about an investment of £14.99. Of which I get

10%. That's what you'll be paying me. Because let's get this absolutely straight. We're going to be examining with ruthless honesty the relationship between Zack and Precious, so let's start off by getting *our* relationship clear. It's written down here in my contract, look, signed and countersigned. 'A royalty of 10% on the first 2,500 copies.' That's the total extent of the emotional demand I am making upon you – a fraction of a penny under £1.50. All right? Just go over to the cash-desk and get your credit card out.

On the other hand, there was a noticeable cross-wind blowing, which might carry the body a little off course, and deposit it on top of the kids sniffing glue behind the rubbish-bins . . .

What, you're still hesitating? Look, I'd like to give it to you for a pound – I'd like to make you a present of it. No, that's not true, I wouldn't. Not because I care about the money, but because I don't think that would be a true or healthy relationship between us. We're trying to start a business connection, not a love-affair. The cash-desk. Over there by the door, look.

Suddenly the old man uttered a terrible groan. 'He's still alive,' said Precious. Zack gave up trying to work out the exact point of impact, and began to ease the body out into space. He didn't want to rush something like this, but he also didn't want any further discussion with the old man about a European currency . . .

No? You think this is exploitation, £1.50? How far can you go in a cab for £1.50? For £1.50 with me you can go all the way from the dark heart of the urban jungle in Balham to the glittering high life of newly-rich derivatives traders in Barnet. And you don't end up as a slippery pulp spread across a major traffic intersection in West Norwood, like Zack on page 397, causing a busload of orphans to run into a truck carrying weapons-grade plutonium. You don't get secretly dumped from a sludge-carrier in the North Sea, entombed in fifteen separate concrete nuclear-waste containers, as part of a global hush-up involving the White House and the Vatican.

You arrive home on page 463, shaken and seared, but fit and well, sitting in your own armchair with a glass of lightly chilled chardonnay in your hand and a bowl of taco chips in front of you. For £1.50! No hidden extras. No airport tax, no gratuities to guides. You buy the wine and the taco chips, the rest's on me. I think you have a pretty good deal.

Or maybe you're not one of those first 2,500 pioneers who rushed to the bookshops as soon as stocks arrived. Maybe you're one of the readers numbered 2,501 to 5,000, from whom my contract stipulates that I get 12.5%. All right, so we have a slightly different relationship. We have a £1.87375 relationship. How do we feel about this? I'll tell you how I feel about it. I feel good about it. I feel I'm selling you something that people want to buy. I believe you feel good, too. You think, OK, so I'm paying a little over the odds for this, but that's the kind of person I am – someone who's ready to pay a premium price for a premium product. This is the kind of novel that 2,500 people have bought already This novel is beginning to be hot. Hot costs.

Unless you're the 5,001st customer – unless you re one of the people who are paying me 15% thereafter. You see me getting my hands on a cool £2.2485 of your money, and you feel you're being taken for a ride. Well, why not? I mean, frankly, you're a Johnny-come-lately. You should have run down to the bookshop along with my fashion-conscious friends 2,501 to 5,000, as soon as they saw it lying on the coffee-tables of their innovative neighbours 1 to 2,500.

Or did you by any chance pick this up off the remainders table? Because if you did I'm getting nothing at all. You know what I think of a reader like you? I despise you. You're cheap. You get to the scene where they torture

Precious to death with an electric toothbrush, you'll have a heart-attack, you'll die.

Get out of the shop! Go home! You think I'm going to give you bizarre forms of intercourse and violence for nothing? This is what you get for nothing:

> *Zack grabbed the old man by the ankles as he fell, and with a huge effort hauled him back into the window. 'Sorry,' he said. 'Just kidding.'*
>
> *And they all sat down together and had a good laugh and a nice cup of tea.*

(1994)

Gift to the nation

I felt terribly guilty when I read that the Treasury had received small sums of money as gifts from private citizens who were 'anxious to do their best to help in the present situation.'

I hadn't realised that the Government would be ready to accept charity. I thought they'd be too proud – I thought they'd be dreadfully hurt if one tried. As soon as I heard that they were prepared to be helped out, of course, I put a pound in an envelope at once, with a brief note to say it was just a little something to see them through to the brighter days we all knew lay ahead.

But, as I was on the point of sealing the envelope up, it suddenly occurred to me that perhaps I was being a bit irresponsible handing out charity like this without having any idea how it was going to be used. Giving people hand-outs which they use merely to debauch themselves further is no kindness at all.

'PS,' I added at the bottom of the note. 'You will use this money *sensibly*, won't you? You're entirely free to use it as you think best, naturally – but you won't go spending it on inessentials, will you?'

Just a brief word of advice – that's all that's needed on these occasions. People thank you for it in the end. But on reflection I realised that perhaps I'd put it in rather a misleading way.

'PPS,' I added. 'I don't mean by this that you should spend it on essentials. Don't spend it on either inessentials or essentials. I'm trying to reduce the pressure of domestic demand by sending you this pound – I'm trying to take purchasing power out of the home market. If I hear you've been putting the purchasing power back by spending my pound in the home market I shall be *rather cross*.'

Obvious, of course. But just as I was licking the flap it struck me that this last bit was open to the most terrible interpretation, too.

'PPPS,' I scribbled hastily. 'I don't, of course, mean go spending the money *abroad*! I'm certainly not giving you a pound to pay for an increase in imports, and to aggravate the flight of sterling to foreign parts!'

I thought that made it pretty clear what they weren't to do with the money. But perhaps I ought to drop a hint about what they *could* do with it?

'The point is,' I explained, 'I don't want you to think of this as spending money at all. I want you to *save it up sensibly* for a rainy day. *Invest it wisely* in British enterprise and British skill. Think to what good use dynamic, go-ahead British firms like Screwe Steel Spoons or the Eccleston Ready-Buttered Muffin Co. could put an extra pound!

'I happen to know for a fact that if Eccleston's could raise any capital they would buy some of the modern automatic muffin-buttering plant which they can't afford at the moment because of this terrible credit squeeze. And that would mean that they could really flatten their competitors in Germany and Japan . . . .'

But hey! It would also mean that the pound had got spent

after all! The whole pound's worth of pent-up purchasing power would have been unchained upon the reeling economy! Muffin-buttering machines which would otherwise have gone for export would have been sold at home – operatives in the muffin-buttering machine factory would have drawn my pound in overtime, and squandered it wildly on essentials and inessentials of every kind! Bit of a slip here – I saw that at once.

'On second thoughts,' I wrote, 'I see that a more subtle investment policy is called for. Now how about this? You invest the pound in a German or Japanese ready-buttered muffin firm! Then it will be their economy which gets rocked by the inflationary effect, not ours!

'It's a low trick to play on anyone, I admit, but all's fair in love and economic competition, isn't it? Just a moment, though – supposing their re-equipped muffin industry plays a low trick back, and puts ours out of business?

'All right, don't invest the pound. What I meant all along was this: put my pound in the reserves. Keep it by you until there's another run on sterling, and you have to buy pounds to support the exchange rate. You may well be glad of the odd pound to buy the odd pound with . . .

'No, I haven't put that very well. I mean you'll be glad of some dollars to buy pounds with. So buy a pound's worth of dollars to keep by you. I mean, don't *sell the pound*, of course. I'm not giving you this pound for you to go around selling it, as if you didn't have any confidence in the currency and you wanted to unload it in favour of dollars, like some damned Continental speculator. I mean, what I want you to do is . . . well . . .

'Now let's work this out calmly. There must be some way of using the pound to make the country rich without actually letting go of it. Let's say you borrow a pound's worth of dollars against the security of the pound. Then you use the dollars to support sterling by buying a pound's worth of pounds. Then with the pound's worth of pounds you buy a pound's worth of dollars ... And there we go again, selling pounds!

'Look, are you sure that my giving you this pound isn't just going to make things worse instead of better? The more I think about it, the more ways I can see that you might cause trouble with it.

'It seems to me on mature reflection that the most constructive thing you could do would be to neutralise its purchasing-power and general potential for harm by burning it, provided that you can do this without spending money on matches and paraffin.

'On second thoughts I recall that there is a national shortage of banknotes. Perhaps the best solution all round would be if I kept the pound, and sent you a cheque for the amount instead. Then you can burn the cheque, and I'll give the pound to the milkman.

'A little nearer Christmas I'll send you a bundle of clean cast-offs for the winter.'

(1966)

H & C

One of the rewards of reading Marshall McLuhan is that it enables me to make my friend Horace Morris feel uneasy about not having read it, just as in the past I've made him feel very insecure for not understanding commitment and alienation, and not knowing what charisma was, and thinking that pop music was a bad thing after all the rest of us had realised it was a good thing.

The way the dissemination of ideas works around our way is that first my good friend Christopher Crumble gets to hear about them, and makes me feel insecure. Then I catch up and make Horace Morris feel insecure. By the time Horace had discovered the meaning and omnipresence of charisma, for example, I was right off it – no one seemed charismatic to me any more, not even Harold Wilson or David Frost. I was on to 'symbiosis' – and Christopher Crumble, the Speedy Gonzales of the intellect, was already out of 'symbiosis' and into 'I-Thou,' or even 'freakout.'

What happens to ideas after Horace has cast them off I can't imagine. That far down in the market their second-hand value must have reached vanishing point.

Anyway, now it's McLuhan, and almost everything in the world, as I now realise, is *iconic*. Including McLuhan's own book, 'Understanding Media.' I've never come across anything more iconic, as I said to Horace.

'Iconic?' repeated Horace uneasily.

'Oh, tremendously iconic. I didn't know it was possible for a book to be so iconic. Have you read it, Horace?'

'Well, not exactly . . .'

'I think your lack of interest in books is very significant and interesting, Horace. Even without reading McLuhan you instinctively reject the print culture, and the whole repetitive, mechanical approach to life of which printing is the archetype. You realise that print means centralisation and uniformity. You're not satisfied with the shallow participation which is all books demand – the specialisation and fragmentation of human life which the print culture suggests.'

'Well, you know, Michael . . .'

'You understand instinctively that print is a hot medium.'

'Well . . .'

'You feel in your bones that this is the electric age – the age of the total involvement of the individual in humanity at large by way of television. You didn't need McLuhan to tell you that television was a cool medium – that it's low-definition, that it requires the participation of the viewer to give the image meaning. The truth is that you're a natural twentieth-century man, Horace!'

'Well, I watch a certain amount of television,' he said uneasily. 'But I must admit, I do read *some* books . . .'

'Oh, *some* books, sure. But how about medieval manuscripts. Horace? Do you read manuscripts at all?'

'Manuscripts? Oh God no, I certainly don't read manuscripts I think I can truthfully claim that I've never read a single medieval manuscript in my life.'

At this, of course, I became somewhat pensive.

'Oh,' I said. 'Oh. That's rather a pity. Manuscript is a cool medium.'

'Well, of course, I've read a few modern . . .'

'Quite. How do you stand on strip cartoons, Horace? Do you look at the strip cartoons at all?'

He thought for some time, shifting uneasily about in his chair.

'N-o-o-o-o,' he said at last. 'No, I don't. I think I've always realised somehow that they were part of the print culture business – you know, very standardised and mechanical and . . .'

'I see. Well, *McLuhan* thinks strip cartoons are a cool medium. He may be wrong, of course.'

'Oh, I wouldn't say that . . .'

'Do you listen to the radio at all, Horace?'

'Oh God yes! Oh God, I mean, I really feel that radio is an essential part of the electric culture . . .'

I was looking very grave at this point in the interrogation, as you can imagine.

'Radio is a hot medium,' I told him, as kindly as I could. 'High definition. Involves visualisation. Caused the rise of Hitler, according to McLuhan. Still, no reason why you shouldn't enjoy it, if you want to. I suppose you like using the phone?'

'Oh God no!' said Horace hurriedly. 'I mean, oh God yes! I mean no! Hate it! Can't stand all that visualisation, and so on . . .'

'Wrong again, I'm afraid, Horace,' I said, shaking my head sadly. 'The telephone's a cool medium. Low definition – involves participation. Still, you do watch television. That's something. What do you watch, Horace? 'Panorama'?'

'Yes – no! No, no, no, no! I watch things like – well old movies.'

'*Old movies,* Horace?'

'Bad old movies,' he added hastily. But he could see from my expression that there was something wrong here. 'I thought bad old movies were good?' he cried. 'I thought bad old movies were the new thing?'

'My God, Horace!' I shouted, my tactful reserve breaking down at last. 'Bad old movies were new three years ago! Bad old movies were back in the days of Susan Sontag! Listen, Horace, films are high-definition. Films don't involve the total participation of the viewer. Films are a relic of the mechnical print culture. Films are *hot*, Horace!'

So much for Horace Morris's pretensions to be cool electric man. Though after he'd had time to think about it, he said that he watched the old movies on BBC 2, with an inside aerial. Definition was so poor, he said, with three or four overlapping images and the picture going jump-jump-jump every minute, and viewer participation was so high, with the viewer springing up to shift the aerial back and forth round the room all the time, that the medium was cool enough to neutralise the heat of even the hottest film.

And when you consider that he's short-sighted, too ... Maybe he *is* cool electric man after all.

(1967)

Hamlet OBE

The one heavy industry that shows no sign of declining is the vast enterprise which turns all that crude Shakespeare the country possesses into finished Peter Hall and Peter Brook.

I sometimes wonder if the workers in this industry ever worry lest one day they exhaust all the possible permutations of interpretation, editing, punctuation, fancy dress, and general joking up, and find themselves reduced to the shameful expedient of putting the stuff on more or less as the old fool wrote it.

I'm not *advocating* this; I couldn't sit through a *Hamlet* uncut and unrelieved by cheering breaks for swordplay. All the same, as time goes on the variations left to try are going to become pretty esoteric. Particularly when the National Foundation Stone on the South Bank gets under way with all the brainpower at its command.

They may bulk the programme out with *Roots, Look Back in Anger, The Caretaker, Roots* done in Second Empire costume, *Look Back in Anger* in Gestapo uniforms and riding boots, *The Caretaker* in Melanesian ritual masks, *Roots* chanted by antiphonal choruses of

Manchester schoolgirls, *Look Back in Anger* danced to music by Chopin and Rachmaninov, *The Caretaker* mimed by actors from the Kabuki Theatre, and so on and so forth, but in between whiles it's going to be Shakespeare, Shakespear, Shaksper.

By the end of the century they should be very far out indeed. Here's a preview of what Lord Olivier of Elstree, Sir Kenneth Tynan, Sir Sean Kenny, Sir Lionel Bart Bart, and Dame Kayser Bondor will be giving us for the winter season of 1999 – *Hamlet OBE.*

Act One

[*Enter Ghost, in phosphorescent buskins.*]

HORATIO: Look! My! Lord, it comes!

[*He flexes his thighs.*]

HAMLET: Angels and ministers of grace defend us!

[*While the Ghost mimes telling his tale, angels and ministers of grace appear dressed as fighter-pilots and Ministers of Defence and burlesque defending us in a satirical anti-war masque.*]

GHOST: Adieu, adieu! Hamlet, remember me.

[*Exit, pursued by a bear.*]

HAMLET: O that! This too? Too solid!

   Flesh would melt,

   Thaw – and resolve itself in two.

   Adieu!

[*He slaps his buskins.*]

OPHELIA: O! what a noble! Mind is here o'erthrown!

[*They fight.*]

Act Two

[*Hamlet, Horatio, Laertes, and attendant Knights Commander. They flex their thighs and slap their buskins.*]

HAMLET: How long hast thou been grave, mucker?

[*The grave diggers perform a very grave digging dance,*

*while newsreel shots of the assassination of Archduke
Ferdinand are shown in back projection.*]
HAMLET: The play's the thing
   Wherein I'll slap the buskins of the king.
[*They fight.*]

Act Three

[*Another part of the plot. The King, Rosencrantz, Guilden-
stern, etc. They flex their buskins and slap their thighs.*]
POLONIUS [*aside*]: Though this be madness, yet there is
      Method in't.
[*They fight.*]

Act Four

HAMLET: To be or not.
   To be *that*
   Is the question whether.
[*He thighs, and busks his slapkins. They fight.*]

Act Five

HAMLET: The rest is silence.
[*Dies.*]
HORATIO: Now cracks a noble.
[*A noble cracks. Horatio auscults him.*]
                        Heart good.
[*Yawning, and offering a chocolate to Fortinbras.*]
                           'Night! Sweet, Prince?
FORTINBRAS: Let four captains bear *Hamlet*, like a
      soldier, from the stage;
   For it was likely, had it been put on,
   To have prov'd most royally.
[*A dead march. Exeunt, bearing knighthoods.*]

                                          (1963)

A hand of cards

Bernard –

> *With All Good Wishes*
> *for a Merry Christmas*
> *and a Happy New Year!*

> – from Charles (Edwards!)

I don't know whether you remember me – we used to prop up the bar of the Rose and Crown together occasionally in the good old days, in dear old London town. How are you keeping back there in England, you old reprobate? Look me up if you're ever passing through New Zealand.

*

Bernard and Jean –

> *Wishing you a Very*
> *Merry Christmas and the*
> *Happiest of New Years*

> – from Charles

Congratulations on your marriage – saw it in *The Times* air-mail edition. Nice work if you can get it. Meant to write on the spot. Anyway, cheers to you both.

*

Bernard, Jean and Baby Flora(!) –

> *All Best Wishes for*
> *Xmas and the New Year*

> – from Charles and Kitty(!)

Charles took the plunge at last, as you can see! Many congrats on the Flora effort – saw it in *The Times* – meant to write. You must come out and see us some time.

*

Bernard, Jean, Flora, and Polly(!) –

> *To Wish you a*
> *Joyous Christmas*

>> – from Charles, Kitty, Gareth(!),
>> and Luke(!!)

Yes, you did hear right – twins! Identical – fair, with Charles's nose and mouth. Born 14 July – same day as Fall of Bastille! Charles had to be revived with brandy. Gareth ate earring last month, otherwise everything OK. Tremendous congrats on Polly – meant to write.

*

Jean, Flora, and Polly –

> *The mail coach dashes thru' the snowy ways*
> *To bring good cheer and news of happy days!*

>> – from Charles, Kitty, Gareth,
>> Luke, Lionel(!), and Mother.

Dreadfully sorry about you and Bernard, but I'm sure you're usually better off apart in these cases. Great shock when we got your last year's card, meant to write at once, but you know how it is, particularly with Lionel and all the rest of it. Lionel was a slight mistake, of course! Mother's moved in to help out.

*

Bernard, Jean, Flora, Polly, and Daisy(!) –

Peace on Earth, Goodwill to Men

> – from Kitty and Walter
> (CRAIGIE!), not to mention
> Gareth, Luke, Lionel, Mother,
> Victoria and Georgina!

Heartiest congrats on you and Bernard getting together again – further hearty congrats on weighing in so smartly with Daisy! Meant to write as soon as your last Xmas card arrived. Walter and I were married in Auckland on 9 June, reception for 120, two days' honeymoon at Rotorua while Mother looked after children. Victoria and Georgina are Walter's children by first marriage, of course(!). Walter is engineer – low temperature. Poor Charles is coming over to England in New Year, told him to look you up.

*

Bernard, Jean, Flora, Polly, Daisy, and James(!) –

> *Hearty Good Wishes for*
> *a Merry Xmas and a*
> *Prosperous New Year!*

> – from Kitty, Walter, Gareth,
> Luke, Lionel, Mother,
> Victoria, Georgina, Murray,
> Lester and Baby Linda.

Congrats on James – my word you keep at it! Victoria and Georgina had lovely joint wedding at St Margaret's, Wanganui, in Feb. Vicky married Murray West (his father's in agricultural machinery down near Christchurch), Georgie married Lester Dewie – nice young man, went to school in England (Thorpehurst – know it?), now learning hotel business. Georgie's baby Linda born (prematurely!) 3 Aug. Did poor Charles ever show up in UK?

*

Charles(!), Jean, Flora, Polly, Daisy, and James –

> *When the Yule log brightly burns*
> *And brings its Christmas cheer,*
> *To days gone by fond Mem'ry turns,*
> *And old friends far and near!*

>> – from Kitty, Walter, Gareth,
>> Luke, Lionel, Victoria, Murray,
>> Georgina, Lester, Linda,
>> Sukie, and Simon.

Heartiest congrats from all of us on you and Charles! V. best wishes – all tickled pink. Shameful of me not to write in summer when I heard news but Vicky was just producing Simon, and then Georgie was having Sukie while I looked after Linda, then Mother passed quietly away.

*

Charles, Jean, Flora, Polly, Daisy, James, Dinah(!), Gareth, Luke, and Lionel –

> *Yuletide Greetings!*

>> – from Kitty, Walter, Victoria,
>> Murray, Georgina, Lester,
>> Linda, Sukie, Simon, and
>> Gabriel.

Congratulations on Dinah! Don't know how you do it! Gabriel (Simon's brother) born 7 Oct. in flood. Hope Gareth, Luke, and Lionel are settling down all right with

their father for Xmas, seems very quiet here without them,
though Lester's mother is coming for Xmas Day (she's just
lost her husband, sadly) plus his two sisters Charmian and
Henrietta, so house will be quite full. Walter has ulcer.

*

Charles, Jean, Flora, Polly, Daisy, James, Dinah, Gareth,
Luke, Lionel, Georgina, Lester, Linda, Sukie, and Jane –

> *Christmas Comes But Once a Year*
> *and When it Comes it Brings Good Cheer!*

> – from Kitty, Walter, Victoria,
> Murray, Simon, Gabriel,
> Nicholas, Charmian, Henrietta,
> *Bernard*(!), Cecilia and Timothy.

Hope the boys are enjoying their Xmas jaunt as usual and
behaving themselves. So good of you to have Georgie
and Lester and the girls for Xmas while they're over in
England, hope Charles will be up and about again soon.
Guess what, Bernard's here! Coming for Xmas Day with his
new wife Cecilia and their baby Timothy (three months).
Sends his love – says he doesn't send Xmas cards any more.
I know what he means – once you start it never ends.

(1967)

He said, she said

'What was that?' he said suddenly.

She looked up sharply, frightened by the alarm in his
voice.

'I thought I saw . . .' he began, then stopped. 'There they

are again!' he said softly. 'Yes, and now there's two more of
them!'

He seemed to be trying to brush something away from
around his face, like a man bothered by flies. There were no
flies, however. She looked around her uneasily.

'I can't see anything . . .' she began, but then stopped in
her turn, because no sooner had she uttered the words than
she could. She could see them quite clearly. They were very
small, but for an instant their heads and their characteristic curving tails were absolutely distinct.

'You, too?' he said.

She nodded.

'Yes,' she replied grimly, brushing them away from her
hair. 'Inverted commas. Quotation marks.'

'Right,' he agreed. 'And not just the odd couple, here and
there. They're all around us. Swarms and swarms of them.'

'Well,' she said. 'We both know perfectly well what it
means. The fact is, we're in the middle of a passage of
dialogue.'

'Oh God,' he agonised softly.

'I know,' she sympathised. She put her hand on his arm
for a moment and smiled at him. He managed a smile in
return.

There seemed to be nothing more to say.

*

Many long paragraphs of narrative and description
followed during which not a word was uttered. Then:

'They're back,' he said.

'So I see,' she replied, trudging on without looking up.
'But I think the thing is to pay no attention – just to get on
with other things at the same time and keep ourselves
distracted.'

She took out a few useful gerunds that she always kept
with her, and passed a handful to him.

'You mean, saying what one has to say,' he said, running his hand reflectively through his thinning hair, 'and at the same time doing something like running one's hand reflectively through one's thinning hair?'

'Yes, or fixing the person you're talking to with a gaze that goes on and on,' she suggested, fixing him with a gaze that went on and on.

'I see,' he said, not seeing at all.

'Or even just thinking something to yourself, or feeling some sort of feeling,' she went on, thinking to herself that he wouldn't even know that she *was* thinking to herself, and feeling rather pleased about it. 'Though it doesn't even have to be a gerund,' she went on, throwing in another gerund all the same.

'How do you mean?' he asked, wrinkling his forehead in a puzzled frown.

'You can just put in a full stop and then do something else,' she replied. She put in a full stop, just like that, with a wonderful insouciance. 'It doesn't even have to have anything to do with what you're saying.' She began to manufacture a double bass out of a pile of firebricks and a ball of pale blue wool. 'Anything, just so long as it holds off the inverted commas for a bit.'

He thought about this in silence. He hated trying to do two different things at once.

'What I've noticed,' he said at last, 'is that even if one doesn't do other things while one's speaking, other things often seem to do themselves.'

As he spoke, an aircraft appeared in the sky, heavily laden with symbolic reference, and crashed portentously behind the pigsties.

*

'*He said*,' he said, a few pages later.

'What?' she said.

'*She said*! There we go again! Didn't you hear it?'

'Oh, that. Yes. You always get that.'

'So who's saying it?' he demanded. 'Who's saying all this *she said* and *he demanded*?'

'Not me,' she shrugged.

'*She shrugged*! Oh, honestly! Before we know where we are we'll be getting *he gritted*.'

There was a slight pause. Then – *he expostulated*.

They stopped talking and listened for some moments, waiting to hear what variations they would be reduced to next. But nothing happened. There was silence.

'I can stand the inverted commas . . .' he began, and stopped. 'There it goes again – *he began*! Every time I open my mouth! It's getting on my nerves.'

'It's as if someone was listening in to everything we said,' she complained.

'It's so unnecessary, that's what maddens me.'

'Everyone knows we're saying things. They don't have to keep being told.'

'Just a moment, though . . .'

'What?'

'I think it's stopped!'

'Has it . . . ? Yes, so it has!'

'They must have realised we could hear them.'

'Well, thank heavens for that!'

'Yes . . . Only . . .'

'Only what?'

'Well, this is rather silly, but I've forgotten which of us is which.'

'Which of us is which? That's easy. You just count back to the last *he said* or *she said*.'

'Oh, I see. Hold on, then . . . You, me, you, me . . . Or, just a moment, was it Me, you . . . ? No, no – I know – You, me, you, me, you, me, you, me . . . Good God – I'm *she*!'

'Don't be silly. Can't you tell from the kind of thing you're saying? That's the way *he* speaks!'

'Is it? Hold on . . . You, me, you, me, you, me, you, me, you . . . Yes! You're she and I'm you! No . . .'

They looked up at the sky, hoping to hear even the faintest *he said* or *she said* echoing through the universe. But the sky was very clear and very empty.

*

For several pages they vanished altogether. Other people took their place, and said this and said that in their turn, and explained and gasped and riposted, and got murdered in various strikingly horrible ways.

'What I really object to,' he said, as soon as they were back, but she stopped him.

'You see?' she said. 'I *knew* it was going to turn out to be you and not me when we got our bearings again. Sorry. Go on.'

'What I object to,' he pursued, 'is being pushed back into the past all the time. When I say something – when I say what I'm saying now, for instance – I feel as if I'm saying it, well, *now*, in the present. But as soon as I've finished – wham! – *he said* – and I realise it was way back in the past. I feel I'm being robbed of my life.'

'I know what you mean,' she said hesitantly. 'But I think one just has to have faith. One has to believe that one day we'll . . . catch up.'

'Catch up?' he queried.

'Get right through the book, to the very last page.' Her eyes were shining. Her eyes were shining because it was an interestingly different way of indicating that she was the one who had been doing the speaking.

'And then at last it will be all *he says* and *she grinds out*?' His ears reddened, for much the same reason as her eyes had been shining.

She shook her head, meaning no, but meaning also that she was the next one to speak.

'No,' she said, just to make it doubly clear. 'But if we can get to the last page we might just get a glimpse of the back of the jacket. Because that's where he lives, this person who keeps saying *he said* and *she said*.'

He looked at her. 'You mean, we might talk to him? Might even shout *he said* every time he opens his mouth?'

She smiled. 'I don't think we'll ever get ahead of him. He's too clever for that. But we might, just for a moment, catch a glimpse of his photograph. We might find out where he went to school, and whether he's married or not.'

And so on they went. Though neither of them knew it yet, they had another 359 pages to go, including 2,769 more *he* and *she said*s, and no less than 4,833 pairs of inverted commas.

So, by the time they got there, the photograph on the back of the jacket would be as out of date as everything else.

(1994)

Head to head

. . . gives me very great pleasure to be here – to see your beautiful and historic country for myself, and to bring greetings from my people across the sea to the people of Fandangia.

And here I must say what especial pleasure it gives me to be in Fandangia as the guest of President Goizi (*Applause*). In the hearts and in the affections of my countrymen, President Goizi will always hold a special place. We know how faithfully he served Fandangia. We have watched him at the helm through times that have not always been easy, amidst the perilous shoals of our world today.

I may say that I had the privilege and good fortune to

meet the previous President, President Fasces. It seems only yesterday that I was paying tribute to him at a not entirely dissimilar occasion. But it was in fact the day before yesterday, and since his tragic death early this morning President Goizi has shown himself in every way a worthy successor.

But we, in our country, have a special reason for the affection in which we hold President Goizi. For we know that the warm and friendly relations that exist between our two nations today are due in no small measure to his interest and to his unremitting efforts. It is perhaps not out of place to recall that President Goizi has visited us. He has seen us at work and play. He has tasted a sample of our national cooking (*Laughter*) – and, I am assured, pronounced it not greatly inferior to Fandangian cooking (*Laughter*). He has watched our national game (*Laughter*) – and, I believe, declared himself mystified by it (*Loud laughter*). In short, we know that he has seen us at first hand, in times that have not always been easy, and observed how we have faced the perils that confront every nation in the world today. It is bonds like these that unite our two peoples (*Applause*).

But we must not let our sense of history make us unaware of the changing world in which we live. We must not let our regard for tradition, and for the preservation of what is best in our way of life – important as these things are – blind us to the events which are taking place about us. And at this point it is perhaps not inappropriate that I should say how particularly pleased I am to find myself in Fandangia as the guest of President Bombardos (*Applause*).

In terms of the time in which these things are measured, it might perhaps be said that President Bombardos has not been responsible for guiding Fandangia's destinies for very long. But already, since he took over the duties which were so unexpectedly thrust upon him after the sudden retirement for health reasons of his predecessor, President Goizi, this evening, he has proved himself to be a worthy successor.

He has brought Fandangia through times which for all of us have not been without their difficulties. It is perhaps scarcely an exaggeration to say that he has made this nation what it is at the moment. And in the hearts and minds of my countrymen, President Bombardos will always be assured of a special place. Already we have come to learn that in President Bombardos we have a true friend. I believe that it is not entirely inappropriate to recollect that he has spent some time among our people. One of his special concerns was to study our police forces – which he was kind enough to say were 'wonderful' (*Laughter*). I believe he also had a taste of our weather (*Laughter*), though there is no record of his saying the same thing about that (*Loud laughter*).

In other words, President Bombardos has seen us as we are, looked at the best and worst in our nation, and, as we like to think, come to understand us. For us, President Bombardos *is* Fandangia (*Prolonged applause*).

But I should not like you to think that this close and friendly interest in every latest development is not fully reciprocated. I cannot therefore finish without paying personal tribute to the President of the Fandangian Republic, President Goizi, who, with the exception of a brief interregnum very recently, has guided your destinies for so long . . .

(1962)

Heart-cry from beautiful Yvonne Romaine

It was pure chivalry which stayed my hand in the act of consigning to the waste-paper basket a publicity handout entitled *The Curse of the Werewolf*, News Sheet No. 3. My eye, usually afflicted by temporary blindness at the sight of a handout, had caught the headline 'Heart-Cry From Beautiful Yvonne Romaine'. Whipping out my Boy Scout penknife, which has an attachment for helping maidens in distress, I quickly read on. The piteous complaint welling up from the tortured depths of Miss Romaine's heart turned out to be: 'I Always Seem To Be More Corpse Than Cutie!'

Here was a girl in trouble and no mistake. She had played a corpse in *Circus of Horrors*, explained News Sheet No. 3, hurled herself to destruction over a cliff in *Interpol*, and been shot dead in *Danger Man*. Now beautiful twenty-two-year-old Yvonne Romaine is acting in *The Curse of the Werewolf*, and she really seems to have reached the end of the line. She plays the part of a deaf-mute girl who dies in childbirth after being delivered of a werewolf cub. 'I confess,' she lisps fetchingly, 'I froze like an ice-cube when I started reading the script.'

I have nothing but sympathy – unlike her so-called friends. This stony hearted bunch, according to News Sheet No. 3, find Miss Romaine's tendency to freeze like an ice-cube 'strange', pointing out with what passes for logic in their part of the world that she is half Maltese and combines the earthy beauty of Magnano with the smouldering fire of Loren. Goodness me, I've known earthy, smouldering folk, pure-blooded Maltese on both sides of the family, who fainted dead away at the mere sight of a werewolf.

'No,' she says in answer to the question hovering on the lips of a thousand journalists, 'I cannot really explain my fear of the macabre. I am not naturally nervous. I am not afraid of heights, high speeds, or stunting in airplanes. I'm not morally uncourageous.' Except to add that she is married to a man who 'feeds comedy lines and gags to distinguished funsters', that seems more or less to complete the case history of Miss Yvonne Romaine.

Aunty Frayn replies:

Dear Yvonne,

Troubles never come singly, do they, my dear? But I'm sure the dark days will not last for ever, and that your moral courage and your fearless readiness for stunting in airplanes will win through to a brighter dawn ahead.

I know how difficult it is, believe me, when one feels one is more corpse than cutie. But it's no good fretting, my dear. Some of us are born to be cuties, and some to be corpses. No man whose love is worth anything at all will turn away from you simply because you are a corpse. And you can improve your appearance tremendously, you know, by the use of a good embalming fluid.

As for your other trouble, I am putting you in touch with a society which exists to help girls in just your position. It seems a pity you are dying in childbirth, though, for you will not have the opportunity to live down your moment of weakness in the years of self-less work for others which I usually recommend. A werewolf cub can be great fun, you know, and I am sending you under separate cover a book entitled *The Complete Practical Werewolf Breeder*. Perhaps after you are gone your husband will rally round. Try to persuade him to cease feeding gags to distinguished funsters and start feeding the werewolf instead.

(1960)

H.I.5

In the peeling, anonymous lobby, Costello showed his pass to the security man. He took a lift to the fourth floor, showed his pass again, and went straight to Control's office, the advance copy of the List still in his hand.

'I'll tell him you're here,' said Control's pretty secretary, giving him a specially sympathetic smile. No doubt everyone would give him a specially sympathetic smile today. One of his best men was blown; already it was vaguely known in the office that be had put up some sort of black. He kept his face wooden.

'Would you go in?' said the pretty secretary, smiling again.

It was hot inside Control's office. Probably the window latch was broken, like everything else in the room. Control sat visibly sweating in his tweed suit, mortifying his flesh by removing neither jacket nor waistcoat. A cup of ancient office tea stood on his copy of the Birthday Honours List. It had left several wet rings on the Companions of Honour, Costello noticed.

'I'm sorry about Spode,' said Control, nodding at the List.

'Yes,' said Costello flatly.

'Doing a drunk driving on you like that, after you'd cleared him to KCMG level. We only just got him out in time.'

'Yes.'

'Three others in the last couple of years, weren't there, who went down one way or another? One for embezzling, one co-respondent, and one who defected to the Russians?'

'Yes.'

'It doesn't look too good, you know. The Committee don't like it.'

'Naturally not.'

'I only mention it. No use crying over spilt milk, of course.

We've got to get down to the next batch for the New Year list. I'm putting you down to do a chap called Sneame – G. B. J. Sneame. He's been Head Gardener at the British Hospital in Zurich for 37 years. Roughboys, the Director, nominated him.'

'A head gardener? You mean for an MBE?'

'Now, I don't want you to think of this as a demotion, Costello.'

'But I've been doing Mike and Georges for 10 years now.'

'The Committee feels you'd benefit from vetting a few MBE nominations again. You know, Costello, in Honours Intelligence we don't think any less of a man because he's only been nominated for the MBE. After all, he's a human being just like you and me. I believe we should remember that an MBE a GCMG – even a KG – are all equal in the sight of God.'

'Yes. You want me to find out if this man's any good at gardening?'

'Oh, he's good all right. We know that much. You'll find it all on the file. But is he *damned* good? That's what we want to know. Is he MBE good?'

'All right.'

'I want you to go out there as a representative of a firm selling specialised pesticides. I take it you can handle a spraygun if the need arises?'

'Yes.'

'Take a look at his roses, Costello. That's the kind of thing the Committee wants to know about. Is he growing first-class English roses out there, with good size, colour, and scent? Is he free of aphids? Has he kept his nose clean on slugs? That's the kind of stuff I can make out a case with. Roughboys says he's strong on miniature cactus. The Committee doesn't want to know about his miniature cactus, Costello, or his pondweed or his herb-garden. You can't give a man the MBE for growing pots of miniature cactus. Do you see what I mean?'

'I've done MBEs before, Control.'

'You've been off them for years. Don't forget that.'

'I shan't forget it.'

'Roses, Costello. It's absolutely vital that we should know the truth about Sneame's roses.'

Control took a reflective sip of cold tea.

'We'd need photographs, Costello – blueprints – actual measurements. Look, what we want to know is the strategic effect of these roses. Is this man filling the whole of Zurich with the unmistakable perfume of an English rose-garden all summer? Is he making Englishmen in Zurich step a little more proudly? Is he making hard-headed Swiss buyers dream of business trips to Britain? We could pay for information like that, Costello?'

'Just leave it to me.'

Control gazed at the tea-stained Honours List for some minutes, playing with a broken stapling machine.

'Then again,' he said, 'we'd need to know what sort of man he is. A loyal worker. But how loyal? Has he ever asked for a rise?'

'Look, I did 20 gardeners for MBEs in my first year down from Oxford.'

'Roughboys says he's unfailingly cheerful. How cheerful is that, Costello? Does he have a smile for everyone? Including the Swiss? Or does he just grin sycophantically at Roughboys and the senior surgeons? *Exactly* how many times a day does he smile? How many times does he laugh? Does he whistle a merry tune as he dungs those roses, Costello? Or does he just produce a tuneless noise that gets on everybody's nerves?'

'I'll measure the exact pitch, Control.'

'And another thing. Find out how many arms and legs he's got. Even if the roses all had green-fly and he only forced a grin on pay-day we could probably swing it if he was a leg or two short.

'I'll count up, Control. You know I always do.'

'All right, then. But Costello. Take care on this one, will you? Just remember I'm nominated for the KCB myself in this next lot.'

(1964)

Housebiz

I wonder if a little more interest in politics might be aroused if politicians cast modesty aside and displayed that total self-absorption which film stars always seem to be able to put over so effectively in interviews. Well, here's a trial run I did with Mr Nigel Sharpe-Groomsman MP, star of Parliament and Tory Party Conference.

Good morning, Mr Sharpe-Groomsman.

Call me Nigel, Mike.

Nigel, you're appearing at the moment in the Infectious Aliens (Exclusion) Bill, aren't you?

That's right, Mike. It's a fearless, controversial bill, of course, but it's immensely human and worthwhile. My role is to stand up and speak out in favour of the brotherhood of man. Of course everyone thinks I'm letting the side down, but in the end I turn out to be loyal after all when I produce horrifying figures of Danes and Dutchmen arriving with influenza, and I vote with the Government.

It sounds a great debate, Nigel.

Yes, it is. The bill's being introduced by my old friend Chris Smoothe. He's a wonderful, wonderful politician, and it's been great fun working with him on this. But then the whole team is absolutely wonderful, and I think we've produced a wonderful, wonderful bill that everyone's going to enjoy a lot.

Is this the first bill you've done with Christopher Smoothe?

No, we were in the Landlords' Protection Bill together in

1960, with Harry Debenture and Simon Sheermurder, and again this year in the Welfare Services (Curtailment) Bill, which broke all records in gross savings at the Treasury. Landlords' Protection, of course, was my first starring part.

You've certainly shot to the top, Nigel. Nigel, is it true that you were first discovered modelling for menswear advertisements?

Yes, I got my first break through the photograph that caused all the scandal – the one of me in underwear and suspenders. A Conservative Party agent saw it and snapped me up at once.

Tell me, Nigel . . .

Call me Nige, Mike.

Nige, you've sometimes been described as the new Harold Macmillan.

Yes, Mike, I have. But I've also been called 'the new Duncan Sandys,' 'the new Ernest Marples,' and 'the new Lord Salisbury.' I don't like these labels. I should like to be thought of just as myself, Nigel Sharpe-Groomsman. I mean, after all, I'm fundamentally a person in my own right. That's what I want to get over.

You don't think there's any truth in the labels, then?

Oh, I wouldn't say that. I think it's true that I have Duncan's nose and Ernest's legs. But people say I smile like Harold Macmillan. I don't think that's entirely true. When I smile – so I'm told by many critics and political commentators – my whole face lights up in a very individual way. And I don't want to get typecast. I don't always want to be the sort of member who appears to let the side down by talking about the brotherhood of man but who always rallies round and votes for the Government in the end. I mean, I want the public to realise – I want Ministers to realise – that I'm a serious politician. It's not that I haven't enjoyed doing this wonderful, wonderful Infectious Aliens (Exclusion) Bill with Chris, but one has one's career to think of.

One last question, Nige . . .

Call me Ni, Mike.

What sort of bill would you most like to appear in, Ni?

Well, Mike, I'd like to do a bill which offered a role with a greater chance to express the real me. A war bill, for example, with a debate where I call for courage and sacrifice from the nation in the face of overwhelming odds. I mean, basically I'm the Churchill type. My friends all tell me I've got Churchill's ears.

Thanks for coming along, Ni. I'm sure we'll all be watching you tomorrow in the Infectious Aliens (Exclusion) Bill.

(1961)

I said, 'My Name is "Ozzy" Manders, Dean of King's'

I must not tell lies.

I must not tell pointless lies.

I must not tell pointless lies at parties.

I must not tell pointless lies at parties when they are plainly going to be found out in the next 10 minutes.

I must not:

1: Let it be thought that I have caught the name of anyone I am ever introduced to, because statistics show that I have never caught anyone's name until I have heard it at least twelve times.

2: Give it to be understood that I have already heard of the owner of the inaudible name, because tests show that apart from one or two obvious exceptions like William Shakespeare and Sir Harold Sidewinder I haven't heard of anyone.

3: Say I have read the man's books, or admired his architecture, or used his firm's brake-linings, or seen his agency's advertisements, or always been interested in his field of research, or know his home town, because I do hereby make a solemn and unconditional declaration, being before witnesses and in sober realisation of my past wrongdoing, that I have done none of these things.

4: Say that I know any of the people he is sure I must know, or have heard of any of the names he takes to be common knowledge, because I don't and haven't, or if I do and have, I've got them all hopelessly mixed up, and when he says Appel I'm thinking of Riopelle, and when he says Buffet I'm thinking of Dubuffet, and when he says Palma I'm thinking of Palermo, and when he says syncretism I'm thinking of syndicalism, and when he says a man called 'Pop' Tuddenham who hired a barrage balloon and dressed it up to look like an elephant I'm thinking of a man called 'Tubby' Poppleton who hired a horse and dressed it up to look like the Senior Tutor.

5: Try to sustain the fiction that I have heard anything he has said to me over the noise, because I have not, and because he has heard nothing I have said, either, so that by analogy he *knows* I am lying just as surely as I know he is lying.

6: Bend my lips in an attempt to counterfeit a smile unless I am absolutely assured by the raising of a flag with the word JOKE on it that the man has made a joke and not announced that his mother has died.

7: In short, get involved in any more conversations that go:

'I've long been a great admirer of your, er . . . stuff, Mr . . . er . . . er . . .'

'How kind of you.'

'Oh, all kinds.'

'No, I'm afraid some critics haven't been at all kind.'

'The tall kind? I see. I see.'

(A long silence. I think.)

'I particularly liked your last boo . . . er, pla . . . , um, one.'

'Last what?'

'One.'

'One what?'

'Um, thing you, well, did.'

'Really? The Press panned it.'

' "The Press Bandit" – of course, it was on the tip of my tongue.'

'Well, the Irish banned it.'

'I mean "The Irish Bandit", of course. How stupid of me.'

'But everyone else panned it.'

'Oh, Elsie Pandit. You mean *Mrs* Pandit?'

'Who – your missus panned it?'

'No, India's Mrs Pandit.'
'They panned it in India, too, did they?'
'Did they? I suppose Mrs Pandit banned it.'
'Ah. You know India, do you?'
'No. You do, do you?'
'No.'
'Ah.'
'Hm.'

(I smile a cryptic knowing smile. He smiles a cryptic, knowing smile. We are getting on wonderfully. Just then my wife comes up and wants to be introduced, and I have to ask the man who he is.)

Why do I do these things? Do I think the man's going to give me a fiver, or a year's free supply of his works for having heard of his name? Do I think he's going to twist my arm and kick me on the kneecap if I don't like his stuff? He doesn't *expect* me to like it. No one likes it except his wife and the editor of *Spasm* and 780 former pupils of F. R. Leavis. Anyway, I've got him mixed up with someone else, and he didn't do it, and even what he didn't do isn't what I think he did. For heaven's sake, am *I* going to strike *him* because he thinks I'm called Freen, and that I write articles for the Lord's Day Observance Society?

I must not waste my valuable talent for deceit on lies which have no conceivable purpose when I could be saving it up for lies which would show a cash return.

I must instead say 'I'm sorry, I didn't quite catch your name.'

I must say 'I'm sorry, I still haven't quite . . .'

I must say 'I'm sorry – did you say "Green" or "Queen"? Ah. Queen who? Come again . . . Queen *Elizabeth?* Elizabeth what?'

I must say 'I expect I should know, but I'm afraid I don't – what do you do? I beg your pardon? Rain? You study it, do you – rainfall statistics and so on? No? You rain? You mean you actually rain yourself? I see. I see.'

I must say 'No, I *don't* see. What do you mean, you rain . . . ?'

I must . . .

I must not, on second thoughts, be pointlessly honest, either.

(1963)

I say Toronto, you say Topeka

Flying, I gather, is not such a high-stress occupation as it used to be, because the stress is being shifted from the aircrew on to computers. But it's increasingly a wrong-stress occupation, as the stress is shifted off the significant word in cabin announcements on to the auxiliary verb.

It used to be just on American airlines. But now even British cabin staff are telling us that the plane *will* be landing shortly at London Heathrow. Passengers *will* be disembarking from the front of the aircraft, they insist. We *are* requested to make sure we *have* all our belongings with us.

I used to think this was because airlines were hiring actors or theatre directors to coach their cabin crew in diction. Actors and directors who perform the classics *have* to find new ways of stressing the lines, to stop themselves going crazy. Or rather, they have to *find* new ways, they have to find new *ways*, new ways of *stressing*, of stressing the *lines*. They are acutely aware that this is not the first time in history that someone has gone on to a stage and said, 'Oh what a rogue and peasant slave am *I*!' They know that at least twenty-seven other actors are going to be saying it somewhere in the world at that very same moment. Their soul revolts! 'Oh, *what a rogue!*' they find themselves gurgling. And a new reading of the part – the prince as queen – has come into being even before they're halfway through the line.

Some actors I've worked with can effortlessly hit every stress in a line except the right one. I am overcome by stress-blindness myself, reading my own plays through to directors. I can't remember for the life of me what stress I had in mind when I wrote the line. All I know is that it's certainly not the *one* I'm managing to produce.

But now another explanation altogether has come to me. We're surprised to be told that the cabin staff *will* be serving lunch because we were taking it for granted that they would be. But maybe we were taking it entirely too much for granted. Maybe the serving of lunch is no more pre-ordained than anything else in life. Cabin staff are human beings, not automata. They are free citizens, not slaves. They have ideas of their own about whether lunch should be served or not – and a tremendous debate has probably been going on about it in the galley ever since take-off. 'We *won't* serve lunch!' say some of the attendants. 'We *may*, in certain circumstances,' say others. 'We *could* ... we *should* ... we *must*' – the argument rages. The passengers ought to be asking each other, 'Will they, or won't they?' They should be taking bets on the outcome. So that when the Chief Stewardess comes out of the negotiating chamber and goes on the air to announce 'We *will* be!' she is issuing hot news. We should all cheer.

Evidently the same kind of thing is going on up there in the cockpit. A battle royal has been raging about the flight-plan, ever since the Chief Stewardess predicted confidently, shortly before take-off, 'We *will* be departing for Cincinnati.' This was in line with well-informed forecasts by both the airline and air-traffic control. But now, up there in the cockpit, the Captain has suddenly raised the possibility of flying to somewhere else altogether.

'I favour Decatur, Illinois,' he tells the First Officer. 'I've heard good things of Decatur.'

The First Officer, a man of little imagination and rigid

principles, is frankly astonished. 'I don't understand,' he says. 'We're cleared through to Cincinnati.'

'I don't much care for Cincinnati,' says the Captain.

'But this is Flight JQ407,' says the First Officer. 'For Cincinnati.'

'As I understand it from Operation Control,' says the Captain, 'Flight JQ407 went to Cincinnati yesterday.'

'Exactly!' says the First Officer.

'I believe it also went to Cincinnati the day before yesterday,' says the Captain, 'and the day before that.'

'It goes to Cincinnati every day,' says the First Officer.

'Then it has gone to Cincinnati often enough,' says the Captain. 'The possibilities of flying to Cincinnati have been very adequately explored. We have had Cincinnati.'

'But we are *contractually* bound to go to Cincinnati!' cries the First Officer, who read jurisprudence at North-Western before he went to air college. 'The front office sold the passengers their tickets on the basis of an *implied undertaking* to go to Cincinnati!'

These powerful stresses have no effect upon the Captain, because captains don't normally stress any words at all. When they talk to the passengers, as you may have noticed, they remain notably laid-back and unemphatic. And this particular captain happens to have read moral philosophy at UCLA.

'We also have a duty to ourselves,' he explains calmly, 'to realise our true potential, to behave with spontaneity and authenticity. I don't think that can best be done by going to Cincinnati.'

For some reason this catches the imagination of the Flight Engineer. 'It's not just *us*!' he cries, with hitherto unsuspected passion, and a wild storm of emphases. 'It's all those poor grey *passengers* back there! Let's bring a little colour into *their* lives! A little of the romance of the *unknown*! Some faint echo of the days of the great *clippers*, when you were at the mercy of the four winds of *heaven*, and you never knew for sure which *continent* you were going to end *up* in!'

No one pays any attention to him. Too many stresses, possibly.

'We don't even know if there's an *airport* at Decatur!' says the First Officer.

'OK,' says the Captain, 'so here's what we do. We go down to treetop height and bop around for a bit, see what we can see. There may be a field. There may be a freeway where things are reasonably quiet.'

'I've got *another* idea!' says the Flight Engineer. There's this *girl* I know in Cedar Rapids, Iowa . . .'

'Well, *I* say we're going to Cincinnati!' shouts the First Officer.

'I say we're *not*,' says the Captain, finally driven to emphasising words himself. 'And *I* am the Captain.'

'You *are* the Captain, right!' says the First Officer, by which he means that *if* the Captain is the Captain then he should *behave* like the Captain.

But the Captain misses this implication. They didn't do rhetoric at UCLA.

'I *am* the Captain?' he says. 'OK, if that's the way you prefer it – I *am* the Captain. No, hold on, I was right the first time, I am the *Captain*. Is that what I said? You're getting me a little confused here.'

'What do you mean, *I'm* getting *you* confused?' screams the First Officer.

'No? OK. You're getting me *confused* . . . You're *getting* me confused . . . It sounds funny whichever way. It's these damned stresses! I am *the* Captain . . . I have a feeling that language is becoming meaningless. I don't know where I am, or what I'm doing. It's all like a dream . . .'

You probably noticed that the cabin staff didn't serve lunch immediately in spite of having been so very insistent that they were going to. That's because they were all in the cockpit, tying up the Captain. And that supposed turbulence, somewhere over Altoona? That's when they were disarming the First Officer, and trying to resuscitate the Flight Engineer.

Don't worry – the plane is being flown by a very level-headed stewardess who saw a film once where this kind of thing happened. But clearly a firm statement had to be issued before rumours began to circulate back in the cabin. Well, you heard what the Chief Stewardess said: 'We *will* shortly be landing in Cincinnati!'

It was Churchillian.

Though when she added: 'We *hope* you've enjoyed flying with us,' I thought I detected the faintest note of doubt.

(1994)

I think I'm right in saying

Orators of any standing no longer orate, and it's a pretty third-rate writer nowadays who is reduced to writing, These antique forms of communication have been replaced by the interview. Would you agree, Mr Frayn?

– Oh yes, entirely.

I believe I'm right in saying that you yourself have given up writing, Mr Frayn, and have instead put yourself in the hands of a competent interviewer. Tell me, is this forward-looking move aimed at easing the strain of thinking, or is it purely an attempt to gain status?

– A bit of both, I think.

I wonder if you agree with me that this technique is capable of considerable extension? It seems to me demeaning in the extreme for Lord Mayors and others to be forced back on the monologue form at ceremonial occasions. It would surely add tone and dignity to the occasion if a good interviewer asked the Lord Mayor:

'What does it give you, sir, to be present here today?'

'Very great pleasure,' the Lord Mayor would reply.

'And what organ is this good cause very close to?'

'My heart.'

'I see. But I believe you're sure that people haven't come here to do one thing?'

'To listen to me talking.'

'So what do you intend to proceed without?'

'Any further ado.'

'One last question, sir. What do you declare this home for asthmatic engine-drivers?'

'Open.'

What do you think of these proposals, Mr Frayn?

– Oh, *admirable*.

I feel (perhaps you will agree with me) that the whole course of human history would have had much more tone and class if these techniques had been put into practice earlier.

– Yes, I suppose so.

I was thinking, for instance, of the rather tedious monologue which Mark Antony delivered to the crowd in the Forum. How much more satisfactory it would have been if some well-informed commentator had introduced him.

'Friends, Romans, countrymen,' he might have started off, 'lend that well-known personality, Mark Antony, your ears. Mr Antony, it's a great honour to have you with us here in the Forum. What exactly is the purpose of your visit?'

'I come to bury Caesar,' Antony would reply.

'Not to praise him?'

'Definitely not.'

'Mr Antony, you've been quoted in some of the Londinium papers as saying that the evil that men do is oft interred with their bones. Would you care to comment on this?'

'I'm afraid they've got hold of the wrong end of the stick

entirely. What I actually said was that the evil that men do lives after them. It was the good, I said, which was oft interred with their bones.'

'And your attitude is, if I may put words into your mouth, "So let it be with Caesar"?'

'Exactly.'

The mob would have remained completely calm and orderly under these circumstances, don't you think, Mr Frayn?

– What? Oh, yes.

Do you think the technique could also be used in the parliamentary and political fields? Would it add interest and variety to speeches that of necessity contain lists of proposals? For instance, I can imagine a good political journalist helping out with:

'Welcome back to the dispatch box, Mr Churchill. I think the question that's uppermost in all our minds tonight is what you, as Prime Minister, have to offer the English people.'

'Nothing but blood and sweat.'

'Nothing else at all?'

'I'm afraid not.'

'How about tears?'

'Oh well, yes, some tears, if you like.'

The same man could have done wonders at the Labour Party Conference at Scarborough.

'What do you propose to do, Mr Gaitskell? Fight or not?'

'Oh, rather.'

'Which, fight?'

'I beg your pardon?'

'I said "fight" again.'

'Oh, again and again and again.'

Well, thank you, Mr Frayn, for coming along and answering my questions so frankly.

As a matter of fact, Mr Frayn's gone to bed, suffering from creative exhaustion. I'm the interviewer who's come

to interview you. Perhaps you'd care to start off by telling
us all what it's like to be a famous interviewer . . .

(1961)

In funland

Sigismund Cortex, that keen Psychomanian student of
British affairs, is greatly excited by the idea of Miss Joan
Littlewood's Fun Palace. The only trouble is, he can't
understand exactly what a Fun Palace is.

He keeps alternately interrogating me and hunting
through a stack of English–Psychomanian dictionaries. He
says they have plenty of palaces in his country, but so
far as he can tell they don't have any fun. I mean *I* know
what a Fun Palace is, but it's damned difficult to explain it
to *him*.

'Is a Palace of Culture?' he asks keenly.

'Not exactly,' I reply helpfully.

'Is a Palace of Varieties?'

'I don't think so.'

'Is a sports stadium?'

'Oh no.'

'Ah, now I see! Is a house of prostitution?'

'Certainly not.'

He turns some more pages in the dictionary.

'You see, Michael, it is important that we in our country
keep up with the technologically more advanced nations.
We refuse to be excluded from the comity of fun-loving
nations. Now excuse me, please. I read in a newspaper
that this Fun Palace would contain six-screen cinemas,
mobile cycloramas, warm-air curtains, optical barriers
and static-vapour zones. Tell me, please, are these the
funs?'

'No, the fun's what goes on the screens and between the barriers.'

'Describe this fun, please.'

'Well, I don't think they've decided what sort of fun they're going to have in there yet.'

'No? They build the building first and then find the fun afterwards?'

'I think that's the idea, Sigismund.'

He suddenly finds a new word in the dictionary.

'Ah, now I understand!' he cries. 'Is a funfair!'

'I'm sure it's not. I'm sure it's dedicated to a much higher and broader concept of fun than that. You see, Sigismund, we have more and more fun in our country these days because we have more and more leisure to have fun in. What we believe now is that almost anything can be fun, if you go about it in the right spirit.'

'Almost anything?'

'If it's fun to do.'

'Aaaaaaaah! You *do* fun? Fun is something you *do*?'

'Oh no – fun's something you *have*.'

'Aaaaaaaah! You *have* fun! Like you have flu?'

'Exactly.'

'You mean, if this dictionary has fun I catch fun?'

'No, if the dictionary is, you have.'

'Excuse me, please. Where is the fun? In me or in the book?'

'I'm not absolutely sure.'

'But the book does not have fun?'

'Certainly not.'

Sigismund makes a careful note of these points.

'In Psychomania,' he says, 'we have sports, pastimes, amusements, diversions, hobbies and various erotic activities. We also have jokes and laughter. You know laughter? Laughter goes ha, ha, ha.'

'We have jokes and laughter in our country, too.'

'Ah! Now, is jokes and laughter fun?'

'Certainly. But fun isn't just jokes and laughter, you know.'

Sigismund starts to plough through the dictionary again, his eyes great pools of blankness.

'Look, Sigismund, the point is this. Nice things can be fun. But in this country we believe that nasty things can be fun, too. Mathematics can be fun. Culture can be fun. Even *work* can be fun.'

'Work can be fun?'

'Certainly. No man of real integrity in this country would dream of working if he didn't find it fun. Otherwise he'd just be selling out, wouldn't he? Why do you think the Prime Minister is slogging away up there in Downing Street?'

'Well, now, because he feels a patriotic duty to . . .'

'That's an unkind thing to say, Sigismund. I can assure you he does it simply because it's fun. Why do you think perfectly intelligent university graduates go into advertising?'

'Surely, because they are paid a lot of money . . .'

'Good heavens, Sigismund, you are a cynic! No, they do it because everyone knows advertising is tremendous fun. Why do you think Milton wrote that damned great poem of his? Because he was a fun person and it was a fun thing to do. "I had a lot of fun writing it," he told reporters, as you probably know, "and all I hope is that people have as much fun reading it."'

'He said that?'

'Certainly he did. We live in a fun culture, Sigismund. It's fun to dance till dawn in a topless dinner-jacket at the Reform Club. It's fun to get down on your hands and knees and scrub the floor with new magic Elbo-Grees.'

'Michael, this I never knew. But what are the symptoms of having fun?'

'Well, one finds oneself saying "Gosh, this is fun!" Or "Heavens, I am having fun!"'

'Excuse me, I make a note . . .'

'Yes, write it down, Sigismund. P-E-O-P-L-E A-R-E
F-U-N. That's our great humanistic creed. It's fun to be
alive. It's fun to drop dead.'

(1964)

In the Morris manner

Two very different styles of life are defined by the two
styles of architecture which seem most pervasively influen-
tial in our time – the austere classicism of Mies van der
Rohe and his followers on the one hand, and the currently
more fashionable informality of Charles and Ray Eames on
the other.

It's not easy to know which to aspire to. So I think it's
worth saying that there is a *third* lifestyle, fundamentally
different again, which has been developed over the years by
our friends Horace and Doris Morris and indeed our good
selves. All we lack at the moment is an architecture to put
around it.

In the Miesian canon, if I understand it, the overriding
goal is perfection of form. The skin of the building is the
most formally perfect solution possible of its function,
expressed (usually) in terms of glass to keep the weather
out and steel to hold up the glass. The contents are as
important to the form of the whole as the transparent skin;
so they, too – furniture, carpets, pictures, the lot – are as
strictly located by the architect as the drains.

An architect friend of mine who recently visited the
famous Glass House that Philip Johnson, Mies's associate,
built for himself in Connecticut reports that discreet marks
are placed on the carpet, when new staff are engaged, to
show exactly where each chair is to stand.

I see the attractions: four days out of seven I should like

nothing better than to have an authoritarian architect design my life for me. But then I see the attractions of the opposite conception, too, as developed out of the Mies tradition by Mr and Mrs Eames, and enshrined in the house they have built for themselves at Santa Monica, in California.

According to Geoffrey Holroyd, in an issue of *Architectural Design* devoted to the Eameses recently, 'the house is filled with a huge collection of toys – objects of indigenous Santa Fe folk culture, tumbleweed, driftwood, desert finds of great variety – placed everywhere . . . Mies wants all glass and no clutter; Eames wants clutter, "functioning decoration." ' The house is also full of Eames chairs – 'the first chairs,' according to another contributor, 'which can be put into any position in an empty room.'

This bald description makes the Eames lifestyle sound superficially rather similar to Horace and Doris Morris's and our own. The concept of *clutter* is certainly very special to our thinking. Our houses contain huge collections of toys, mostly broken, together with a random precipitation of pieces of wood, pebbles, old tin cans and cardboard boxes, broken chalk, dolls' legs, scattered heads, empty bottles, and torn envelopes with examples of indigenous child-art on the back. Our chairs, too, are arranged all kind of anyhow.

But a glance at photographs of the interior of the Eameses' house shows that their clutter is clutter only in the loosest sense; it's not clutter in the strict sense that we and Horace and Doris Morris mean at all. The Eameses' tumbleweed has tumbled neatly on to rows of hooks on the wall. The driftwood has drifted into an elegant complex just outside the garden door. The objects of indigenous Santa Fé folk culture have arranged themselves on a square board squared off with a square table, and the chairs have rained down from heaven into positions of the most geometrical exactitude.

The general appearance, in fact, places Charles and Ray Eames pretty firmly in the tradition of our good friends Christopher and Lavinia Crumble, whose extensive collection of folk junk and *objets achetés* has also arranged itself about the living-room with an effortless casual elegance which is entirely alien to the Horace and Doris Morris style.

A completely different approach to the organic development of the clutter is involved. When Christopher Crumble finishes reading a book, for instance, and tosses it casually down on the coffee-table, it lands squarely on top of 'Giovanni Battista Piranesi and the Origins of Op Art' (Limburger & Brie. 7gn.), the edges parallel, the diagonal extending the diagonal of the alabaster lamp-base standing at the golden section of the table. When Horace Morris or I toss a book down, however, it behaves in a much more radically casual fashion. It hits an abandoned Wellington boot standing in an empty soup bowl, perhaps, loses its jacket, and comes down half-open, halfway into an ashtray which is teetering half off the table and half on, kept in balance only by being half-covered with a pair of old trousers which have been put out for mending.

Later, one throws down the daily paper, half-open, on top of the ashtray, the book, the boot, the trousers, and all the rest of it, whereupon half the paper slides down the side of the heap, and wafts away to fetch up along with the book, half under the sofa and half out.

One's wife comes tramping through the broken chalks, pebbles, and amputated dolls' legs, carrying a large cardboard box marked Heinz Spaghetti with Tomato Sauce, and full of bills and grey woollen socks. With unthinking deftness she half folds up the half-open newspaper to half make room for it, so that the box forms, some days later, an attractively unstable podium on which to rest the load of old colour supplements which have finally slipped off the top of the television set.

Within a week or two one is hacking one's way back down to table level again, hefting the sliding sea of colour supplements up by the armful and dumping them into a Sainsbury's Australian Pear Halves box, which one shoves into the kitchen while one tries to think what the hell has happened to a Wellington boot and a book which have mysteriously gone missing. And didn't one have a spare pair of trousers at one stage of one's career . . . ?

It's a style of life all right. All we need is a style of architecture that makes sense of it.

(1967)

In the superurbs

The suburbs are all right after all. They are not, as has been commonly supposed, deserts of boredom, conformity, competitiveness and wife-swapping. They are not a dreadful social aberration which will in time be mercifully blotted out by enlightened town-planning, and living in them is not spiritually or morally inferior to living in the centre of cities.

These, at any rate, are the general conclusions which are to be drawn from the study of one particular lower-middle-class suburb in New Jersey made by the American sociologist Herbert J. Gans, and reported in his book 'The Levittowners.' His findings are said to have been violently attacked by orthodox professional opinion in America; a sure sign that they will eventually be violently accepted.

I accept Mr Gan's findings right now, ahead of the rush, and only wish I'd had the wit to find them first. For a long time now I've nursed the vague project of writing a guidebook to my native London suburbs. Like most guidebooks, it would touch upon the geography, history, architecture, customs and economy of the region. Whenever I've mentioned it to people they've either laughed and said it could be devastating, or asked if the suburban joke wasn't a bit played out. The idea of actually *describing* the suburbs, without either laughing at them or moralising about them, evidently seems to most people about as far-fetched as mapping a plate of mashed potato.

One of the reasons why the suburbs are thought to be such hotbeds, or perhaps coldbeds, of boring conformity is that they boringly *fail* to conform to the tastes of intellectuals. So anyone with intellectual leanings leaves at the first opportunity. Somewhere in the centre of the city, of course, they run into other disaffected intellectuals fleeing from *their* suburbs, and settle down on the spot to set up a boring conformity of their own.

Of course, the boring conformity of the intellectual community doesn't seem like boring conformity to the intellectuals, any more than the boring conformity of the suburbs seems like boring conformity to the suburbanites; each, to its adherents, seems full of the most stimulating diversity.

Let us not forget Progel's First Law of Social Appearances, which states: 'The homogeneity of a group seen from outside is in direct proportion to its heterogeneity seen from within.' Or as Samuel Crink (1721–1897) puts it: 'Likeness is in the eye of the unlike; the like see nothing but their unlikeness.'

All the same, if I had money invested in the future prospenty of the suburbs, I think I should at this point discreetly begin to withdraw it. When moderate people like you and me, and all the others who will eventually come round to Mr Gans's ideas, start thinking that an institution is a good thing after all, its prime is past; nothing but stagnation and decay lie ahead.

Remember what we thought of Victorian architecture, until it started to become ripe for demolition? Remember

what filthy things we thought steam trains and steam-
ships were, until just before the rise of the motorcar and
the aeroplane? Now, of course, we know that it is the motorcar and the aeroplane which are ruining our countryside
and destroying our character. We shall come round to them
only when they invent the . . . whatever it is that will mark
the end of our civilisation next.

This is the general moral history of ideas: in their
mewling infancy they are interesting and challenging and
on the point of opening up a wonderful new age. Then,
when they grow strong and effective, and start opening up
the wonderful new age, it turns out that they are inhuman,
soul-destroying, contemptible, and ridiculous. And finally,
in old age, when their strength begins to fail, they are
regarded with understanding and affection, and showered
with honours.

Remember how television was turning us all into a
nation of square-eyed morons until McLuhan said really
it was doing us all a world of good and the young were
growing up as a new electronic super-race? Immediately, of
course, we hear that fewer and fewer young people are
watching television.

The other day I heard an architect talking nostalgically
about pre-fabs as the best attempt yet at popular housing.
High-rise flats − created in a messianic attempt to avoid
the suburban sprawl we now think might be fine after all,
and currently reviled in their turn − even these we shall
one day come to feel affection for. Truly, there is almost no
limit to the capacity of human beings to adapt themselves
to the ideas imposed upon them for their own good.

It's odd how we feel impelled to react to everything in
moral terms. Why does *everything* have to seem good or bad
to us? Particularly when we know that whatever we now
think good we shall eventually think bad, and vice versa.
We're like tossed pennies, that can register nothing but
heads or tails! Good God, is there really no aspect of the

universe that we don't feel compelled either to encourage or discourage with our little smiles and frowns?

Let us put ten minutes aside each day to practise feeling morally numb. The more things in the universe which we can contemplate with neither approbation nor disapprobation, the more moral energy we shall have left to concentrate on the things which really do need something done about them. Let our commonest moral reaction be a shrug, our commonest moral discourse 'I dunno,' and 'Sawright Ispose.'

Then, faced with new ideas like adolescent self-determination and the spread of unfamiliar intoxicants, we might learn to express our unease and fear just as plain unease and fear, and instead of leaping in to condemn and ridicule, just modestly shuffle from foot to foot, and lick our lips uneasily and tremble.

From the moral point of view (if one can say this) it would be a great improvement.

(1967)

Inside the Krankenhaus

I'm learning a lot from the series the *Daily Mirror* is publishing by Auberon Waugh and his wife ('the brilliant young Waughs,' as the *Mirror* calls them). They're travelling about Europe, sending back a piece a week on the national characteristics of each country they visit.

The Germans are the latest race to come under their microscope. 'Our idea of the country,' writes Mr Waugh, 'had been formed by seeing war films in which all Germans shout "Ach, so! Gott in Himmel!"' He was agreeably surprised to find that this was not the case in the Federal Republic today, and almost as surprised by the sheer variety of the German race. 'Germans come in all sizes,' he reports, 'fat, thin, tall, short, dark, fair. Some are cheerful, some gloomy.'

Ach *so?* one feels like gasping. Thin as well as fat? Short as well as tall? Some cheerful, some gloomy? Well, dash it all! Gott, as one might say, in Himmel!

So the old prejudices and misconceptions are at last exposed. There's only one thing in which Mr Waugh thinks the Germans might be deficient, and that's a sense of the ridiculous – a grave flaw, of course, which sets them apart from visiting British journalists and others. Mr Waugh thinks that their language might be in some way to blame.

'It must be very difficult to keep a straight face,' he writes, 'if, when you go to visit a relative in hospital you have to ask for the Krankenhaus, or when you want the way out, if you have to ask for the Ausfahrt.'

I suppose it must. I'd never thought of it that way before. I suppose life must be just one long struggle to keep themselves from bursting out laughing at their own language.

It would explain a lot, of course. That's what the object of all that iron Prussian discipline must have been. That's what all those duelling scars were for – to camouflage the dirty grins on the face of people inquiring about the Ausfahrt.

Now that the old traditional codes of discipline have gone it's terrible. The approach to every Ausfahrt, Einfahrt, and Krankenhaus in the Federal Republic is jammed with people falling about and holding their sides. But that's nothing to what it's like *inside* the Krankenhaus. Inside it sounds like 14 different studio audiences trying to earn their free tickets simultaneously, as the patients describe their various comic-sounding symptoms to the staff. Here's a new admission scarcely able to speak for giggles as he tells the doctor he has a pain in his elbow.

'A Schmerz in your Ellenbogen?' repeats the doctor without any sign of amusement – he's heard the joke before, of course. 'Which Ellenbogen?'

'Both Ellenbogens,' replies the patient, trying to pull himself together. 'I also get agonising twinges which run up and down my leg from my . . . from my . . .'

But it's no good – he's off again. Unable to get the words out for laughing, he points silently from his thigh to his ankle.

'From your Schenkel to your Knöchel?' says the doctor, the corner of his mouth twitching very slightly in spite of himself. The patient nods helplessly.

'And sometimes,' he gasps, 'and sometimes . . . all the way down my . . .'

He closes his eyes and vibrates silently, shaking his head from time to time to indicate that speech is beyond him.

'Come on,' says the doctor, frankly grinning himself now. 'Get it out.'

'All the way down my . . . my . . . my Wirbel . . .'

'You'll start me off if you're not careful. Your what?'

'My Wirbelsäu-häu-häu-häu-häu-häu-häu . . .'

'Your Wirbelsäule? Your backbone?'

The patient nods, his eyes covered with his hand, his shoulders shaking rhythmically. The doctor bites his lip hard to stop himself giving way.

'Any other symptoms?' he demands gruffly.

'Yes,' croaks the patient weakly, 'Verstopfung!'

At this the doctor can hold out no longer. A great snort of laughter forces its way past his clenched jaw muscles, and he puts his head back and laughs until he cries.

'Verstopft, are you?' he manages at last. 'Constipated?'

'Verstopft up solid!'

Eventually they both simmer down a bit, and sigh, and wipe their eyes, smiling anywhere but at each other.

'You know what your trouble is?' says the doctor. 'You've got Kniescheibenentzündung. Housemaid's knee.'

'Don't!' pleads the patient, 'You'll start me off again!'

'And a rather bad dose of . . .'

'No, honestly, I've got a pain as it is . . .'

'No, listen, a rather bad dose of Windpo-ho-ho-ho-ho-ho . . . !'

'Stop! Sto-ho-ho-ho-ho-ho . . . !'

'Wind . . . Wind-hi-hi-hi-hi-hi . . . !'

'Oh . . . ! I swear I'm dying . . . !'

'Windpocken! Chickenpox!'

'No, honestly, shut up . . . !'

'*And* . . .'

'I'm not listening!'

'. . . You've sprained your – no, listen – your nostril, your Nasenflügel . . . !'

Well, the poor devil's in stitches already, of course. By the time he's had a splint applied to his Nasenflügel and been wheeled out towards the Ausfahrt, he's probably just about what German doctors call *blühendekopfabgelacht* – laughed his blooming head off. That's going to take a stitch or two to fix; it's yet another case of someone coming out of the Krankenhaus a whole lot kranker than he went in.

Gott in Himmel! It makes you glad to be English.

(1966)

Ivan Kudovbin

It's a weirdly fascinating business watching sober and fair-minded human beings trying to work out a formula for the circumstances in which abortion should be permitted. All possible reasons and permutations of reasons are canvassed and debated; excepting only the reason that the woman concerned wants an abortion, which no one mentions as having any relevance to the question at all.

Of course, this way of thinking is very congenial to a bureaucracy-loving socialist like me, who believes that people shouldn't be allowed any freedom to choose for themselves, but should have all their decisions made for them by faceless officials and so-called experts who think they know what's best for everyone. But I'm rather surprised that the tireless defenders of personal liberty whom we usually find ourselves up against in our insidious erosion of citizen rights haven't been exposing controls and snoopers in this sector with quite their usual vigour.

No, I was being gently ironical. I'm aware that those who deny that a pregnant woman has any personal right to choose whether she wants to give birth do so because they are trying to protect the right of the unborn to be born. And there are two arguments often advanced in this direction which I must admit I find rather compelling.

The first is that few people (if any), once having got themselves born and in a position to say, would prefer not to have been born, however reluctant or unsuitable their mother, or however exhausted and inadequate she subsequently became. The second (and logically similar) argument is that if abortion had been freely available in the past, the world might have been deprived of individuals like Leonardo da Vinci and William the Conqueror (who were illegitimate), and Bach (the eighth of eight children).

These arguments are good ones. The only trouble with them is that they're *too* good. Take the case of that astonishing sixteenth-century figure Ivan Kudovbin. He invented a primitive form of gas-mantle; he wrote 123 flute sonatas, before the sonata form had been invented; he experimented with cheap money and deficit budgeting; he raised a citizen army which drove the Galicians right out of Galicia into Silesia, and the Silesians right out of Silesia into Galicia. He was undoubtedly a genius. But, as we know from studying the history of the period, he was one of the unlucky ones who didn't get born. He Kudovbin, but he wasn't. If he *had* been born he would have preferred to have been born, I'm pretty sure. His loss is a tragedy both to himself and to mankind.

Perhaps Kudovbin was aborted or miscarried – I'm not sure. But I think the trouble was quite probably that he never got conceived. I don't know what went wrong exactly. Perhaps he was the twelfth child in the family, and his parents stopped at eleven. Perhaps his mother was a nun, under vows of chastity. Perhaps his father was away on a business trip the night he should have been commenced. But what seems fairly certain mathematically is that the tragedy of his non-birth could have been averted if everyone had really taken the matter seriously.

Think of it. If the available reproductive plant had been fully utilised from the beginning of time, and every woman had been kept bearing a child a year from puberty to menopause, billions upon billions more people would have been born. Nearly all of them, once born, would have preferred to have been born. And among them, presumably, would have been the usual proportion of geniuses. Kudovbin after Kudovbin – composers who wrote greater polyphonic music than Bach; Elizabethan dramatists more universal than Shakespeare; Elizabethan monarchs more Elizabethan than Elizabeth.

The steamboat would have been invented in time to take people to the Crusades; the United Nations in time to reach a negotiated settlement instead. Frozen fish-fingers would have come in about the beginning of the Renaissance.

Just think for a start how many innocent babes – potential great men among them – have been kept out of this world because of legal or moral sanctions against fornication, adultery, rape, and intercourse below the age of consent! Sentimentalists have opposed these creative and life-enhancing activities on various short-sighted grounds, such as the well-being of the woman concerned, and the desirability of stable family and social life. Have they ever stopped to consider the well-being of poor little Vsevolod and Tatiana Kudovbin, who as a result of their interference never even started being, well or ill?

But then, people never stop to think about the rights of the unborn. So-called reformers struggled for years to get slavery abolished, using a variety of spurious moral arguments, but really on the shallow hedonistic grounds that the slaves themselves didn't much care for it. Didn't they, indeed! Nobody stopped to consider that without slavery there would in years to come be no Buddy Bolden, no Jelly Roll Morton, no Blind Lemon Jefferson; hence no syncopated popular music of any sort; hence no Beatles and no Cilla Black. So much for Cilla Black, for all Wilberforce cared.

The simple truth is that it's an ill wind that blows nobody any silver linings. So carry on persecuting people; they may be Dostoyevsky. And don't hesitate to martyr any likely-looking candidate; remember, he may not get canonised otherwise.

(1966)

A letter from the publisher

Michael Frankenstein

Every week in this column we tell you the wonderful story of how one section of SPACE MAGAZINE was born. Today we are telling a nativity story so holy, so pregnant with awe, that no man has dared to tell it before – the story of the birth of this column, the Publisher's Letter, itself.

Here at SPACE-DEATH INTERNATIONAL we venerate the Publetter as the inmost shrine of SPACE journalism, the revealed word of the SPACE world-mind. No ordinary column this, but a steely skein of newsprose which is the result of a vast co-ordinated effort by all the manpower at our command. To make the column you are now reading, 1,200 SPACE staffers around the globe filed a word each – and each word was one they had already digested from all the millions of words which were used during the week in the capitals they cover.

An operation like this entails risks, dangers. On his way to file the word 'which,' *Miguel Freños,* 42, covering the Corunna, Spain, beat, fell into a hole in the road ordered by Corunna's genial public works boss Juan Pepito, 54, and broke his rugged, much-tanned neck.

It also entails long-range planning. Off to Kano, Nigeria, flew Communications Editor *Milo Frangle* to organise the complex task of getting word from remote up-country stringer *Nmikel Mfrayn.* Beaten out over the first stage on jungle drums, the message was taken by camel caravan to Kallamiti, then by age-old traditional post-chaise drawn by highly prized, aphrodisiac-horned rhinoceroses to Katastrofee. Here a specially chartered jet air-liner waited at runway's end with engines blasting. But fog kiboshed a take-off, and at the last moment the whole mammoth organisation was altered to switch to Plan Two – a picture postcard, on the flip side of which resourceful family man Mfrayn had written the sought-for word – 'and.'

Back at SPACE-DEATH headquarters, Non-Executive Editor *Martin Faine* spread the collected words over a football-pitch-sized floor area, while Advisory Editor *Max Phrane* indexed and cross-indexed them. But Editorial Editor *Magnus Frenner* was still not satisfied. After an all-night conference with the heads of editorial departments, he ordered a search of the dictionaries. Snapped thrice-fired Frenner, 35: 'We've got good words, but there may be better.'

Seventy researchers flipped 15,000 pages of ten diction-aries in 25 hours. So heavy was the yield of words from this operation that snowploughs had to be called in to bulldoze a way out of ten-foot word-drifts for word-weary staffers. Only then could Co-ordinating Editor *Morag Sprain* and his team begin the awesome task of sifting out the 700 most telling terms – the weekly winnowing known to hardened SPACE word-birds as 'the Big Weed.'

Over in the laboratories Analytical Director *Micah F. Ryan* submitted each of the elite 700 to elaborate tests of spelling and syntax, while behind the scenes SPACE's own corps of undercover men checked the background of even the humblest preposition for Red influence. Woman's Editor *Mabel Brain* – wife of Pulitzer Prizewinning Dogs Editor *Mumbo Brain* – was summoned from her bed by special messenger at 2 a.m. to come and add the woman's angle, followed shortly by Manipulating Editor *Morry Fryable,* who gave the words the usual slant.

At 6 a.m. world-famous writer *Misha Fraenev* was rushed to the office with siren-wailing squad-car escort to advise on arrangement of words. Said Fraenev – now through his sixth word-order assignment: 'Ask some folk "How so successful?" Reply I – "Write I like I speak in backward-running, adjective-rich mother tongue Russian."'

Four Punctuating Editors went without breakfast to get this edition of SPACE out on the streets in time for our mammoth staff of Junior Sales Editors to begin their weekly stint – trying to find anyone not on SPACE staff left in the world to be enrolled as Paying Reading Editors. Even so they'd never have done it, if some compositor hadn't had the sense to dash this alternative piece off and set it up the night before.

(1962)

Listener sport

Why people watch sport baffles me. But why they listen in their millions to a wireless commentator watching it on their behalf numbs even my faculty of bafflement. I wonder if it's just sport they are eager to experience vicariously, or whether they would find a new pleasure in, say, discussion programmes presented this way?

. . . And here in the studio in Maida Vale we're just waiting for the team to emerge from the Hospitality Room for the 143rd session of Top Topic. It was rather cold in the studio earlier on, but it's warming up now, and the patches of damp you could see around the walls in the early afternoon have almost dried out.

And now here comes the team, led by their chairman, O. J. Sprout, the well-known literary critic and man of letters, followed by Sir Harold Sidewinder, the grand old man of so many walks of life, Lady Frigate, woman of opinion, and Ken Nocker, the teenage satirist.

Now, while they take their places round the table, let's look at the form. Sir Harold Sidewinder, of course, has appeared in this programme 18 times before, though only twice in this studio, and on those two occasions he seemed slightly worried by the tricky north-east draught for which this studio is notorious . . . And now I think O. J. Sprout is about to deliver the first topic. No, there's still some delay about positioning the team. As I was saying, Sir Harold's analysis over the 18 programmes was 147,000 words for 31 topics raised, which . . .

Oh, the first topic's away, and it's a beauty! Sprout raised it very easily and naturally, almost as if he was lobbing a topic of conversation on to his own breakfast-table. And he's nodded to Lady Frigate. Lady Frigate moves in smoothly to pick it up – you can see from her technique that she is an old What's My Salary? player. On the top of her form this season, too. With a quick flutter of the eyelashes she rephrases the topic so that yes – so that its meaning is reversed, and swiftly dismisses it. Away goes the first topic of the programme, with all the sting taken out of it, into Sir Harold Sidewinder's lap.

Sir Harold swings at it easily, as if he had all the time in the world. What a grand old exponent of the game he is! There are few men half his age who could put yet another twist on an already twisted meaning with that aplomb. What's he up to? Is he . . . ? Yes, he is – he's explaining very steadily and easily that the topic as he has now formulated it reminds him of something Lord Curzon told him in 1910.

Now while Sir Harold is telling his story – with the score standing at one down and one to play on the first topic of the 143rd session of Top Topic – I'll just say a word about Ken Nocker, whose first appearance in Top Topic this is. He's a forceful young player who has attracted a great deal of attention by his immensely aggressive, hard-hitting approach. It's the sort of play that the crowd finds very attractive, and . . .

Hello, what's this? Ken has cut in on Sir Harold's graceful stone-walling with a very sharp tackle. Sprout intervenes. But now it's Nocker again, going like the wind.

Nocker to Sidewinder. Sidewinder to Nocker. Sprout tries to tackle Nocker, but Frigate cuts in ... And it's Frigate to Nocker, Nocker to Sidewinder, Sidewinder to Sprout, Nocker again, still Nocker ...

Now there's a general free-for-all, with the topic in the middle somewhere, I think, and everyone going like mad. I can't quite ... I think it's Frigate ... no, it's Sidewinder ... no, I'm wrong, it's Nocker, and this is sensational, it's unbelievable ... Sidewinder's leaning back looking very tired – I don't think he can last much longer – and it's Nocker, Nocker all the way. No! Yes! No! Yes, it is. It's Nocker's point, and the applause-meter shows that at the end of the first topic in the 143rd Top Topic the score is 1–0, with the topic 'Is the crime wave due to all this psychology we hear so much about?' voted as likely to get into this week's top twenty topics in the news.

And now, while we're waiting for the next topic to be raised, I'll just give you a words-per-topic analysis of the last 50 programmes ...

(1961)

The literature of coexistentialism

The last time I was in Moscow an article I wrote for the *Guardian* describing my impressions of that city called forth half a column of personal abuse in *Izvestia*, in which I was described as 'a stinking rocket of the Cold War'. So I was delighted to find this week a model of the sort of article I should have written – a piece by Mr Alexei Adzhubei, the editor-in-chief of *Izvestia*, on his impressions of London.

The article was written at the request of the *Sunday Express*, after Mr Adzhubei had visited Britain for the unofficial talks at Wiston House (and incidentally offered to take over the editorial chair of the *Daily Mail* and double the paper's readership in two months). When the *Sunday Express* saw the finished product, however, they turned it down, on the grounds that it did not 'quite measure up to the standard of interest and entertainment that we aim to provide'.

It was rescued from the waste-paper basket by the *Sunday Pictorial*, who published it together with a reproach for the 'puny and frivolous' attitude of the *Sunday Express* towards the problem of understanding the Russians.

Just how considerable this problem is you can discover for yourself by reading Mr Adzhubei's article. I will make my little contribution to solving it by admitting that by Adzhubei standards my piece on Moscow was simply not up to scratch. Humbly confessing my past errors, I present it again, entirely rewritten in the peaceful coexistence style. *Izvestia* may reprint it if they want to, but if it doesn't quite measure up to their standard of interest and entertainment I'll submit it for the 'What I did in my holidays' competition in *Chicks' Own*.

MOSCOW

Moscow is an interesting city. I am happy to have the opportunity of describing my impressions of it. Perhaps this is because it is such an interesting city. Or perhaps there is some other explanation.

I will be as brief as possible. I must say first that we in England have already heard of your city. It is, in my opinion, a big city. There are many buildings and streets in it. I do not want to trespass on your countrymen's most intimate national feelings, but as I walked round the streets I could not help thinking, 'This is a big city, and it is an interesting one.'

In a short article like this there is not enough space to list all the sights I saw. But I must mention the Kremlin, an old building which I find most interesting. I also saw Red Square and the Bolshoi Theatre. I don't have to tell you that, by and large, and on whole, they are impressive and interesting. There were also many other sights of historical interest I saw in Moscow. I have no space to mention them all, but as I looked at them I was most strongly impressed by how interesting they were. Need I add that some of them were also big?

While I was in Moscow I heard Russian spoken. It was spoken by Russians, quite fluently. To all you Russians, whether in Moscow, Leningrad, Kiev, or Odessa, I bring greetings from the people of London, Manchester, Birmingham, and Bury St Edmunds. I talked to some of you about subjects too numerous to mention here. We did not attempt to listen to one another. Everyone must decide for himself how to live, without listening to anyone else.

Unless the editor has any objection, I should like to give some more of my impressions of Moscow, although space is too limited to mention more than a few. I saw cars and buses in the streets. I saw trains going along by the ingenious use of wheels running on rails. All this is the Moscow one does not read about in guide books. I find it very interesting.

Very soon now there won't be any more space left before the end of the article. I should like to use what there is to say that even if there were more space left, which there is not, I rather doubt if I could have given a better impression of your big and interesting town. To sum up, I saw the Kremlin, Red Square, the Bolshoi Theatre, and many other historical monuments which lack of space prevents me mentioning by name. On this note I must conclude my article, which I am writing on paper, sitting at a table.

(1961)

Lives and likenesses

Mr Ken Russell seems to have hit upon a simple but important new biographical principle in his films for 'Monitor' on BBC Television. According to sympathetic critics, he makes each film in the style of the artist it is about.

Thus, according to Peter Black, 'his Elgar was straightforward and sentimentalised, his Debussy misty and complex.' His Douanier Rousseau, similarly, was naïve and primitive. In fact it was considerably *more* naïve and primitive than Rousseau. It takes a real hardened professional to get as naïve and primitive as that. These amateur innocents like Rousseau never knew the tricks of the trade.

Writers have obviously been missing an opportunity. In fact, it's rather presumptuous, when you come to think about it, for old Strachey to have written 'Queen Victoria' in his own style and not Queen Victoria's. And why didn't Mr Alan Bullock couch his study of Hitler rather more in the familiar Nuremberg vein? A touch of egomania here?

Now Mr Russell has shown the way, no doubt the idea will be taken up. Here are trailers for one or two biographies I hope to be seeing in the bookshops soon.

Firstly I should like to say this – and I make no apology for mentioning it: Harold Wilson was born – and I choose that word advisedly – on the eleventh of March 1916. Not on the tenth, or the twelfth, as some people would like you to believe – and here I intend no disrespect to the many men and women up and down the country who I know *were* born on the tenth or the twelfth, and who have given loyal and unstinting service to the community, and whose special needs – I say this to them now – have not been forgotten.

But – and it's a big but – if this book is to make any real headway, if we're really going to bring it up to date, we simply cannot afford – and this cannot be said too often –

we simply cannot afford to sit back and rest content with our progress so far. Because make no mistake – and there's none of us who doesn't make mistakes at times – if we're forced to go on breaking off like this for modifications, concessions, and reassuring asides, we shan't reach Mr Wilson's first birthday until about Chapter 23.

A (indef. art.) man who might with some justice be called the
AARDVARK (noun) of English letters, whose
AARONIC (adj.) pronouncements upon anything from the
AASVOGEL (noun) to the
ABACA (noun) often took his companions
ABACK (adv.), and frequently caused them to
ABANDON (verb) themselves to mirth, Dr Johnson was never known to let anyone
ABASE (verb) or
ABASH (verb) him, and would wallow agreeably
ABASK (adv.) in what others might have found to be a veritable conversational
ABATTOIR (noun).

Mozart:
Chapter No. 21 *in D Minor*

In 1779 Mozart returned to Salzburg. In the year 1779 Mozart returned to Salzburg. Back to his native city in the year after 1778 Wolfgang Amadeus Mozart came.

And was made court organist, was appointed organist at the court, the organ-player at the court he was created. Having come back to Salzburg in 1779 he became court organist, the court organist is what he became after his return to Salzburg in 1779.

He was oppressed with debts. He owed money. Goods and services had been credited to him for which he had not yet paid. He was oppressed with debt, debts weighed him down. Money was outstanding. He owed. Money was what he owed.

In 1779 Mozart returned to Salzburg. Back to his home town came he. And was appointed court organist.

To Salzburg, the well-known town in Austria. That was where, in 1779, Mozart returned.

*

A Life of T. S. Eliot:
Acknowledgements

> How can I begin to thank
> Professor Pomattox, or Doctor Frack,
> The Misses Fischbein, or Monsignor Blum?
> Words lose their meaning, and grow slack.
>
> Some typed upon Remingtons in obscure rooms.
> Some made suggestions.
> Some read the proofs. Some wept. One smiled:
> 'The world is full of questions.'
>
> Mrs Crupper came and went
> With tiny jars of liniment.
>
> The finished pages flutter to the floor.
> La lune éternue et s'endort.
> All this, and so much more,
> And so much more.

(1965)

Lloyd

A HISTORICAL TRAGI-BUDGET, OR BUDGI-TRAGEDY, IN FIVE ACTS

(commissioned for the Hoylake Festival, 1994)

Act Three, Scene Four – A Chamber in the Treasury
(Sennets and tuckets. Enter the Chancellor of the Ex-chequer, the Lord Privy Purposes, and the Lord Footstool, followed by Under-Secretaries, Parliamentary Private Sec-retaries, Joint Permanent Secretaries, Under-Secretaries' Private Secretaries, Joint Permanent Secretaries' Under-Secretaries, Fools, and Knaves.)
Chancellor:

> I saw it in his eyes: he turn'd his gaze
> Upon me, wondrous soft, avuncular,
> Beseech'd me with those pouched eyes of his
> As might a man urge on his faithful hound
> To some high eager feat of houndly valour,
> Yea, with an uncle's smile he bade me forth
> To save beloved England's tottering cause
> With one bold coup-de-main of fiscal arms!

Under-Secretaries, etc.:

> Hurrah!
> *(Trumpets, cannons, etc.)*

Lord Footstool:

> 'Tis well said, Chancellor, for Fortune frowns:
> And faceless men do undermine the boroughs,
> Unsettling vacant loons we once call'd ours.

Lord Privy Purposes:

> You mean to take a budget to our woes –
> To beat from metal tempered by the times
> And edg'd upon Necessity's hard stone
> A budget e'en to budget them to death?

Chancellor:

> I do. And with such high intent this day
> Are we three met to forge the cutting steel.

Lord Privy Purposes:

> Acquaint us with your stratagems.

Chancellor:

> Then hark:
> First will I ease the groaning discontent

> Which freights unjustly those our countrymen
> Whose lawful aspirations soar no higher
> Than purchasing a humble toasting-fork.
> Eleven per cent off toasting-forks, I say!

Lord Footstool:

> This is a wise and bounteous act: the poor
> Will count your name as blessed this day forth.

Chancellor:

> Then will I buy the love of every man
> Who holds the common mousetrap dear: the tax
> On mousetraps swoops from nine to eight per
>   cent!

Lord Footstool:

> O admirable Chancellor!

Chancellor:

>   But now,
> Our forces swoln by loyal mousestrap-men,
> And grateful liegemen of the toasting-fork,
> We fall like falcons on those jack-a-dandies
> Whose foul-brained appetite doth feed on hats,
> And scourge them with an added four per cent.

Lord Privy Purposes:

> 'Tis well. A hatted man is gallows-bait.

Chancellor:

> And yet my devious stratagem goes further –
> Makes pepper-mills more dear, salt-cellars
>   cheap,
> Brings Jew's harps down, sends plated shoe-
>   trees up,
> Puts two per cent on fire-dogs, cheapens pins,
> Tacks tax on tacks, attacks the tax on ticking.

Lord Privy Purposes:

> Hurt barrel-organs, Chancellor, I pray –
> Their monkeys satirise us publicly.

Chancellor:

> Why, so I will. Yet list, we do proceed,

> These hair's-weight-balanced dispositions
>   made,
> These plots complotted, nimble gin-traps
>   sprung,
> At last to strike the boldest blow of all!
> And gentlemen not in the Treasury
> Will count themselves accurst they were not here
> To ride forth on St Crispin Crispian
> And cry: Fifteen per cent on lollipops!

Under Secretaries, etc.:

> Hurrah!
>
> *(Trumpets, cannonades. The Chancellor of the
> Exchequer draws his red dispatch-box from its
> scabbard, and holding it aloft gallops off in the
> direction of Agincourt.)*

Lord Privy Purposes:

> Such hair-springs drive the clock of destiny:
> Small wonder it still stands at ten to three.

(1962)

The long and the short of it

British Telecom, out of the goodness of their hearts, are running a major advertising campaign to persuade men to be more communicative. We don't talk for long enough on the phone; this is our problem, apparently. We compare unfavourably, in BT's view, with women, who are quite likely to sit down for chats with each other lasting half an hour at a time. BT approve of these 'simple joys'. They are pained by men's propensity to be 'short, sharp and to the point'.

A characteristic man's telephone conversation, they say, runs like this: 'Meet you down the pub, all right? See you there.' They find this 'abrupt'. I find it distinctly garrulous. 'Meet you there . . . see you there' – the poor fellow's saying everything twice. He also appears to be arranging to exchange a lot more conversation. Curious that this doesn't elicit BT's approval. Perhaps its beneficial spiritual qualities will be more appreciated by the brewers.

I can't imagine my friend W rambling on like this. BT would be even more deeply pained by *his* telephone calls – they're almost subliminally short. This has never been a problem between us, so far as I know. Quite the contrary. We have been good friends for thirty-seven years now and in all that time we've never had a cross word. There wasn't a chance. The receivers were back on their rests before either of us had had an instant to check whether we had any grievances outstanding.

The last call I had from him was entirely characteristic. He announced his name and asked me for a telephone number he needed. I told him the number. He said thank you, and put the phone down.

I have run through it again from memory, stopwatch in hand, and it lasted for approximately thirteen seconds. Thirteen seconds of pure communication – it seems to me to come close to the ideal. He could have left out telling me who he was, now I come to think about it, since I know that, and the 'thank you' was a rather time-consuming concession to convention. I suppose we could have got it down to about seven seconds, with a little more ruthlessness. But in an imperfect world thirteen seconds is not bad.

I can claim little of the credit for this exemplary brevity. The determining factor is W's iron self-discipline. Note, in the conversation recorded above, that he did not begin, as a less self-controlled person might have done, by asking if I was well. Nor did he finish up by doing it. A lot of people manage to stay off the subject until the last moment of a call, when their nerve suddenly goes. 'Oh, and how are you, by the way?' they say, with a concern so belated as to be insulting.

What you can't see, in the transcript above, is that W left no pause, either, between his courteous 'thank you' and his putting the phone down, for me to weaken, as I might well have done otherwise, not having his character and determination, and enquire after *his* health. 'Are you well?' I should have said, if there had been a finger's width of opportunity to say it in, in spite of not having the faintest desire for a medical bulletin. Why should I suddenly want to know how he was? He's been well for thirty-seven years now – and even if by some remote chance he'd suddenly stopped being well he wouldn't have dreamt of telling me.

'*Very* well,' he would have had to reply – simultaneously, for all I should have known at my end of the phone, trying to apply a tourniquet to a severed artery. Only four or five more seconds lost, it's true – but once we'd got this far politeness would have required him to add at least two more syllables. 'And you?' he would have had to enquire. 'Fine,' I should have been obliged to inform him, for all he knew with only my mouth still functioning among the bandages.

One more word from him – 'Good' – and we could have got back to what was left of our lives. But by this stage it would have been difficult for him to put the receiver down without an infinitesimal pause to see if I was proposing to say anything else. I *shouldn't* have been proposing to utter another word, of course. But now that this small hole had opened up in the fabric of the universe I should have felt compelled to fill it. I should have found myself telling him that it was very nice to hear from him. Before either of us knew what was happening I should have been enquiring after his wife and children, and various mutual friends. I should have forgotten the names of some of the people I was enquiring after, and should have had to filibuster in the hope of recalling them, or at any rate of making up for my apparent lack of concern in forgetting their names by the sheer amount of time I devoted to discussing them.

Somewhere around this point I should have remembered that we hadn't seen each other for some time. He would have felt obliged to suggest that we must bring this state of affairs to an end. We might even have got out our diaries, and negotiated vaguely back and forth over various more or less unsuitable dates in an indeterminate number of the weeks to come.

By now it would be dimly coming back to me that there was actually something of importance that I'd been meaning to tell him. So then I should have had to keep the conversation going until I'd remembered what it was.

It's even within the bounds of possibility that I should have asked him what the weather was like at his end. Admittedly he was not phoning from another country, when mutual enquiries about the weather are required by international law. But he *was* on the other side of London. It's not particularly surprising if the weather's different in Australia, but it would be worthy of note if some completely different weather system had moved in on another Inner London borough.

Now that the conversation had acquired this much momentum, bringing it to an end would have been as difficult as halting a fully-laden container vessel. Eventually, however, driven by growing hunger if nothing else, one or the other of us would have had to make preliminary moves towards coaxing the great craft into its moorings. 'Well,' my friend might have said, 'I must get back to work.' And in the slight regretful pause that would naturally have followed this I should have heard myself asking: 'What are you working on at the moment?'

He would have told me. Very succinctly, of course, given his character – so succinctly that I should have had to pose a number of polite supplementaries.

Whereupon he would have had to ask me what *I* was

working on. I should have given him a brief outline. As I did so I should have found myself warming to my theme. I should have begun to recall various small professional triumphs which had been insufficiently appreciated elsewhere, various major professional injustices to which I had been subjected, and for which I had not yet had sufficient sympathy.

I should have told him how difficult my life seemed to have become these days – how little time there was to get anything done. He would have told me how little time he had. By now everyone but us would have left their workplaces and gone away to the country for the weekend, so it would have been too late for him to make the telephone call he had originally wanted the number for.

By now in any case, night would have fallen. In the darkness, the scrap of paper on which he had noted down the number would have got brushed off his desk, and have disappeared behind some piece of furniture. He would not have instituted any search for it, because by this time he would have forgotten that he had ever wanted it.

As the dawn came up we should have told each other how nice it had been talking to each other. We should have asked each other to give our respective love to wives, children, aunts, neighbours. Just after he had finally managed to put the phone down I should have remembered what it was I had been meaning to tell him.

Crucial pieces of work now having been ruined on both sides, our respective careers would have languished, and we should both have fallen upon hard times. Since neither of us would have known about the other's plight, each of us would have been too proud to reveal his own, so we should never have rung each other again. Our thirty-seven years of friendship would have come to an end.

Thinking gratefully about how my friend's firmness of character had saved us from all this, I rang one of my daughters on some small point of information, and while I was about it I asked her for all her news, and she told me, and she asked me for mine, and I told her. In fact we gossiped away for the best part of an hour. British Telecom thought it was wonderful.

So did I, curiously enough.

(1994)

The Magic Mobile

When the curtain rises on Act Two of my opera *The Magic Mobile* the scene is set in the Check-In Hall of a major international Airport.

S~1_mn Muzak is heard, and Sarastro, the Airport Manager, enters. He informs the assembled Staff that a Traveller is approaching the doors of the Airport, seeking admission to their Mysteries. The Traveller, he tells them, wishes to throw off everything that shackles him to the Earth below, and ascend towards the Light and Purity of Heaven.

The Airport Staff remind the Manager that in a major international Airport this Goal can be reached only through diligence and suffering, and they question whether the Traveller will be able to endure the process. The Manager tells them to perform their sacred office, and to test the Traveller's resolve by a series of rituals and tests, so that he progresses towards his symbolic Enlightenment only by gradual stages.

The glass doors now slide back, and the Traveller, Papageno, enters. He is carrying a Mobile Phone, and as he hurries distractedly towards the Ticket Desk, which is the first stage of his Ordeal, he is playing a cheerful little tune upon its musical buttons. He is ringing his partner, Papagena, and explaining to her in a dramatically charged aria ('You're not going to believe this, but') that in Act One he had to leave home in too much of a hurry to use public transport, as he had planned, and that he has been forced to take the car instead, which he knows she is shortly going to be needing herself, for some spiritual odyssey of her own.

But before Papagena in reply has had time to develop her feelings about this musically, Papageno is undergoing his first ritual purification at the hands of the Ticket Staff. In a short cavatina ('The flight is heavily') the Sales Person makes a preliminary assessment of the Traveller's seriousness of purpose by declaring that there are now only Euro-Business seats available, at a substantial premium. After some earthily comic hesitation, Papageno expresses resignation to his fate, and is quietly relieved of a substantial proportion of his worldly wealth.

He is rewarded with a Passenger Ticket entitling him to proceed to the second stage of his Initiation at the Check-In Desk. The jaunty little theme for mobile phone is heard several times more, but before he can get through to Papagena and clarify their evidently now troubled relationship he has to present the Ticket, find his Passport, and answer a solemn ritual Interrogation about the Contents of his Suitcase. His answers proving satisfactory, the symbolically burdensome suitcase, and the various pieces of Electrical Apparatus he has confessed it contains, is spirited away, and his Passenger Ticket is returned, now accompanied by a Boarding Card marked with certain cabbalistic signs. Armed with Ticket, Passport, and Boarding Card, he proceeds to the Bank to acquire Currency suitable for the world he is hoping to reach. Again and again the Mobile Phone theme is heard, until he is at last able to explain with breathless haste to Papagena in the prestissimo 'Listen, listen, listen' that he is going to post the Parking Ticket to her, so that she can come down to the Airport at her leisure and collect the car.

His relations with Papagena seem to be still in a somewhat equivocal state as he runs back and forth trying to find where to buy an Envelope and a Stamp, and then hastens to the barrier of the Inner Sanctuary, beyond which only Postulants holding a Boarding Card are admitted. Papageno is indeed, as we know, holding the precious Boarding Card, but since he is also holding the Passenger Ticket, the Passport, the Foreign Currency, the Parking Ticket, the

Envelope and the Stamp he has the opportunity for further comic business, accompanied by the delightfully desperate 'I know I had it when' before he is allowed to proceed, and is consequently in a state of some confusion at his next Ordeal in Security Control, as the Body Scanner plays the ominous Body Scanner theme, and he is forced to empty his pockets of the Mobile Phone, his Pocket Calculator, his Keys, and his remaining Small Change.

It only remains for him to have his Passport checked once again in Passport Control before he is rewarded by admission to the manifold delights of the Departure Lounge. Here he is offered food and drink, and gratefully accepts a Takeaway Coffee and a Freshly Baked Croissant, since he missed breakfast, before he hastens to purchase a small phial of Duty-Free Perfume to enclose with the Parking Ticket in the hope of rescuing his threatened relationship with Papagena. Sarastro and the secretly watching Security Men almost give up hope for Papageno when he seems tempted by some of the other earthly goods on offer, and for a moment contemplates purchasing a duty-free 48-inch television with quadrophonic speakers, which they doubt can ever be got airborne. But he is saved by the disembodied voice of the Queen of Flight singing the famous coloratura aria 'This is the final call for passengers on'.

He now enters the most arduous stage of his Initiation – the long walk to Gate 73, checking as he goes that he still has the Passenger Ticket, the Passport, the Boarding Card, the Foreign Currency, the Parking Ticket, the Envelope, the Stamp, the Pocket Calculator, the Keys, the Small Change, the Takeaway Coffee, the Freshly Baked Croissant, and the Perfume. Many times he almost forgets where he is going. Many times he is tempted to settle for Gate 35 and Helsinki, or Gate 51 and Philadelphia. All that drives him on is the need to find somewhere to sit down for a moment and lighten his burden by putting the Passenger Ticket in the Envelope, and the Parking Ticket in the back of the

Passport, after which he will need only a Rubbish Bin where he can post the Envelope, and a Post Box where he can dump the greasy remains of the Croissant.

A trio of smiling sopranos greets him as he at last totters up to Gate 73. 'Boarding Card and Passport,' they brightly sing. As he spreads all his possessions out over the floor to locate them once again, they inform him that the nearest Post Box is in the Check-In Hall – part of a profane world that has long since closed behind him forever.

He stumbles on into the Final Departure Lounge. He has one last chance to phone Papagena and try to explain what has happened before the use of Mobile Phones is forbidden during the heavenward Ascent. His fingers form the familiar jaunty pattern on the buttons. But, in a musical master-stroke of heart-breaking poignancy, all we hear is silence. There are no buttons for him to play upon, because he has left the Mobile Phone lying on the table at Security Control.

Only now is he sufficiently chastened to enter the winding narrow corridor that leads to the ultimate Goal of his Ordeal. He bows his head abjectly to pass through the last low doorway – and when he raises it again he is in a new and better world, with heavenly Muzak playing, and the Cabin Crew welcoming him in the joyous finale, 'Thank you for choosing'. They hope he has a pleasant flight, they sing, as the triumphant clunking of Seat-Belts is heard and the curtain falls.

So now all our victorious hero has to face is Act Three, and Disenlightenment at the other end.

(1994)

The mails must go through

Dear Joyce,
    Just a line to say thank you for your letter. Lots of news

to tell you, but must rush, so excuse scrawl.

I hope you and Howard are keeping well, and that Nicholas and Simonetta are in 'rude health'. Dominic and Nicolette are both 'blooming'. They've got through the summer with no coughs or sneezes so far, though I suppose there's plenty of time yet, so we're 'keeping our fingers crossed!' John sends his love. Had a letter from Ida on Monday – she and Ralph are both well. She asks to be remembered to you, and says Simon and Nicola are both 'blooming.' Ralph sends his love.

Well, I must stop rambling on like this or I will go on all night. Must rush to catch the post.

All my love,

Eileen

Dear Eileen,

I expect you will almost faint with surprise to find your ever-loving sister-in-law replying already! Wonders will never cease. The trouble is you're such a virtuous correspondent you make a girl feel the still, small voice pricking away like mad! Wild horses couldn't drag me to take up pen and paper normally, but Duty calls!

Glad to hear Dominic and Nicolette are blossoming. Nicholas and Simonetta are disgustingly healthy, needless to say. Also had a letter from Ida (not usually the world's greatest correspondent, so you see the age of miracles is not past!), and she says Simon and Nicola are flourishing like the proverbial green bay tree. She and Ralph send you their love. Howard sends his love too of course.

Forgive the horrible scrawl. Lots more to tell, but must stop now or shall have to go over on to new page, and it's not worth it just for a line or two.

All my love,

Joyce

Dear Joyce,

Just a line to thank you for your letter. Been meaning to write ever since it arrived last Wednesday (first post), but I've been putting it off and putting it off, you know how it is. I feel very guilty for not 'doing my duty' more promptly, but I always was a poor correspondent. Somehow I never seem to have the time – I expect you find it much the same. How you manage to keep it up I simply do not know. I suppose some people are just 'born' letter-writers! Not me, worse luck, it's a terrible chore.

Dominic and Nicolette are very well – no coughs or sneezes so far, touch wood. Ralph and Ida were over with Simon and Nicola – all in the 'pink.' They send their love. How are Nicholas and Simonetta?

Well, I mustn't go on, I'm just indulging myself. I must rush, or you won't get this first post. Please excuse scrawl.

All my love,

Eileen

Dear Eileen,

Don't faint with surprise, but it really is a letter from me. Wonders will never cease. Give a girl the prize. Believe it or not, I feel the stern call of Duty sometimes! I'm quite the little model correspondent – I must be shamed into it by your sterling example! I feel sorry for you having to decipher yet another dollop of my famous horrible scrawl, but on your own head be it – don't say I didn't warn you!

First and foremost, I had a letter from Ida (yes, you did hear right!). Ralph sends his love, and apparently Simon and Nicola are both A1 at Lloyd's. I trust Dominic and Nicolette are likewise and ditto. Nicholas and Simonetta I am glad to inform you are their usual sweet (ha, ha!) selves. Howard sends his love.

Well, the bottom of the page is already raising its ugly

head, so I must restrain what Howard calls my boundless gift for gossip, and dash to catch the post.

All my love,

Joyce

PS. Must go over on to a new page to tell you – so funny. Had an extraordinary epistle from Our Mutual Mum-in-law – rambling on about everything under the sun from French history to politics. Yes, politics, *for heaven's sake, in a letter! I didn't read it all, of course, but the general gist of it seemed to be that she was well and sent her love.*

Dear Joyce,

Just a line 'in haste' to apologise for not writing before, so excuse the scrawl. Keep promising myself I'll sit down and write you a really good long letter one of these days, but never seem to get the chance. You're such a good letter-writer it makes me feel ashamed of my own poor efforts. I suppose it's the way you 'put' things. I always feel 'I wish I'd thought of that' – but then you've got the gift, haven't you? When I sit down to write it all flies out of my head. But one of these days I really will sit down and write a good long letter.

Well, sorry to have 'gone on' so long – I never 'know when to stop,' that's my trouble. Must rush to catch post, so I'm afraid I'll have to close.

All my love,

Eileen

PS. Knew there was something I meant to say – everyone is well and sends their love.

(1963)

Major minor

1 The press pack concerning the vision of Zebediah, the son of Ud.

2 Like unto rotten medlar fruits are the harlotries of Ashkelon, and the whoredoms of Moab cry unto heaven as the howling of wolves in the wilderness of Geshur. And the day shall come when the sons and daughters of Ashkelon are devoured by the cankerworm. In that day shall the fire of the Lord fall upon the husbandmen of Moab, and fry them like the potatoes of Shechem.

3 This urgent warning to the world is the message of the *Book of Zebediah*, the forthcoming major prophetic work from the publishers of the *Book of Obadiah* and the *Book of Habbakuk*. (Publication date: 6 June 635 BC. Price: 14.99 shekels.)

4 Controversial prophet Zebediah's raunchy study of lust and decadence in the sunbaked desert settlements of Judah and Gilead is certain to be the big headline-grabber of the season. Already a major religion is bidding for biblical rights.

5 Leading prophets who have seen the *Book of Zebediah* prior to publication predict that it could repeat the huge popular success of the *Book of Jonah*. Zebediah, says Hosea, will do for cankerworms what Jonah did for whales.

6 Often regarded by critics as a member of the so-called Minor Prophets group, Zebediah himself prefers not to be labelled. 'Woe unto the pigeonholers and them that cry minor,' he says, 'for their inkhorns shall run dry and their retainers shall be cut off.'

7 Although he respects the great classical prophets of the past such as Isaiah and Jeremiah, he believes the whole prophecy scene has changed. 'The six and sixty chapters of Isaiah, yea, and the two and fifty chapters of Jeremiah also, are as great oaks that darken the sun,' he says

thoughtfully. 'But this generation is a generation of grass-hoppers. Their attention flareth like dry grass in the fire, and dieth as quickly away. Under two and fifty chapters they sink as an over-laden she-ass, and six and sixty shall be drowned by the snoring of fools.'

8 The modern prophet, he believes, has to adapt to the audience's taste. 'Let him tarry not in his task. Let him jump nimbly from the striking of thunderbolts upon the mountains of Ziph to the opening of graves in Dothan, let him haste from the depredations of locusts in Ataroth to the roaring of lions in Aphek, as the bee passeth quickly from the lily to the asphodel, nor lingereth long upon any blossom.

9 'And he that crieth Oh, how are the prophets of this generation become short of breath, how they have become minor, let him beware, for the day shall surely come when the twain do meet, and then woe unto him that hath raised his voice against us, for strong drink shall be thrown in his face, and backs most markedly turned.'

10 Zebediah will be doing a seventeen-city author tour of the Holy Land, from Dan to Beersheba, featuring readings and author signings. Beth-shemesh shall hear his words, and woe shall it be unto Beth-shemesh in that day! (12 June). Beth-horon shall be read the full horrific details of what it's like to be devoured by cankerworms, even as a dead sheep is devoured among the thorn-bushes of Gezer, and the prophecy-lovers of Beth-horon shall be as sick as the dogs of Tishbe.

11 Zebediah will be at Prophetic Writing Week in Jezreel in July, taking part in a brains-trust with fellow-prophets Nabum and Micah on 'Whither Prophecy?'. At the Ashdod Festival in August he will give a seminar with Amos on Prophecy as a Career Option.

12 Like all prophets, Zebediah is often asked whether he prophesies regularly, or only when he feels inspired. 'The wise prophet,' he says sagely, 'sitteth down to prophesy

directly he hath broken his fast, nor shall he first answer letters from them that have heard his words, nor linger to read reports of new abominations. But when the sun standeth high in the heavens, and the signs and portents visit him less readily, then is it pleasant to go to the well, and drink a stoop or two with others that labour in the same vineyard.'

13 Haggai and Malachi are among the fellow-prophets he often sees. Sometimes, he says, they talk about the semiotics of eschatology. 'But more often,' he admits laughingly, 'we raise our voices against the exactions of agents, and the faint-heartedness of publishers.'

14 In fact Zebediah has something of a reputation as a hell-raiser, which some people find surprising. 'Yet if the prophets go not among winebibbers and harlots,' he demands reasonably, 'how shall the transgressions of these be known?

15 'And he that passeth the night in this manner, when he awaketh, the light of the sun shall be heavy upon his eyelids. And there shall be a rolling of great rocks inside his head, and his mouth shall be as the dust of the wilderness. Then shall he know more fully the fruits of wickedness, and cry out more perspicaciously for repentance.'

16 He admits, like most prophets, to occasional depression and bad patches. 'There cometh haply a morning when the prophet riseth up, and his head is as clear as the fishpools in Heshbon,' he says wryly. 'And, lo, the evil things he saw have receded away like melting snow, the harlotries of the people seem not so much harlotries as formerly; and their whoredoms understandable. Then murmureth the prophet unto himself. It may yet come to pass that the cankerworm will cease from his devourings, and the anger of the Lord will be turned aside. It may hap that we are entering upon a time of prosperity and sustained growth without concomitant inflation.'

17 In fact the horrifying consequences of this scenario for the whole future of prophetic writing are the subject of the sequel he is working on now, *2 Zebediah*, extracts from which be will be performing from September onwards as work in progress. In leading wildernesses everywhere.

(1995)

Making a name for yourself

Writing a novel, as any novelist will tell you, is hard. Writing a short story, as any short story writer will be eager to add, is harder still. The shorter the form the harder it gets. Poems are hell. Haiku are hell concentrated into seventeen syllables.

Until finally you get down to the shortest literary form of all, which is the title of whatever it is you're writing. Long-distance novelists who can happily write several thousand words a day for months on end then go into creative agonies when the time comes to compose the two or three words that will go on the spine. Battle-hardened samurai of the haiku take instruction from Zen masters before they attempt to extract an odd syllable out of their hard-won seventeen to go in the index.

This year, for various reasons, four different works of mine have reached the point where they need titles, and I've reached the point where I need hospitalisation. It's not that I can't write titles. I've written far more titles than anything else in my life. For one of these four projects I have 107 titles. For another – 74. For the third – 134. 134 titles! For one short book! 134 pretty good titles, though I say so myself. The trouble is you don't want 134 pretty good titles. You want one perfect title.

No titles at all so far for the fourth project, but this is

because I haven't written the thing yet. Though after the agonies I've had with the other three I'm starting to wonder if I shouldn't write the title of this one first, then dash down a few thousand words to fit it.

The curious thing is that you usually do have a title first. You have the working title, that you put on the front of the file when you begin, just so that you know which file's which. The working title, as its name suggests, works. That's to say, it actually succeeds in telling you which file's which, and it does it without being pretentious, or facetious, or unintentionally obscene. But the publisher, or the producer, or whoever it is, doesn't like it. Your agent doesn't like it – your partner doesn't like it. No one likes it. This may be because they don't know about it – you haven't told them. You know you can't use the working title. Life has to be harder than that.

One of the troubles with a list of 134 titles is that it offers odds of at least 133 to 1 against getting it right. I've got it wrong many times in the past. There's only one novel of mine that anyone ever remembers – and for all practical purposes it's called *The One About Fleet Street*, because even the people who remember the book can't remember the title I gave it. I wrote another book called *Constructions*. I think I realised even before publication that I'd picked a dud here, when my own agent referred to it in the course of the same conversation once as *Conceptions* and once as *Contractions*.

I suppose it must be even worse being ennobled, and having to find a title to give yourself. *You're* not going to go out of print and be pulped. You're going to be stuck with being Lord Conceptions, or Baroness Contractions, for the rest of your life. The thought of the torments that new peers must go through makes me look at the House of Lords with a fresh respect.

As with a book, of course, you start with a perfectly good little working title. When the Prime Minister's office writes with the good news you're G. E. Bodd, of The Moorings, Oakdene Avenue, Carshalton Beeches. You could perfectly well become Lord Bodd of somewhere. Lord Bodd of Carshalton, why not? Lord Bodd of The Moorings? Or Lord Moorings of the Beeches, perhaps? You never consider any of them for a moment. You'd be ashamed to mention them to the College of Arms.

You let your imagination take flight a little. You want something that celebrates the rise of the Bodds of Carshalton with some suitable panache – something that brings a touch of good old-fashioned romance to the world – something that your friends can remember. Lord Mountfitchet of Compton Pauncefoot? The future Lady Mountfitchet doesn't like it. Lord Lafite-Rothschild of Sampford Peverell? Too many syllables, says Garter King of Arms – toastmasters will never be able to say it. So how about something nice and Scottish? That always sounds attractively baronial. Lord McDrumlin of Dundreggan? Rouge Dragon says there's a superstition in the business that Scottish titles bring bad luck.

You play with the idea of something extravagantly modest and self-deprecating. Lord Dymm of Dull. Lord Little of Mere. But Rouge Croix says that in the highly competitive peerage of today you are liable to be overlooked if you don't sell yourself hard. You go to the opposite extreme. For the whole of one afternoon you have absolutely decided that you will be Lord Magnificence of Belgravia. One of the Pursuivants – Portcullis, probably – says this is too abstract. You wake up in the middle of the night knowing with absolute conviction that you want to be Lord Lashings of Styal. Portcullis quite likes it, but it doesn't really speak to Bluemantle.

You decide to forget grandeur, and be entirely up-to-date and straightforwardly commercial. You flirt with Lord Brookside of Coronation Street. Then you think, no, if we're going down into the marketplace, let's get right down there and quite frankly sell ourselves. You submit a shortlist to the Heralds that includes Lord Knight of Passion and Lord Stirrings of Lust. There is no reply from the Heralds.

You'd really like to find something absolutely plain and straightforward that reflected your character in some way. Lord Baggs of Enthusiasm, perhaps? The Heralds say there is already a Lord Baggs of Foulness. Then you go through a whimsical phase, when you fancy spending the rest of your life as Lord Much of Amuchness. The Chester Herald loves it, but the Windsor Herald can't find Amuchness, even on the large-scale Ordnance Survey. He can find Sale and Hay, it's true, but there's already a Lord Conditions and the Lancaster Herald for some reason hates Lord Bundles. You feel that Lord Fax of Uckfield has a certain ring, or alternatively Lord Hunt of Cuckfield. The Heralds turn them both down. They will not explain why.

By the time you have gone through 134 permutations you are ready to grasp at anything. Anything! Yes, why not? Lord Anything of Interest. Lord Anything of Anywhere . . .

In the end you go back to your working title. Lord Bodd. It has the advantage of saying what it means. Bodd is who you are, after all. You still jib at Carshalton, though. Then you remember you have a great-aunt living in Budleigh Salterton. At the eleventh hour you settle blindly for your 135th effort – Lord Bodd of Budleigh. As soon as you've sent it in you realise it's a disaster, but it's too late for 136th thoughts.

No one's going to remember, anyway. The first time you go to the House, Lord Doss of Liss introduces you to Lord Loss of Diss as Lord Budd of Dudley, whereupon Lord Loss of Diss introduces you to Lord Ladd of Lydd as Lord Dudd of Didley.

And what most people are going to call you is Lord What's He Called, the One Who Used To Be What Was His Name, Only He Got the Sack.

(1995)

The manual writer's manual

Congratulations! You are a highly-qualified expert in various scientific fields, and you have just been engaged by some leading electronics corporation or software manufacturer to write the instruction manual and Help files for their product. This simple step-by-step guide will assist you to get the most out of your career.

This is an interactive programme. Convenient gaps have been left between the various sentences so that you can stop and go back at any point if you have not understood.

Lesson 1. The purpose of this lesson is to calm your fears about the difficulties of the subject, and to foster a sense of optimism about the work in hand. So:

   a. Unscrew the top of your fountain pen. (If you are intending to write your manual on a word-processor, open the instruction manual supplied.)

   b. Test that there is ink in the pen. (For word-processor users: read the opening sections of the manual, which you will find are encouragingly simple to understand.)

   c. Feel rather pleased with yourself. Wonder why anyone ever thought there was much to writing instruction manuals for leading electronics corporations and software manufacturers.

Lesson 2. The purpose of this lesson is to help you preserve some sense of mystery in your manual. (Hint: for many of your readers technology is taking the place of traditional religious belief. In the past they might have been reading the Scriptures, now they are dependent upon your work to learn an attitude of respect towards the deeper unknow-

ability of the universe, and of deference towards authority
– particularly yours!) So:

  a. Unscrew the top of your fountain-pen again, if you
     replaced it at the end of Lesson 1, and

  b. Suddenly introduce some quasi-hieratic protocol. If this
     should cause problems, maximise the heuristic opacity
     of the procedure by ellipsis or recursiveness in the
     hermeneutics. The sudden contrast with the somewhat
     pleonastic exegesis adumbrated in the prolegomena . . .

(Yes, I haven't forgotten it's an interactive programme, and
I can see you've got your hand up. Just wait till we get to
the end of the sentence.)

  . . . will induce in the neophyte a characteristic dis-
  orientation and frustration similar to the feelings
  notoriously engendered in a child by the unpredictable
  alternation of maternal love and punishment.

All right. You're confused. Don't worry! You can go back to
the beginning at any point. So . . .

  *Congratulations! You are a highly-qualified expert in
  various scientific fields, and you have . . .*

What . . . ? Oh, you understood that bit . . . You mean
further on? All right . . .

  Unscrew the top of your fountain-pen . . .

No? You don't mean *quasi-hieratic protocol* . . . ? Oh, I see
. . . No – not the slightest objection to explaining. A *quasi-
hieratic protocol* is an expression introduced into the
discourse by the initiate without vouchsafed profane
signification, with the intention of preserving sacerdotal
prerogative. All right . . . ?

   What do I mean by *an expression introduced into the
discourse etc* . . . ? I mean an expression such as *quasi-
hieratic protocol.*

No, I'm sorry – I'm not going to explain it again. I've already given you a simple ostensive self-referential formulation which I should have thought was comprehensible to a child of $^3\sqrt{8}$ . . . Yes, certainly – it's an interactive manual. But interactivity doesn't mean constant interruption! It doesn't mean asking about things that I understand perfectly well.

Now where was I? Yes – and you might like to note this – I was telling you to *maximise the heuristic opacity of the procedure by ellipsis or recursiveness in the hermeneutics* . . . And before you open your mouth again, please don't ask me what heuristics and hermeneutics are! Look them up for yourself! You're a big grown-up scientist!

No, no – I'm not going to tell you where to look them up . . . ! All right, then, don't whine – under Epistemology. For heaven's sake! Come *on* . . . !

Where's Epistemology? How should I know? In the back of the book somewhere. In the index. You want me to write the index for you, as well as everything else? Somebody else is doing that! Some specialist index-writer . . . ! No, I *don't* look to see what he's put in his index . . . No, he *doesn't* read the text before he writes the index. He's an index-writer, not a manual-reader . . . What does he put in his index? The same as any other writer puts into what he writes! Whatever comes into his head! Which in his case I should think is more probably words like 'fountain-pen' and 'congratulations', because if I know anything about index-writers he's as baffled as you are.

Keep calm, keep calm! There's no need to raise your voice! They did explain to you in the shop, did they, that you need at least a degree in semantics to run this programme . . . ? They didn't? Oh, I see. Never mind, press on, do the best we can with the material we've got. So, just check that you *have* taken the top off your fountain-pen . . . Right, good, well done, don't shout. Now, simply bring the nib of the fountain-pen into contact with the paper – right?

– and *introduce the crypto-hieratic whatever it was*!

What? Speak up ... I know, I know – I said *quasi-hieratic* before. I've changed my mind ... What's the difference? That's my business. It's *my* mind I've changed, not yours. *I* know what I'm talking about ...

Look, don't scream at me! This is the way manuals are written! I can't change the system! Pull yourself together! You're behaving in a most extraordinary manner. Lying down and drumming your heels on the floor like that! This may be an interactive programme, but interactive doesn't mean screaming abuse, and it doesn't mean hurling the manual across the room. It affords me a certain pleasure to watch you, it's true – but interactive goes both ways, you know. No pudding for you this evening unless you stop this tantrum. My word, even if I did know what pseudo-hieratic whichwhats are I shouldn't tell you now, not after the way you've behaved.

I mean proto-hieratic ... Or rather hiero-proleptic ... No ... What am I talking about? You're getting *me* confused now!

Don't snivel. You'll see the point of all the suffering you've endured in the course of your education when you go out into the world at the end of it and make your own pupils' lives a misery in their turn.

(1994)

The meteorological school

All afternoon the great fleets of slow-moving summer cumulus were coming up out of the south-west, solid and intricately moulded, touched in places with a hot coppery burnish, gravely pacing the immensity of the steppe. Sergei lay in the long grass and watched them, thinking about Anton Fyodorovich's house in Ryazan Province . . .

That's how one of my great unwritten novels starts. Another begins:

The fog crept among the houses and patrolled the streets like the spies and pickets of an occupying army. All the sounds of the city were muted by its grey presence. Familiar landmarks loomed strange and menacing as one walked about, as if no old loyalty could be taken for granted under the new dispensation. Somewhere out in the great grey limbo in one of the open squares, Van der Velde caught the raw wetness of the air in his throat, and coughed. 'Damn this fog,' he said . . .

And another:

Just before noon a fine, warm, soaking rain began to fall, turning the dusty grey slates on the roof of the church a glossy black, and whispering monotonously in the topmost branches of the elms. The rain covered Mrs Morton-Wise's spectacles with a film of fine droplets, making it increasingly difficult for her to see from where she stood what was happening on the other side of the churchyard . . .

That's how they start, and that's how they stop. I'm all right on the measured periods describing the weather. It's the entry of Sergei, Van Der Velde, Mrs Morton-Wise, and the rest, that puts the curse on them.

Who are these people, anyway? I'm not sure that I'm terribly interested. If Van der Velde's not fat he's thin, if he hasn't got good digestion he's got bad digestion. All right, let's say he's thin with bad digestion. He hates his father, say; he marries a depressive heiress who deceives him with an art dealer; he's accused of supressing the truth about conditions in a desiccated coconut factory. I don't know. Maybe he writes a novel about a fat man with good digestion who runs off with the wife of a schizoid bicycle designer ... So what? How can I write fine prose about people's digestive troubles and bicycle designers' wives?

The weather – that's what I want to write about. What immensely evocative stuff weather is! Whenever I look out of the window and observe the meteorological condition of the day I can feel the grand periods pulsing in the blood, the nostalgic phrases ringing in my head. Whenever I look at the typewriter and see a blank piece of paper, the thin Atlantic cloud-wrack starts to scud across it immediately.

I dare say I'm not the only one. Anyone with a liberal education and a maritime climate probably feels the same. English novelists on the whole keep the reader fairly continuously informed about the temperature, humidity and wind velocity in which their man reveals his inner nature and gets the girl.

Most of my literary tastes were formed by the twin volumes of prose passages for translation into and out of French which we used in the sixth form at school – not surprisingly, since translation is one of the few occasions on which one is obliged to examine prose in close and intimate detail. I believe my addiction to meteorological romanticism is no exception. All the extracts seemed to be about nocturnal storms, the ending of great droughts, or summer nights spent out of doors in warm airs and brilliant starlight, and by the time one had looked it up in Mr Mansion's invaluable French dictionary and decided whether the mist rising from the reed-beds as the dusk drew on was *brume, embrun, brouillard, brouillasse* or *brumasse,* the meteorological subtleties had made a considerable impression on one's subconscious.

One can of course revert to the weather pretty frequently

during a novel (for instance, I can see that a day of gathering oppression, followed by a terrible nocturnal thunderstorm and a clear, sparkling morning, are going to take our minds off Sergei some time in the near future). But between whiles it's people, people, people. Before I can make a career for myself as a novelist (and is there any other honourable career for an arts graduate?), the people problem will have to be solved. Either I shall have to collaborate with someone who's good with people but lost when faced with the fine, steaming drizzle from the iron-grey overcast, or I shall have to found the meteorological school of novel writing.

It happened in painting. Once upon a time such weather and landscape as there was occurred only in portraits, fitted in very small between the subject's left ear and the frame. But the weather and the landscape expanded, and the heads shrank in the steadily increasing rainfall, until eventually the sun shone and the snow fell upon insignificant little fellows in the middle distance, or upon no one at all.

Now it's happening in the novel. Take what some critics consider the greatest of my unwritten works in this genre, 'My Sun, My Sun.' This is a ruthless and entirely un-inhabited exposure of a high-pressure system centred over the Azores, which on a trip to Southern Ireland meets a weak trough of low pressure moving down from Iceland. Their encounter is tempestuous, and a cold front is born, which brings a routed cavalry of storm clouds trooping in from the sea, with scattered showers like torn banners streaming in the wind . . .

And so on. It's one of the saddest things in the world that so much which is a pleasure to write is a pain in the neck to read.

(1964)

Money well changed

No more Wechsel. The last of the summer Cambio. The real sadness of the Single European Currency is that it would mean the end of European moneychanging as we know it.

I recall many delightfully unhurried exchanges of currency and traveller's cheques all over Europe, many delicious stews of noughts and decimal points, many entertaining failures to have my passport with me or to remember that banks close for lunch. But if I had to select just one occasion to recall in the bleak years ahead it would be a certain Monday morning in late June at the Banque de France in Laon.

Laon, appropriately enough, is at the crossroads of Europe. It's in the Aisne, in Northern France, situated just off the motorway that runs from Strasbourg and Germany to the French Channel ports, at the point where it crosses the N2 from Paris to Brussels. Whichever road you're on you can see it coming from miles off – two ancient Gothic cathedral towers perched on a fortified hilltop islanded in the great agricultural plain. Two stars in the Michelin – three for the nave of the cathedral – wonderful views.

This charming town was full of sunshine and the bustle of market day when we found ourselves in need of a little financial refreshment there. We were on our way back from South Germany, and we needed a little more French currency to see us through to Calais. We had it in mind to change some forty pounds' worth of left-over German marks, together with a £20 sterling traveller's cheque. The Banque de France seemed like a good choice for our custom. Its appearance was discreetly imposing, its name suggested solidity and extensive reserves. We were right. The feast of fine banking that ensued was worth another three stars in the Michelin. I was so impressed that I made a complete note of it, course by course, from the moment we pressed the yellow button beside the heavily-armoured front door.

1 A red light comes on to indicate that our application for entry is being considered. We are instructed to wait for a green light before attempting to push the door.

2 The green light comes on, and we enter, to be confronted by a second door, with a second yellow button. A second red light comes on, while our credentials are examined all over again.

3 We pass through the second door, and enter a great hall divided by a counter. On the other side of the counter are a dozen or so employees of the bank. On this side is a spacious emptiness occupied only by us. We are the only people in Laon to have passed both tests.

4 We advance towards the counter and the waiting staff. We choose the nearest clerk, on the righthand side of the bank, and present our £20 traveller's cheque, our passport, and our 130 Deutschmarks. The clerk examines the cheque. She examines the passport, then takes a printed form and writes down by hand the number of the passport, together with my name and address. She examines the fifty Deutschmark note, then the three twenties, then the ten and the two fives. She goes away to consult the bank's files.

5 She comes back and performs various computations upon a small pocket calculator. The calculator is for some reason balanced half on and half off a ledger, so that it gives to the touch like a pudding. She writes down by hand on the printed form the quantities of sterling and Deutschmarks involved, the rates for each currency, and the two subtotals in francs. She performs another wobbly computation, and writes down the total. So far, a dignified but not unusual display of traditional handcraft moneychanging.

6 But this is merely the *amuse-gueule* before the meal proper. The clerk takes the form she has filled up,

together with the passport, the traveller's cheque, and the seven Deutschmark bills, to a more senior-looking woman, who has drawn-back grey hair and steel-rimmed spectacles. She checks the two multiplications and the addition. She re-examines the passport, the traveller's cheque, and the German banknotes, and returns them to the clerk. Everything is in order. The clerk returns to the counter and hands us back our passport. She retains the traveller's cheque – but she hands back our Deutschmarks. What?

7 She indicates a male cashier in a small fortified enclosure a kilometre or two away on the lefthand side of the great hall. Of course. A division of functions familiar from many such occasions in the past.

8 We walk across to the cashier. The clerk, on the other side of the counter, also walks across to the cashier. We are holding the passport and the returned DM 130, *she* is holding the £20 traveller's cheque and the form she has filled up, as checked and authenticated by her senior. We wait for the cashier to take the Deutschmarks through the front of the security grille, she waits for the cashier to open a special window in the back of it and take the traveller's cheque and the form.

9 The clerk returns to her post on the righthand side of the bank.

10 The cashier examines the traveller's cheque once again, then consults another set of files. He reworks the computations on the completed form. He takes the seven Deutschmark bills from us, and examines them again in their turn – first the fifty, then the three twenties, then the ten and the two fives. They all apparently pass muster once again. Nothing has changed, in this rapidly changing world, since they were first examined and re-examined on the righthand side of the bank.

11 Or has it? The cashier is evidently shaken by a sudden

doubt. How about the exchange rates? Some fair amount of time has now gone by since they were checked and double-checked on the other side of the bank. There may have been dramatic developments in the markets since then. The Federal Government may have fallen. The pound may be soaring even as the Deutschmark goes into free fall. He looks up both the rates again. Nothing has happened. Pound and mark alike are rock steady.

12 This steadiness in the markets makes a pleasing contrast with the cashier's pocket calculator, which is balanced half on and half off a ledger, just like the clerk's, so that it gives like a second helping of pudding as he punches each button, and recomputes all the computations that he has just reworked manually.

13 There is evidently something a little unsettling about the result of this fourth trip through the sums. I suspect the trouble is that the new results are *exactly the same* as the earlier ones, which may of course tend to confirm them, but which may on the other hand suggest the possibility of systematic error in the bank's methodology for multiplication and addition. The cashier summons a second cashier, who goes through all the rates and calculations for a fifth time. I notice that he too keeps the calculator balanced half on and half off the ledger as he works. Sponge *calculatrice* is obviously a *spécialité de la maison*.

14 And yes – steps are being taken. Action is in hand. The first cashier has let himself out of his cage. He is walking all the way back across the bank towards the righthand side. We cross back as well, separated from him by the counter, in parallel, anxious to stay in touch with events. I believe he is carrying the traveller's cheques and the German banknotes, but he evidently doesn't have everything with him, because

after he has spoken to the clerk on the righthand side she leaves her position, and we all walk back again to the lefthand side.

15 I'm not sure that it's the correctness of the mathematics that are at issue now – the calculator has been left to one side. I have the impression that they have moved on to more general questions. After all, not two but three different currencies are involved in this transaction, and there may be problems of protocol and precedence. Should the Bundesbank or the Bank of England be informed first?

16 A long time goes by. It is very quiet and still inside the bank, and my attention wanders. I find myself covertly watching some of the other staff. I become fascinated by one particular man. He is recklessly handsome, with a moustache and a three-piece suit, and he has nothing at all to do. The desk in front of him is completely empty. He rubs his hands together and gazes into space, with a look of wistful tenderness. I don't believe he is thinking about high-interest savings accounts, or even ways of making the bank's foreign exchange procedures more secure. I believe he is thinking about some member of the opposite sex.

17 I notice that there is in fact a young woman sitting just in front of him, typing rapidly, until there is nothing more to type, when she, too, leans on her empty desk and gazes into the great spaces of the room. I believe her thoughts have also strayed back to her private life. They do not talk to each other. They do not look at each other. I get the impression that it's not each other that they are thinking about. Their separate reveries seem strangely deep and poignant in the quiet lofty room.

18 Just a moment. Something's happened . . . I don't know what it was, but the clerk is walking back to her place on the righthand side of the bank. It's been

settled. Everyone's anxieties over the transaction have been set to rest.

19 The clerk fills out a second form to replace the first one.

20 She walks back to the cashier with the new edition of the form. I have the impression that she is moving a little more slowly than before. Her footwear, I think, is not entirely suitable for active pursuits like currency exchange.

21 The cashier checks the new figures and the current state of the foreign exchange market. He pays over Fr. 636.27.

22 We exit through the double security system.

The sun is still shining. We are in no hurry, and Laon is a delightful place to be. I look at my watch, the whole entertainment has taken twenty-five minutes.

So what's going to happen to everyone in the Banque de France in Laon when the ecu comes? How are the rest of us going to fill our time? We're *all* going to end up staring into space, thinking about our loved ones.

(1992)

The monolithic view of mirrors

It is with a close and warmly sympathetic interest that all men of good will, whatever their creed, are following the vigorous debate now going on within the Carthaginian Monolithic Church on the vexed question of rear-view mirrors.

It has long been the teaching of the Church that looking backwards while travelling forwards is categorically and explicitly forbidden by God, since it was for doing this that He visited instant fossilisation upon Lot's wife.

In this context 'looking back' has always been interpreted

as frustrating the natural forward gaze of the traveller, whether by turning the head (*visus interruptus*), or by the interposition of a mechanical device such as a mirror.

Carthaginian Monolithic theologians claim that looking back is not only divinely prohibited, but can also be seen by the light of reason to be contrary to natural law, since it is patently interfering with nature to inhibit the inherent tendency of fast-moving objects to collide, and is frustrating the natural consequences of the act of driving.

Moreover, they argue, there is a strong aesthetic objection to looking back, since it must plainly detract from the spontaneity of the driving act, and they point out how much more insipid life becomes if the spice of the unexpected is removed altogether. It must in all fairness be pointed out that the keen interest of the Monolithic clergy in preserving spontaneity and avoiding insipidity is entirely altruistic, since they do not themselves drive.

These arguments notwithstanding, the Church has long recognised the need to prevent cars smashing into the back of one another indiscriminately, and Monolithics are permitted to avoid it by abstaining from driving altogether, or by driving only during the so-called 'safe period,' between midnight and six a.m., when the chances of being crashed into are greatly reduced.

Nevertheless, there is a sympathetic – indeed, anguished – realisation among many Monolithic leaders today that self-restraint alone may be inadequate to meet the situation. The question was less crucial in the days when the main effect of the doctrine was to prohibit Monolithics from sitting with their back to the engine in railway carriages. But the increasing popularity of the motor car is putting an intolerable burden upon the accident wards of the world's hospitals.

There is intense sympathy, too, for the great strain undergone by Monolithic drivers who have heen run into from behind perhaps thirteen or fourteen times already, and who now scarcely dare drive home to see their wives if it involves turning right, or pulling out to pass a parked car.

It is to this agonising problem that 'the box' may provide an answer. 'The box' is a rearward radar scanning device which scientists are still testing. 'Liberal' Monolithics believe that a scanning aerial cannot be said to 'look' back in the natural sense of looking, and that the radar screen does not deflect the natural forward gaze of the driver, like a mirror, but is a natural part of his natural forward view.

It is emphasised that even if 'the box' were to be accepted, it could never be used for merely selfish purposes, to avoid a crash simply because a crash was not desired, but only where a driver had already had three or four crashes, and there were genuine grounds for believing that another one might have a serious effect upon his health.

(O. J. SPROUT: *I must say, I'm greatly struck by the responsibility and fair-mindedness with which Mr Frayn is treating this thorny subject.*

MRS SPROUT: *I agree with you, Sprout. He's not a Carthaginian Monolithic himself, is he?*)

All the same, some authorities doubt if the box could ever be an acceptable compromise. They believe that the only hope would be to develop a device which would make the safe period principle more reliable – making absolutely sure that the road behind the car was kept clear by scattering perhaps nails or broken glass, perhaps small high explosive bombs.

(SPROUT: *You know, I don't think he's a Carthaginian Monolithic at all, Mrs Sprout. That's the beauty of it. To me the whole article suggests the best tradition of agnostic liberal journalism.*)

Non-Monolithic observers can only look on at this debate with sympathy and understanding. They may be sure that it will be carried through with utter sincerity and a genuine sense of urgency, and that everyone on both sides

will do his best, and play the game according to the rules.
(MRS SPROUT: *There were tears in his eyes in the last paragraph, Sprout.*
SPROUT: *In mine too, Mrs Sprout. I can only say that the whole inquiry was conducted with the beautiful reverence and respect which the subject demands.*)

(1964)

My life and loves

Distinguished civil servants and others, when they realise they are being observed by a journalist, hastily leap up from their armchairs and with rather unexpected quiet passion and rather unexpectedly engaging smiles begin to play badminton, collect seventeenth-century Irish egg-whisks, write the standard work on the lesser celandine, reveal a rather unexpected line in wry humour, take a rather unexpectedly serious interest in the campaign to preserve the death-watch beetle, and beget ten rather brilliant children; continuing this dazzling simultaneous exhibition until the journalist leaves, when (I should imagine) they slump heavily back into their armchairs rather unexpectedly exhausted.

The behaviour of distinguished actors and actresses when a journalist or handout writer comes over the horizon is entirely different. They don't start *doing* anything at all. They just start believing in and being intensely moved by and being utterly realistic about. They simply come vibrantly, richly, and passively into contact with life.

Here, for instance, is the throbbing voice of an actress called Yvette Mimieux in a newspaper cutting I have: 'I like snails and hot chocolate and dancing and tangy cheese and soft lead pencils and thick, strong coffee and tangerines and racing cars.'

Imagine the Permanent Secretary at the Ministry of Waste Disposal taking this sort of line. ' "I adore walking in the rain," lisped Mr O. R. Strood, the tough-minded *éminence grise* behind Britain's newest rubbish tip, "and the smell of new bread and comfortably worn dispatch-boxes and thinking and Ministry cars and mid-morning biscuits and chewing my pencil and – oh – heaps of things." ' Be rather unexpected, to say the least.

But it looked perfectly natural when Mr Nicol Williamson, actor, listed his loves to Mr Marshall Pugh, journalist, in the *Daily Mail* last week. Mr Williamson, it appears, loves old wooden houses, Bach, good stew and ale, pubs, belting tennis balls about, and diving into the sea and coming back and scattering his records all over the room.

How he stands on hot chocolate and tangy cheese and soft lead pencils he doesn't say. But he did come out for humility – 'I'm humble in some ways,' he told Mr Pugh, 'much humbler than you think' – and faith. 'Faith bothered him constantly,' reported Mr Pugh. 'It was so bloody personal, such bloody agony.'

Yes! Oh God, yes! Oh God, I absolutely bloody agree! The smell of coffee roasting, sunlight falling on hair, the clouds coming down on the mountains – I love them all, too. I may not have mentioned it before, but I'm involved in life up to my bloody eyebrows. Gregorian plainsong, hot, strong cheese and tangy snails – I'm deeply committed to every corny, wonderful, bloody experience in the book. I've never tried diving in the sea and coming back and scattering my records all over the room, but oh God, it sounds marvellous! I'll give it a whirl at the very first opportunity I have.

And there's the snag – opportunity. As Mr Williamson says: 'I want to live intensively, 101 per cent. But how can I do it in this job?'

God, I know the feeling! How can I do it, either, in my job, or you in yours? And if it's not the job stopping us living it's something else. Just as you're about to start living, really

101 per cent living, it's lunchtime. Or some damned person rings up. You get inside some lovable pub and you never have a chance to really experience it, because you have to spend all the time either trying to break into your friends' conversation to ask them what they want to drink, or trying to catch the barmaid's eye.

And the hot chocolate – that turns up just when you feel like the thick, strong coffee, and the thick, strong coffee is wheeled on just about bedtime, when the only thing you want is hot chocolate. Nor is it possible to listen to the Bach properly when you're hunting high and low for something to write with, because all you can find is some damned joky soft lead pencil.

No, if you want to live – *really* live – you've got to get away from life. You've got to find somewhere where you can be completely idle, so that if you want to spend all morning walking in the rain you can, for the simple reason that there's nothing else to do. And if you happen to come across a smell of coffee roasting you can stop and inhale it – and go on inhaling it until you're fed up with it. Then you can sit down in a café somewhere and have a hot chocolate. Have two hot chocolates if you feel like it – there's nothing else to do. Go on guzzling hot chocolate until you're chocolate-coloured in the face. Then you can start walking about in the rain again, trying to get up an appetite for that lunch of stew and ale.

After lunch you could go and look at some wooden houses. Look at them from the front, look at them from the back. Really get an eyeful of them – there's no earthly hurry. Then perhaps you could stroll along and smell the coffee roasting again. Have another hot chocolate. If the weather's cleared up you might go and take a dive in the sea, then go up to your room and chuck the records about. After that you might go out and take another dive, and chuck the records about all over again – you've probably still got about four hours left before dinner . . .

No, if you're really going to live – really 101 per cent live – you need some purpose in life. You need to work. Oh God, think of that bloody marvellous little pub you used to slip out to after a hard day's work! And the Goldberg Variations tinkling quietly away in the background as you worked with the soft lead pencil! Oh God, how bloody wonderful such moments are – in recollection, if you didn't think about them when they happened!

(1965)

My nature diary

JANUARY: Out and about, as usual, striding across the local public recreation ground, observing Nature and the slow turning of the seasons. Brace of children gambolling and snapping at heel, ready for anything, particularly a sudden encounter with a bag of sweets or a television programme. Can't help noticing the grass – blade after blade of it, with a fine display of common brown mud (*terra fusca vulgaris*) coming through.

How one longs for February, the *real* fag-end month of winter, with its raw, murky, desolate afternoons expiring in sodden fields! Plan richly gloomy afternoon trips throughout February to the Fens and the dank industrial landscapes of the Thames Estuary.

FEBRUARY: Out and about on the public recreation ground. Grass still doing well. Children put up an old cock Smarties packet, its brilliant colouring showing up vividly against the mud. Order them to put it down again.

Weather oddly unsuitable for fens or marshes. Sudden warm, bright days occur, making one unable to think of anything except those sudden warm, bright days which will occur in March and touch one's heart with the first advance publicity for spring. Swear that for once I will be ready to make the most of them by dashing out to Kentish oast-houses surrounded by blossom, to the crocuses on King's Backs.

MARCH: Neat green and brown of native recreation ground spoiled by disgusting litter of old almond blossom. These blossom-louts should be prosecuted.

Too busy thinking about April to go anywhere. Ah, April! When the first brilliant greenery softens the gnarled timber of this ancient winter world! And we shall see it happen along the Quai d'Anjou and in the gardens of the Hotel Biron. Because in April we shall be in Paris! Or in Amsterdam. Or possibly in Venice, still fresh and cool and sparkling!

APRIL: I mean, of course, that we shall be there in May. Always expect the spring to happen in April, and realise only when April arrives that it happens in May. Meanwhile, observe the immutable march of Nature's timetable on the recreation ground, as the local dogs are brought out each day to move their bowels.

MAY: May somehow goes by before I have time to notice what Nature's doing on the recreation ground, let alone get tickets to fail to notice it elsewhere. *June's* the month, of course. Midsummer; full leaf; the fresh prime of the year. To hell with the tawdry pleasures of foreign cities – in June I will take a knapsack and a stout stick and stride through the heartlands of England. Through Warwickshire, Worcestershire, Gloucestershire, Oxfordshire; through old towns full of bells and strong ale; through ancient green forests where temporarily dispossessed dukes wander with their courts, hunting the deer and communing in blank verse as fresh as spring-water.

JUNE: Take up my stout umbrella and stride through the heartlands of the recreation ground, now gaily bedecked with the Lesser and Greater Paper Bag, the Common Orangeskin, and the shyly peeping Lolly Stick.

How half-hearted, wishy-washy June makes one long for the great heats of July! They'll find me and my family in the simmering uplands of the Aveyron – no, in the sweltering, dusty plains of Emilia – no, no, in the burnt brown hills of Umbria! Solid iron heat will enclose us! Pulsating, suffocating heat! Ah!

JULY: While waiting for the great heats to arrive, walk about the recreation ground with my old 12-bore umbrella in the crook of my arm, unable to see anything but a vision of August. August is water, of course. Sunlit blue water, creaming surf. Have now saved such an enormous amount of money by not going to Paris or Amsterdam or Emilia or Umbria, and not buying a stout stick, that we could surely afford to spend August in Cyrenaica, or on the wild coast of Maine.

AUGUST: Funny – we couldn't. Spend August at home, thinking about September. My God, in September we'll go *anywhere.*

SEPTEMBER: And, indeed, in the ghastly little resort of N'Importe-Où we end up. Exercise our children by walking them on the local *terrain de récréation.* The yellowing leaves are being brought down by the rains and the equinoctial gales. Makes one deeply nostalgic for the golden-red autumn melancholy of England in October.

OCTOBER: Observe, on my rambles across the home recreation ground, that grass and mud do not in fact turn golden-red in autumn. The month we're all waiting for is November, when London really comes into its own, and the afternoon sun goes down blood-red into the foggy mercantile exhalations of the city. You'll find me in November mooning among the cranes and warehouses of Bankside, and calling at tea-and-crumpet time on friends with houses in Queen's Gate and Onslow Square and the Boltons, as the nannies dawdle home from the smoky Park with children in leggings.

NOVEMBER: I remember now – I haven't got any friends in Queen's Gate, Onslow Sqaure, or the Boltons. Well, to hell with South Kensington and November. My own rude native recreation ground will look incomparably beautiful when December comes, and the green grass and brown mud disappear beneath that first soft snowfall of winter.

DECEMBER: Get out and about on the recreation ground, children at heel, yapping after ice-creams. Make a rainman for them and organise a rainball fight. How one longs for January and February, the *real* winter months, when one starts to feel the first intimations of spring – spring, with all its sweet anticipation of a summer pregnant with winter-heralding autumn . . .

(1966)

Never put off to Gomorrah

... the proposals in your Note can only meet with unqualified rejection, while the proposals I have set forth above, on the other hand, contain the basis of equitable negotiation in the cause of world virtue, leading eventually to the total liquidation of unrighteousness which is undoubtedly the dearest and most heartfelt wish of the peoples of our two great cities.

N. S. LESS, *Lord Mayor of Sodom*

My dear lord Mayor,

I have now been able to study very carefully your reply of February 22 to my Note of February 12 to your reply of February 10, for which I thank you. I see with regret that its main proposal is the one which you put forward in your earlier Notes, of October 14, November 1, December 9, January 12, January 20, etc., calling for any conference on reducing the level of unrighteousness to be preceded by a meeting of the civic heads of our two cities.

This, as I explained in my Notes of October 17, November 3, December 12, January 15, January 28, and February 12, is unacceptable. I do not believe, as I said in those Notes, that any useful purpose would be served by an unprepared meeting of civic heads at this stage. What we have to do before we meet, I am convinced, is to create confidence by achieving some actual progress in reducing the dangerously high level of unrighteousness in our two cities before – as so many experts have warned us is possible – it leads to a disastrous holocaust in which both our cities would be destroyed.

Let me say once again that I believe – and my Corporation believes – that before there can be any agreement to reduce unrighteousness, provision must be made for adequate intercity inspection to ensure that the agreed level is not exceeded. Here I must reject as entirely false your allegation, set forth in your Notes of October 14, etc., and previously rebutted in my Notes of October 17, etc., that my intention in putting forward this plan is to establish, under a cloak of respectability, an espionage service for discovering details of your secret and advanced vices which would be commercially useful to us. Such a suggestion can only be intended to serve the purpose of propaganda. The real reason, as I have explained in earlier notes, is to obviate the danger – presented by your proposal for unverified reduction – that one of the parties, while storing up credit in Heaven by publicly liquidating the forces of vice, might in secret be building up other vices, so obtaining an unfair advantage in the tourist trade.

I do not wish at this stage to go into this too deeply. My point is that here is a clearly defined area of disagreement between us of the sort which would have to be explored by specialists in moral hygiene with positive results before any general question of morals could be usefully discussed at the summit. It was with the aim of obtaining expert exploration of these areas that I proposed a disunrighteousness conference to take place first (my Notes of October 14, etc.). I suggest, as a measure of compromise, that this conference should be preceded by a meeting of town clerks to prepare an agenda for the conference, though with the limitation, naturally, that this agenda should exclude any consideration of an unverified reduction.

It is in no spirit of mere propaganda, but in the hope that you will respond to the desperate yearnings of the common people in both our cities for righteousness that I urge you to consider this proposal.

J. F. MORE, *Lord Mayor of Gomorrah*

My dear Lord Mayor,

I must say frankly that I am deeply grieved by the negative attitude adopted in your reply of February 25 to my note of February 22 to your reply of February 12 to my note of February 10 to your . . .

(1962)

New man coming

One's personality is a remarkably stable structure; and the most stable element in it is one's steadfast conviction that it is just on the point of being entirely transformed.

Transformed, needless to say, not by any efforts of one's own, but by magic objects and events outside oneself. One's dissatisfactions and limitations will be suddenly and wonderfully sloughed off, one comes to believe, when one has acquired a striped suit, or a red car; when one has got married; when one has written a book, or found God, or learnt Italian; when one has reached the age of ten; when one has moved house; when summer comes.

It is strange that so much of one's action is motivated by such patent witchcraft. But in a society where unhappiness is regarded rather like fleas, as an unappealing state that people ought to be ashamed of getting into, I suppose it is congenial to see oneself as a naturally happy soul hindered from achieving perfect contentment only by external causes. All these extraordinary superstitions are ways of concealing from oneself the painful fact that most of one's discontents are the inevitable by-products of one's own nature.

I rely a bit on almost all these superstitions, but most particularly on those that involve straightforward covetousness. If I had a certain material object, I have repeatedly felt, my whole life would be entirely changed. From its small corner the totem would radiate such a powerful field of rightness and delight that everything else would come to glow in sympathy.

The first thing I can remember coveting as a child was a propelling pencil that wrote in five colours, after I had seen the teacher correcting exercise books with one. Other little boys might have conceived a passion for the teacher, but I fell in love with the propelling pencil. It was beautiful, and I desired it. The provocative glimpses of the coloured leads through the slots in the side inflamed my senses. I longed to touch the exquisite texture of the nickel-plating.

My parents were driven to say they would buy me one – but, torment of hopes raised only to be the more savagely hurled down, there was none in the shops! I raged about the house like a tiny junkie deprived of his fix, while they ransacked London, and after days of great misery for all of us, ran one to earth in far-off Peckham Rye. But so supremely unimportant did it become as soon as I possessed it that I cannot even remember what happened to it.

It sometimes seems to me that the whole story of my life could be adequately told in the catalogue of these love affairs. There was the affair with the ten-and-sixpenny plastic crystal set (purchased – never worked); the affair with the miniature starting-pistol (owned by a friend – fiercely desired through long centuries of time – swapped for about half my possessions – instantly devalued, and allowed to fall to pieces before it could fire the five blank cartridges which my friend's father was keeping locked up to celebrate the end of the war with); the affair with the second-hand sports car (£180 – 'Take you anywhere, that car,' said the salesman. 'Take you to Land's End and back'), snatched away at the last moment by a providential failure to raise the money.

One learns, of course. I don't think I shall ever fall in love with another propelling pencil, or another plastic crystal set. But the inoculation is against the particular ju-jus I've tried, not against ju-jus in general. It doesn't in any way deter me from my present mania, for example, which is coveting a swivel chair. If I had a swivel chair, upholstered in worn leather, I know I should be a new man.

I can see myself very clearly with the swivel chair. I am a calm man, a responsible man, a happy man, a man who can work for eight hours at a stretch without being interrupted by fatigue, boredom, bad temper or incompetence, a man who can take well-earned relaxation with his smiling wife and laughing child in some agreeable but uplifting leisure pursuit. I am a man who keeps an exquisitely selected early June day permanently outside his window. I am a man who does not get telephone calls from people who think they are phoning the South Eastern Gas Board.

I am a man who is swinging gently from side to side in his worn leather swivel chair as he decides whether to spend the sunlit working day ahead on finishing his play about the ultimate essence of man, or starting the essay in which the ultimate nature of the universe is set forth in 500 exact and simple words.

Manufacturers of swivel chairs, join me in happy contemplation of the picture! Sooner or later I shall have the swivel chair, and you will have the money for it. How would you sell me a swivel chair I do not need if I did not believe I was buying a complete new personality? How would any five-colour propelling pencils ever be sold if other people did not share my disorder? How would the evangelists and travel agents survive?

And just as surely as I know that the man in the swivel chair will be a new and perfect man, so I know he will be the same inadequate one, not only depressed by the weather, interrupted by the telephone, unable to find a pen that works, and confused about exactly what he is supposed to be doing, but also driven to final exasperation because the swivel on the blasted chair is broken.

I know it only too well. Perhaps it's just as well for all concerned that I don't actually believe it.

(1963)

Night thoughts

Impossible to postpone moment of recognition much longer. No no, leave it few moments more. Mustn't jump to conclusions. Never know, might just manage it in last few minutes. Too much effort for tired man to decide. Put it off for minute – half-a-minute, then – just a few more seconds . . .

All right, I surrender. I admit, I AM NOT ASLEEP. I have not been asleep, am not asleep now, nor ever will be asleep. Inside of head feels like armaments factory on night shift, every particle of it alive and occupied with teeming, meaningless activity. Three o'clock! Half night gone and no sleep to show for it. I shall get up tired, go through day in haze, and go to bed too tired to sleep tomorrow night. Was there ever anyone in such a pitiful case? Was there ever anyone so ill-used by his own cerebral cortex? I shall get tic, grow old before time, go mad. Be permanently exhausted. Never manage to sleep again. Oh, unfortunate me, how I pity my condition!

Now, calm. Think. Get up, take bracing breath of cold night air at window, fetch water, wake up properly, start all over again. Aaaaugh! Bare toe stubbed on misplaced furniture. Wife stirs, asks the matter. Explain just fetching water. Tone hopelessly matter-of-fact. Couldn't I have produced something more tragic, more martyred, more wife-awakening? Wife asleep again already. Some failure of communication here? Some indifference to husband's mortal predicament? Marriage breaking up? Divorce courts looming?

Lie down again, full of air and water. Arrange limbs with utmost care, relaxing each muscle in turn. Method prescribed in book I once read – infallible cure for insomnia. Unfortunately have to unrelax right arm to deal with itch in scalp. Rearrange arm again, relaxing each muscle individually as prescribed – though scarcely enough muscle in bicep section to know whether relaxed or not.

Peace. Hopes rising every moment. Alas, itch breaks out in foot. Have to disarrange right arm and left leg to scratch. Rearrange limbs with difficulty, since right leg and left arm have also become disarranged and unrelaxed in process. Wait anxiously. If sleep doesn't come in next fifteen seconds, doubt whether will be able to remain relaxed in this hopelessly uncomfortable posture. Suddenly get itch between shoulder-blades. Contortion of every muscle in body necessary to scratch it.

So much for that method. Will now try just lying on left side like normal human being, as always have done. Funny – something deeply unsatisfactory about left-hand edge of body. Couldn't remain lying on that side if I was paid to. Twist with insane speed on to right-hand side. Too fast, too fast! Can feel nerves still twanging like strings of piano thrown downstairs. Right-hand edge of body, curiously enough, in precisely same state as left-hand. Never mind, will make a stand here – retreat has to be halted somewhere. Not another inch will I cede. I am on my right-hand side, and on my right-hand side I remain, till I have taken sleep at bayonet-point.

One minute. Two minutes. It's more than flesh and blood can stand. Retire in disorder – hurl self on to back. At last discover reason for sleeplessness – too hot. Fling back covers. By tremendous effort of will blot out all thought processes, concentrate on featureless field of cerulean blue – another infallible trick for inducing sleep I read in another book. Feel pain in temples at sheer effort of keeping whole mental horizon sky-blue. Watch aghast and helpless as jet airliner flies in from lower edge, on way to Rome. Reminds me of worrying problem – where going for holidays? Must think. Must *not*! Sit up hastily. Discover another reason for sleeplessness – freezing cold, because no covers on.

Still awake! Hell and damnation! Outrageous injustice of

distribution of sleep in world! What sort of welfare state is this? What am I supposed to do – lie there till breakfast time without anyone caring? Go through life sleepless – while all around me sleep-millionaires are positively wallowing in the stuff? Must use the leisure to plot Insomniacs' Revolution, to take sleep from sleepers and redistribute to sleepless . . .

Hm. Greyness. Daybreak. Daybreak!? Quick, quick – relax muscles, think of sky, no, no, drink water, relax muscles, but first turn over, fling back covers, now relax muscles, drink water . . .

(1962)

No one could be kinder

You hear a lot about the growing harshness of life. You don't hear so much about the good side of things, though – the huge increase there has been in politeness and kindness.

In the old days, if you rang up Associated Swill Industries, what did they say? They said 'Associated Swill Industries.' Just like that. 'Associated Swill Industries.' Take it or leave it. Or more probably just 'Ndustries'. Because people on switchboards frequently didn't bother to turn on their microphones until they'd almost finished explaining who they were, so you were always talking to firms call 'Umpany', or 'Orporated', or 'Imited'.

It's completely different nowadays. 'Thank you for calling Associated Swill Industries!' they cry, with absolute delight. You're taken aback. You hadn't realised you were doing *them* a favour. You suddenly feel a warm glow, a slight lump in your throat. So, someone in this world does appreciate the efforts you make after all! Your ears are red. 'That's all right,' you feel like mumbling. 'Don't mention it.

My pleasure. Least I could do. Any time.'

But before you can say anything – on they go again. 'In what way may I help you?' they say – and you know, from the sheer eager eloquence of the words, that they really mean it. This is astonishing – you scarcely know these people! You find yourself saying: 'Well, I wouldn't mention it if I could think of any other way of doing it – but if you could possibly – I know this is a lot to ask – but I should be eternally grateful if you could somehow, well . . . *put this call through for me.*'

You were going to say 'To Customer Accounts' – you have a query about your bill. But now the words die on your lips. If someone takes the trouble to talk to you as lengthily as Associated Swill Industries now have, if they have told you how grateful they are to you, and begged you to tell them of any way in which they could possibly make your life better, then you can't just ask for Customer Accounts and start niggling about your bill. They offer you the moon – and you ask for Customer Accounts! It's an inadequate response. It's worse than that – it's a deliberate rebuff, a cold refusal of intimacy.

You feel you should explain about your personal problems. Ask them for advice about where to go on holiday, and how to get on with your parents-in-law – perhaps even request a small unsecured personal loan. Or would this be going too far? You've only known them for such a short while, after all. Though it seems much longer. In fact you suddenly feel as if you had been sitting there talking to Associated Swill Industries for half your life. So you ask if they could possibly put you through not to anywhere as mundane as Customer Accounts, but to the Chairman himself.

Then you can threaten him with legal action for the amount of your time and your capacity for emotional response that his firm has wasted.

I'm also rather overcome when people I've never met

before tell me, usually over a public address system, often on aircraft, that I'm *kindly requested* to do this, or not do that. In the bad old days they used to say, 'Will you kindly do this? Will you kindly not do that?' In other words they expected all the kindness to be provided by us in doing as they asked. Why should we have to start laying out stocks of kindness, when we're not getting paid for it? Particularly when we'd no idea in what spirit the request was being made. Were they requesting us kindly? Or were they doing it unkindly? Quite unfeelingly, perhaps – cruelly, even? And then they expect us to be kind to *them*!

Now we know that a warm heart and a generous nature are concealed behind that loudspeaker. I just wonder, though, if it's fair that they should have to tell us this themselves. Suppose there was no one to introduce a distinguished visiting lecturer, and he had to start off by telling us himself how witty and erudite he was, and how he was going to enlighten and entertain us!

Couldn't some of the switchboard operators who have spent so much time helping callers that their employers have gone into receivership – couldn't they travel aboard planes and introduce the speakers? They wouldn't be hampered by any lingering modesty. 'Mr Clake, your Director of Passenger Services, is known wherever aircraft fly not only for the kindness with which he makes his requests, but also for the refined accent that he does it in. Critics have praised the sheer courage and determination of his requesting, its exuberance, its technical virtuosity – and at the same time its engaging modesty. So, here, to ask you to leave the aircraft by the forward exit – the great requester himself! Ladies and gentlemen, will you please welcome – Mr Clake!'

Politeness hangs in the air these days even when there's no one there to utter it. It's not just switchboard operators who thank you for calling them – so do answering machines. Slot machines thank you for putting money into them. Tills send you courteous little bread-and-butter letters, as if you'd had them to stay for the weekend.

Towns and villages have been welcoming arriving motorists for many years – even at night, even in the rain, when there's no one around, and all the petrol stations and cafés are shut. But now so do railway stations. Welcome to Wolverhampton (High Level)! they cry silently. Welcome to West Wittering! The grimy paintwork is attempting to smile, the empty fire-buckets seem to be offering flowers. As they get the technology of politeness better even small suburban stations, deserted in the freezing dusk, will bank up the fire in the waiting-room for us. Invite us to stay to dinner with the vending machine. They are but humble establishments, notices will explain, but we should be welcome to share their modest fare, if we don't mind a simple bag of crisps, perhaps washed down with a cup of the local instant tea, or instant cocoa if we'd be kind enough to press the button on the right. They would account it an honour if we would spend the night on one of their broken benches, alongside any other derelicts who haven't yet been moved on by the police.

They do mean it all, do they? They're not just saying these things?

I'd be happier if they could offer us some reassurance about the spirit they were saying them in. 'You are kindly welcomed,' the notices on the stations might say. 'You are eloquently thanked,' the till receipts might cry. 'And we say this with absolute sincerity and deep conviction! If we had eyes there would be real tears in them! If we had hearts they would be overflowing most painfully! How can mere stove-enamelled signs, mere scraps of printed paper, adequately bear witness to the turbulence of the emotions surging through our keyboards, raging through our public conveniences? You are kindly requested to look in the till and see for yourself how full its heart is! You are benevolently begged to listen to the wind howling through the broken windows of the ticket-office, and hear for yourself its genuine sense of pain!'

And, finally convinced, we should fold the receipts carefully away next to our hearts, and press our lips against Network SouthEast's cold and rainswept logo.

(1994)

The normal fifth

The normal home contains a pet, and the normal pet is a cat or a budgerigar, according to the statistics in the Official Handbook published by the Central Office of Information. The normal man, it appears, spends the normal evening at home with his cat or his budgerigar in front of his television set.

The leader-writer in the *Daily Mail* is appalled by the piture the figures conjure up. 'What a miserable collection of stick-in-the-muds we are!' he writes. 'Why don't we go out and enjoy ourselves? Why don't we throng the streets, talk to our neighbours, or sit about in cafés just looking at people?'

Sit about in cafés just looking at people? Sit about in which cafés, just looking at what people? In the Nell Gwynne Tea Shoppe in the High Street? Looking at old Mrs Poorly and her friend Ida Know eating buttered scones?

And throng which streets, pray? Throng Delamere Gardens, NW12? Throng Jubilee Road, Screwe? There are some streets which in my experience are really pretty well unthrongable.

Anyway, whatever the pleasures of street-thronging, it's 'splendidly normal people' that the National Children Adoption Association are looking out for to become adoptive parents, according to the secretary in *The Times*. What seems splendidly normal to the NCAA turns out to be remarkably similar to what seems normal to the Central Office of Information, except that the NCAA's standards of normality are so searching that only one in five of their applicants turns out to be splendidly normal enough to qualify. The ideal couple, says the secretary, probably live in the outer suburbs, and have a middle-sized detached or semi-detached house with a garden. 'They are splendidly normal people, in good health and completely without neuroses now or in the past. He probably goes up to the City every day and she has no ambitions outside her home and her family. They usually have a pet – a cat or a budgerigar – and they don't have a lot of outside interests. But this doesn't mean to say they need to be exactly dull.'

Of course, when one hears about all the splendidly normal people like this, one cannot help worrying once again about the abnormal ones, and what can be done to help them. Because, let's face it, there *are* abnormal people around; we can't just shrug the problem off and pretend they don't exist.

Some of them have only mild abnormalities, such as living in large houses, or keeping dogs, which might disqualify them from adopting children, but which need not otherwise prevent them leading decent and useful lives.

But a few of them do suffer from gross abnormalities, like not working in the City. Progel, in 'The Abnormal Englishman,' identifies this condition as dysmetropolia, and attributes it to the absence or inadequacy of the patient's uncle-figures during adolescence. He sees working in other parts of the country as a subconscious evasion of reality – a symptom of neurosis allied to, and often co-present with, neurotic manifestations such as dropping aitches, doing manual work and playing out masochistic guilt-fantasies by refusing to earn a normal middle-sized salary.

Hergstrom takes a more radical view. He believes that everyone, however disturbed, *knows* somewhere inside him that he works in the City and lives in a middle-sized suburban house with a budgerigar, and that delusions to the contrary are merely hysterical.

McStride and Leastways, in their classic study 'Behaviour Patterns of Budgerigarlessness,' put more emphasis on learned reflexes. One of their most grossly disturbed patients presented an extraordinary range of symptoms. He lived in a *terraced house* in Sheffield, worked in a *factory,* and confessed that he often *went out in the evening.*

McStride and Leastways achieved a partial cure by attaching electrodes to the patient, and administering painful electric shocks when he went to work, and when he came home, and when he went out again at night. After prolonged treatment the patient moved to Nottingham, which was at any rate 37 miles along the road to recovery from his dysmetropolia. (When last heard of he was undergoing further conditioning therapy to overcome his irrational dread of electricity.)

The abnormality symptoms presented by women can sometimes be even more serious. In his survey of married women arrested for reading in Beckenham Public Library, Didbold estimates that there may be as many as 200 or even 300 married women in this country suffering from ambitions outside the home and family.

According to Meany, outside ambitions in women are the result of emotional deprivation in infancy, possibly aggravated by over-intense educational experience. He wants the Government to launch a crash programme for the early detection of unnatural ambition, and warns that if nothing is done the country may in a year or two's time face a full-scale epidemic.

In both men and women, ambitions and interests outside the home tend to be the most dangerous abnormalities, if allowed to go unchecked. Strabolgi, for instance, has demonstrated a definite correlation between extra-domiciliary interests and certain forms of criminal behaviour. In his sample of 317 men and women in the Barnet area, *not one* committed burglary, simony, or robbery with violence while sitting at home watching the television.

It's true that 14 were later convicted of tax offences, six of wounding their wives, and one of strangling his budgerigar.

But that's normal.

(1967)

Now then

My feeling that archaeology is not so much an exact science as a sort of high-class blind man's buff has been considerably fortified by the Knossos affair. Professor L. R. Palmer has just proved that Knossos in Crete was not, as had been supposed, the cradle of European civilisation, but simply another offshoot of the Mycenaean Empire on the Greek mainland.

Apparently Sir Arthur Evans, who excavated Knossos, grossly misreported what he found, and as a result dated it all some two hunded years too early. Even leaving misreporting aside, the archaeological evidence from which the course of prehistory is deduced is dark, ambiguous stuff. One of the clues which put Professor Palmer on the trail in the Knossos case, for example, was a sentence in a Minoan Linear B script from another site which had previously been translated as 'Aigeus the Cretan brought it' but which he amended after further study of the handwriting to 'of Cretan workmanship with goats' head handles'.

You can see the difficulties facing archaeologists by imagining what they will conclude when, 2,000 years from now, they dig down through the hundred feet of soil which covered Britain after the Great Nuclear War in 1965, and excavate what turns out to be the remains of your house. Professor Snodgrass's report runs (as closely as it will go in English):

The excavation was our first glimpse into that period of prehistory about which almost nothing is known, the Neoplastic Age. Although only a few fragments of the site were intact, we were fortunate enough to find several letter-containers (not unlike our modern envelopes) obviously addressed to the Neoplastic occupant of the site, which established his identity as a man called On Her Majesty's Service.

On Her Majesty's Service, or On as he was probably called for short, was clearly a priest, and the building he occupied a temple. Several things point to this – particularly the steel box found in one of the chambers which contained the mummified remains of offerings to the gods – the severed leg of a sheep and the carcase of a chicken, both of which seemed to have been subjected to some ritual treatment by fire. The box also contained an exquisitely worked glass container, presumably for holding holy oil, inscribed in raised letters with the magical rubric 'United Dairies'.

In one of the chambers we found a letter that On had kept in its original envelope, which suggests he placed some considerable value on it. Professor Grabowski, our philologist, has been unable so far to translate it exactly, but the address at the top is clearly a town called Income Tax in the province of Demand Note.

Our most valuable find was perhaps that of the holy texts used in the temple – four enormous, closely printed volumes of verse in head-rhyme. They are as yet imperfectly understood, but Professor Grabowski believes he has isolated a primitive creation legend in one of them. The first few lines are reproduced below. (The expressions in the righthand column are probably responsions to be made by the congregation as the priest read aloud):

A1 Adhesives Ltd, Arlington Avenue Wks,
   Arlington Av., N1   CANonbry 7126
A1 Bureau, 66 Peckham Rd, SE5   RODney 4581
A1 Café, 299 Borough High St, SE1   HOP 3294

There is no doubt about where the rites were performed – a small chamber set apart as a holy of holies, big enough for only the priest to enter. The central object in the chamber is a hollowed-out altar, about waist-high, and made of white porcelain. To it are affixed a pair of metal figurines representing seated gods, one inscribed with the name 'Hot', the other 'Cold'.

It was perhaps fanciful, but as we stood in that holy place it required but little imagination to see before us On Her Majesty's Service, one of the last Neoplastic men, offering up a sheep's leg to the implacable Hot and Cold, chanting the endless litany of the Post Office Telephone Directory (London Postal Area), as the congregation in the outer chamber roared forth 'CANonbry 7126 . . . RODney 4581 . . . HOP 3294 . . .' It is of such moments of insight as these that the stuff of archaeology is woven.

(1960)

Oh, un peu, vous savez, un peu

Considering how much at home middle-class intellectuals like you and me feel in the presence of the middle-class intellectuals from the rest of Europe we meet on holiday, it's astonishing how little we can actually communicate. Or, to put in another way, considering the ratio of effort to information in those long holiday sessions of laboured English or paraplegic French, it's amazing we can go on seeing ourselves as having that broad understanding of the world we feel so comfortably in the abstract.

It's different for the spying classes, of course. If the novels do not lie, any plain English spy having difficulties in Bulgaria, say, finds that the smattering of Bulgarian he picked up from collecting stamps as a boy is quite adequate for passing himself off as a used horse dealer from Plovdiv. And when in Chapter 16 he finds himself in the clutches of the notorious Bulgarian police chief, Colonel Khaskovo, communication doesn't falter for an instant.

'So, my friend,' says Khaskovo in beautifully starched English, 'your foolish inquisitiveness has necessitated our taking certain precautions. It grieves me deeply, believe me, that you will unfortunately not be in a position to appreciate the full fiendish ingenuity with which your so clumsy blunderings will be brought to an end.'

How different it all is when the kindly-looking lady at the next table in the *pensione,* whom one for some reason takes to be a German, tries to establish some elementary communication by showing a polite interest in one's child. Taking one to be French, she remarks:

'Quel âge?'

In any other circumstances the phrase would be transparently comprehensible. But somehow, spoken in an

Italian *pensione* by a woman one takes to be German, a curious obscurity hangs over it. Kellarzh? Kellarzh? Ah, I see – 'Qu'elle large!' – obviously Teutonic pidgin French for 'How wide she is!'

'Er, ja,' one says, tactfully helping the poor soul back into her native language.

'Jahr? Ein Jahr?'

'Ja. Er, ja.'

'Ein Jahr! Fantastisch!'

'Oh, *Jahr*. Er, nein Jahr. I mean . . .'

'*Nine* Jahr? Neun year?'

'Oh, nein, nein!'

'Neun Monat? Neuf mois?'

'Nein nine! I mean, nein neun. Nicht nein – er, neun. Er, excuse me – ich muss à la plage, er, gehen.'

Of course, one gets beyond this stage, because the woman and her husband (who are in fact Psychomanian) turn out to speak quite good English. But the further one gets beyond, the heavier the going becomes. For one curious thing, they admire and wish to discuss a whole Pantheon of famous Englishmen of whom one has never oneself heard.

What do we think of Spencer Philips, the philosopher? Oh, really? In their country he is *very* widely read. How privileged we are to belong to the nation that has produced Gordon Roberts, the great modern dramatist, and Philip Gordons, the celebrated novelist. *No?* In their country even the children read translations of them. We shall be saying next that we have never heard of Gordon Spencer, the sociologist, or the world-famous Spencer Roberts, whose political writings have had such an influence on modern Psychomanian thinking!

One tries to return the national compliment, by expressing one's admiration for that grand old man of Psychomanian letters, Sigismund Cortex. Or does one mean Siegfried Catalept? Either way they haven't heard of him.

Worse, whatever level a conversation starts on, it soon comes sprawling down among an unavoidable undergrowth of explanation and counter-explanation. One may start by talking about the ethical well-springs of government, say, but within minutes one is down with one's face in this sort of mud:

'Ah, I must explain. In our country, in each small part of land we have committee governing. What is this called in English?'

'Rural district councils, perhaps?'

'Rura distry council. Yes. In each divided part of land is rura distry council. But in the towns also is rura distry council.'

'No, in the towns we call them urban district councils. Or do I mean borough councils?'

'Yes. Of course, the urban distry councils are the underdogs – idiomatic word I learned – the underdogs of the rura distry councils.'

'Oh, no.'

'In our country oh yes. In our country in the country – can I say that? – is also what you call *country* councils. But I think our country councils are not just the same as your country councils. I must explain . . .'

I sometimes wonder if Colonel Khaskovo and his friend were correctly reported. What the dreaded Bulgarian police chief really said, I suspect, in the confusion of at last confronting the British master-spy in the secret atomic pile was:

'Mein Gott! Wer ist dies?'

'Wer?' repeats the British master of espionage stupidly, his grasp of German interrogative pronouns slipping somewhat in the stress of the moment. 'Dies ist die Pile.'

'D. Pile?' repeats the Colonel, momentarily taken aback. 'Nicht J. Standish, of British Intelligence?'

'Oh, who, ich?'

'O. Whuish or J. Standish is no matter. Lay down your arms and put up your arms. Can I say that?'

'Hands.'

'Ah, hands, yes. I must explain. I have a firehand here, and if you are not putting up your arms I will pull the – what is in English the little thing hereunder which when one is pulling it makes bang bang . . . ?'

Yes, as our wonderful English poet Markson Spencer said: North is north and south is south/ They can only talk with their foot in their mouth.

(1962)

On the receiving end

> I see . . . I see . . . Yes, yes . . . I see . . .
> Oh, really . . . ? Is that so . . . ?
> I see . . . I see . . . ! Good Lord . . . ! Good God . . . !
> No . . . ! Heavens . . . ! Really . . . ? *No* . . . !
>
> You *didn't* . . . ! Did you . . . ? How fantastic . . . !
> Of course . . . Oh, naturally . . .
> Fantastic . . . No . . . ! Incredible . . . !
> An *albatross* . . . ! Blow me . . . !

This is an extract from my long poem: 'The Rime of the Wedding-Guest'. My intention is that it should be recited, or rather murmured, simultaneously with the recitation of 'The Rime of the Ancient Mariner' as a sort of accompanying ostinato.

The position of the man who tells a story has been very fully explored in literature, of course – but the role and problems of the person who has a story told to him have scarcely been touched upon. It's not as easy as it looks to be on the receiving end. One has to find ways of expressing one's continued interest and comprehension – whether sincerely or not – without interrupting the flow, and yet without seeming to have passed into a state of trance, or of mindless repetitive grunting.

Where do you look, for a start? The narrator's eyes seem the logical place. But which eye – the left or the right? And can one stand gazing at either of them for more than a few seconds at a time?

A psychologist called Michael Argyle has been doing some experiments on this sort of problem at Oxford. The farther away his subjects sat from their interlocutor, he found, the more they kept their eyes on the interlocutor's eyes during the conversation. The closer the subjects sat, the more they tended to avoid the interlocutor's eyes (I suspect because of this difficulty of deciding which eye to choose at close range). The optimum distance turned out to be between four and six feet.

But even at this distance the subjects were noticeably disconcerted when the interlocutor's eyes were concealed behind dark glasses; and more disconcerted still when the eyes were visible but the rest of the interlocutor was hidden.

The Ancient Mariner, of course, was partially concealed behind a long grey beard, from the midst of which he held the Wedding-Guest with his glittering eye. He also held him with his skinny hand, which suggests an eyeball-to-eyeball distance of two feet or less. The whole situation for the Wedding-Guest, on Argyle's showing, can scarcely have been more disturbing. No wonder that he left afterwards like one that hath been stunn'd, and that a sadder and a wiser man he rose the morrow morn.

And while one shifts one's gaze uneasily about between right eye, left eye, and Adam's apple, one hears the sort of depressing subarticulate noise issuing from one's lips which occupies the Wedding-Guest in my poem from stanza 57 to stanza 79 inclusive. Thus:

Um, um . . . um, um . . . yep, yep . . . um, um . . .
Aha . . . uh-huh . . . ah . . . oh . . . ?

Sure . . . quite . . . uh-huh . . . yep, yep . . . yop, yop . . .
Yup, yup . . . aha . . . oho . . .

And one nods. Or I nod. I can't stop myself – there seems
to be some direct link between my eardrums and my
nodding muscles.

I find myself nodding even when I'm only one among an
audience of many. Lecturers catch sight of me, nodding
away in apparently eager agreement with every point they
make, and they gradually get round to delivering the
lecture exclusively to me, unmindful of my surreptitious
attempts to seize hold of my head and keep it still.

But it's worse to be an audience of one among one, as on
guided tours of remote caves and castles on rainy days in
late September. When I was an undergraduate I attended a
course of lectures with an audience which dwindled swiftly
as the weeks went by from six to one. The one was me, and
I couldn't dwindle any further because the lecturer was my
supervisor, which encouraged him to take the liberty of
calling to collect me on his way to the lecture-room.

They were nine o'clock lectures, and on several occasions I
was in bed when he arrived. He would wait politely while
I got up and got dressed. Then we would walk to the
lecture-room together, and I would sit down somewhere
around row three, while he leant over the lectern and
delivered at me the lecture he had always given at nine
o'clock on that particular Wednesday of the Michaelmas
term ever since he had first written it as a young graduate
in 1915 or so.

If I so much as blew my nose or glanced out of the
window, of course, he'd lost his entire audience. It was a
fearful responsibility. I thought several times that I'd have
nodded my head right off on to the floor by ten o'clock.

One feels an overwhelming need in this sort of situation
to vary the nodding and grunting with a few intelligent
questions. One of the reasons the Wedding-Guest has such

a glazed look in my poem from stanzas 13 to 21 is that he's working out some keen questions for stanza 22, which goes:

> What was the tonnage of this ship?
> For what port was she bound?
> And was she gimbel-rigged, or gyved?
> And were her gaskets sound?

Then he's looking glazed again from stanzas 72 to 79 because he's thinking, My God, it's 50 stanzas now since I last made an articulate remark of any sort! I must tell the old boy some anecdote about myself, to show how much I sympathise. So in stanza 80 he suddenly compresses his lips and looks into the distance and says:

> It's odd, you know, your saying this,
> Because when I was staying
> At Brightlingsea I hired a boat . . .
> – I'm sorry, you were saying . . . ?

Because the old bloke is just sweeping on regardless – and getting all the credit from the critics.

Take my advice: Don't wait to be told – get telling first.

(1967)

On the subject of objects

I expect you're pretty used to people lying here in your consulting-room and telling you the most terrible things about themselves, aren't you, Dr Wienerkreis? I mean, thinking they've got all sorts of frightful things wrong with them which turn out to be nothing but . . . ?

Yes, well, anyway, the point is, Dr Wienerkreis, I'm

suffering from, I mean, I think I might possibly have got a
. . . well, *a serendipity deficiency.*

I mean, I never *find* things. Everyone I know but me
seems to find things. What sort of things? Well, they find,
sort of, *objects.* They come across fantastic sea-shells on the
beach. They stumble on oddly shaped pieces of wood in
fields. They glance into a junk shop and pick up an elegant
brass letter balance for seven-and-six, say, or an amusing
Victorian steel engraving for tenpence-halfpenny. Well,
you know, *objects.*

What? Well, they take them home and arrange them as
it were casually in their living-rooms. What do they do
then? Well, I suppose they look at them. I mean, they're
intriguing things. I suppose they look at them and
feel intrigued. When they have guests the guests look at
them and feel intrigued.

For example, we have some friends called the Crumbles.
When one goes into the Crumbles' living-room one's surrounded on all sides by patch-boxes, astrolabes, sticks of
Victorian rock, model Dreadnoughts, lumps of quartz-
porphyry, eighteenth-century milking stools, Chinese tooth-
picks. One's intrigued. It gives one something to talk about.

What does one say? Well, I don't know, one says perhaps
'What's this intriguing little object, then?' Something like
that. And Christopher Crumble says, more or less. *'That?
Oh, that's an early Georgian dentist's forceps I found by
sheerest chance at a little shop I know down in Devizes.'* Or
something along those lines. Well, then you're away on a
sort of whimsical-cultural, or cultural-whimsical, conversation that will see you through until the soup's on the table.

I know, I know . . . Of course I don't think everyone collects
intriguing objects. Some people collect beer-mats and
miniature liqueur bottles. Some people collect Louis XV
candle-snuffers or Baroque doorknobs. But the people I know
are too sophisticated for beer-mats and too poor for Baroque
doorknobs. So they collect amusing objects. The point is, Dr

Wienerkreis, I have a social context I have to try to fit into.

The trouble is, the fields I walk through are just full of earth. Whenever I look into a junk shop the contents consist exclusively of junk. I never see any amusing Victorian ship's chronometers. All I see is heaps of rusty ice-skates, broken clockwork trains, warped rattan cakestands, and chipped mauve cocktail sets that someone got for 1,700 cigarette tokens in 1938. The only thing I've ever found anywhere is the word *serendipity,* which I came across by absolute chance in a little dictionary I know . . .

Yes, of course it matters. When the Crumbles come to dinner with us they're surrounded by great quantities of nothing. Yes, nothing at all. Well, to be absolutely precise, I suppose there are usually a few things lying around like plastic giveaways out of cereal packets, week-old copies of the *Daily Mirror,* broken sunglasses, bits of paper with 'No milk Sunday' written on them, that sort of thing.

I mean, our living-room is a cultural desert. You can't expect people to say '*Where did you get this intriguing little "Daily Mirror" from?*' You can't show guests the plastic television personalities, and explain how you just picked them up by sheerest chance as they fell out of a little Fungles packet you know down behind the refrigerator.

Of course, the plastic television personalities may come to be amusing objects in time. By the turn of the century the graciously ageing Crumbles may well have a small but distinguished collection of them in their living-room, together with an amusing old wireless valve, a highly intriguing Dun-in-a-Jiff patent potato peeler (c. 1960), and a number of nostalgically beautiful and rather valuable photographs from *Reveille* of *le pin-up de cheesecake* school. Not us, though – we'll just have a couple of week-old number of the *Times-Mirror* and some broken bits of the central heating reactor lying on the floor.

I need help, Dr Wienerkreis. Help myself? You mean,

practise? Start off modestly and work up to normal serendipity by easy stages?

I see what you mean. I could begin by arranging the old *Daily Mirrors* and the broken sunglasses in a tasteful way Is that the sort of thing you have in mind? Then I could try finding slightly unusual looking pebbles and bits of twig. I could buy some of the less rusty ice-skates and the less chipped mauve cocktail-shakers. Then I could gradually work back through 1930s toothbrush-holders, 1920s false teeth, and Edwardian rubber dog-bones, to Diamond Jubilee shoe-trees and Great Exhibition bradawls.

But Dr Wienerkreis, I have a bad block here – I'd feel such a damned fool having an Edwardian rubber dog-bone about the house without having an Edwardian dog to chew it. Do you think I'd get over that? I'm afraid I might retreat into gross psychotic delusion – decide I was the only one who was sane, and start writing articles trying to make everyone else feel a damned fool for not feeling a damned fool.

(1963)

Our pleasure, Captain!

Good morning, ladies and gentlemen. My name's Thork, Peter Thork, I'm one of the passengers, I'm sitting in seat 33B . . .

Could we just have a bit of hush in the cabin . . . ? A bit of hush, please . . . ! Thank you. I haven't got a microphone, I'm afraid, unlike Captain Mellowdew! So I'll just have to shout. Can you hear me at the front? Can the cabin attendants hear me . . . ? And Captain Mellowdew and his crew . . . ?

Good. Right. Ladies and gentlemen – Captain Mellowdew and his crew – Director of Passenger Services Clake and his cabin staff – fellow-passengers . . . I won't keep you for long. I only want to say a few words in reply to the various very charming speeches we've heard from Mr Clake and Captain Mellowdew.

I have to fly quite a lot – I'm in international consultancy – and I sometimes can't help feeling a bit ashamed of the way we all just sit here and take the really kind and heart-warming speeches we always hear from the crew so much for granted. I thought that just for once someone ought to get up on his hind legs and say a word or two in reply.

So let me assure Mr Clake that we will indeed keep our seat-belts fastened when the sign is on, and that we won't smoke in the toilets. Thank you, Mr Clake, for your concern.

We were all, I think, particularly touched to be welcomed on board by Captain Mellowdew in person. We know how busy he must be up there on the flight deck, and I think we all very much appreciated his finding a moment to talk to us. Particularly since he stressed that he was speaking not only for himself, but on behalf of all his crew, including his First Officer, Mr Timmins, and the Flight Engineer, Mr Huckle. I'd just like to say that we're very pleased to *be* here – and I know I'm speaking on behalf of at any rate Mr Ted Trice, in seat 33A beside me, and Mr G. T. Waddell in seat 33C.

Mr Clake, you'll remember, told us that he was being assisted by Cheryl and Shiree in the forward cabin, and by Lorraine, Fontana, Pearline, and Coralie in the aft cabin. I hope they'll forgive me if I've missed anyone out. Captain Mellowdew was kind enough to say that Mr Clake and his team would be doing their best to make our trip enjoyable. Let me assure him that their efforts are being highly successful, and that we are all enjoying ourselves hugely.

Captain Mellowdew – if I may address myself to you for a moment, if I may be personal – you said something else that particularly touched me. You thanked us for flying with you. I don't know about the others, but for some reason your words really touched a chord in me. I know how easy it is to take it for granted that people will get on your plane. I know how easy it is just to fly off without a word, get people to their destination, and never stop to appreciate their kindness in coming along. It means a lot to us, to know that the contribution we make on these occasions has been noted.

So let me tell you, Captain Mellowdew, very sincerely, what an honour it is for us to be able to play our part. We know things have been a little difficult for this airline in the past year, what with the record trading losses, and that slight mishap one of your planes had on touchdown at . . . well, on a happy occasion like this I don't want to intrude upon what must be a very sensitive area. I'm confident, though, that when the report of the inquiry is published the blame will be put firmly on the local air-traffic control. And if we've been able to help just a little bit with the money side of things then it's all been worth while. What are passengers for, after all?

And, Captain Mellowdew, thank you so much for that very helpful information you gave us about the height we were flying at. I guessed it was 32,000 feet, Mr Trice thought 34,000. So when you told us it was in fact 33,000, we both felt our minds had been put at rest. Well worth being woken up for!

It occurs to me that you up there on the flight deck might like to know a little more about what's going on back here in the cabin. Well, some of us have been sleeping – or trying to! – and some of us have been reading or working. I couldn't help noting that Mr Trice was doing his expenses during the early part of the route, and that Mr Waddell has been wearing his headphones, lost in a world of his own. Mr Trice, I should perhaps tell you, informs me that he has a little back trouble, but I gather it's not too serious, and it's not expepted to hold him up today.

So God bless you, Captain Mellowdew! And you, Mr

Timmins and Mr Huckle! And you, Mr Clake, and you, Cheryl and Shiree in the forward cabin, together with Lorraine, Fontana, Pearline, and Coralie in the aft cabin! We won't forget you! We look forward to travelling with you again very soon. And I personally, now I've got started, look forward to the chance of letting you hear this very same speech, many, many more times in the future. Thank you.

(1994)

Outside story

. . . So, provided the scheme to build low-cost weekend housing on the estate is accepted by the local planning authority, it looks as if the cherry orchard itself has been saved from the axe. More on that later. Now back to the main story of the evening. Are you there, Michael?

Yes, Trevor, I am.

How are things outside the National Theatre?

Well, it's a fine night out here, Trevor, with a bit of a breeze off the river. But inside it's pretty tense. The good news is that they're still in there, and they're still talking. Some of the talking, by all accounts, has been pretty tough – Hamlet himself, I gather, has not pulled his punches. It's been a long evening – this is the feeling here – and it's going to go on for quite a bit longer yet.

Any developments in the situation since we last talked to you?

Trevor, it's too early to tell. But I was talking to someone who was inside the theatre in the last half-hour or so, and he said there were plans at court for a bit of a family get-together, which must I think be a good sign.

A get-together?

I understand it involves some sort of home theatricals.

No fears that the King might be tempted to take a tougher line?

Oh, I don't think so, Trevor.

There were some pretty wild allegations flying about earlier.

Yes, but there is a great determination here not to let the peace process be derailed, and most of the people I've spoken to remain pretty hopeful about the outcome.

There's no sense of déjà-vu *about all this?*

Yes, Trevor, some old hands have been saying 'We've seen all this before, and if we don't learn from past mistakes we could just end up with a real disaster on our hands.'

So the next hour or two could be crucial?

They could, Trevor, but the King has already brought two younger men on to his team who are known to be close to Hamlet, in a very clear gesture of conciliation. It may or may not be significant that the Prince is to make an official visit to England, which should help to take the steam out of the situation a little.

Is the Prince showing any signs of strain?

He has been showing some signs of the enormous pressure he is under, yes. He's made a number of major speeches in the last hour or two, but quite what effect they've had on opinion here it's too early to tell.

Is that the Prince we can see now, just behind you?

No, that's one of the local dossers being thrown out of the theatre by security men. If you'd been here earlier you'd have seen quite a lot of coming and going just behind me there. Quite a lot of stiff drinks being drunk. Quite a lot of visits to the toilets. But things have quietened down in the last few minutes.

So you feel the signs are good?

I'm pretty hopeful, Trevor, provided they can just keep talking. They've been talking now for the best part of two hours, and the longer they go on the more likely it is we're going to see them shake hands and issue a joint communiqué.

But if the talks do break down . . . ?

Then it's anybody's guess. The consequences are incalculable. We could, I think, see a distinct worsening of relations. We might even end up with the King and the Prince not on speaking terms.

No chance that it could even end in violence?

Well, we hope it won't come to that! It's in everybody's interest to keep calm and behave sensibly. They'll probably keep us all on tenterhooks until the last possible moment, but the smart money here is on wedding bells before too long.

Michael Brunson, thank you. Now, the rest of the news. Fire broke out this evening in Valhalla, home of many of the world's best-known gods. Local fire chiefs say that the blaze is now under control. And in Spain a wealthy playboy has had the novel idea of inviting a statue to dinner! The statue duly turned up, and by all accounts thoroughly enjoyed its evening out. That's it for now! Have a good weekend.

(1994)

Pas devant les enfants

It's not television which is the greatest threat to the art of conversation, in my experience; it's children.

The Victorians were certainly a hundred years ahead of their time on this problem, with their doctrine of children being seen and not heard. If the children are heard then any adults present are not; and the Victorians, with their usual sensitive concern for parent-care, realised that the most frightful psychic damage could be inflicted upon adults whose natural drive to communication and self-expression was persistently frustrated.

What I don't quite understand, though, is the Victorians' inexplicable permissiveness in letting children be *seen*. A child, at any rate a small child, doesn't need to be heard to disrupt all rational intercourse in the vicinity; its visible presence is quite enough.

A child is rather like a television set, in fact – and turning the sound down when company comes isn't enough to prevent all eyes in the room from being irresistibly drawn towards it. How often has one seen a whole roomful of normally artictulate adults sitting bemused around their assembled offspring, bereft of all powers of speech, apart from the sort of desultory facetious comment which is usually reserved for the Westerns? And television sets have the great advantage that they can be switched off.

Of course, if children are disruptive with the sound turned down, they're worse still when it's turned up. Sound and vision tend to be deployed to their fullest communication-destroying effect just when a matter of some delicacy and importance has to be conveyed between husband and wife. Just when Mr Ricardo was trying to explain to Mrs Ricardo about Marginal Utility – that's when the children would have switched on the jammers: just when the Tsar and Tsarina were discussing whether to invade Poland next season.

Or take the afternoon that Pythagoras came out of his study looking rather pleased with himself.

'You know this work I've been doing recently on hypotenuses?' he says to his wife, trying to sound casual. 'Well, a rather interesting point struck me this afternoon – I don't know whether you think it sounds reasonable – that the square on the hypotenuse must be equal to . . .'

But at this point a ringing cry from the lavatory interrupts the exposition.

'Will you wipe my b-o-o-o-t-tom!'

'Sorry,' says his wife when she gets back. 'What were you saying? Something about hypotenuses.'

'I was just going to say that the square on the hypotenuse . . .'

'Mummy!'

'Sh, Jemima! Daddy's talking.'

'. . . that the square on the hypotenuse is equal to . . .'

'But *Mummy* . . .'

'*Sh,* Jemima! You musn't interrupt when someone's speaking! How many times have I had to tell you?'

'. . . equal to the sum of the squares on the other two sides!'

'I see. Now, what's the trouble, Jemima?'

'James is being horrible to me! He's taken my zoetrope!'

'James, give Jemima back her zoetrope at once! Sorry, Py. What were you saying?'

'I said it.'

'All hypotenuses are equal . . . ?'

'God give me strength! Why do you *never* listen to what I say? I said the square on the hypotenuse is equal to the sum . . .'

'The what?'

'The *sum* . . . the SUM . . . ! My God. I can't hear myself speak! Will you SHUT UP, you two! If I hear one more word out of either of you, I'll throw that damned zoetrope into the Aegean, and that'll be the end of it! Now, the *square* on the *hypotenuse* . . .'

'Yes, yes, I got that bit . . . Just a moment – James, what *have* you been doing to your face . . . ? Well, go and wash it off at once . . . Sorry – "the square on the hypotenuse" – I *am* listening . . . Don't just rub it on your sleeve, James . . . ! Sorry, Py, but if he's left to go wandering round in that condition there'll be shaving cream all over the house . . . Anyway, the square on the hypotenuse . . .'

'Will you wipe my b-o-o-o-o-t-tom!'

It's Pythagoras's turn this time. 'Where were we?' he asks wearily when he returns. 'Oh, yes, the square on the hypotenuse. Well, all I was going to say was that it's equal to the sum of the squares . . . *Now* what are you doing? What the hell do you keep turning round for?'

'Sorry – I was just trying to see why Jemima was so quiet all of a sudden.'

'Oh, for God's sake!'

'Go on about the square on the hypotenuse.'

'It was nothing.'

'Don't be silly.'

'It wasn't of the slightest importance . . . Well, I was merely going to say that it was equal to the sum of the squares on the other two sides. That's all.'

'But, Py, that's absolutely *fascinating*! I'd never have guessed it! Marvellous . . . ! What is Jemima up to, by the way? Is she sulking? Can you see? She's not sucking her thumb, is she?'

'Yes . . . No . . . I don't know! She's not there . . . Look, are you interested in my work on the hypotenuse or aren't you?'

'Of course I am. I think it's tremendously important . . . I'd better just make sure she hasn't wandered out into the street . . .'

'I mean, I don't care whether you are or not. I just

thought you *were,* that's all. It's just that once upon a time
you used to *ask* me . . .'

'Will you wipe my b-o-o-o-o-t-tom!'

It's the trailing clouds of glory which Wordsworth
observed hanging about children – that's what really dis-
rupts communication. Glorious-looking clouds, certainly;
but when you're in amongst them, like most clouds, pretty
well indistinguishable from dense fog.

(1967)

Plain speaking on S'Agaro

Having just come back from a holiday in Spain I can tell
you one thing about that part of the world; they speak a
pretty peculiar sort of language down there. I was given
a trilingual guidebook to the Costa Brava – or, rather, to
what it insisted on calling the 'main accidents' of the area
– which has tied several reef-knots and a running bowline
in my powers of communication. The accident the author
cares most about is a town called S'Agaro. Well, it's a non-
town. I mean, it's a happy conjuncture. I mean – well, let
him explain it:

S'AGARO TODAY

S'Agaro is neither a town nor a history: S'Agaro is a
happy conjuncture, an inquietude felt since few years
– 25 – and in its boundaries, everthing except the
Nature is recent. This is why S'Agaro becomes
unistakable.

Besides being a personal discovery (it is known to be
the work of the sole man) it is a harmony become
possible where heretofore was not anything else than
savage rocks, rough, full with thick woods and wild

vegetation, where the beach of San Pol, belonging to San Feliu de Guixols, ended. Mr Ensesa felt once the calling of S'Agaro. that landscape, hostile and rejected, was keenly studied with the collaboration of the architect Mr Santiago Maso Valenti. After four years they gave rise to this light and wonderful reality of the S'Agaro of today, abridgement of beauty, harmony, good taste, and selectness.

The general plann, ruled to the least details, has become his miracle of synchronism in the style and the ambient. The buildings in their totality the same as the wonderful gardens and works to embellish the whole urbinisation have followed the same rule and have not deserted the collective soul. There is not in S'Agaro a single eccentricity for the edge of those architectonic monsters with which another urbinisations are so full . . . In S'Agaro the tourist finds that 'it' he missed. This 'it' so social, and elegant, so subtle and poetic. Within its district the whole 'grand monde' collects in formal parties, international sport contests, all this gives it the fame that enjoys everywhere in the world.

After this, the author apparently felt too confused and exhausted to go on to 'S'Agaro, Tomorrow.' But here, for those who care, is a play entitled *S'Agaro, Yesterday*, an unhappy conjuncture of inquietudes I shall be putting on out there before the grand monde next season. All cheques for tickets should be made payable to the English-Speaking Union.

(Scene: S'Agaro heretofore. Not anything else is there than savage rocks, rough, full with wild orange peel. On that savage rock sits Mr Ensesa and Mr Valenti, neither towns nor histories, but a felicitous condouble-ment of humane beings.)

Mr Ensesa *(jumping upwards)*: I felt the calling of S'Agaro!

Mr Valenti: Make no attention, Mr Ensesa. It is probably just an inquietude felt since eating bad paella for lunch.

S'Agaro *(calling)*: Mr Ensesa!

Mr Ensesa *(excitedly)*: The calling is now a two-timing re-duplicature!

(They keenly study that landscape, hostile and rejected.)

Mr Ensesa: I am missing 'it', Mr Valenti. In all that wild waste of broken sun-tan-lotion bottles is not 'it'.

Mr Valenti: You mean that 'it' so explicative, so deliquescent, so uneccentric, Mr Ensesa?

Mr Ensesa: It is unistakable. We are missing the 'big world' (I translate, of course) collecting in formal parties to play clock-golf and international deck-quoits contests. We are missing – how we say it in Spanish – the *'pesetas'*.

Mr Valenti: Permit me to urbanise this unfelicitous inquietude, Mr Ensesa. I am architect, well known for urbanising without a single eccentricity for the edge of those architectonic monsters with which some urbinisations I could mention are so full.

Mr Ensesa: If your plans are as harmonious as your words, Mr Valenti, S'Agaro will indeed be a dish for the dogs. Can you give rise to abridgments?

Mr Valenti: Abridgments, atunnelments, ahousements, anything.

Mr Ensesa: Then give rise to an abridgment of beauty, harmony, good taste and selectness.

(While Mr Valenti savagely abridges these, reducing them to mere shadows of their former selves, a kind of prophetic radiance plays about Mr Ensesa's head.)

Mr Ensesa *(rhapsodically)*: In years to come, all the peoples will be regarding our happy inquietude and calling it 'a miracle of synchronism in the style and the ambient.' Or maybe 'a stylistic synchro-mesh in ambulating mirror-cells.' Or perhaps even 'an ambidextrous cyclotron called Mirabelle Stylites.'

(He stops to consider the point, but by this time, so thoroughly has Mr Valenti abridged everything, the curtain has come down and the band is playing 'God Save Our Gracious Dictator.' Oh, well, I've just realised what the guidebook is getting at when it calls S'Agaro an inquietude and happy conjuncture – it means it's a noisy but cheerful joint. Let's dance.)

(1960)

Please be seated

Breakfast in bed – there's nothing like it! Nothing like it for making you realise what wonderful inventions the table and chair are.

The position forced upon you by having breakfast in bed is a torment in itself. Making prisoners sit up with their legs straight out in front of them and their back unsupported is (I hope) outlawed under United Nations conventions on torture. But now here you are, not detained without charge in the jails of a Third World dictatorship, but on a well-earned holiday in a rather expensive hotel covered by the protocols of the European Community, and your wife has said that she would like breakfast in bed, so the humanitarian efforts of the United Nations do not apply.

But, as the meal proceeds, your position deteriorates still further. You have of course been eating with extreme circumspection so as not to get toast-crumbs into the bed. You have stomach-cramp from leaning forwards over the tray, and in fact you haven't even touched the toast, because you're not such a fool as to think you can eat toast in bed in any way at all, even with a bag over your head, without getting the crumbs into the bed with you. You have eaten nothing so far but the grapefruit – and you haven't even eaten the grapefruit, because trying to prise the segments free shook the tray, and made the coffeepot rock wildly from side to side. In spite of all this care, however, crumbs have mysteriously begun to break off the toast of their own accord, and creep surreptitiously off the tray and down into the sheets. These toast-crumbs, by the feel of it, are now enjoying breakfast in bed themselves. The breakfast they are enjoying is you.

With extreme circumspection, since you have this complex array of uneaten toast and brimming hot liquids balanced across your knees, you shift your bottom away from the crumbs. So now you are no longer quite sitting up. You are sustaining yourself at a slight angle to the vertical, in even more flagrant contravention of international law. Gradually the angle increases, and you begin to slide down the bed. The strain becomes unbearable. But, since you don't wish to share the bed with half-a-litre of scalding coffee as well as the toast-crumbs, you do not make any of the sudden or convulsive movements that you long to make. You put your hands on the bed and gently . . . gently . . . ease yourself . . . together with the tray on top of you . . . into a better position.

But now you realise with dismay that the butter and marmalade which have somehow got on your fingers, in spite of your never having touched them, have transferred themselves to the sheets. The entire bed is becoming a toast and marmalade sandwich. You look for the napkin to clean things up. It has withdrawn in a cowardly manner to the relative safety of the floor. You lean with infinite precaution sideways over the edge of the bed to reach it . . . The napkin seems be withdrawing still further as your fingers approach. For one brief moment you take your eye off the tray to see what's going on . . . And at that moment the tray moves quietly and decisively out of the horizontal.

I see why bed-bugs like having breakfast in bed. Why women do I find rather more obscure.

It scarcely bears thinking about, but there must have been a time, before civilisation began, when people had to have breakfast in bed every morning, because there wasn't anywhere else to have it – neither the table nor the chair had yet been invented. In fact people must have had lunch in bed as well. And tea, and dinner. In fact, sitting, in the sense that we know it, with knees bent, and feet stored on a lower level, had not been discovered! Apart from sitting up in a right-angle with a tray across your knees, there were only two known positions that the human body could take up – vertical and horizontal. The only alternative to sitting up in bed to eat was to do it lying down, and choking to death. Or else to go to someone's party, and eat standing up.

This last alternative was so awful that it's almost certainly what inspired the crucial advance to the table and chair. Archaeologists believe that it occurred during the Sumerian civilisation, some time after the invention of the wheel, around 2100 BC. King Ur-Nammu, the founder of the third dynasty of Ur, is thought to have held a particularly important banquet at about this time, where the guests would have been required to remain vertical all the way from cocktails at 7.00 p.m. until the brandy and cigars, somewhere around midnight.

For five hours they would have been holding massive gold plates, with huge silver goblets of wine clipped to them by the newly-invented wineglass-holder (in light-weight plastic, it's true, but encrusted with large uncut chalcedonies), transferring the knife from the right hand to the left after cutting up each mouthful of meat, and simultaneously transferring the fork from the left to the right in order to eat it, then transferring the entire plate from one hand to the other before the wrist finally gave way under the strain, and in so doing dropping the knife or the fork, or both, and then, in recovering the knife and fork, tipping gravy down the front of some great court official's shirt, then searching for the napkin to wipe him down, and finding it . . . not on the floor, where you would expect a napkin to be, but clenched underneath the plate in fingers which had by now become so paralysed that the napkin could not be prised free without dropping the plate.

Alcohol had already been invented, specifically in order to offer some hope of escape from this situation into the horizontal and the unconscious. But how to get at the alcohol with one's hands tied up like this?

And then, somewhere around midnight at this particular banquet, it is believed, Ur-Nammu himself suddenly buckled at the knees. By chance he was standing in front of the radiogram (as the audio system was then called). The sound of Carroll Gibbons and his Savoy Orpheans ended in a noise like a sword ripping through chainmail, and in the terrible silence that followed everyone looked round to see that the king was no longer vertical.

But then neither was he horizontal. He was caught in a curious position hallway between the two, his bottom resting on the radiogram, folded at the waist and again at the knees, so that he formed a kind of zigzag. It was a profoundly comic sight, but no one dared to laugh. Then Ur-Nammu smiled. 'This is delightful,' he said, so far as can be made out from the hieroglyphs in the society columns next morning. 'It is a huge advance upon standing up. I shall call this *sitting down*.'

Sitting down became all the rage. Everyone in Ur, Kish, Ahkshak, Hamazi, and the other cities of Mesopotamia sat. Some sat on record-players or television-sets, some (agonisingly) on radiators, some on ashtrays and umbrella stands, some on discarded sandwiches. Very soon the first purpose-built *chairs* began to appear (though of course their full potential couldn't be realised until the invention of leaning back). It may be a coincidence, but life-expectancy in the Sumerian world rose by forty-seven per cent about this time.

Life was still not perfect. People still had to balance their plates on their knees, together with glasses of red and white wine and Perrier water, plus napkin, cutlery, side-plates, crackers, balloons, going-home presents, and the text of any speeches which they proposed to make, and there were some who found this difficult. Another thirty years elapsed before Ur-Nammu's successor Amar-Su'en made the next great advance. He was still a student at the time, and although he was himself sitting on a specialised development of the chair called a throne, a lot of his fellow-students were sprawling about on the floor, as students will. Among them was a delightful girl reading Social Sciences and Early Hittite, who was sitting literally at his feet, and laughing in a most satisfactory way at all his jokes. She was saying quite amusing things herself, too, and Amar-Su'en was suddenly taken with the desire to slap his thighs to demonstrate his appreciation. So, to clear his thighs for slapping, he had the idea of balancing his plate on her head.

After that he took the girl to all the parties he went to, and grew so attached to her that he stood everything on her head, from vases of flowers to typewriters. When she subsequently died of pressure on the brain he was heart-broken. But the custom spread, until political developments began to make it increasingly difficult to find volunteers for the task. Soon cheap substitutes made of marble or carved mahogany took their place – and the table as we know it today took shape.

At last the human race was getting somewhere. Nouvelle cuisine and quantum theory followed in short order. So let us give thanks for the table and chair – and please, *please*, let us make full use of them.

(1994)

A pleasure shared

Do you spit? No? You don't mind if I do, though . . . ?

Khhghm . . . Hold on – can you see a spittoon on the table anywhere . . . ? Never mind. Sit down, sit down! I can use my empty soup-bowl. Khhghm – *thpp*!

My God, that's better. No, I've been sitting here all the way through the first course just dying for one. Iron self-control, but I do think it's rather bad manners to spit while one's eating. I mean, at a dinner-party like this. Your mouth full of the hostess's soup, and suddenly . . . kkhghm – *thpp*!

You *have* finished yourself, haven't you? You haven't! I'm so sorry . . . ! Oh, you don't want the rest.

Very nice of you not to . . . khhghm – *thpp*! . . . not to mind. One has to be so careful these days not to offend people's prejudices. I always ask first, of course. People never raise any objection, in my experience. In fact they usually never say anything at all. They generally do what you did – smile rather charmingly and kind of wave their hand about. Quite surprised even to be asked, I think, most of them.

Khhghm . . . Where's the soup-bowl gone . . . ? No, no – sit down! Don't keep jumping up! I'll use yours! You did say you'd finished . . . ? *Thpp*!

I'm glad you're not one of these hysterical people who try to stop other people enjoying themselves. It's so onesided. I don't try to stop anyone not spitting over me! In fact this is something I feel rather strongly about. People used to spit all the time in the good old days, and no one so much as raised an eyebrow. Spittoons everywhere you went – sawdust on the floor. It was only about fifty years ago, you know, that all this anti-spitting nonsense started. Suddenly everyone went mad. Notices up in the buses – 'No Spitting. Penalty £5.' And before we knew what had happened we'd lost another of our ancient liberties.

So, quite honestly, I . . . Khhghm . . . Oh, they've taken the soup-bowls away . . . No, no, stay right where you are! *Thpp*! . . . Keeps the moth out of the tablecloth . . . Yes, I spit very largely as a matter of principle.

And I hawk. As you can hear. Khhghm . . . ! In fact I hawk deeply, also as a matter of principle. *Khhhhhghhhhm* . . . ! Because I believe that if you're going to spit you might as well get the full benefit of it, and shift the entire contents of your lungs out into the atmosphere. Why keep all that stuff festering inside you, when you could so easily . . . Khhghm – *thpp*! . . . spread it around a bit . . . ?

Didn't spit in your face then, did I? Hold on – I think I did! I'm so sorry I'll just give it a wipe with the corner of the tablecloth . . . Come back, come back! The tablecloth's perfectly . . . no, sorry, hold on, I'll try another bit . . . There we are. It's very nice of you to go on smiling about it, but I know even the most broad-minded non-spitters sometimes feel a little sensitive about getting a faceful of the stuff.

Anyway, point taken! I'll be very careful henceforth to turn my head aside, look, and . . . Khhghm – thpp! . . . spit in your very lovely hair, or down your very charming dress.

Why don't I sit a little closer? There . . . It's the alluring way you're . . . khhghm – *thpp*! . . . wriggling around! I beg your pardon . . . ? It tickles? What tickles . . . ? You mean it ran down inside your dress? It gets everywhere, doesn't it! Anyway; don't worry. Just hang your underwear up in some airy place when you get home tonight, and it'll be dry in no time.

Look, you wouldn't mind, would you, if . . . No, come here! Don't lean away! I'm trying to whisper a few private words in your ear. You wouldn't mind, would you, if I gave you a ring some time? I thought perhaps you might like to come round one evening. I could give you a quiet spot of . . . Khhghm – *thpp*! Or we might go out and do something a little more exciting. I don't know. Maybe

– Khhghhkhkhkhm – *thppshmk*!

You keep shaking your head. Did you get some in your ear? Don't worry – it's not as if you were inhaling it . . . What? Oh, you're saying no? I see. I see. You're not somehow offended because you got a tiny bit in your eye . . . ? I *thought* so! I thought that smile of yours was beginning to get a little fixed. My God! I did *ask*, if you remember. I did ask if you minded!

So you're one of these anti-spitting fanatics, are you? I'm not allowed to spit – is that what you're telling me? – but it's perfectly all right for you to go round leaning away from people, and grinning that ghastly glassy grin at them.

God, the *intolerance* of you lot! It makes me want to . . . Well, I'll tell you what it makes me want to do. It makes me want to *khhhhhhghhhhhm* – Oh, and here's the next course. I'll put that one back for later.

(1989)

A princess in disguise

I believe society women are becoming more ambitious and serious-minded. In an earlier century they all wanted to take up careers as shepherdesses – now they want to become actresses. I put it down to education and female suffrage.

Ex-Queen Soraya of Iran shot to stardom in the film industry recently. Now Lee Bouvier – otherwise known as Princess Lee Radziwill, and sister of Jacqueline Kennedy – has fought her way to the top of the ladder, and crowned a dazzling career with her appearance on the world's television screens in 'Laura.'

A hard struggle it was, as recounted in the *TV Times* last week. The first thing she did was to take some lessons in acting. She didn't just rush out and book six half-hours with the local elocution and tap-dancing teacher, of course; you can't take short cuts in this business. What she did was, 'she mentioned her ambition to Alan Lerner (author of the musical "My Fair Lady"); he mentioned it to an impresario, who recommended a coach to give her private drama lessons.'

Her studies completed, she made her modest debut on the stage – playing the lead in 'The Philadelphia Story' in Chicago. After this rich and varied experience in the provinces she was ready to tackle anything. ... 'Her friend Truman Capote went to David Susskind and suggested putting her in a TV production. Capote . . . offered to write the script. He turned in the adaptation of "Laura."'

One can only wonder what the next step will be. Lucia di Lammermoor? Giselle? Or is her song and dance a little rusty? She told the *TV Times* that it was difficult to find good directors to work with. I suppose all the talented young millionaires and aristocrats one sees around simply don't have the dedication and stamina it takes. They only have to think of giving up every Thursday evening for a month and serving a week's apprenticeship in Glasgow or St Louis, and their hearts fail them.

What I like is the very chivalrous and helpful part played by Mr Lerner and Mr Capote in Miss Bouvier's success story. Real knights in shining armour. Well, that's the way we writers are. Take my friend Ken Nocker and myself. We're besieged with requests from great ladies who want us to write verse-dramas for them, or get them parts in 'The Avengers,' and we always do our best to oblige.

Did you see ex-Queen Beatrice of Savoy in that play of Ken's at the Victoria Theatre, Screwe, recently? Ken rang me up in great excitement the day he discovered her.

'What a find!' he shouted. 'She has a first-class figure, wonderfully expressive eyes, and very substantial holdings in De Beers and blue chip industrials.'

'Yes, but can she act?' I queried keenly.

'Can she act?' he cried. *'Can she act?* Listen, that gracious lady is twelfth in succession to the throne of Romania, and a second cousin by marriage to the Duke of Kent! Anyway, she wants me to write a kind of light-hearted black comedy, with a part for her as a golden-hearted whore. A *kooky* golden-hearted whore, to be precise.'

'Aren't kooky golden-hearted whores a little *passé*, at the moment?'

'Well, that's what she wants to play. Either that or Lady Macbeth, and I felt at this stage of her career . . . you know . . . Anyway, I shall have a completely free hand. Her only condition is that she isn't asked to do anything undignified or unbecoming, and that her skirt comes down to the knee.'

'She's not going to be standing on her dignity all the time, is she?'

'No, that's the wonderful thing about her! She just wants to start right at the bottom of the top, and be treated exactly like any other beginner. Of course, I'll have to see that each character calls her "Your Majesty" on entering.'

'Oh, of course.'

'But thereafter it's just plain "Ma'am." In fact, I was thinking of making her not so much a golden-hearted whore as a golden-hearted madam. That would make it sound more natural, I think. It's very important that the other characters behave absolutely naturally with her, just as if they really were in a brothel – so long as they don't speak until she's spoken first.'

Well, it all went off very well. Sir John Gielgud injured his back – he tripped over the footlights and fell into the orchestra pit while walking backwards out of the brothel bowing – but apart from that it was all very enjoyable, and surprisingly audible. In the front stalls, at any rate.

Of course, it's not just acting ambitions that Ken Nocker and I try to fulfil. Some of our rich friends want to be architects, or airline pilots. There was the lovely Lady

Dimity Mincing, who couldn't rest until she had appeared
as a barrister at the Old Bailey, and defended some
innocent person wrongfully charged with a serious offence.
We managed to pull strings and fix it for her, and it gave
her a great sense of personal fulfilment; though I think she
was a little disappointed with the verdict.

Our greatest triumph was arranging for Mrs Jefferson T.
Doppelganger III to fly over and perform a heart transplant
at Guy's, before an invited audience. Of course, we insisted
that she did a Red Cross first-aid course beforehand.

Anyway, *our* secret ambition is that some of our good
friends will be able to repay our little kindnesses, and
arrange with the millionaires of their acquaintance for us
to have a go at being rich.

(1968)

Private collections

I wish people weren't so coy about showing their slides and
films and snapshots. You have to drag the stuff out of them,
as though it were their first efforts at poetry.

They let themselves be frightened off by the convention
that one's snaps are boring to others. But the truth is more
or less the opposite. It's oneself who is likely to be bored,
since one has seen it all before; to others they're almost
certainly fascinating.

At any rate, they are to me, in any reasonable moderation.
I find the prospect of sorting a huge muddled parcel of
somebody else's snapshots over the carpet on a winter's afternoon, or of sitting in the calm after-dinner darkness watching
the brilliantly coloured images of someone else's life succeed
one another on the screen, a distinctly cheering one.

I don't mean so much the pictures of the Baptistry at
Pisa, or the barefoot boy driving goats on Naxos, or the

Hopi initiation ceremony in New Mexico (though I must admit I enjoy these too). I mean the really basic stuff – the pictures taken by our old friend Horace Morris of his wife Doris, with the sun in her eyes and a telegraph pole growing out of her head; the pictures of Horace by Doris where he is striking a humorous attitude on top of a rock, with his feet bigger than his head, half his head missing, and the horizon at 10 degrees to the horizontal.

I suppose it's partly plain curiosity about how other people live their lives when one's not around to watch. But there's more to it than that. I think one is perhaps soothed to have some nagging unconscious solipsism stilled by this evidence of the world's independent existence.

'The mystical thing,' wrote Wittgenstein in the *Tractatus*, 'is not *how* the world is, but *that* it is.' And since the arrangement of things in these pictures is unimportant, we are brought face to face with this fundamental aspect – the sheer fact that there was a moment in the history of the world when Doris Morris stood in front of a telegraph pole, and screwed up her eyes against the sun; that whatever was or was not, a rock with Horace Morris on top of it was.

The moment has gone. The state of affairs that united Horace and rock has disappeared beneath a thousand million succeeding states of affairs, and minute by minute grows remoter still. Horace will become too old to climb upon rocks; the rock will be worn down to sand by the sea; the photograph itself will fade and disintegrate. But nothing will ever destroy the fact it recorded for long enough to be appreciated – that at one particular moment this one particular state of affairs did obtain.

I suppose newspaper photographs and television images say no less. But I suspect that we don't entirely believe them. We accept them, as we do the accounts given by physicists of molecular structure, but we don't intimately feel the reality of them, as we do of the things which touch upon our own existence and identity. If we registered all those pictures of suffering, wealth, and action as anything more than a sort of factual fairyland, they would overwhelm us.

But poor old Horace Morris I *know*. My total belief in his reality might falter if I saw him on television, discussing the country's economic situation. But to the top of that only too probable rock, to a position 10 degrees out of the vertical, with too much foot and too little head, my belief will follow him unquestioningly.

And on, by extension, beyond him, to the world outside the frame of the picture. To the cigarette packet lying half-buried in the sand, just seven feet to the right. To the two men who walked by, three minutes earlier, gazing down at the sand as they talked, the one absently swinging at pieces of seaweed with a child's plastic spade, while the other gestured with his right hand, and said, 'That may be so, I don't dispute that for a moment, it may very well be so, I wouldn't argue with you on that . . .' To the faint drone of aircraft passing high overhead, on their way out from that particular time and place to other countries, other days.

I like the modesty of snapshots – the fact that they make no claims, imply no principles, demand no reactions. They don't, like news photographs, claim to show anything typical, or illustrative, of matters outside themselves. They don't, like advertising pictures, attempt to suggest attitudes or courses of action.

They make a counterpoise to art, too. For the convention of all art is that things can be arranged, or selected, or lighted, or simplified, or emphasised, to bring out some significance within or beyond the objects themselves; or that events can be represented as falling out in such a way that they cast some special illumination upon human behaviour; or that men can be driven by the pressure of extreme circumstances to some special self-knowledge or self-revelation.

One accepts this as the convention which makes art possible. But so universal is it that it comes to seem more like a natural law. And what *that* suggests is that there really is, in the external world, some special 'truth' which the everyday appearance of things conceals; and that the real significance of these appearances is that they can be manipulated by the artist to reveal this truth.

The snapshot, however, reminds us that the world is not like this – that things are what they are, and that they are significant in themselves, for their own sake. Horace Morris, on his rock, stands for nothing, except Horace Morris on a rock; typifies nothing except Horace Morris on a rock; purports to reveal no truth about the nature of Horace Morris or the rock, except that at this particular moment of time the one was standing on the other, and that together they looked thus and so.

Horace for Horace's sake – a good working principle.

(1967)

A question of character

Canon Montefiore's suggestion that Christ might have been homosexual was bound to cause a stir, but it would still have caused offence, I think, if the Canon had speculated about Christ's heterosexual proclivities. Or, indeed, about the working of his digestion, or whether he had corns on his feet.

The truth is that there's not much you can say about Christ without its seeming inappropriate. There's even less you can say about God. 'All-powerful,' 'eternal,' 'merciful,' 'just,' and a number of other compliments are in order, but not, I feel, 'shrewd,' 'charming,' 'keen,' 'cheerful,' 'tidy,' 'sporting,' or 'brave.' In fact we've got in a rather odd tongue-tied state about our gods altogether, considering that the medieval schoolmen used to maintain that God had all possible attributes. That should have provided plenty to say about him.

Shrewd and charming he would of necessity be on this analysis. An inadequate father, of course – though this would be balanced out by his being a perfectly adequate father, too. He would also be hexagonal, Chinese, mother-fixated, 12 years old, soluble in dilute sulphuric acid, south-westerly veering to westerly, and entirely composed of blotting-paper soaked in minestrone.

Yet few people took the opportunity to describe him as such.

Other theologians maintained that he was the sum of all possible perfections, which would have reduced his range a good deal, but still left him with perfect conductivity, perfect insulation, 20/20 eyesight, and first-class honours in social anthropology.

But these characteristics were little remarked upon at the time.

And quite what's being asserted of God when it's said that he's merciful, etc., is difficult to know. Because if one queries whether God really is quite as merciful as he is cracked up to be, given the astonishing number of quite merciless things which occur under his jurisdiction, and which in any other organisation would lead to vociferous demands for his resignation, religious people are astonished at the naïvety of one's interpretation.

'Good heavens!' they cry, often laughing cheerfully as well. 'when we say that God's merciful we don't mean that he's merciful in any merely human sense of the word! With our miserably limited understanding, and our pathetically inadequate language, we couldn't hope to make anything but the most incomplete and misleading attempt at describing him.

'There's no way of knowing what we mean when we say that he is merciful. For all we know, *God's* mercifulness may consist in just those very things which we, with our poor understanding, think of as merci*less*!'

Gods weren't always as indescribable as this. The Greeks didn't hesitate to characterise their team as lecherous meaning lecherous, jealous meaning jealous, and drunken meaning drunken. God is very clearly characterised by the Old Testament, too. He's the local dictator who invents his own laws as he goes along and insatiably demands flattery; the unsleeping father of his people and architect of their victories, who bullies his courtiers and plays cruel tricks on them, and who murders individuals and destroys whole communities who step out of line – a small-time Stalin, with something of Castro's showmanship.

Now that's what I *call* a god. Nobody could read the Old Testament without being stirred to wholesome indignation. But then the producers got worried about the series – felt it didn't reflect the changing tastes of the age, thought it might be having an anti-social influence. So they tried to make the chief character turn on goodness instead of sheer power. They stopped him murdering people, and had him helping them in distress instead.

A weaker piece of characterisation, in my opinion. And when people began to complain that the new character was implausible, and viewing figures dropped off, the producers made a disastrous series of concessions. Instead of strengthening the character again, they weakened him still further.

'All right,' they said. 'If people don't believe there could be this all-powerful magic character going round doing good deeds, let's have him *not* going round doing good deeds. Let's have him doing nothing – just being good, and feeling agonised by the awfulness of things, and trying to make everything all right in the end.'

Down went the viewing figures again, naturally.

'No, listen, all right, we've got it now,' said the producers desperately. 'This is a kind of more subtle thing. When we say he's good, we don't mean he's good in any ordinary, obvious way. We mean he's got this secret code of his own which . . .'

And down went the figures once more.

'Hey, no, stop, we've rethought the whole product!' shouted the producers. 'He's not a person at all! No, listen, you'll love this – he's a kind of scientific principle, a sort of abstract emotional kind of . . . No, hey . . .'

I think it's a pity to see the whole series go down the drain. Of course, we can't go back to the old characterisation now. We need something more sophisticated, a character which suggests a certain psychological insight; and this, I suppose, is what Canon Montefiore is attempting to provide. We also need some sort of recognition of the moral ambivalence you'd expect in a god, and of the essentially illusory nature of power.

My advice to the company is to get the theologians off the programme. No theologian ever wrote a good legend.

(1967)

A question of downbringing

My wife's studying sociology. She comes home from the lectures and teaches it to me over dinner, and one of the most interesting nuggets of sociological information I've been tossed across the cheese and biscuits so far is that my wife (a doctor's daughter) has married beneath her.

'It hadn't really struck me before,' she said. 'Journalists are lower-middle class.'

'Don't talk tripe,' I replied, with my usual scientific detachment.

'I'm not using the term with any emotive connotation,' said my wife. 'It's just a simple sociological fact. I had it from the lecturer less than an hour ago.'

'Class is a matter of supreme indifference to me personally, as you know, so leave me out of it. But are you trying to tell me that people like the editor of the *Spectator* with his £40,000 house are lower-middle class? You take a look at the lads soaking up the hock in El Vino's and you won't go round screaming "lower-middle class" like that.'

'I'm not screaming anything. I'm giving you a piece of completely objective sociological information. Where do *you* think you come on the social scale, anyway?'

'Just about anywhere except the lower-middle class, if you really want to know. Working class, upper-middle class – I don't mind, just so long as it's not lower-middle.'

'Because deep inside you know lower-middle's what you are. Everybody struggles to get off his own particular pin, and just succeeds in impaling himself harder and harder.'

She showed me the tables – the Registrar-General's classification of social classes; the Hall-Jones scale; the A/B scale used by the Institute of Practitioners in Advertising. It was difficult to get round it, certainly. I'm clearly not a member of a learned profession (the top of everybody's list), or the daughter of one. I don't manage or administer anything. I'm not a skilled manual worker. The only possible hole for a man in my position seems to be Hall-Jones group 3 or 4 (Inspectional and Supervisory) or IPA group C 1 (Supervisory and Clerical), on the grounds that I mind or supervise other people's business. And Group C 1 is clearly down in black and white as lower-middle class.

'Are you trying to tell me I'm worse than some crooked accountant or fly-by-night lawyer?' I shouted calmly.

'Who said anything about better or worse?' said my wife. You're just lower down the social scale, that's all. There's no need to get upset about it.'

'As if I'd get upset about some obsolete pseudo-concept like class!' I snarled, doing my best to be reasonable and conciliatory. 'Look, I'm not trying to say I'm upper-middle class, or even middle-middle class. But as a matter of sober and objective self-assessment I do happen to believe that I'm *upper-lower-middle.* Or, at any rate upper-middle-middle lower-middle.'

'It's no good trying to persuade me,' said my wife. 'Take it up with the Registrar-General. Argue it out with the IPA *I* can't change natural laws to suit your convenience.'

'But don't you remember, before you started doing sociology, how we always used to feel tremendously middle-middle class together?'

'Michael, everyone thinks he's middle-middle class. It's just a romantic notion one has to grow out of. Let's face up to reality. You happen to be two or three social classes below me. That's all. I'm sure that with good will and understanding on both sides this needn't prove an insurmountable barrier.'

It's a difficult subject all right, class. When Anthony Powell appeared on television, the *Radio Times* described him as a novelist who 'satirises the upper-middle classes with a brilliant sense of social nuance.'

The upper-middle classes? The Earl of Warminster, Sir

Gavin Walpole-Wilson, General Conyers, Sir Magnus
Donners-Brebner, Lady Ardglass, Lady Molly Jeavons,
Prince Theodoric, and all the rest of those magnificent
characters, *upper-middle* class?

Well, stap me! I thought they were the *upper* classes! I
suppose that just shows my embarrassing lower-middle
class naïvety. The *Radio Times,* with its brilliant sense of
social nuance, saw immediately that all Powell's earls,
courtiers, and great industrialists were really horribly
bourgeois. And indeed, the whole upper class recedes like
the horizon as you approach it. What could be more middle
class than an earl or a courtier, when you come to think
about it? Except perhaps a royal duke, or an oil millionaire?

Indeed, as my wife pointed out when I raised the matter
at my next tutorial, for sociological purposes the upper
classes simply don't exist. The Registrar-General's classification and the Hall-Jones scale both start with the
professional classes, the IPA grading with group A, the
upper-middle class.

'But look,' I protested, 'the middle classes must be in the
middle of something. They can't just be sandwiched
between the lower classes and God.' *'Lower classes?'* said
my wife. 'What are they? You don't mean the working
classes, do you?'

'What I'm getting at is, are you trying to tell me that you
and your professional pals are higher up the social scale
than earls and kings and so on?'

'It depends how the earls and kings spend their time,
Michael. If they just inspect their troops and supervise
the running of their estates I suppose they come in the
Inspectional and Supervisory category along with you.'

'What? You honestly think a doctor's daughter's higher
up than a full-blown belted earl!'

'This is a surprisingly reactionary attitude you're taking
up, Michael.'

'Well, for heaven's sake! I mean, one does know certain things instinctively.'

No, let's be bold and radical. The upper classes have got to have somewhere to live, after all. I don't mind having them down here with me in the lower-middle classes. Just so long as they don't tell my smart friends they saw me down here.

(1966)

Ready, steady . . . no . . .

Now have I got everything?

Shoulder-bag with my various bits and pieces in – yes, on my shoulder. I think that's all I need, isn't it? I'm only going to Tunbridge Wells. I'm only going to be away for two or three hours. Oh, keys, of course . . . Not still lying on the hall table, are they, as has been known to happen occasionally in the past . . . ? No, here in my hand, just where they ought to be.

Very satisfyng. I do believe that for once I'm setting out in reasonably good time for something. I'm going to catch the train without any hurry at all.

So, just set the burglar-alarm, and I can . . .

Hold on. Better check I've got some money in my pocket . . . I did pick up my wallet . . . ? Yes, I did. And my little organiser thing, and my penknife? I don't want to find myself in Tunbridge Wells for two hours without a penknife . . .

Yes, everything's under control . . . Oh, have I closed the bathroom window? Better look. Don't want to get halfway down the street and have to come running back . . . Yes, window closed. I did switch off the copier . . . ? Oh, come on! Just set the burglar-alarm and . . . Ticket! Where's my ticket? I've forgotten my ticket!

No, here it is, neatly tucked away in the ticket section of my wallet. Perhaps I am finally beginning to get organised in life. Got my money, got my ticket, got my passport . . .

No, I haven't! I've forgotten my passport!

Now, don't be silly. Tunbridge Wells – remember? Tell the Tunbridge Wells Writers' Circle how to organise their professional lives, then home again. I don't need sun cream, I don't need a mosquito coil . . . Might need a spare sweater, though. I've no idea what the weather's doing down there in Kent. Might be pouring with rain . . . Rain, yes! Umbrella – where is it? And a comb. Gale blowing up Tunbridge Wells High Street – last few hairs seriously deranged. Not the kind of thing they like in Tunbridge Wells.

Anything else, before I definitely set the burglar-alarm? How about something to read on the train? Quick look along the shelves – grab anything – haven't got all that much time now . . . *The Brothers Karamazov* . . . My God, it weighs a ton . . .

Right – burglar-alarm on . . . This departure has now taken slightly longer than the last act of *The Cherry Orchard*. Yes – I haven't left any aged retainers locked inside, have I? No, but I *am* leaving without a handkerchief! I was going to spend the entire talk wiping my nose on my sleeve!

Switch off the burglar alarm . . . Take a spare handkerchief as well, perhaps. Driving rain coming under the umbrella – I might suddenly find I've got a cold coming on. Yes – better put some aspirin in . . . And throat-lozenges . . . What's this packet? Plasters . . . Well, why not? Sensible precaution. Antiseptic cream, too. Pair of tweezers for getting splinters out . . .

Spare socks? No, no, I'm not on a walking tour. Nice to have a map, though. And the map-measurer? Well . . . why not . . . ? And the compass? Come on, this is getting out of hand . . . Though since it takes up so little room . . .

So . . . This bag's going to burst. I'll just quickly transfer everything into a suitcase . . .

Actually there's room for one or two more things, now I'm taking the suitcase. How about a few apples to eat on the train? We might break down between stations – get stuck overnight in a snowdrift. Look round the kitchen as I collect the apples. That ball of string might come in handy. A few elastic bands.

Right – burglar-alarm on and out of the door before I

think of anything else! Double-lock the Yale. Lock the Chubb . . . Only now I'm outside it feels distinctly warm. Supposing it turned out to be a heatwave? Better just run back in and take my vest off . . .

Quick, quick – unlock the Chubb, unlock the Yale – switch off the burglar-alarm . . . Coat off, shirt off, vest off – shirt on, coat on, alarm on . . . On the other hand, ne'er cast a clout . . . Alarm off, coat off, shirt off – vest on, shirt on, coat on, alarm on . . . Stop! Where are the keys! I've put them down on the hall table, unbelievably. I'm going to lock myself out again! Grab keys – out of the door before the burglar-alarm goes off . . . Lock Yale, lock Chubb. I'm going to have to hurry.

I can't hurry! Not with this load! Unlock, unlock. Alarm off. *Brothers Karamazov* out. Apples out. Spare handkerchief out. Elastic bands out . . . Alarm on. Lock, lock. Now – *run*!

Run back! The talk! The text of my talk!

Unlock, unlock. Alarm off . . . Where is it? Right . . . Alarm on. Lock, lock. Run, run . . . !

I did lock up . . . ? Back, back! Unlock Chubb – *was* locked – relock it. Unlock Yale – also locked – relock. Run! Except . . . I never put the alarm on! Unlock, unlock. Beep beep . . . I *did* put the alarm on! So – lock, lock. Run, run, run, run. . . . SCREECH SCREECH!

What . . .? Oh, my God, I never switched it *off*! Back, back! Fumble, fumble – SCREECH SCREECH! Fumble, fumble, fumble – SCREECH, SCREECH, SCREECH! Fumble, fumble, fumble, fumble . . .

Finally restore peace. Reassure the neighbours. Put the keys and the suitcase very calmly and unhurriedly back on the hall table, and reassess the situation. OK, I've missed the train. Does that matter so very much, in the great scale of things? I'll get the next one! I simply ring Tunbridge Wells and tell them they'll have to talk quietly amongst themselves for an hour or two, sort out their own problems.

At least I've now got plenty of time to take a last look round . . . put the ball of string back in the kitchen, the plasters back in the medicine cabinet . . . take my vest off again . . . transfer the text of the talk and a few other bare essentials back into the shoulder-bag . . . put the shoulder-bag neatly back beside the keys on the hall table . . . turn on the burglar-alarm . . . and close the door behind me in unhurried dignity.

Shoulder-bag . . . I've left it on the hall table. Never mind – no rush now. Just quietly unlock the door and . . . Keys . . . They're not . . .? They can't be . . . !

(1995)

Return match

What really makes a holiday of course, is not the sun or the landscape or the architecture; it's the people.

It's the people who give the place its character, after all, and the intelligent holidaymaker makes a great effort to get to know them. They may be a bit shy at first, but you can be sure there's nothing they like more than a visitor really taking an interest in them. You stop and chat with them about their work. You find out how they live. You try to enter into the communal life of the place for a week or two. That's how real international understanding is created.

All the same, as I stroll about that delightful little unspoilt Psychomanian village chatting with the goatherds and dropping in for a glass of something with the old wattle-dauber, a worrying thought sometimes comes to me. Supposing they take it into their heads to get to know me back?

One day when I am back at home the front door bell is

going to ring, and there on the doorstep will be a colourful Psychomanian peasant with his wrinkled wife, their wonderful timeless quality looking unpleasantly out of place among the sodium lights.

'Good morning!' he will say, with an ingratiating smile and irritatingly grammatical English. 'Marvellous weather we're having, are we not?'

'Ah,' I shall reply guardedly, my eyes narrowing with shrewd middle-class cautiousness.

'Of course, everyone knows the weather is never right for you townspeople! Ha, ha, ha! But the truth is, you people don't know how lucky you are to live in a suburb like this. The air's so thick and fumy – it's like wine. For poor devils like us who have to spend the rest of the year cooped up in the countryside breathing that thin country air it's as good as a tonic.

'I just dropped in to pass the time of day. Do you mind if I take a photograph of you as we talk? You look so typical, somehow, standing there in the door of your little home . . . Head up, please. Look into the camera, will you, with that stupefied sort of expression? Thanks. Well, I expect you've got work to do.'

'Yes.'

'*Marvellous* accent,' he whispers to his wife in Psycho-manian.

'Honestly,' he says to me, 'don't worry about us. You must get on with your work and we'll watch you. No, truly, there's nothing I'd enjoy more.'

When he discovers that I am an article writer by trade he is very excited.

'As a matter of fact,' he says, 'I'm by way of being something of a connoisseur of articles – I'm a member of the literary club at home, and we have regular article tastings. I you want my honest opinion, I'd swap any of your overpraised vintage Hazlitt and Addison for the sort of unpretentious rough stuff I expect you're turning out, if

I could read it where it was meant to be read, in the rain,
next to an English gasworks.'

While his wife, who apparently doesn't speak English,
goes out to the kitchen, smiling with wordless benevolence,
to watch and make notes while my wife opens a tin of
ravioli for lunch, he takes photographs of me operating the
traditional typewriter. He asks me what all the different
keys are for, and begs to be allowed to have a go himself.

'It looks easy when you do it,' he says admiringly, as he
crashes his thick peasant fingers up and down. 'But I can't
seem to get any sort of article out of it at all.'

'Takes practice,' I mumble, flattered into loquacity.

'What a marvellously true thing to say! God, you people
really have got a salty bourgeois wit, haven't you? How
about singing one or two of your suburban songs for me?
No? Well, then, what are the local superstitions round
here? Do people hereabouts believe in little electrons, and
all that sort of thing? Come on now – have you ever seen an
electron yourself?'

I could tell him a thing or two about electrons all right,
but I prefer to keep myself to myself, so I just shrug my
shoulders and grunt expressively. With a little cry of
delight the peasant discovers the telephone and asks if I
would be prepared to sell it to him.

'I've got quite a little collection of English urban
artefacts,' he explains. 'I find them rather amusing. Let's
say a shilling, shall we?

'You know, it's a great privilege, being invited into such
an ordinary home as this. But the really *marvellous* thing
is to find oneself among people who've got time to sit down
and talk. At home life is just one long rush to get the
ground ploughed, the seed sown, the crop harvested. And of
course it's a terrible rat-race, you know, the peasant world
– everyone trying to be just that little bit shrewder and
more obstinate than everyone else all the time.

'But then the – whole pace of ancient life is killing. The

trouble is, things are still so simple that there's nothing to think about but money, money, money. There are no chemicals in the bread – the eggs still taste like eggs – we plod senselessly from place to place at four miles an hour. I must say, I sometimes wonder where it will ever start.

'But it really is a wonderful break to sit here listening to you talk. You're so remote from the earth, somehow. Oh, is this ravioli for me? Gosh, thanks. Incidentally, I've heard a lot about the complex urban merry-making that goes on at cocktail parties. I don't know whether it would be possible to get into one?

'I mean, it is people who take one out of oneself on holiday, isn't it? And they cost so much less than all the other forms of entertainment I can think of.'

(1964)

Ron Number

Whatever other unseen beings we do or do not believe in, we are all believers in Ron Number. Ron Number is mysterious, unpredictable, unknowable. But undeniably, Ron Number is.

He speaks to us all at one time or another, and when he speaks, there is no denying the call. The telephone rings. 'REPugnance 4278,' one says. 'Oh,' replies the voice, 'Ron Number.' And rings off.

Ron Number never forgets us. He speaks to us on our birthdays; at Candlemas, Martinmas, Lammastide, and Septuagesima. He remembers us on Mondays. He remembers us on Tuesdays. He remembers us on Wednesdays, Thursdays, and Fridays. He does not forget us at the weekend.

He calls us when we least expect it – saving us from the

tedium of being asleep at six o'clock in the morning and interrupting our idle reverie as we sit in the lavatory. When one's guests have been warmed with food and wine to the point where they are just beginning to speak openly and directly from the depths of themselves, Ron Number phones. 'Oh,' he says, 'Ron Number.' And afterwards nothing is quite the same again.

What is Ron Number trying to tell us? His utterances are oblique and cryptic. I have humbly recorded the ones vouchsafed to me in the Book of Ron Number, which in the Improved Version comes between the book of Usually Reliable Sources and the Book of Celebrities. Here is a reading from Ron Number, vii 3–10 as a sample:

'And when the bell chymed, he made answer according to the law and to the usage of his house, saying: "REPugnance 4278." And Ron Number spake unto him, saying: "Oh," And Ron Number spake further with him saying: "Ron Number." And Ron Number here made an end to his speaking.

'And on another occasion Ron Number spake unto him saying: "Oh. Oh."

'And at another chyming of the bell Ron Number saith: "Oh, terribly sorry."

'And at another: "Terribly sorry. Frightfully sorry."

'And at another: "I wish to speak to Mr Chatterjee, in the small room on the first floor."

'And at another: "Is that REPugnance 4728? That's right – 4728. That's what I *said* – 4728. Yes, 47 . . . – oh' 4278? Oh. Sorry." '

'And at another Ron Number saith nothing, but silently departed. Yet was he known even by his silence.'

A great deal, of course, has been written by commentators attempting to elucidate these utterances. Most commentators have pointed to the remarkable insistence on a sense of grief for transgression. Others have pointed out that the sum of 4278 and 4728 is exactly 9006. Some have seen the mysterious Mr Chatterjee as a textual corruption of Mt Chimborazo.

Almost everyone has been struck by the constant repetition of 'Oh,' or 'O.' A minority of somewhat eccentric commentators have taken this to be a revelation of the Golden Number, and have attempted to use the figure zero to compute the date of the invention of the telephone. The usual interpretation up to now has been that it stood for Operator, and was intended as giving a metaphorical corporeal identity to Ron Number to make him comprehensible to the human intelligence. But the most modern commentators read the whole phrase as 'O Ron Number!' and regard Ron Number as a self-worshipping entity, a sort of abstraction inherent in the telephone system,

One day, almost all of us more or less believe, Ron Number will come in person. He will ring the front-door bell. 'Oh, Ron Number,' he will say, and stand there mysterious and awful, the miraculous visual equivalent of the universal way he sounds, as he speaks with the tongues of old ladies, wizened Chinamen, fat company directors, and burly West Indians.

Not, of course, that Ron Numberism is entirely undivided in its beliefs. There is, for example, a sect of telephone subscribers in Bexleyheath, the principal tenet of whose creed seems to be that I am an incarnation of the South Eastern Gas Board.

They ring me up and pray to me. 'Oh, South Eastern Gas Board?' ask the more agnostic members of the faith, sceptically. 'O South Eastern Gas Board!' the true believers proclaim in resounding vocatives.

As an orthodox Ron Numberist I try to put them right. But you can't combat faith with reason, and the really convinced believers go right ahead and pray to me to heal a sick gas water heater, or provide them with a refrigerator, or even sometimes to take from them an old and ailing gas cooker.

Perhaps they are sustained in their faith by a miracle –

a time when after earnest prayers had been offered up to REPugnance 4278 a palsied gas water heater suddenly and wondrously filled with gas and blew up, killing seven. Perhaps they have a chapel of their own, and a wise old preacher who tells them that if when they phone REPugnance 4278 they imagine they hear someone denying that REPugnance 4278 is the South Eastern Gas Board it is only a temptation put in their way to test their faith, and that they should strengthen themselves to overcome it by telephoning twice as often. Perhaps they sing simple gas hymns, like:

> *Oh how the weary heart desires*
> *The golden streets, the pearly gate,*
> *The gaseous heaven of the wires –*
> *REPugnance 4278.*

Only, of course, an argument breaks out as to whether the number is 4278 or 4872, and a schism occurs. But the more schisms they have the better; the more combinations of numbers they try the more people to whom they will have to say 'Oh, Ron Number.' Yes, whatever our beliefs, and whether we know it or not, we are all doing Ron Number's work.

(1962)

The sad tale of P-t-r B-nnykin

Once upon a time there was a naughty little rabbit called Peter Bunnykin.

This sentence is almost certainly actionable (noted Mr K. J. Writweather, barrister-at-law and libel-reader for *Chicks' Own,* in the margin of the galley-proof) unless we are absolutely certain that Mr Bunnykin is no longer alive.

'Naughty' is indefensible, and I think to be on the safe side we should also remove the name, since a jury might conceivably hold that calling Mr Bunnykin 'a little rabbit' was damaging.

Even so, Mr Bunnykin might be able to show that the phrase 'a little rabbit' identified him to those who knew him, and I should feel happier if it were removed. If you think 'Once upon a time there was,' is not strong enough as an opening sentence on its own I should be prepared to accept a completely fictitious description – 'a big griffin,' say, or 'a medium-sized dodo.'

Peter Bunnykin lived in a cosy little rabbit-hole in Bluebell Woods.

Any hole in the ground, however innocent it seems, may, unknown to the author, be a Regional Seat of Government, and as such covered by D-notices. I suggest: 'He lived in a cosy little dwelling in a wooded location.'

One day he decided to go along to Farmer Barleycorn's lettuce-patch and steal a lettuce.

This imputation upon the good faith of Mr Bunnykin's intentions would be impossible to substantiate. Either 'steal' must be changed to 'purchase,' or else the link with Mr Bunnykin must be weakened by changing the sentence to 'Later, a rabbit went to Farmer Barleycorn's lettuce-patch, etc.' Then if Mr Bunnykin ever did bring a case I think it could be argued with some success that it was never intended to suggest that the rabbit who took the lettuce was the same rabbit that was mentioned earlier.

Off he went, hippity-hop, hippity-hop.

I suppose this might just pass as fair comment.

With two snip-snaps of his little front teeth he was through the fence around the lettuce-patch.

I suggest: 'At another point, a rabbit was in the lettuce-patch.' By the sound of it, an action may well lie against the manufacturers of the fencing material, and by the time this story is in print the whole matter may be *sub judice.*

What a bad rabbit he was!

The nearest I can get to preserving the rhythm of this sentence and avoiding any resetting is 'What a brown rabbit he was!' I realise this is not very close to the original sense. The best I can do in that direction is 'What a broad-minded rabbit he was!'

But he had eaten only two lettuces when Farmer Barleycorn leapt out from behind a hedge and gave him a terrible spanking!

'But only two lettuces had been eaten . . .' – the passive is in general a much less dangerous voice – 'But only two lettuces had been eaten when a rabbit and a hand were in collision.'

And Farmer Barleycorn said, It's not the first time I've caught you stealing my lettuces, young Peter Bunnykin.'

I think the nearest we can get here, if you are prepared to take a calculated risk, is 'Farmer Barleycorn then made a statement.'

But coming on top of everything else I'm afraid there is still an element of innuendo even in this. I must admit I should feel safer if it was changed to 'Someone said something.' Though here again we must ask ourselves, as always, 'Will someone sue?' I'm afraid that in my experience someone always sues. I should sleep easier if we changed it to 'No one said something,' or better still, 'No one said nothing.'

Poor Peter Bunnykin slunk off home with his tail between his legs, feeling very small and wishing the earth would swallow him up.

I have as you suggested taken the opinion of leading counsel on this passage, and the more we discussed it, the more ways we could see in which it could be taken to be tendentious. Adding together all our reservations, we suggest: 'A certain animal went home in a certain manner, with his tail in a certain position, feeling a certain size, and wishing that a certain object would perform a certain action.'

And so Peter Bunnykin lived happily ever after, with a permanent house-guest who was a model with plenty of men-friends: his name connected with members of the Royal Family in vile rumours published by scandal-mongering children's comics on the Continent: being frequently helped home in a state of collapse after gay parties suffering from influenza: with a trunkful of letters from the Under-Secretary for Rabbit Affairs addressing him as 'My dear Bunnykin': and described by a Divorce Court judge as a thoroughly rotten, contemptible little rabbit without a single spark of common decency.

This bit seems more or less all right.

Sir, – We are instructed on behalf of our client Mr Lybell Laws, whose attention has been drawn to an article containing certain extremely damaging innuendoes . . .

(1963)

Sandra sesame

You have dealings from time to time with various large and complex organisations – international corporations, professional bodies, public authorities. You're a humble private citizen, and your business with them is modest.

You ring them to get one replacement part, one small piece of information, one minor adjustment to your account. They are publishing your thesis on Carolingian funeral customs, perhaps, or manufacturing some little range of armaments you've designed. You have never set foot inside their doors, but you know that at the other end of the line are dozens, hundreds, thousands of people, organised into departments and divisions, structured into grades and hierarchies, in ways that are completely opaque to you and the rest of the outside world.

'How can I help you?' asks the impersonal corporate voice that answers their phone. What do you say? How *can* it help you? How do you, in your lowly state of singleness and ignorance, enter into communication with this mighty complex of manifold unknowability?

Well, you have a magic formula. Two simple words.

'Sandra Sprott,' you tell the corporate voice authoritatively.

How did you first get hold of this name? You can't remember. Someone you met at a party told you. Or the first time you rang the organisation they put you through to various people with various names and positions, who put you through to various other people, with various other names and positions, and the one name you somehow caught was Sandra Sprott, though you never quite understood what it was she actually did. You wrote it down on the back of an envelope nevertheless, and somehow the envelope was still lying on your desk the next time you had to call them. So you asked for Sandra Sprott, and Sandra Sprott seemed to have a dim recollection of dealing with you before. On this fragile basis you have built some kind of continuing human relationship. You still don't know what she does, even so, or very much else about her, except her name. You know that she once told you how to fill in a GX/33/Y (Exemption) form, and that raises some faint hope that this time she will also be able to help you get the washing-machine repaired, or obtain tickets for the opera.

Or possibly not. You may be asking her to do things which are not part of her professional responsibility at all, since you have so little idea what her professional responsibility is. *She* knows that applications for exemption go to Documentation, and exemptions from documentation go to Applications – but *not* to Lynette Swordsmith, who only deals with Overseas, except in the absence of Peter Cork, who is also responsible for Foreign (not to be confused with Overseas!), and certainly *not* to Elwyn Eady, who is notoriously difficult about such things – probably not even to the ever-reliable Jane, in Ted Thorough's office, since she is moving next week to run the vehicle fleet in the Devotional Software Division.

Nothing of this is vouchsafed to you, though. So of course you worry about your helpless dependence upon Ms Sprott. Are you embarrassing her by asking her to do things which are beyond her, or beneath her? Is she coping with you merely out of the goodness of her heart? Are you her private welfare case?

Probably when you first got put through to her it was because she was so junior that she was the person to whom everyone who didn't know anyone in the organisation got put through. She was so humble that she didn't like to tell you you'd got the wrong department altogether, so raw that she didn't even realise herself. Maybe she's nothing to do with the publication of academic theses – she's in the Industrial Paints Division. To get your awful thesis published she had to get on to someone *she* knows in the Trade Directories and Gazetteers section, and get them to do a favour for *her*, even though they're obviously not the right person, either – it's just that they've *always* done favours for her, and they don't like to start saying no now that they've become a Deputy Controller.

And of course she's been promoted herself since the far-off day when you established that first tremulous contact. She's now *Director* of the Industrial Paints Division. She's sitting there trying to think large strategic thoughts about expansion in the Pacific Basin and down-sizing in the North Sea, and there's this idiot on the line who wants to make a correction to a footnote on eighth-century shroud-weaving techniques.

You're not to know this, of course. But there's something about her voice that makes you suspect. Every time you ring her you apologise at length for wasting her time – and waste minutes more of it in the process.

All this is bad enough, for a sensitive person like yourself. But then something even worse happens. A terrible day comes when you phone, and she's not there. She's left the organisation. Probably she made a mess of the Pacific Basin expansion programme, thanks to perpetual distractions and interruptions. Your magic formula no longer works. Your pass has been cancelled, your thread into the labyrinth has snapped.

You get put through instead to someone whose name you don't catch. You tell them your name. They don't catch it. You explain what you want. They sigh. You ask them humbly who else you should speak to. They don't know. You are out in the cold again.

And now your phone's ringing, and there's someone called Sandra Sprott on the line for you. 'I'm terribly sorry to bother you – I know how busy you must be.' You are very busy, it's true, but you don't like to say so because there's something vaguely familiar about the name – you have a feeling that she may be the relative of a friend, or the friend of a relative. 'No, no,' you lie, and you have to wait while she wastes yet more time on expressions of gratitude before she explains that her children are doing a project at school on the Industrial Revolution, and that she remembered your name because you were something to do with history . . .

(1994)

Save it for the stairs

Esprit de l'escalier is a maddening form of cerebral activity; but *politesse de l'escalier* is a good deal worse. I'm an expert on all branches of the subject; I think of pretty well everything in life, from witty replies to fundamental moral attitudes, only afterwards, on the way downstairs, and it's the belated realisation of my failure to have made the appropriate polite remarks which casts me into the greatest despair of all.

It's not only on *escaliers* that the point comes sickeningly home to one, of course, but in the *rue,* the *bain,* and perhaps most frequently of all, in the *lit,* in the *milieu* of the *nuit.* Suddenly the faulty connection sparks, and a dismal shock goes through one. Oh, God – one never asked O. J. Sprout how his poor wife was! Holy heaven – one never thanked Christopher and Lavinia Crumble for putting one in touch with that marvellous little man of theirs in Market Strayborough! One never congratulated Thorsten Trouncer on the birth of his son! Never asked Diminua Pinn if she'd got that job she was up for! Never evinced any surprise or pleasure to see Mrs Haddock out of hospital again!

And once more it's borne in upon one what an insufferable egotist one is – indifferent to other people's triumphs and sufferings, forgetful of their kindness as soon as one has made use of it. How hurt all those poor souls must have felt, as they struggled bravely to smile and talk about politics, when all they really wanted was to hear some passing word of interest in the size of their family, some grudging expression of sympathy on the state of their pancreas!

Except, of course, that they almost certainly wanted nothing of the sort.

Because the odd truth about the expression of polite interest – impossible as this is to believe when one has failed to offer it – is that people really *don't* want to be on the receiving end of it. It's not pleasing but irritating to have to explain for the twentieth time why one's hand is in bandages; not gratifying but embarrassing to announce for the thirtieth time that one got the job, or the prize, or the nomination; and not soothing but humiliating to have to report, for the fortieth time, that one failed to. Pregnancy is a great condition for attracting polite interest, various women have told me. They have sometimes felt, they said, that if one more kindly inquirer asked politely when the baby was due they would fall into screaming hysterics and give birth on the spot.

In fact, as modern politeness analysis shows, the principal – and often the only – beneficiary from the expression of polite interest is the interest-taker, and not the subject of the interest at all. The subject is merely being exploited to increase the interest-taker's sense of psychosocial well-being. Or so some of us at the Self-Justification Research Centre feel.

Let us examine a typical case in our records. 'James,' a chronically inadequate interest-taker, has been subject since childhood to *politesse de l'escalier* and subsequent bouts of remorse. In a recurring situation, he finds himself up against 'Oscar,' a skilled and relentless interest-taker with deeply sympathetic eyes and a forehead already wrinkled with altruistic anxiety. The following typical encounter makes it fairly clear which of them it is who is gaining the greater psychosocial profit from the relationship.

'Are you feeling better?' asks Oscar as soon as they meet,

with a specially solicitous smile.

'Better?' queries James nervously. 'Better than what?'

'Better than you were last time we met. You had a dreadful cold, if you remember.'

'Oh, did I?'

'Oh, a terrible one. You still look a tiny bit under the weather, as a matter of fact. How do you feel?'

James starts to explain that he does have a slight but tiresome catarrh, and is still coughing a little. Oscar nods earnestly, evidently appalled by every symptom. Then suddenly James's tone becomes a little uncertain. He has just been struck, as any competent politeness analyst would realise immediately, by the faint but troubling recollection that Oscar himself is a martyr to some very serious and painful disease.

But before he can remember exactly what it is, Oscar is asking him how he enjoyed his recent trip to Boulogne. James holds forth at some length on the amusing ubiquity of English fish and chips in the town, etc., etc. – when suddenly the ancedotes falter, and a strained look comes over his face. The uneasy suspicion has just come to him, as we politeness analysts see at once, that Oscar has just got back from Peru. Or is just off to Peking. Or was born and brought up in Boulogne. Or . . .

But already Oscar is asking if James's son enjoyed his birthday the previous week. Open alarm seizes James. Does this mean that Oscar sent a present, he thinks, and that I'm supposed to thank him for it? Did I send his child a present on its birthday? Does he *have* children?

'And that reminds me,' says Oscar, his brow wrinkling anxiously once more. 'How is Deirdre, your second cousin once removed? Has she recovered from that rather nasty fall she had the year before last?'

James mumbles in incoherent consternation. What fall? What second cousin once removed? How does Oscar know more about his family than he does himself?

'You were telling me about it,' says Oscar helpfully, 'when you came to dinner last (and I really must thank you once again for your kindness in coming). Remember?'

Almost certainly not. But he will, Oscar, he will. On the *escalier* afterwards. Together with the fact that you got a Nobel Prize last week, are just about to swim the Atlantic single-handed, and have still not had back the dinner-jacket, the electric drill, and the copy of 'Finnegans Wake' you lent him.

But it's James, as we at the Self-Justification Research Centre believe, who will go to heaven.

(1967)

School of applied art

There's a lady in Kensington, according to the papers, called Mrs Thorne, who runs conversation classes 'for the sophisticate who finds small talk difficult.' In seven hours, at 10 guineas the course, she teaches her case-load of sophisticates to get round their incapacity by talking about art.

We sophisticates have long known about the old art dodge, of course. The trouble has been up to now (if my own case is typical) that while we find small talk difficult, we don't get on too well with the big stuff, either. This has cost some of us dear in lost opportunities for business and romance.

Mrs Thorne has hit upon two great complementary principles which make big topics accessible to small talkers. 'It's just a question of learning what to say,' she insists; and, 'It doesn't matter what people say as long as they say something.'

Armed before and behind with these two weapons of war, the sophisticate advances into any social gathering and merely looks round the room until his eye falls upon a picture. If it happens to be a Constable, Mrs Thorne advises that you should mention you have just come back from the Constable country. If it's a Van Gogh, she suggests greeting it with a remark like 'I always wonder what sort of painting he'd have done if he'd been entirely sane.' (If you want to know what to say if it happens to be a Vermeer or a Leonardo, or a Guardi or a Braque, take your 10 guineas along and ask Mrs Thorne.)

Anyway, it's clear that Mrs Thorne is providing in seven hours what at the universities it still takes three solid years to acquire – a thorough practical grounding in the humanities, of the sort which years of experience have shown to fit graduates for a career in industry or government, for the management of scientists, and for the selection of a wife or husband.

Take the case of Harley Sparrowdew, bachelor and sophisticate. In the documentary film I am preparing on the Thorne system for Unesco, we see him at a brilliant gathering of industrialists, playwrights and Cabinet Ministers, a vodkatini in one beautifully manicured hand, gazing profoundly at a rather unsophisticated painting of a yellow chair. Suddenly be becomes aware that the lovely sophisticate Soignée Cheroot is standing silently beside him, lost in contemplation of the picture, too.

'What I always wonder,' breathes Soignée raptly, 'is what sort of painting he'd have done if he'd been entirely sane.'

Sparrowdew turns and gazes at her. For a moment the world seems to stand still.

'You wonder that?' he asks softly. 'Because so do I. Always. Night and day I ask myself, "What kind of thing would this man have done if he'd been normal?"'

'I know. I know. The question haunts one. Oh *God,* I know the feeling!'

'It seems to me that if he could just have got away from this terrible sick obsession with chairs, he might – who knows? – have painted something quite normal. A table – a sideboard.'

'Yes! Or a hatstand, or a cocktail-cabinet. Something clean and wholesome! Something that says yes to life!'

'Yes! That's it *exactly* . . .'

A century later – or is it only 10 minutes? – they have slipped away from the vacuous social throng, and are sitting at a sidewalk café beneath the stars. Somewhere, soft music is playing.

'I realised you were an Old Thornian, too, from the first moment,' Sparrowdew is saying, gazing into her eyes. 'I felt at once that we had the same background, that we were interested in the same things. I felt – oh, I don't know – we spoke each other's language. When you said that wonderful thing about Van Gogh – "I always wonder," you said (I shall never forget it), "what sort of painting would he have done if he had been entirely sane" – when you said that I felt somehow it was all preordained. I felt as if our whole thing was written down somewhere in some great book. You know what I mean?'

'Yes! I feel that if I hadn't said it first you would have said it yourself.'

'I feel that, too. It's your tenderness, your deep *concern* for Van Gogh, that moves me.'

'Our education taught us both to ask questions.'

'To wonder. To have a sense of wonder.'

'Yes! And the tremendous freedom with which one learnt to speak!'

'The feeling that it didn't matter what one said – all that mattered was the act of saying, the act of being articulate!'

They sit in silence for some minutes, absorbed in the thoughts they have conjured up.

'It was terrible when one first came down from Mrs Thorne's,' says Sparrowdew slowly. 'One's first contact with the real world outside. It seemed so – so bleak and grimy. One went from party to party, and nowhere did one see a Constable or a Van Gogh on the wall. One's education seemed wasted, irrelevant.'

'I felt exactly the same. Exactly!'

'The odd Piper lithograph, perhaps, the occasional Colquhoun sketch. The phrases one had learnt sounded hollow in one's mouth.'

'But gradually . . .'

'Gradually it began to make sense. People listened. Personnel officers – managing directors. Older and wiser heads than one's own saw the advantage of having a man with a sense of curiousity about Van Gogh in charge of research.'

'Or on the Board.'

'Slowly everything fell into place. One perhaps bought one's Constable or one's Van Gogh. Bit by bit, with maturity, the point of it all became clear. All one lacked was someone who understood to share it with.'

'Until tonight . . .'

'Until tonight . . . Did I tell you I'd just come back from the Constable country, incidentally? I've got one or two slides I took of it, if it's not too late to come back to my place and have a look at them . . .'

(1965)

Scrapbook for 1964

It was a wonderful summer that year. Everyone seemed to be at the seaside, enjoying the long sunlit days without a care in the world . . .

It was the year of the Mods and Rockers . . . of 'Can't Buy Me Love' and 'Anyone Who Had a Heart'. Everyone was dancing the Shake, the Block and the Blue Beat. In America a man brought out a two-piece swimsuit with only one piece . . .

But over it all hung a shadow. For this was 1964 – the twenty-fifth anniversary of the outbreak of the Second

World War. In grim sunless offices all over Europe hard-faced men in shirtsleeves were plotting to unleash upon the world the most terrible campaign of war memoirs, war films, war poetry, war photographs, war histories and war reappraisals that mankind had ever seen . . .

Among the crowds in Britain as the crisis drew on that fateful summer was one man who sunbathed and danced the Shake with a somewhat pensive expression. From time to time he would stop singing 'Anyone Who Had a Heart' for a moment, and thoughtfully jot down something on a scrap of paper. A perfectly ordinary man, you might have said, jotting something down on a perfectly ordinary scrap of paper . . .

But what he was writing was a diary – a minute-by-minute account of his experiences in that fateful year. His intention was to place it in a sealed envelope for publication on the twenty-fifth anniversary of the outbreak of the Great Memoir War, as a form of endowment assurance for his old age. We are privileged to be able to publish it now, twenty-five years ahead of its time.

Thursday: Lunch at Reggie Tooth's with the Dicky Dymchurches and Sandy Troon. The talk is of nothing but the crisis – the papers are full of it every day. Only the *Daily Express* strikes a more hopeful note – 'No War Anniversary This Year'. They argue that only a hopeless pessimist could believe that the silver anniversary of the Second World War would fall in the same year as the golden anniversary of the First. They say the conjunction must be the result of some official muddle.

I ask Reggie, who has highly placed contacts in the diary and calendar industry, if he thinks there might be anything in this. He says he thinks not, and I'm afraid he is right. We have managed to turn a blind eye to the ominous events of the last few years – we did nothing about the anniversary of Caesar's invasion of Britain in 1945; we looked the other way in 1955, when we were faced with the

500th anniversary of the outbreak of the Wars of the Roses. But I've met no one who doesn't think we're in for it this time.

Friday: Sunshine, ripe corn, red apples warm to the touch – the grim old portents of impending war memoirs are everywhere. I cannot help recalling with a shudder the blazing summer of 1959, when we numbly watched the remorseless approach of the 105th anniversary of the Crimean War.

Spend the afternoon looking at the grey, sunless holiday snaps of happier years.

Saturday: Down to the Dymchurches' place for the weekend, with Reggie, Arthur Wissop, Eddie Nockstruck, and some of the Bewers-Loadwater crowd. Over lunch Arthur says the situation is even more serious than we suppose – he has private information that 1964 is also the 225th anniversary of the War of Jenkin's Ear.

Eddie suggests that there might still be a chance to avoid it, if the Government took the bold step of going over to the duodecimal system, which would make it only the 189th anniversary.

'That would merely postpone the evil day, Eddie,' said Reggie wisely. 'We should soon be landed with the 200th duodecimal anniversary. You have to face up to these things one way or another.'

Eddie began to mutter something under his breath. 'What was that?' asked Reggie sharply. 'I said it's exactly 2,182 years since the outbreak of the Second Punic War,' replied Eddie. 'Why aren't you worrying about that?'

'Dammit, Eddie,' said Reggie coldly, 'there are *some* rules in this game.'

Sunday: Gathered around the Dymchurches' television set after dinner to watch for the latest bulletins. A queer, tense atmosphere. After the news Huw Wheldon broadcasts to the nation. 'It is my duty to inform you,' he says, his voice almost breaking, 'of two grave new developments in the situation. It is now clear that this year is the 140th anniversary of the First Burmese War, and the 125th anniversary of the China War of 1839. We must all be ready for celebrations at any moment.'

After the broadcast we sit in silence for some minutes, each absorbed in his own thoughts. Then Reggie says levelly that we have a long haul ahead of us – he mentions among other things the centenary of the Franco–Prussian War in 1970, and the bicentenary of the American War of Independence in 1975. Eddie begins to say that he can see no earthly reason for commemorating the American War of Independence, since we lost it, but even his friends shout him down. I do not think he speaks for Britain in her new mood.

Monday: Spend the day on war memoir work, patrolling the streets recording the hours of sunshine, and looking for apparently ordinary men doing apparently ordinary things. Meet Guppy Trottle outside Boodle's. 'Do you realise,' he says, 'that it is now exactly twenty-four hours since this time yesterday?' Make a note of it. Seems of little meaning or consequence now, like everything else, but one knows how solid and significant it will appear when it is recalled twenty-five years hence.

(1964)

Service with a smile

'As you are aware,' begins a letter that arrived the other day, '*x* Computer Services is your encumbrant service provider.'

Well, no, in point of fact, I was *not* aware that *x* Computer Services was (or even were) my encumbrant service provider. I thought they were the people I had a maintenance contract with to repair various pieces of electronic apparatus when they go wrong. It comes as a slight surprise to discover that I have such a thing as an encumbrant service provider.

A pleasant surprise, certainly. I shall drop it into the conversation when you are going on rather tiresomely about the wonderful little man you have who adjusts your bannisters, or tunes your euphonium. 'If you ever need any encumbrant service,' I shall say, 'you might do worse than try the provider I have.' You'll be shaken. You haven't got an encumbrant service provider yourself. The need for encumbrant service has never arisen in your rather less sophisticated lifestyle. You're not absolutely certain, if you're honest, what encumbrant service is.

So you probably wouldn't understand the rest of the letter, either. It's all written in a very elevated style, which I think may be a little above your head, but which evokes confidence and respect in those of us who know how to appreciate the finer things of life.

'We understand,' it says, 'in times like these IT Departments are under extreme pressure to provide internal services to there users. We are uniquely positioned to assist your organisation with a full portfolio of additional value added services . . . As you are already a valued customer of x, we can . . . encompass additional services within your existing contract.' And they offer me a choice of On-site Resource and Outsourcing.

You gape. You didn't know I was an IT Department, as well as a man of letters and connoisseur of fine wines. You never realised what pressure I was under to provide internal service to various there users. The concept of a there user is probably beyond you for a start. Look, there are here users like me, yes? Here I am, using here in various ways – sitting, talking, etc. No mystery about it. You understand that? Well, then there are also users who are not here but there. There they are, using there. But to do this they require internal services from here.

Which we poor IT Departments have to provide! Oh, yes, we earn our outsourcing all right, especially in times like these – because I don't have to tell you what times like these are like. So I'm particularly glad to be offered not only additional services but *value-added* ones. And to be offered them not in a plastic carrier-bag, but in a *portfolio*, ready to be *encompassed*. And not by some scruffy street-trader propped up against a lamp-post, but by someone *uniquely positioned*.

It's embarrassing to watch you struggle with all this. All right, let me go back to the beginning and explain to you what *encumbrant service* is. It's service so elaborate and gracious as to be a positive encumbrance to the less socially adept. You remember when you were staying in a grand hotel somewhere, and you picked up the phone to order a boiled egg from room-service? And you knew you'd get such a flourishing of napery and single-stemmed roses, such a flashing of smiles and a whipping-off of covers, and that you'd be required to perform such a nervous jumping up and down and smiling and thanking in return, such a juggling with gratuities which may or may not have been included in the bill, that you put the phone down again?

Well, that's encumbrant service, and a man of the world like myself is perfectly at home with it. One of the machines that *x* Computer Services look after is on the blink now as it happens. If it were yours you'd pick the phone up, then realise you couldn't just blurt out in ordinary uncultivated English to service providers as grand as these that the screen was all kind of jiggering about, and you'd give up and go out for a hamburger once again.

Whereas I put on my special voice for talking to earls and above, and I say easily . . . Well, let me just practise in front of the mirror for a moment.

'I do most tremendously regret being encumbrant upon you, but I seem to be positioned so that I am requirant . . .

requisant . . . of on-site resourcing . . . outsourcing . . . out-site onsourcing. Could you encompass this? I should explain that I am a servicee of yours. A receivee of your valued service . . . your value-added service . . . your valuable additional service with added value. I am, I should perhaps explain, a here user. A here and now user. A here and in-times-like-these user.

'Or rather was, until my equipment became service-requisant. I am a here and formerly in-times-like-these user. An existing here and formerly in-this-day-and-age user. An ex-existing user who is urgently desirous of becoming a re-existing user.

'The thing is, the screen's on the blink . . . Sorry! – I mean on the nictitate . . . It's gone all kind of funny . . . has become in some sense inducive of cacchination . . . inductive of risibility . . . Well, let's not beat about the bush, let's not flagellate about the berberis. It's afflicted by an encumbrancy . . . positioned in discommodant mode . . . internally subfunctional . . . functionally value-deficient . . . defective in its functional modality . . .

'Anyway, I am desirous of achieving disencumbrancy of this encumbrancy. Would you be positioned to offer, ex-portfolio, external service to which value had been added, where the value in question resides in the successful encompassment of the value-added service?

'And if so, could you do it in times like these? I mean, in times *remarkably* like these? In times more like these than tomorrow will be?

'May I say how much value I should esteem to be added to your already valued offer if you could extend its presently existing potentiality into fully potentialised existence?'

You see? That's what I call *style*. It needs a little effort, but it's so encumbering.

(1995)

Services rendered

FIRST SERVICE

Tonight they are holding my favourite service, the Annual Service for People in Advertising, in All Souls, Langham Place – and the sixth in the series, no less.

Still, not everyone in the advertising industry will find the somewhat traditional atmosphere of All Souls congenial. Since the moral welfare of advertising men is a subject close to my heart, may I recommend the Harvest Festival which CADCAR (the Congress of Advertising, Confidence, and Allied Racketeers) is holding in St Swiz's, and which many in the industry will find more up-to-date and relevant in its approach? For those who are thinking of going, here is the order of service:

HYMN

We put our trust in Swiz,
For only Swiz has Fiz, etc.

LESSON

From the Book of Amazing Free Offers

1. These are the generations of Swiz. Thomas Noggin begat Joseph Noggin; and Thomas Noggin and Son begat Noggin *Holdings*; and Noggin Holdings begat Noggin (England) Ltd; *and* Noggin (England) Ltd begat Oho.

2. And Oho begat Fub; and Fub begat Guf; and Guf begat Swiz; and Swiz begat twelve million pounds.

RESPONSES

Blessed be the name of Swiz.
Let the name of Swiz be praised.
The hoardings shall blazon it forth.
And the air shall be loud with the clamour of it.

On the page it shall be written.
On the page, yea, across two pages.
In special supplements shall it be sounded forth.
And bruited even in the editorials.

(The copywriters and public relations men walk in procession to the front, bearing pieces of copy, designs for cereal packets, plastic giveaways, samples of tournedos and whisky they have bought for journalists, and newspaper cuttings of stories they have originated. These offerings are judged by a panel of well-known television personalities, and Golden Calf statuettes are awarded as prizes.)

(Here endeth the first part)

> *It's new! It's true! It's made for you!*
> *For knees in trousers, knees in cassocks,*
> *You cannot better CADCAR HASSOCKS!*
> *CADCAR! CADCAR! CADCAR!*

(Here beginneth part two)

LESSON

From the Second Book of Unsolicited Testimonials

1. There dwelt in the *town* of Screwe, that is over against Twicester, a certain poor woman.

2. And it came to pass that unto her appeared a man in *shining raiment* that said: I am come from Swiz, and am sent forth by him to inquire if there be any in this city that *keep* his name in honour.

3. For unto him that keepeth his name in honour shall be given cause for rejoicing, and great increase shall be his.

4. Then saith the poor woman: all my life I have kept faith with Swiz, and *have not deserted* him. And lo, she shewed the man her Swiz, which was of *family size*. And he drew forth from his scrip two more Swiz, and gave them to the woman, saying: Thou faithful servant, thy treasure is multiplied threefold.

5. And he saith unto her: Unto those that keep faith with
Swiz, with them shall Swiz also keep faith. For that which
is white shall be whitest; and that which is whitest shall be
whiter than white. Ten thousand are the women that have
witnessed unto this miracle, and it is written: Can ten
thousand women be wrong?

6. And the woman was amazed, and gave thanks, and
magnified the name of Swiz.

SERMON

On the text from the Book of Fub: 'Shall a man labour for
truth, when that which is not true comforteth multitudes?
For truth is like the butter that was put unto the test. An
hundred women partook thereof, and of those hundred
were there nine and ninety that were deceived, and knew
not the false butter from the true. For the false butter was
smooth and finely apparelled, and they knew it not.'

HYMN

Who would an adman be
Hymning sweet fictions,
Must labour valiantly
'Gainst state restrictions.

Consumers flee away,
I'll fear not what they say,
I'll call the night the day,
To be an adman.

(1961)

SECOND SERVICE

I'm sorry to say that the helping hand I tried to offer my
friends in the advertising industry in the last piece by
announcing (free of charge) the order of service for the
advertising men's Harvest Festival at St Swiz's was not too
well received.

The hardest things of all were said by Mr Mark Chapman-Walker, a director of Television Wales and West, about the extract from the article which later appeared on BBC Television. It was, he said, 'so staggering in its irreverence, bad taste, and general unfunniness that I am not surprised that a large number of people complained'.

Mr Chapman-Walker is also a director of the *News of the World*, so his views on matters of taste command respect. In fact I have decided that the best thing I can do is to go right back to the beginning, and give the details of the service in St Swiz's with an attempt at the reverence, good taste, and general funniness which in the good old days made Mr Chapman-Walker's paper the trusted and respected companion of eight million families every sabbath.

THE VICAR AND THE WOMAN IN THE FRONT PEW

What a vicar alleged he saw going on quite openly in his own church at Harvest Festival was described yesterday when Michael Frayn, a journalist, of 29 Tregunter Road, Screwe, was found guilty on three charges of irreverent staggeringness, gustatory badness, and general humourlessness.

The Reverend Harold Admore, vicar of St Swiz's, said that he had held a Harvest Festival for advertising men. But his first reaction to what met his eyes on entering the church was one of disgust. In answer to a question, he replied it was the smallness of the congregation that had disgusted him.

SEX MIX-UP

Admore said that besides the men there were a number of women present. The sexes were mixed. He thought that some of the women had been brought by the men, but that others had 'simply walked in on their own from the street'. Many of the women were wearing make-up and high heels.

ASSOCIATED WITH COLOURED MAN

Admore stated that he took as the subject of his sermon man's quest for good, likening it to the skilled tracking which was associated with the Red Indian. His intentions throughout the alleged incidents, he said, had been entirely honourable.

Miss E. Grewsom said that she had been sitting in the front pew all the time that the events mentioned were alleged to have been taking place. She agreed that the vicar had used certain words. They were clearly audible from where she was sitting. She also saw him make certain gestures.

SHOCKED

She recalled distinctly that at the end of the first hymn, and on several other occasions, the vicar had used a four-lettered word. It had stuck in her mind, she said, because of the tone of voice in which he had uttered it, and because it seemed to be constantly on the lips of everyone present, women as well as men.

Under cross-examination, Miss Grewsom admitted that she had been shell-shocked while serving with the ATS.

NOT HIS BABY

Mr P. J. Nunbetter, a church-warden, gave evidence that he had heard Admore make a certain suggestion to a younger man. As a result of this suggestion, the younger man had played the first hymn.

Nunbetter said he did not remember which hymn it was, since the musical side was 'not his baby'.

INDULGED IN ORGY

Questioned about money that was alleged to have changed hands during the evening, Mr R. O. Platter, another church-warden, admitted that he had collected it.

He said he did not know how much was involved, and that it was none of his business to ask what services were expected in return for the money.

'My job is simply to collect it,' he said. 'You seem to think I had nothing better to do than to indulge in an orgy of speculation.'

NOTHING ON

In a statement, Admore was alleged to have admitted being a miserable sinner, but to have added: 'The police have nothing on me.' His wife gave evidence that he had always behaved perfectly normally, so far as she knew.

As stated, Frayn was found guilty on all three charges, and sentenced to five years' corrective reading of the *News of the World*.

(1961)

The sleepy sickness

The ailment of the age seems to be a combination of sickness and tiredness. Everyone's suffering from it.

The Duke of Edinburgh is sick and tired of making excuses for this country. A great many of us, according to Sidney Silverman, are sick and tired of the North Vietnamese always getting the blame.

'People are sick and tired of listening to criticism of the Holy Church,' declared Father Joseph Christie, the acting Catholic chaplain at Cambridge, after cutting short his fellow-Jesuit Archbishop Roberts in the middle of an address to Catholic undergraduates on the grounds that it was heretical, and closing the meeting.

'I am convinced,' said Father Christie, 'that there will be an enormous amount of approval for myself.' I dare say there will. All sorts and conditions of men, I gather from the papers, are sick and tired of something. If it's not hearing their Church criticised that they're sick and tired of, it's seeing traditional morality and family life undermined, or hearing oaths on television, or all this soft treatment for criminals.

And if there's any one group that's sicker and tireder than the rest, it's *some of us*. Some of us, if some of us are to be believed (particularly Labour politicians), are sick and tired of pretty well everything.

No wonder we had to abandon the National Plan. There can scarcely be a soul left well and fresh in the country.

Nor are sickness and tiredness the only symptoms produced on these occasions. Mr Patrick Wall MP last week defended the removal of Father McCabe from the editorship of the *New Blackfriars* magazine on the grounds that its criticisms of the Catholic Church would 'cause distress to millions of Roman Catholics in Britain and elsewhere.'

The *New Blackfriars* has a circulation of 2,000, but of course distress, like sickness and tiredness, is very catching. Great outbreaks of distress are perpetually being diagnosed or predicted among people of all denominations and outlooks as a result of exposure to unfamiliar ideas.

What is not always appreciated, I think, is that we humanists, agnostics, Britain-knockers, morality-underminers, and so on, get sick and tired, and suffer distress, just like anyone else when the ideas and values that we hold precious are called into question. Day in, day out, we are sniped at. Often I can hardly finish reading the morning papers, there is so much in them that offends my susceptibilities.

'What's the matter, dear?' asks my wife anxiously. 'You look rather sick and tired again this morning.'

'Oh, it's nothing,' I lie bravely, my face grey with fatigue, my brow fevered. 'It's just that there's a rather clever fellow in the paper here pouring scorn upon all that some of us hold most sacred. You remember that rather beautiful idea some of us had of arranging for humanist school-children to say special humanist prayers at morning assembly? Well, this clever gentleman apparently finds something rather funny in it. That's all.'

'Perhaps some of you ought to go back to bed today,' suggests my wife solicitously.

'Perhaps some of us ought to. Some of us *were* going to try to make a personal contribution towards raising national output today by writing slashing attacks on various reactionary prejudices and superstitions. Now, of course, the country will just have to do without that.'

But that's nothing compared with what some of us have been through on other days. There have been occasions when my wife has found me suffering really acute spiritual distress after hearing ideas at variance with my own publicly disseminated.

'I can't think why it's allowed!' she has heard me cry, my voice breaking. 'Fancy letting someone appear on television, in front of millions of people – some of them impressionable teenagers, some of them mere children – and say he believes in original sin!'

'There, there,' she murmurs.

'He was wearing a clerical collar!' I moan, shuddering at the recollection.

'You must be brave, Michael.'

'But I can't help feeling that my trust has been abused. That's what upsets me, you see. I put the television on expecting some sort of wholesome, decent entertainment – people bashing each other over the head and having babies and saying "bloody" – you know, our sort of thing. And what do they spring on me . . . ?'

'Try to take a broad view, Michael.'

'I mean, we are a *minority*, after all, aren't we? We deserve the same consideration that other minorities get, don't we? Goodness me, some of us go to the most inordinate lengths to be respectful about the Catholics. Never mention their little troubles except in the most hushed and reverent tones.'

'You're not all that respectful about the Methodists, are you?'

'The Methodists? Oh, for heaven's sake! You don't have to be respectful about the *Methodists*! That's a different sort of thing entirely. But we're very careful about of the feelings of Jews.'

'What about Jehovah's Witnesses and Plymouth Brethren?'

'Oh, come, come! But take the Sikhs and the Quakers. We're very reverent about them.'

'And the Communists?'

'Certainly not. Everyone's nasty to the Communists. That's what Communists are for.'

I wonder if perhaps some of us shouldn't bury our little differences, and get together on a broad platform of being sick and tired of all the rest of us. It could bring the brotherhood of man a little nearer.

(1967)

Smoothe's law

Of course, I'm entirely on the side of the nurses, God bless 'em (*said Rollo Swavely, the well-known public relations consultant*), but all this shindig about their pay has been damned unfair on Christopher Smoothe. I handle his private account, as you know, and I've seen the strain, the terrible sense of injustice, that he's been labouring under these last few weeks.

You see, Mike, everyone thinks it's rotten luck that nurses get five pounds a week, or five pounds a month, or whatever it is. And of course luck's the responsibility of

Christopher, as Minister of Chance and Speculation. It's not as if it was just the nurses – it's been civil servants, teachers, railwaymen – one after the other. 'What bad luck!' says everyone – and Christopher gets the blame once again. Well, he's just a human being like you and me, Mike. He can't help worrying about it.

That's why some time ago he set up this National Wages Explanation Council ('Nwexie' to you), under the chairmanship of Arthur Weefellow, the Professor of Ancient Economics at Twicester. It's not that he's for one moment doubting the fundamental Conservative principle of leaving all human affairs to the free operation of chance. But he believes fervently that all the Government's present difficulties can be solved by public relations, and as a genuinely constructive step in this direction he's given Nwexie the task of discovering some general principles that would explain to the layman without mentioning the word chance just why the nation's wage-structure takes the form it does.

It's a damned complicated business, Mike. I've been looking at their preliminary report on wages in what we call the devotional field. Take nursing, for instance – a job that clearly requires unlimited devotion. Obviously the general principle here is to make the wages as low as possible to keep out undesirable elements who would otherwise pour into nursing just to make a fast buck. But now we come up against a snag. What about surgeons? Don't they need devotion? Does their high pay mean that all the operating-theatres in the country are full of undesirables just out for the cash?

Well, I can tell you Nwexie took evidence on the last point from the PRO of the British Surgeons' Association, and he assured them at first hand that in the case of surgeons high salaries and devotion are entirely compatible. So they had to amend the principle to read: 'The greater the devotion required for a job, the lower the wages – except where applicants are likely to have a standing conferred by class or education which would put them above sordid financial considerations.'

But what about schoolteachers? A lot of them have a university education – and their salaries are derisory. So Nwexie amended the end of the formula to read: '. . . above sordid financial considerations – unless the work involves contact with minors, who could be corrupted by the flaunting of great wealth.'

You'd have thought that covered just about every complexity wage-structure in the devotional field could possess. Far from it. What about bishops? Aren't they well paid? And don't they confirm children? So Nwexie had to go to work once again and add: '. . . corrupted by the flaunting of great wealth – save where the noxious effects of such flaunting are neutralised by suitably uplifting ecclesiastical surroundings.'

We're still not out of the wood, though. What about people in other devotional jobs, like advertising or public relations? What about all the advertisers who sell things to children? Am I supposed to go and conduct my 'Meths for Men' campaign, to get teenagers drinking methylated spirits, in church, just so that I can justify being paid more than five pounds a week? So they had to add something about either uplifting ecclesiastical surroundings or a beneficial effect on profits.

And so on, and so on, until they had a formula twelve pages long. It certainly brings a gleam of logic into what at first sight one might think was entirely illogical. Nwexie wanted to reduce it to a simpler formula for the benefit of the man in the street. Christopher turned down 'You get what you grab' as being against the public interest. So it looks as if Smoothe's First Law of the Diffusion of Income, as I've suggested calling it, is going to read: 'Wages are what they are.' Drink up, old boy.

(1962)

Songs without words

The news that English National Opera were proposing to introduce surtitles, even though they always sing in English, has had much the same effect upon a lot of people as the news of Edgardo's betrayal upon her betrothed in *Lucia di Lammermoor*. They went mad. Hands have been wrung, letters have rained down upon editors. An article in the *Independent* described the decision as 'corporate suicide'. Surtitles, said its author, Mark Pappenheim, result in 'an undue emphasis on "what's going on". As if any real opera was ever about anything as banal as narrative action.'

Verdi, he argued, 'never expected every word to be heard – he tried instead to make a few key words (*parole sceniche*, he called them) really come across – words like *madre, amore, morte*.' Every syllable of Mr Pappenheim's argument was clearly distinguishable.

Apparently ENO agree, because the report, like the report of Edgardo's faithlessness, turns out to be false. The surtitles will be merely an experiment at some performances, to replace signing for the hard of hearing.

When it comes to operatic dialogue, though, even sung in English, we're all hard of hearing. I certainly longed for a surtitle or two during ENO's current *Khovanshchina*. This magnificent production of Mussorgsky's great historical epic, which portrays seventeenth-century Russia's belated emergence from mediaeval barbarism into Peter the Great's slightly more up-to-date variant of it, has (for once) been properly and universally acclaimed by the critics. But, as they have also noted, its plot is as tangled as tights in a washing machine.

This is not the fault of the production, or of ENO (who have provided no less than three separate accounts of the plot in the programme, together with an excellent

historical background and the genealogy of the Romanovs).
It caused me particular difficulties, though. I saw it with a
group of friends who in each interval flatteringly turned to
me, as someone who knows Russian, and asked me to tell
them – well, yes – what was *going on*.

Who were the Streltsy, they demanded. Why were they
Archers in some versions, and Musketeers in others? Why
did Khovansky appear to be supporting the Tsar in Scene
One, and then getting murdered by him in Scene Five?
Which side was Golitsyn on? Which side was anyone on?
What did the Old Believers believe? Who was this Susanna
who suddenly appears out of nowhere in Scene Three and
starts hurling accusations around? Had she and Figaro fled
to Moscow to escape the attentions of Almaviva? Why were
there three accounts of the plot in the programme?

My knowledge of Russian didn't help me very much,
since it was being sung in English. For myself, of course, I
am far above any banal interest in the narrative content
of opera, but my companions seemed to place an undue
emphasis on the question, even without surtitles to encourage them, and my reputation and authority declined
from interval to interval.

It was not as if I hadn't prepared myself – I'd read the
three accounts of the plot in the programme, and studied
two different works of reference in advance. All five
versions went out of my head as soon as the curtain went
up. I listened hard for any helpful *parole sceniche*. But you
needed a little more to go on in this case than *madre,
amore, morte*. You were hoping for something more like
'. . . son of Tsar Fyodor III's father Alexei not by Maria
Miloslavskaya but by Natalia Naryshkina . . . Vasili
Grigorievich, arrested on false testimony for plotting to
usurp the deputy-chairmanship of the Moscow City
Council Cleansing Department . . . Grigory Vasilievich,
supposed second cousin of the disgraced ex-sub-Metro-
politan of Kiev . . .'

But the bits you actually do catch on these occasions tend not to be quite as *sceniche* as you require. They're more usually things like: 'Alas . . . Extraordinary to relate . . . nevertheless . . . Aha . . . ! Oho . . . ! Oh . . . ! Ah . . . !' (Because of course there's nothing singers sing more distinctly than open vowel sounds, unconstrained by consonants.) Also: 'Who is this . . . ? What are you saying . . . ? What is *going on* . . . ?' Because probably the characters can't catch much more than we can of what's being said. Most of them in *Khovanshchina* are also illiterate – they haven't even been able to read the programme.

If only Mussorgsky, who wrote his own libretto, had realised that opera wasn't about anything as banal as narrative action he could have saved himself, the singers, and us a great deal of trouble. The discovery has certainly simplified the titanic struggle I have been having with my commission from ENO to write the libretto for *Euroshchina*, Harrison Birtwistle's vast new historical opera about the crucial negotiations involved in the emergence of the European Union in its present form.

In this mighty confrontation of historical forces as I now conceive it, the singers will make up their own text as they go along in all the inaudible sections, with as many open vowels and as few consonants as they like. All I'm going to provide them with is the audible bits. The job's as good as done.

Act I. *The Grand' Place in Brussels. A vast crowd of under-secretaries, lobbyists, political columnists, disgruntled pig-farmers, speechwriters, and Autocue drivers is surging colourfully around, singing with great conviction about some policy they are strongly in favour of – possibly connected with set-aside payments for turnips, possibly with standardised inflation pressures for children's balloons. A bloody confrontation ensues with another crowd who are strongly opposed to it.*

Enter LANCELOT HIGGLE (*baritone*), *a journalist who can usually be relied upon for a few quick pars of historical background, to fill us in on the development of the Union so far.*

HIGGLE (*espansivo*)
Ah! Long and meandering is the path
That led us hither . . . You recall
The basket of currencies . . . the shadowed
    Mark . . .
(Not Mark Thatcher – another one . . .)
But long, long before . . . joint working-parties at
    ministerial level . . .
Agenda . . . referenda . . . An end
To centuries of conflict . . . Alsace-Lorraine . . .
Franco-Prussian War . . .
Holy Roman Empire . . . Huns . . . Gauls . . .
Neolithic peoples . . . Ah! Oh . . . !
500 words, invoice follows.

He drinks himself to death. Enter the COMMISSIONER *of some country whose identity is completely obliterated by a blast on the trombones just as his name is announced. He is deep in conversation with a* SECRET EMISSARY FROM THE CZECH REPUBLIC. *Unless it's* A COMPLETE IMBECILE TO CHECK THE PLUMBING.

COMMISSIONER (*molto moderato*)
Annexe B to Directive 5Z9 . . .
Revised draft . . . Amendment
To Clause 15g . . .
Your Government's views . . . ?
EMISSARY   Ah!
COMMISSIONER Are? This is most interesting . . .
Are what?
EMISSARY   Aha!

COMMISSIONER Are hard? And fast? I see . . .
Well – a helpful and constructive
exchange of views . . .
So vital . . . maintaining a dialogue . . .
Each other's point of view . . .
EMISSARY What?
COMMISSIONER Remarkably . . . For the time of year . . .

Enter HUGH PAYNE (*tenor*), *a British MP who was intending to vote for the European budget, but who failed to hear the division bell because of a sudden tutti. Unless it's* BILL *someone* (*bass*), *who was going to vote against, but who failed to hear the voice of conscience for much the same reason.*

COMMISSIONER . . . Hugh Payne?
PAYNE Who's paying? Who's paying what . . . ?
COMMISSIONER I mean, you're Bill . . . You're Bill . . .
PAYNE My bill? What bill? Not my bill at the
Ritz . . . ?
COMMISSIONER The writs . . . ? What's this about writs?
PAYNE . . . Issuing 'em!
COMMISSIONER Bless you.

Enter LUCIA DI LAMMERMOOR.

LUCIA I seem to be . . . a little confused . . .
Could somebody tell me . . .
What . . . in a word . . . is going on?

Everyone comes surging hopefully downstage and gazes up into the darkness above the proscenium arch. But, fortunately for the aesthetic purity of Europe, up there nothing is going on at all.

(1994)

Spock's Guide to Parent Care

PARENTS ARE JUST LARGE HUMAN BEINGS. It's only natural for a small child to feel a little daunted by the hard work and responsibility of coping with parents. All parents get balky from time to time, and go through phases which worry their children, and all children get tired and discouraged and wonder whether they're doing the right thing.

The important thing to remember is that most parents, deep down inside, want nothing more than to be good ones. A parent may act tough and cocky, but at heart he wants to be one of the gang. He wants to learn what's expected of him as parent and do it. What he needs from you above all is plenty of encouragement, and plenty of reassurance that he's doing all right.

EVERY PARENT IS DIFFERENT. This one flies into a fury at the sight of crayoning on the wallpaper. That one bursts into tears. Yet another goes into a sulk and won't say anything all afternoon. All these are perfectly normal, healthy reactions. I'd be inclined to be suspicious of the parent who seems a little too good to be true. He or she may be deprived of emotional experience for lack of opportunity. I think I'd ask myself in this case if I was drawing on the wallpaper enough.

THEY AREN'T AS FRAGILE AS THEY LOOK. Handle them confidently. Many parents look as though they'll have a nervous breakdown if you bang your toy on the table just once more. Don't worry – nine times out of ten they won't.

DON'T BE AFRAID TO INSIST ON YOUR OWN STANDARDS. There's been a great swing away from the over-permissiveness which used to be the fashion, when a parent's every whim was regarded as sacred. Nowadays we've come to realise that on the whole people don't have any very clear ideas about manners or morals until they become parents, when they hastily start to make them up as they go along. They're secretly very grateful for a little firm but tactful guidance.

I don't mean by this that you should squash the parents' own spontaneous efforts to help. But what they eventually learn to think right and proper will be decided very largely by the way you act anyhow.

PLAY IS EDUCATION, TOO. All the time you are with your parents you are educating them in tolerance and self-discipline. Playing games and romping with them is specially useful. It's not only great fun for them – it's helping to form their characters. Various games such as hitting your little brother, and then bursting into tears before he does, train their powers of detection and judgement. Jumping on their stomachs after meals and finding reasons to get them up in the middle of the night develop their resistance to hardship, and generate a sense of righteousness which will enable them to face cheating their colleagues the next day with an easy conscience.

TEMPER TANTRUMS. Almost all parents have temper tantrums from time to time. You have to remember that between the ages of 20 and 60 parents are going through a difficult phase of their development. They have got to a stage in their exploration of the world at which they find it is rather smaller than they thought. They are discovering the surprising limitations of their personality, and learning to be dependent. It's natural enough for them to want to explode at times.

It's no use arguing with a parent who's in this sort of state. The best thing is just to let him cool off. But you might try to distract him and offer him a graceful way out by suggesting something that's fun to do, like taking it out on your little brother instead.

GO EASY ON KIDDING. Most parents enjoy a joke. If you get hold of a good one, try it on them 20 or 30 times, just to show them what it's like being on the receiving end of the family's sense of humour. But I think I'd give it a rest after that, in case it causes nightmares.

JEALOUSY. Most parents are worried, though they probably wouldn't admit it, that they're not really good enough, and that other parents are better at the job than they are. In one parent it will take the form of worrying that his children are not as pretty, or as well-behaved, or as intelligent as other people's. Another will try to resolve his fears by telling himself that other parents don't really look after their children properly.

A parent showing symptoms of jealousy needs lots of love and reassurance. Once in a while it might help to beat the boy next door in a clean fight, or win that scholarship. But you can't do this too often without the risk of spoiling the parent. Once a parent gets the idea that he can just sulk and you'll win a scholarship for him he'll lead you a terrible dance.

BE FRIENDLY BUT FIRM. In general, don't give your parents too much chance to argue. Just quietly get on with whatever you want to do, perhaps chatting amiably to distract their attention. The chances are they won't even notice, or that when they do it will be too late for them to feel like making a fuss.

Parents can sometimes drive a small child almost to distraction by dawdling about in shops, or talking to friends. It doesn't really help to keep nagging, or to try dragging them along by brute force. If I were you I'd hop cheerfully about from foot to foot, and say in a firm, friendly voice: 'I want to go to the lavatory.' If that doesn't work, you could try turning white, and saying you're going to be sick.

REMEMBER YOU'RE HELPING THEM TO GROW UP. It's your job to help your parents grow up into mature, responsible old-age pensioners, self-confident, armed with a workable code of morals and manners, and too exhausted in mind and body to make trouble for anyone else. If you

keep in mind that you're training your children's grand-
parents you won't go far wrong.

(1966)

Strain cook thoroughly before serving

When I was a bachelor I used to dine variously on fried
eggs, fried bacon, fried eggs and fried bacon, or fried bacon
and fried eggs. There were also occasional days when I had
forgotten to buy either eggs or bacon.

My somewhat limited range in the culinary field has
earned me but a menial position in the kitchen now that I
am married. I am allowed to peel the potatoes and empty
the trashcan, provided I stand to attention when spoken to,
but not to prod the soufflés, or baste the beans, or whatever
real cooks do.

There are, however, certain recipes which reduce my
wife to such a state of nervous disintegration that she is
forced to lean on me abjectly. I mean the sort written by
authors who haven't yet heard the good news about the
invention of weights and measures. And if a recipe-writer
still hasn't got round to the concept of ounces and pints (or
for that matter hins and cubic cubits – we're prepared to
make every effort to compromise), you can bet your bottom
tealeaf that he hasn't managed to grasp the principles of
written communication either, or of predicting what tools
and materials he is going to need until he has actually
picked them up.

I hear despairing cries from the kitchen, and find my
wife set on making a recipe which starts off: 'Pour a fair
amount of milk into a medium-sized bowl, and throw in a
generous handful of soya beans. Add a modicum of grated
cheese and the quantity of chopped chives which will lie on
a sovereign piece.'

I help my wife choose a particularly medium-sized looking bowl, and supply the generosity for measuring out the soya beans. 'Take a few eggs,' the recipe goes on, 'and carefully separate the whites from the yolks. Now whisk them into the mixture.' The whites or the yolks? We compromise with a half of each.

'Fry the mixture for a few minutes over a hottish flame, until it is the colour of a walnut sideboard, and there is black edging round the shredded onion.' The shredded onion? 'This should have been added before the soya beans in order to prevent the milk curdling. Now quickly transfer the mixture to a cast-zinc stew-pan.'

'Run out to the corner,' shouts my wife, 'and buy a cast-zinc stew-pan.' I run all the way there and back. 'You'll have to go out again,' she cries on my return. 'After I've transferred the mixture to the cast-zinc stew-pan I've got to add a very large eggcupful of icing-sugar.' Without a word of protest I run all the way back to the corner and get the icing-sugar. 'No, no, no!' shouts my wife as I stumble breathlessly back into the kitchen with it. 'I've got the icing-sugar – I wanted you to buy the very large eggcup.'

When I stagger painfully back into the room again with the eggcup, I find my wife sieving tiny pieces of raw meat out of the mixture. 'The recipe,' she sobs, 'says: "Pour the mixture over a jam-jarful of minced beef." '

'Then why are you taking the beef out again?'

'The next sentence says: "The beef should have been roasted for an hour first."'

We force-roast the beef, and brace ourselves for what lies ahead. 'Place an asbestos mat beneath the dish,' says the recipe, 'and beat it with a wooden spoon. Continue beating until, at the bottom, the top of it is covered underneath with a grey sauce of sodden soya bean. The bottom of it should then rise out of it, coming through the top of it (the pan) until the rest of it (the bottom of it) can be separated from it, and placed in a pie-dish beaten to the consistency of thin gruel. Bake briskly. When a fine blue aromatic smoke begins to rise, the mixture is hopelessly overcooked.'

It is quite late at night when the fine blue aromatic smoke at last curls out of the oven, and we are both very tired and weak with hunger. My wife turns over the page and reads the last sentence of the recipe: 'Before serving, store in a cool place for at least a fortnight to allow fermentation to finish.'

Well, well. But the canned luncheon meat, I must admit, is opened to a turn.

(1961)

Substance without soul

It's curious how plastics are so universally disliked as materials. Or perhaps not so much disliked as despised, as if they were in some way *morally* inferior. Everyone uses them, and everyone despises them, just as the rich use and despise the poor.

Not *you*, of course, open-minded reader. I know you've got an entirely sensible attitude towards plastics, as towards everything else. But take me. In our house we eat off china plates, which break if you drop them. We drink out of glasses, which break if you look at them. We have plaster walls and wooden furniture, neither of which are capable of surviving the proximity of normally active human beings. How is it in your house, open-minded reader?

Most people's first objection to plastics, I think, would be that they frequently try to ape their betters and pass themselves off as other materials. But they disguise themselves only to avoid our contempt for plastics as plastics, and to plastics as plastics I think our principal moral objections are these:

They don't feel right. They're too cold to the touch, or too warm; too smooth, or too tacky. To put it bluntly, they don't feel like leather or stone or wood or metal. They feel like, well, like plastics.

They're unnatural. That is, they're not got by hewing, mining, quarrying, smelting, tanning, or any of the other robust age-old processes by which we get proper materials. I say 'we.' I don't mean 'we' in the sense of 'you and I,' of course – I don't suppose you or I have ever done much quarrying or smelting. I mean 'we' in the sense of 'someone.'

They're too bland. They have no grain or quirkiness – no innate character which imposes itself upon us. Like a subject race they are too obedient to be respected.

Thus, they can be worked too easily. I don't mean that you or I could work them. Of course we couldn't – we haven't got the right tools, and we couldn't tell a polyester from a polyanthus, anyway. I mean that you don't have to roll up your sleeves and forge plastics, or carve them, or otherwise bend them to your will by sheer physical skill, as you do with proper materials. Or as someone does.

Dammit, they're not produced by individual craftsmen at all. They're turned out by faceless industrial organisations equipped with immensely expensive plant, and staffed by ordinary faceless functionaries like you and me.

Anyway, they're too cheap. They're cheaper than the materials for which they're alternatives, which is damning enough in itself; and because they're cheaper, goods made in plastics are usually more widely distributed, to poorer people with commoner tastes.

I'm not sure that this last objection isn't the strongest of the lot. After all, china-clay is bland and easily-worked. Glass is cold and unnatural. Stainless steel and diamonds are produced by immense corporations equipped with remote-controlled electric furnaces.

Still, I dare say we shall come round to the new material eventually. We usually do. I seem to remember that when

I was a child the word 'cotton' had a rather deprecating ring. It went with 'thin' and 'flimsy,' as in descriptions of under-nourished girls wearing cheap make-up and shivering in their thin cotton dresses. Cotton was the poor man's substitute for wool or silk. Then they invented nylon and the rest; and now a genuine cotton shirt is the luxurious alternative to a hard-wearing, drip-dry, artificial one.

Thatch was once endured by the poor, and is now restored by the rich. Fur-coats were no doubt regarded much like denim overalls until someone invented weaving, and hunting declined. Denim, indeed, has risen from overalls to ladies' play-suits. Even poor old chromium plate begins to be treated with respect, now that we can look back with nostalgia from the thin chromium-plating put on cars today to the thick, rich, incorruptible stuff they trowelled on before the war.

One can imagine with what disdain the last of the Neolithics looked upon the incoming tide of flash, cheap bronzewear; and how young married Bronze Agers kept bronze cutlery for the children, and proper flint knives, which broke if you dropped them, for their guests. And how the first grasping entrepreneurs of the Iron Age made their money selling characterless iron teaspoons in Woolworths, and spent it on buying for their own use fine antique bronze teaspoons rescued by astute dealers from the nurseries of an earlier generation.

Not all materials make the grade – corrugated iron hasn't for one. But I confidently expect before I die to be buying back at reassuringly high prices the plastic junk I'm throwing out now, and hanging it reverently round the antique plastic panelling. I see myself at some great age settling back in my cosy old PVC-covered swivel chair and watching a learned team on television discussing the lost glories of the Age of Plastic.

'This delightful little figure of a cowboy,' some expert will be saying, turning it over lovingly in his fingers, 'dates from the early 1960s, and was probably given away with a breakfast food, so general was pride in art and fine craftsmanship then.

'This sort of work was being done in literally hundreds of small workshops up and down the country. It's difficult for us today, I think, to realise what a tremendous atmosphere of creative excitement there must have been in the air at that time. The whole nation must have seemed to be bursting forth into plastic song. Why, the very names of the materials those old craftsmen used are a hymn of praise in themselves – polystyrene, polyethylene, polypropylene, polymer resin, polyurethane, polyolefines; cresylics and phenolics; acrylonitrile-butadiene-styrene . . .'

Not like the ghastly range of materials they'll be using by then. Unnaturally resistant to all forms of damage, with some ludicrous form of grain or texture to boot.

And *outrageously* cheap.

(1966)

Tell us everything

The phone rings. You pick it up. You're a private person, in your own home. What do you say?

You say one word. You say 'Hello.'

And you say it with an upward inflection, with the suggestion of a question mark at the end. This is dialogue of a succinctness and expressiveness that a playwright can only envy. With one short word you are simultaneously announcing your presence, offering a sample of your voice for identification, and asking your caller to identify himself in his turn.

The line can be performed in all kinds of different ways. It can suggest courtesy and patience, or irritation at being interrupted. It can convey character – a confident optimist who expects every call to be good news, a suspicious pessimist who knows it's going to be bad.

All this with one word – 'Hello?' And now here is where your performance achieves true greatness. Because whichever way you said it, at this point you stop. You sense, with the instinct of the true artist, that you have said all that needs to be said, and you say no more.

Now let's take a slightly different situation. Once again you're answering the phone. But this time it hasn't rung – not yet. You're going out, and you're recording the response that your answering machine is going to make to calls in your absence. You press the outgoing message button – and at this point all your artistry deserts you.

'Hello,' you begin, certainly – but as soon as you've said it you realise you haven't said it in the usual way. There was no upward inflection, no note of query. Your voice fell instead of rising. You have no sense of an audience. You know you are talking to yourself, and you have begun to

feel rather foolish. Like an actor on a bad night, you find
that your whole performance is beginning to break up
around you. You are not speaking politely or impatiently,
confidently or cautiously. You are speaking slowly and
carefully. That unresponding audience out there . . . you
have a sudden uneasy feeling that it may not even understand English.

You don't trust the text any more. And so you start to try
and improve upon it. 'You have reached 0467 22 983 3451,'
you say, very distinctly. This is odd – you've never announced your number to me before. You don't need to. I
know it. I've just dialled it. But you suspect you may not
be speaking to me. You think I may be some complete
stranger who has just arrived from Paraguay, ringing from
a darkened phone-box with a number scribbled semi-
legibly on the back of an envelope that was given him by
someone he met years ago in a youth hostel in Turkey. And
I may well be. But if so, why are you treating me to this
great piece of oratory about *having reached* the number?

Yes, this is odder still. You are speaking not just slowly
and carefully – you are speaking portentously. Never mind
this non-existent visitor from Paraguay – you seem to
believe you are making a statement which may be used in
evidence in some future court case. You are broadcasting a
last message to the world from the besieged city. You are
speaking to posterity. Your words will go into the archives
of recorded sound, to be cracklingly broadcast and re-
broadcast in the years to come over newsreel shots of the
mid-nineties.

And on you plunge. 'There is no one here to take your call
right now,' you inform me solemnly. I believe I was beginning to guess as much. I think a faint suspicion was
beginning to dawn upon even the man from Paraguay, who
doesn't understand a word you're saying.

'But,' you say, 'if you wish to leave a message . . .'

If I *wish* to leave a message, I notice. Not if I merely *want* to. We are on a slightly higher plane of human aspiration than mere wanting. If I *wish* or *desire* to. If I *am desirous of* leaving a message. Well, why not, while we're about it? But a message for whom, I ask myself. For the nation? For all mankind?

'. . . for Warrington or Lenticula Shrubbe . . .'

Oh, for my good friends Warrington or Lenticula Shrubbe! For you two! For the very people I phoned, the ones who are not there to take my call right now! How very logical!

'. . . or for their children, Rigida and Reston . . .'

Their children? Rigida and Reston? I thought they were *your* children! What are you telling us?

'. . . or for Craxton Upstruck or Specula Gumm, who are contactable at this number until the 24th . . .'

And who I believe are that very boring couple you met on holiday last year. Yes? Why not tell us so, then? You've told us everything else. Why this sudden abandonment of full public disclosure?

But now a serious question arises. *If*, as you surmise might be the case, I wish, or desire, to leave a message for any of you, how on earth do I go about it? I put it in a bottle, perhaps? I go out and buy a carrier pigeon . . . ? But what's this I hear? You're still speaking! You're telling me what to do!

'. . . then please speak clearly after the tone.'

I see. Thank you. I am to speak – not to shout, or to whistle – and to speak clearly. I am to do it after the tone. But only, of course, *if* I wish to leave a message. *If* I am moved by a volition to communicate an intelligence. If I am not so moved, however, then I imagine I may speak clearly *before* the tone. I may speak *indistinctly*, either before or after it. I may mutter to myself, before, during, *and* after it . . . I may even say nothing.

In which case why don't you tell me this in so many words? Why do you leave me to work it out for myself? Why not say, quite plainly: 'If, on the other hand, you do not feel the advent of any overmastering need to communicate your thoughts to any of the aforementioned, not even to poor Specula, who never gets any messages, then you may elect to replace your receiver in silence, gently but firmly, being careful to keep it properly aligned with the base of the instrument.'

You don't because you're too busy worrying about the mess I shall make of things if I do try to leave a message.

'Kindly leave your name,' you suggest.

My name! Of course! Were desirousness of expression on my part the case then my name, indeed . . .

'And number,' you add.

And number! Yes! A shrewd suggestion! Thank you!

'It would also be helpful if you stated the time you called, and the date, together with the current weather conditions, and a note of your date of birth, next of kin, and National Insurance number.'

But before I can assemble all this information you have moved on once more. And this, I think, is going to be of particular interest to me, because now we have come to the question of what you are offering to do in return for all my efforts.

'We will call you back,' you promise, 'as soon as we can.'

You will call me back. Yes. This is the amazing proposal that your speech has been leading up to. This is what I could never have foreseen when we started out on this great journey together.

And when will you call me back? Not, as I might have guessed, when you happen to feel like it. Not when your children have grown up and left home. You will do it *as soon as you can*.

But when precisely will that be, *as soon as you can*? It will be when I am out, of course. So you won't be greeted by my usual curt 'Hello?' You will get my answering machine. You in your turn will be treated to a torrent of eloquence, a wealth of helpful suggestions about how to proceed. You will be astonished and delighted by my proposal to call *you* back.

If you're still listening at that point. Because you may have put the phone down by then, which is what a lot of my callers seem to do. So they miss all the later parts of the message, when I'm absolutely certain I'm talking to myself, in which I agonise about my terrible sense of isolation, in spite of all my efforts to communicate, and ask myself whether it's something about my manner that puts people off. Should I try to explain the workings of the answering machine more fully? Be more heartbroken about my inability to take your call?

Or should I just go *beep*, and to hell with it?

(1994)

Tête-à-tête-à-tête

'What do you feel about the passing of the shirt tail?' asked my wife suddenly the other day, in a thoughtful tone of voice. If only I'd had the presence of mind to reply:

'I personally – and of course you will understand that I am speaking now purely as an individual – I personally believe that the passing of the shirt tail is something deeply symptomatic of the social crisis of our times – and one to which all too little attention has been paid by the Press and the public alike.'

If I'd managed to say that, we should at last have had the makings of a *television conversation* in our own home. We should have shown that it was possible for ordinary people to emancipate themselves from the old-fashioned private conversation, intended merely as a utilitarian form of communication between those taking part, and to aspire to the new public conversation, held exclusively in order to be overheard. To take an analogy from another art, we should have moved in one step from singing in the bath to the mad scene from *Lucia di Lammermoor*. If not farther.

Well, it will come, it will come. And when it does, my wife can scarcely help but reply:

'I think I'm right in saying, am I not, that to you a shirt which comes untucked from the top of your trousers is a very real symbol of the chaos and violence eternally present beneath the surface of life?'

Self: Yes, I think this symbolism has been a constant theme in my work over the last 10 years – almost an obsession. To me the shirt that comes untucked is the eternal artist and rebel – the Rimbaud, the Raskolnikov – if you like, the Wild One on the beach at Margate – who breaks loose from surroundings he finds intolerably restrictive, and in so doing shows up the hollow pretensions of the trousers from which he has escaped.

Wife: This is of course, is it not, a theme which has fascinated and inspired artists since the invention of the trouser? But what I think many people may not realise is that, *paradoxically,* in your personal life you yourself have made – and indeed to my knowledge still make – the most enormous, one might almost say the most *gigantic,* efforts to keep your own shirt tucked in.

Self: I think this ambivalence, this one might almost say *dichotomy,* is very central, isn't it, is very seminal, to what I think it was C. S. Lewis would have called the noumenon, or as Jung so expressively put it, the mandala. Or, as we know it in our own lives, the shirt tail.

Wife: I remember – with enormous pleasure, if I may say so – the wonderful exhibition you made of yourself with an untucked shirt at Edinburgh in 1961. I hope we shall have a chance to see that performance repeated some time in the very near future.

Self: Thank you. And now, to change the subject. It's a

far cry from shirt tails to bath-water, but all the same, it's bath-water that we're going to talk about now. I think we were all shocked to hear the news today that the bath belonging to our good friends Horace and Doris Morris had overflowed. Now, I believe you were in the area recently, shortly before the flooding occurred. Can you say anything which would help me to evaluate the scale of disaster?

Wife: Well, the bathroom is about 15 ft long by 10 ft wide, with important towel-drying installations on the south side and dense clumps of toothbrush on the north. But I should imagine that the area which was chiefly affected was the floor, in which as I remember it was comparatively low-lying.

Self: As one who knows the Morrises intimately, how do you think they will react to the situation?

Wife: Well, knowing them as I do, and indeed as you do, I believe they will pull together – make a really tremendous united effort to get the damage repaired and put their bathroom back into commission as soon as possible.

Self: Well, we wish them luck. From bath-water it's but a short step to another liquid – tea. I'm going to pass you a cup of tea. Here it is – a cup of tea. Just an ordinary cup, with tea inside it. Now I want you to look at this cup of tea, at this perfectly ordinary cup, with this perfectly ordinary tea inside it, and tell me if you would like sugar in it.

Wife: Just one lump, please, of perfectly ordinary sugar. And from a lump of sugar we move many thousands of miles northwards, from the sugar plantations of Trinidad to these rather less sunny climes – to a lump in the throat here at home. To the lump in the throat, to be precise, without which I cannot recall the time when I was single.

Self: Perhaps I should just interrupt here, if I may, to make it clear that you are now married.

Wife: That is correct.

Self: And what I think is quite interesting to note – and

I believe this is something you are too modest to mention –
you are in fact married to me.

Wife: Yes, I think that's a point worth making. Anyway,
as I was saying, I cannot recall without emotion the time
when I was single, and had no one with whom to hold a
conversation and share my inmost thoughts.

Self: I know this is a painful question, and believe me, I
would not ask it if I did not have to in order to get the
answer I need to round off this unscripted, spontaneous
discussion. What did you do for conversation in those days?

Wife: I just gazed sadly into the teleprompter and talked
to myself.

Self: Mrs Frayn – thank you.

(1964)

That having been said

I've been visiting the local Old Tropes Home.

I'm very concerned about what happens to expressions
and metaphors in their old age. They start out in life so
fresh and colourful, so full of humour, so eager to please.
They're worked day in and day out over the years
until they're exhausted – then they're brutally shoved to
one side to make room for younger and more energetic
expressions. I believe that they shouldn't have to eke out
their last few years of life on the streets, taking any work
they can get, spurned and abused. They should be looked
after among their own kind in quiet and dignified surroundings.

In the place I've found the residents were obviously made
very comfortable. Comfortable with and about everything,
even the most appalling ideas and decisions. In fact they
seemed particularly comfortable about Attila the Hun.
There was a statue of him, placed somewhat to the left of

the building, so that almost everything inside was somewhat to the right of him.

The Matron who showed me round spoke very reassuringly. 'I understand where you're coming from,' she said. 'So let me just bring you up to speed. We're very definitely state of the art here, and I don't need to tell you which art that is – it's the art of living. And if you're up at the sharp end then you've got to get your act together and show your street cred. That having been said, what gets up my nose is that people can't get their heads around this. I mean, what are we talking?'

I said it sounded to me like some dialect of English.

'We're talking serious money,' she said. 'We're talking megabucks. Because what are we looking at here?'

So far as I could see it seemed to be the ancient flagpole outside the window up which things were run to see if anyone saluted them.

'We're looking at ten grand a day,' she said. 'Ten K – and I do mean K. Because, make no mistake, the sky's the limit. That said, you pays your money and you takes your pick.'

The social range of the residents was wide. As she showed me round the Matron pointed out both the Poor Man, to whom many things here were said to belong, curiously enough, and the Thinking Man, who apparently owned much of the rest. But everyone there seemed to be terribly good value. Indeed, they were all getting increasingly better value. Because things in the Home don't just get increasingly whatever, or more whatever. They get increasingly more whatever it is. There seems to be an acceleration involved here which bears the fingerprints of the pace of modern living.

Some of the residents were in poor shape. Things had cost them an arm and a leg – often as a result of prices going through the roof, and the roof falling in, so that the bottom had dropped out of the market. Some of them looked as if they'd had a coach and horses driven through them.

A very decrepit old trope called Arguably buttonholed me in the corridor. 'In the last twenty years or so,' he told me, 'I have become arguably the most common word in the English language. I have arguably been responsible for making more unconfirmed statements possible than ever before in human history, and I've arguably saved writers and speakers more mental effort than the word processor and the dictating machine combined.'

He thought for a little, though not very hard.

'Then again,' he said, 'equally arguably I haven't.'

Couples are not separated in the Home. You can see them wandering along the corridors together, hand in hand, touchingly devoted. This Day and Age – they're still as much in love as ever. If you see First you're bound to see Foremost. Sick and Tired were being wheeled along in a double bathchair by Hale and Hearty. Care and Attention were being utterly devoted to all the Hopes and Fears. Though one Fear had left the family group and gone off with Trepidation. Now they've grown so alike that a lot of people can't tell them apart.

The old tropes are a remarkably lively lot, considering. 'We *have sex* a great deal,' one of them told me. I expressed surprise. 'Oh,' he said, 'we have it pretty well non-stop. Look through this keyhole. You see? People having every single variant of sex listed in the OED! Everything from (1) *either of the two divisions of organic beings distinguished as male and female respectively*, through to (2) *quality in respect of being male or female* – even (3) *the distinction between male and female in general*'!

My informant thumbed through a greasy copy of the OED. 'It doesn't stop there, either,' he whispered hoarsely. 'The OED says that this third usage is now often associated with a *more explicit notion*.' He licked his lips and bent closer towards me as he read it out. '*The sum of those differences in the structure and function of the reproductive organs on the grounds of which beings are distinguished as male and female, and of the other physiological differences consequent on these.'*

These torrid relationships and steamy romances raise the temperature and humidity of the Home so that everyone gets a little hot under the collar. The clouds of vapour given off by all this may be the mysterious *yonks* which so many people haven't seen each other for.

To take the inmates' minds off sex there is a playing-field attached to the Home, and great efforts are made to ensure that it is a level one – though people are apparently always moving the goalposts. Efforts to organise a piss-up in the local brewery have not yet been successful. The local vicar sometimes invites inmates to the original vicarage tea-party. No one ever goes, though, because everything in the Home has been made to look like it already, even the steamiest sessions of distinction between male and female.

In the dining-room residents were making a meal of it – and that was just for starters. Some of the dishes on the menu were out of this world. In fact they were to die for, and if they weren't to die for they were the kind of thing you'd kill to get your hands on. So, one way or another, by the end of meals a fair number of the residents tend to be out of this world as well.

In other words, they'd had their chips, which was just as well, because when the chips are down there's no such thing as a free lunch. It's not a picnic here, after all – naturally enough, since some of the inhabitants are two sandwiches short of one. In the circumstances I was not surprised to be told that most of them were quite frankly out to lunch.

The Home is organised along military lines. I talked to inmates who were proud to belong to the Gin and Tonic Brigade and the Blue Rinse Brigade. The Green Welly Brigade have a reputation for profligacy with the brigade colours – they are always giving things a bit of welly.

I could hear the most alarming noises of protest in the background, but the Matron explained that this was coming from the twentieth century, into which various things were being dragged kicking and screaming, entirely for their own benefit.

I asked why some of the residents were being made to stand in silence with their faces to the wall. The Matron said that they were members of the chattering classes – people who had had the temerity to talk about politics and other public matters that concerned them. She also pointed out a group of luvvies – actors and actresses who had ludicrously attempted to vary their slothful round of unemployment and awards ceremonies with some kind of pretence at seriousness. They were being put down hard and sent up rotten.

In some of the rooms there was scarcely room to swing a cat – though this was impossible to check because, as the Matron explained, the cat was in hell, and it didn't have much chance of surviving. About as much as a snowball, she thought. Though, if the snowball managed to survive until hell froze over it would find itself in a whole new ballgame.

They did have a handcart for going to hell in, said the Matron, if I wanted to go down that particular road, and she wished me the best of British. But before we could get the ball rolling all hell broke loose.

An inmate in bell-bottomed trousers staggered up and flung his money around. He was not, he explained, flinging his money around like a drunken sailor – he was the drunken sailor like whom everybody else flung their money around. Very difficult to know, in that case, I suggested, how he himself was flinging his money around. Was it, I asked, like money was going out of fashion? Not at all, he replied, it was like there was no tomorrow.

It was plainly crunch time, and the Matron cracked down hard, though she papered over the cracks as best she could.

But no way could the crackdown be made to bite unless it was given teeth.

As I left I met a new arrival, still looking relatively fresh-faced. 'Political Correctness,' he introduced himself. 'I feel I'm a bit past my sell-by date. And since the whole idea of a sell-by date has gone down the tubes itself some time ago, like the tubes it went down, I thought I'd join it in here, and we could all pop our clogs together.'

Because that said, what's it all about, at the end of the day? What's the bottom line? Let me spell it out to you in words of one syllable – the bottom line is this.

(1994)

Through the wilderness

It is nice now that all you boys have got cars of your own (*said Mother*). You know how much it means to me when the three of you drive down to see me like this, and we can all have a good old chatter together.

John: That's right, Mother. So, as I was saying, Howard, I came down today through Wroxtead and Sudstow.

Howard: Really? I always come out through Dorris Hill and West Hatcham.

Ralph: I find I tend to turn off at the traffic lights in Manor Park Road myself and follow the 43 bus route through to the White Hart at Broylesden.

Mother: Ralph always was the adventurous one.

John: Last time I tried forking right just past the police station in Broylesden High Street. I wasn't very impressed with it as a route, though.

Howard: Weren't you? That's interesting. I've occasionally tried cutting through the Broylesden Heath Estate. Then you can either go along Mottram Road South or Creese End Broadway. I think it's handy to have the choice.

Ralph: Of course, much the prettiest way for my money is to carry on into Hangmore and go down past the pickles factory in Sunnydeep Lane.

Mother: Your father and I once saw Lloyd George going down Sunnydeep Lane in a *wheelbarrow* . . .

Howard: Did you, Mother? I'm not very keen on the Sunnydeep Lane way personally. I'm a great believer in turning up Hangmore Hill and going round by the pre-fabs on the Common.

Ralph: Yes, yes, there's something to be said for that, too. What was the traffic like in Sudstow, then, John?

John: Getting a bit sticky.

Howard: Yes, it was getting a bit sticky in Broylesden. How was it in Dorris Hill, Ralph?

Ralph: Sticky, pretty sticky.

Mother: The traffic's terrible round here now. There was a most frightful accident yesterday just outside when . . .

Howard: Oh, you're bound to get them in traffic like this. Bound to.

Ralph: Where did you strike the traffic in Sudstow, then, John?

John: At the lights by the railway bridge. Do you know where I mean?

Ralph: Just by that dance hall where they had the trouble?

John: No, no. Next to the neon sign advertising mattresses.

Howard: Oh, you mean by the caravan depot? Just past Acme Motors?

John: Acme Motors? You're getting mixed up with Heaslam Road, Surley.

Howard: I'm pretty sure I'm not, you know.

John: I think you are, you know.

Howard: I don't think I am, you know.

John: Anyway, that's where I struck the traffic.

Ralph: I had a strange experience the other day.

John: Oh, really?

Ralph: I turned left at the lights in Broylesden High Street and cut down round the back of Coalpit Road. Thought I'd come out by the Wemblemore Palais. But what do you think happened? I came out by a new parade of shops, and I thought, hello, this must be Old Hangmore. Then I passed an Odeon –

John: An Odeon? In Old Hangmore?

Ralph: – and I thought, that's strange, there's no Odeon in Old Hangmore. Do you know where I was? In *New* Hangmore!

Howard: Getting lost in New Hangmore's nothing. I got lost last week in Upsome!

John: I went off somewhere into the blue only yesterday not a hundred yards from Sunnydeep Lane!

Mother: I remember I once got lost in the most curious circumstances in Singapore . . .

Ralph: Anybody could get lost in Singapore, Mother.

John: To become personal for a moment, Howard, how's your car?

Howard: Not so bad, thanks, not so bad. And yours?

John: Not so bad, you know. How's yours, Ralph?

Ralph: Oh, not so bad, not so bad at all.

Mother: I had another of my turns last week.

Howard: We're talking about cars, Mother, CARS.

Mother: Oh, I'm sorry.

John: To change the subject a bit – you know where Linden Green Lane comes out, just by Upsome Quadrant?

Howard: Where Tunstall Road joins the Crescent there?

Ralph: Just by the Nervous Diseases Hospital?

John: That's right. Where the new roundabout's being built.

Howard: Almost opposite a truss shop with a giant model of a rupture belt outside?

Ralph: Just before you get to the bus station?

Howard: By the zebra crossing there?

John: That's right. Well, I had a puncture there on Friday.

Ralph: Well, then, I suppose we ought to think about getting back.

Howard: I thought I might turn off by the paint factory on the by-pass this time and give the Apex roundabout a miss.

John: Have either of you tried taking that side road at Tillotsons' Corner?

Ralph: There's a lot to be said for both ways. A lot to be said.

Mother: I'll go and make the tea while you discuss it, then. I know you've got more important things to do than sit here listening to an old woman like me chattering away all afternoon.

(1962)

Total scholarship

I was delighted to hear

I was depressed to see

I was interested to learn that the complete works of the late Charlie Parker, the great master of modern jazz, are being brought out in a variorum edition, including all the false starts and alternative readings.

It surprises me

It does not surprise me

It surprises me that no one has yet suggested publishing a variorum edition of any journalist's works. I should think they must get round to it finally.

As a matter of fact, I have given the matter a certain amount / a great deal of thought, and I am rather inclined / absolutely resolved to make a start in that direction myself. For the benefit of posterity I am going to begin writing my own footnotes.[1] I'm going to stop / cease / desist from crossing out the speeling[2] mistakes, and thoughtlessly chucking / casually flinging / irresponsibly precipitating the material I don't use into the waste-paper basket.[3] In a word, I'm going to compile my *own* ~~voriarum~~[4] ~~viarorum~~[5] variorum edition. It'll save somebody[6] a lot of work, anyway.

James Thurber[7] once remarked that if you saw his first drafts you'd think the cleaning woman[8] had written them. If his first drafts really could have provoked scholars to suppose anything so stimulating to literary research, they were source-material which it was wanton vandalism of Thurber to throw away.[9] DON'T FORGET RING CRUMBLE ABOUT DINNER THURS!!!![10]

This new approach represents a serious criticism of our recieved (check spelling)[11] idea of the function of art. From

1 This is a good example of the *genre*.

2 Mis-spelling for *spieling* – 'persuasive talking.'

3 Reichart remarks that 'basket' was a common euphemism in the Royal Navy c.1930 for 'bastard,' and suggests that by analogy with debased Anglo-Indian usages such as 'janker-wallah' the phrase 'wastepaper basket' may perhaps be understood as 'salvage collector.' But more probably in this context, 'a receptacle for waste-paper.'

4 Voriarum: corruption of *vomitorium*.

5 *Viarorum*: i.e., via Rorum. Rorum is a non-existent place, therefore, 'by way of nowhere,' i.e., 'not by any means' (humorous usage).

6 Exactly whom is a matter of speculation. Reichart suggests that he himself is intended here, but Skimming disputes this.

7 James Grover Thurber (1894–1961).

8 The so-called 'Dark Lady of the Broom Cupboard.' Identified by Skimming as Della (cf. Thurber: 'My World and Welcome To It'). Pilsudsky's theory that it was the Earl of Arran is not generally accepted.

9 Probably intended jocularly, but the simple truth nonetheless.

10 Meaning obscure. For an interesting explanation in Jungian terms, see Rosie (Journ. of Amer. Soc. of Ephem. Lit., vol XXIII).

11 It is typical of the author's 'feel' for language that he sensed this word was mis-spelt.

a superficial point of view, it has always seemed that the whole point of books, articles, poems, and so forth was their form and subject.[12] It has been left to modern scholarship to show that their real significance lies in the light which they cast upon their authors.

In other words

To put it slightly differently

Otherwise speaking (Is this English?)[13] a creative undertaking is nothing less than the autobiography of the undertaker.

That is to say, art is interesting because it tells us about the artists[14] – who are of course interesting because they produce art.

In other words, the whole of art is nothing less than a running gossip column on the art world.[15]

(1964)

12 This observation has been confirmed by many other authorities, e.g. Westland, Boosey, Sidgwick, Fanfani and da Costa.
13 No.
14 Very true.
15 This pungent and devastating conclusion is of the greatest interest because of the light it sheds on the author's ability to reach, in this case, a pungent and devastating conclusion.

Twelfth Night; or, What Will You Have?

The other day my wife bought a jar of what were described on the label as 'Old English Cocktail Olives.' Ah, evocative words! They bring vividly to mind that golden age when England was still covered with primeval olive groves and when the rip-roaring Old English Cocktail Party was in full flower. Like most Old English things, it was at its best in Elizabethan times – to judge, at any rate, from the following fragment, entitled *Ye Cocktayle Partye,* and attributed to Will Shakespeare (by Mike Frayn, at any rate).

(Scene: The Earl of Essex's At Home).

ESSEX: Ah, good Northumberland! Thou com'st betimes!
  What drink'st? Martini? Champagne cup? Or hock?
  Or that wan distillate whose fiery soul
  Is tamed by th' hailstones hurl'd from jealous heaven,
  The draught a breed of men yet unengender'd
  Calls Scotch on th' rocks?

NORTHUMBERLAND: Ay, Scotch, but stint the rocks.

ESSEX: Ah, Gloucester! And your fairest Duchess, too!
  Sweet Leicester! Ah, my Lady Leicester, homage!
  And Worcester, and the Chesters, radiant pair!
  And Ursula, the sister of Lord Bicester!
  Northumberland, methinks thou know'st not Gloucester,
  Nor Gloucester Worcester, nor the Leicesters Chesters.
  Lord Worcester, may I introduce Lord Leicester?
  My noblest Gloucester, meet your brother Chester.
  My Lady Chester and my Lady Leicester,
  Meet Ursula, the sister of Lord Bicester.

ALL: Hail!

GLOUCESTER: Well, now, hath Phoebus quit these climes
    for ever?

WORCESTER: Ay are we now delivered quite to gales,
  And spouting hurricanoes' plashy spite?

CHESTER: Sure, 'tis foul weather.

LEICESTER: Why, so 'tis.

NORTHUMBERLAND: 'Tis so.

(Another part of the battlefield).

ESSEX: What ho, champagne! Crisps, ho! Pass round
    the peanuts!

WORCESTER: A peanut, madam? Pardon me, I pray,
  But when we met, the white-hot dazzlement
  Your beauty rains about like thunderbolts
  Quite seared my eyes; I did not catch your name.

LADY URSULA: Why, Ursula, and sister to Lord Bicester.

WORCESTER: Not Harry Bicester? Known to th' admiring
    world

As Eggy? Wears a red moustache?

URSULA: The same.

WORCESTER: O, Eggy Bicester! and thou, thou art his
    sister?

Then long-lost cousins must we surely be!

ESSEX: Forgive me, Ursula, if I intrude,

But, Worcester, meet our brother Chester here.

He has the royal birthmark on his arm,

Would know if you had, too.

WORCESTER: Why, so I have.

CHESTER: Why, marry then, you are my brother, stol'n

At birth by she-bears.

WORCESTER: Why then, that I am!

LADY LEICESTER: The truth of th' ancient legend now is
    clear:

'When Worcester linkt to Chester prove to be,

Then Gloucester in Northumberland we'll see.'

Northumberland is Gloucester, chang'd at birth,

And Gloucester Worcester, while the aged Earl

Of Leicester plainly must be Lady Chester,

All chang'd, and double-chang'd, and chang'd again,

The Chesters Leicesters and the Leicesters Chesters,

Lord Chester, thus, the proof runs clear, is me,

And Ursula, Lord Bicester, his own sister.

NORTHUMBERLAND: Before the discourse turns again to
    weigh

Apollo's absence and the pluvious times,

We should acquaint our new selves with each other.

My Lady Chester, once the Earl of Leicester,

Meet Lady Leicester, now the Earl of Chester . . .

ESSEX: Old friends 'neath curious titles oft are found

Come, pass th' Old English Cocktail Olives round . . .

(1961)

A very quiet car

Plain ordinary cowardice. That, for what it's worth, is my un-informed personal diagnosis of what's wrong with my car. Cowards, said Caesar, die many times before their death, and my Audi has died seven times in the three years I've had it.

Seven times I've gone to start it, and found it with life entirely extinct. Seven times it has been taken in, by Audi's excellent recovery service, to the excellent local Audi agent, and resuscitated. They have given it two new batteries, and changed a certain control unit, I think, three times. They have kept it under observation for periods of up to a fort-night. They have done everything that motor engineers can do, and done it with genuine concern, intelligence, and determination. The bills have all been met by Audi, even after the guarantee expired, under the heading of 'good-will'. Audi's goodwill seems to be unbounded. It's mine that's becoming just a shade strained.

I bought it because it seemed a quiet, safe, secure, reliable, dark blue kind of car. And so indeed it has turned out. When it's in its inactive mode it's very quiet indeed. The diagnosticians at the garage sometimes ask if it clicks when you turn the ignition key. The answer is no, it doesn't even click. A click would sound like a gun going off in the profundity of its silence. Safe? Yes – the chances of its being involved in an accident in this mode are as close to negli-gible as car-designers are ever likely to achieve. Secure? Unstealable, I think, without a tow-truck or a team of horses. Reliable? So far, at returning sooner or later to its peak performance in terms of quietness, safety, etc. And dark blue? Still dark blue.

It's been back in intensive care this past week, having its

entire electrical system stripped out. Manuel, the recovery driver, is always remarkably good-humoured about being called out. He reminded me, laughingly, that the time before last I had for some reason become a little agitated, and had added considerably to the entertainment value of the occasion by locking the key inside the car. This time I remained very good-humoured myself. I've got used to the routine. I'm becoming institutionalised.

Also, to be fair, the car often goes. In fact it goes more often than not. But sometimes I can't help feeling that it would be nice to have a car that went a little more often still. That utter silence when you turn the key, the sudden realisation that total safety and security have descended once again, is always unnerving, even now I've achieved such serenity myself.

I worry, too, about the *car's* state of mind. I diagnose cowardice, as I said, a reluctance to go out and face the traffic. But seven total breakdowns in three years suggests some quite profound spiritual malaise. We can't just go on tinkering with the physical symptoms. We've got to get to the psychological root of the problem. One certain cure would be to drive the thing over Beachy Head. But then of course it might well not be in active mode at the crucial moment. I think the sensible alternative is to get it qualified psychiatric help.

I know exactly what's going to happen, of course. After half-an-hour on the couch in Dr Einspritz's consulting-room this silent, safe, secure, reliable, dark blue car is suddenly going to burst out in hysterical accusations. Against me, of course – who else? It's going to start sobbing that I never showed it enough affection when it was new. I never washed it by hand, never shared quality time with it. Was always impatient for it to get on in life and go somewhere. The owners of all the other cars it knew bought them toys to dangle from the mirror. I never bought it so much as a yellow duster. Etcetera, etcetera.

Absolute nonsense, of course. All right, I never washed it by hand – I was a busy man – I had its insurance premiums to earn, just for a start. But I used to take it to the carwash from time to time. Buy it hot wax and wheel scrub. Not full valeting and engine clean, I accept that. I didn't think it was the sort of car that wanted to spend all day in a steam bath. I thought it was a dark blue sort of car, interested in serious personal transportation.

Well (it's going to sob), that just shows how little I ever understood it. Didn't I realise it wanted to go out and see a bit of life? To get stuck in traffic-jams occasionally with other cars, engines all going vroom-vroom together, the air thick with exhaust fumes? It was dark blue on the outside, certainly – but couldn't I see that in its heart it was fire red? I never wanted to do much but go slowly along half-empty streets, and park at parking-meters. And all the time it was longing to drive dangerously! Burn up the motorway a little! Be left at rakish angles on double yellow lines! Get towed, for heaven's sake!

Then it's going to start telling Dr Einspritz I always preferred my other machines. My word-processor, my pocket organiser. But it's not true. In my own undemonstrative way I loved that car. It's going to turn out to be jealous of the waste-disposer next! Well, at least the waste-disposer didn't sink into depressive silence. It got blocked, yes – everything gets blocked – but at least it went on struggling to cope, it went on making a kind of strangled noise.

Oh (the car's going to scream), what kind of love was this, that was withdrawn at the first hint of trouble? Dr Einspritz has explained that my failure as an owner has given it low self-esteem. It sees itself as a burden on the road-system, a drain on natural resources, and a threat to the environment. So every now and then it gorges on its own electricity to compensate and renders itself entirely incapable.

Dr Einspritz (it's going to go boring on) has been making a study of my articles, and has discovered that at least half of them seem to be complaints about various bits of machinery. Dr Einspritz believes that the root of the trouble is that I fear and hate machines in general.

What? – I'm going to scream. I *love* machines! I *understand* them! My relationship with machines has always been exceptionally close!

But what do the machines themselves say? With one accord (says Dr Einspritz) they switch off at the sight of me, they jam, they falter, they wipe my words and instructions out of their memories. In all their various languages they conspire to accuse me.

And of course I end up on a couch myself, being treated for abusive relationships with domestic machinery by one of Dr Einspritz's colleagues. Meanwhile Dr Einspritz contemplates my Audi, as it lies back on *his* couch, with considerable professional satisfaction. Its great outburst is over, its conflicts are resolved, it is at peace with itself at last.

Very still and quiet it lies. In fact entirely silent and motionless. Its battery's flat again.

(1995)

A very special collection

I had a letter the other day from the Mugar Memorial Library at Boston University, kindly inviting me to send them my manuscripts and correspondence files so that they could be 'curated under optimum archival conditions in a special Michael Frayn Collection.'

I declined this unexpected honour, for reasons which seemed cogent enough at the time. Now, in silent reproach, the library has sent me a lavishly illustrated brochure about their Special Collections – their 'jewelled showcase,' as they call them – and I realise what a fool I was.

Just to think – by now the precious papers could be inside an acid-free envelope in a humidity-controlled vault, on the sixth floor of a building to which 'Modern Baroque architecture has given special opulence,' instead of on the floor at home being drawn on by the children. They could be taking their turn for revolving display in the exhibition hall, which is framed, as the brochure explains, by a picture window 'draped grey in translucent yarn to give a sense rather than sight of the trolley-infested street outside,' and whose rooms are divided by glass walls 'allowing floor surfaces to flow into each, conspiring for partial illusion and playing with the magic of light.'

The library houses what the brochure claims to be probably the largest collection of its sort in America, with contributors ranging alphabetically from Eric Ambler, 'through torch singer Libby Holman,' to Alec Waugh. Leslie Chatteris is in. So is Ngaio Marsh, and the manuscript of 'Born Free.'

There's not space in the brochure to illustrate all these riches, of course, but they do have a page from one of their real treasures – the typescript of 'Rally Round the Flag, Boys!' by Max Shulman, which makes the value of this sort of collection abundantly clear.

As readers of Shulman will no doubt recall, he describes the life of his character Guido as being 'singularly free of vicissitudes.' But this is not what Shulman originally wrote! He described it initially as 'singularly free *from* vicissitudes.' Then, upon mature reflection, he changed it. 'Free from' to 'free of'; here we have a first-hand picture of the writer at work.

The brochure also contains the facsimile of a page from 'Fantastic Voyage,' by Isaac Asimov, based on a screenplay by Harry Kleiner, which in turn was based upon an original story by Otto Klement and Jay Lewis Bixby. This is another extraordinarily revealing document. For one thing, Asimov types much worse than Shulman. Better than me, but worse than Shulman. That helps to place him, I think.

And the revisions he's made! There's enough material for a thesis in this one page alone! 'Grant nodded,' he typed curtly for a start (p.94, line 14). Then he crossed out 'nodded,' and inserted 'continued to stare about in wonder.' You see? The whole character of Grant has changed. The neutral, merely acquiescent Grant of Harry Kleiner's conception, not to mention Otto Klement's and Jay Lewis Bixby's, has matured through Asimov's rich reworking into Grant the wonderer, Grant the curious observer, Grant the *concerned* – in a word, Grant as he has come down to us today.

The brochure illustrates a composition by Bizet, transcribed and written out by one of the *actual composer's actual contemporaries!* There is a post-card from George Bernard Shaw (*the* George Bernard Shaw) to Claude Rains (*the* Claude Rains), directing him to change two lines in 'Caesar and Cleopatra.' The brochure illustrates not only the message side of the card, but also the address side. It contains the address of Claude Rains, interestingly enough. And a postage stamp.

And here's a scoop – an actual Christmas card sent by John F. Kennedy and his wife to Gladys Hasty Carroll! 'Wishing you a Blessed Christmas and a New Year filled with happiness, Senator and Mrs John F. Kennedy,' reads the printed text, followed by the autograph, 'Best – Jack,' 'Best' is spelt 'B-E-S-T.'

But manuscript is not the only commodity they're curating out there. The Henry Roth Collection includes a mailbox, through which most of the correspondence between Roth and his publishers apparently passed. The mailbox is pictured in the brochure; it carries the autograph 'Roth' on its side in roughly painted capitals, and the lid doesn't close properly.

Looking at it, you can imagine Roth (embittered, according to the text, by the tepid public response to his book 'Call It Sleep') going out into the storm to collect the latest depressing news from his publishers. He is embittered still further to find the rain has got in through the open lid, turning the wad of circulars from the local supermarkets into a sodden pulp, and thereby gravely prejudicing their value as historico-literary documents – you can see it all! Lord, the life we writers lead!

They are also curating Anthony Newley's hat in the Anthony Newley Collection. I'm thinking of applying for a research grant to go and study it. I'd like to see it *in situ* – nestling in its acid-free hatbox in the humidity-controlled vaults, or framed by the picture window with the trolley-infested street beyond, and surrounded by the conspiracy of spatial illusion and the magic play of light.

In the meantime I think I'd better send them a pair or two of my old socks, so that they can start the Michael Frayn Collection after all. I'll throw in a birthday card from my Great Uncle Alexander, and part of the cardboard box I keep my old bank statements in, signed 'Crosse and Blackwell.'

I hate to see the stuff go out of the country, of course. But when scholarship calls, the dustman must take second place.

(1967)

We all say the same

Sir – Are we alone in deploring the alarming decline in the number of Letters to the Editor bearing multiple signatures?

No, Sir, we are not alone! At the foot of this letter you will find 270 signatures, standing in proud columns, shoulder to shoulder, united in deploration. (Or 271 if Renforth Ossett BA MBE signs, as he promised Sir Spencer Fough KCVO he would, though we have been unable to confirm this, in spite of many attempts to telephone him.)

We believe that together we are able to deplore far more deeply than any one of us ever could on his own. Indeed, one of the things we deplore is the shallowness of so much deploring today. It is frankly deplorable that, with the world in the state it is, deploring has so signally failed to rise to the occasion by sinking to the new depths which are only waiting to be plumbed.

It is surely economic madness, at a time when the communications industry is increasingly dominated by large multinational corporations, to leave letter-writing to the backyard efforts of individual correspondents. We believe that no Letter to the Editor should be accepted for publication in this day and age unless it is signed by at least twenty people, of whom half should have some kind of titles or letters after their name. Indeed, as the advent of the fax and e-mail make it ever easier to circulate drafts of proposed letters among ever wider circles of possible signatories, we look forward to lists of signatures numbered not in tens but in thousands.

We are a curious nation. We complain about the overcrowding of our letters columns – but we continue to allow precious column-inches to be taken up by letters selfishly occupied by only one signatory. No wonder our forests are being laid waste to provide writing paper. No wonder carbon dioxide emissions are soaring, as readers light bonfires with newspapers which they have so little personal motivation to preserve.

We should perhaps add that this letter would also have been signed by Tessa Tilling MA PhD FRZS, only she wanted to insist on adding a paragraph about animal rights, whereupon Lord Blastwater, who has financial interests in this area, threatened to withdraw, together with some thirty business colleagues. This, we should explain, is a minority paragraph signed by †Twicester MA DD and (Mrs) Cynthia Treadwell CBE in protest.

In the light of this, may we urge? We should certainly hope we may. Or is this fundamental right to be taken away from us, like so many others, by unelected quangos and faceless bureaucrats in Brussels? If we, who between us have so much experience in urging, are not to be allowed to urge, then what hope is there for freedom of urging in this country?

We therefore call upon the Government. We call upon them daily, but we are never invited in. This is further evidence, if evidence be needed, of the national decline in good manners. We do not expect to be offered lunch, but surely it is not too much to hope for a cup of tea or coffee? It cannot be beyond the wit of man to provide a simple cup of something, together perhaps with cake or biscuits, for 270 tired and hungry letter-writers (or 271, should Ronforth Ossett BA MBE surface at the prospect of free refreshments). If the Government should ever take it into its head to call upon us in return, they will find our door open – indeed, all 270 (or 271) of our doors.

We feel we must at this point sound a note of warning. In our concern for the mass letter-writing market we must not forget the plight of single letter-writers. We should in all fairness make clear that this is a further minority paragraph signed by †Twicester MA DD and (Mrs) Cynthia Treadwell CBE.

What nonsense! We personally feel – and this is the vast majority of us writing now – that quite enough concern has been expressed already for so-called 'single letter-writers'. If they didn't want to be single letter-writers, why didn't they make the simple effort to meet other letter-writers with similar outlooks, as the rest of us have, and set up happy, loving letters together? Every view, in our humble opinion, needs at least two authors to cherish it.

Not in *our* even more humble opinion.

Who wrote that last paragraph? Is this †Twicester MA DD and (Mrs) Cynthia Treadwell CBE breaking ranks once again? It would be helpful if signatories wishing to make some personal comment would identify themselves.

Oh, yes, sorry – (Lady) Frances Huffey CVO and (Sir) Rufus Tort QC and for that matter DSO, though I don't usually mention this in informal contexts.

May we say how much we agree with Lady Huffey and Sir Rufus Tort? And this expression of support, we are not ashamed to say, *does* come from †Twicester MA DD and (Mrs) Cynthia Treadwell CBE. We utterly reject the attempts being made by the big battalions of signatories to suppress the views of minorities amongst us. We can only applaud the sentiments that Lady Huffey and Sir Rufus express about paragraph ten.

May I say (Blastwater, Chairman, Associated Swill Industries), with respect, through the letterhead, that †Twicester and (Mrs) Cynthia Treadwell, for all their display of doctorates and orders, are exactly the kind of perpetually cavilling, sententious, hand-wringing whingers who get the rest of us a bad name, or names?

I for one (D. P Snedding, Deputy-Chairman, Associated Swill Industries) heartily agree with Lord Blastwater.

I for two – B. B. Brumfit, Director of Public Affairs, Associated Swill Industries – would like to know why (Mrs) Treadwell keeps her marital status so carefully wrapped in brackets? Does she view being married as a source of shame? Why for that matter is (Mr) Treadwell not in evidence? Does he not see eye-to-eye with his wife? I should also be interested to hear the views of †Twicester's good lady on her husband's choice of co-signatory.

May I say – and I speak as one who is Charles G. Strumley MD FRCS – in defence of †Twicester MA DD and (Mrs) Cynthia Treadwell CBE, that they are being unnecessarily modest when they say that they 'can only applaud the sentiments' of Lady Huffey and Sir Rufus. To my personal knowledge they can also dance an elegant foxtrot together, as they demonstrated most notably at the last annual get-together of signatories.

Some of us (Grace Threadneedle and others) would prefer to leave personalities aside and get back to the urgent questions facing us all in the world today. First and foremost of these is surely whether paragraph nine of this letter should be allowed to stand in its present form.

If paragraph nine goes (Professor Sir Thirlmere Stagg MA PhD and others) then so do all of us in the Paragraph Nine Support Group!

What some of us (B. B. Brumfit, and all in Associated Swill Industries) want to know is why nothing has been heard of from †Twicester MA DD and (Mrs) Cynthia Treadwell CBE for several paragraphs now. So far as we can see from here their names are no longer in the list of signatories below. Have they perhaps run off together so as to be entirely alone in thinking?

We remain,
Yours, etc.

CRAWFORD ('BILL') STRIVE
MRS CRAWFORD ('BUBU') STRIVE
CRAWFORD STRIVE II (aged 5)
VICTORIA CRAWFORD STRIVE (aged 2 years 5½ months)
GRANDFATHER STRIVE (aged 93)
THE STRIVES' NANNY (aged 22)
MUSWELL TRACTION, a friend and neighbour of the Strives (aged 41, if this is relevant)
MRS MUSWELL TRACTION (also aged 41, though my birthday in fact falls three months after my husband's!)
'DISGUSTED' (age withheld)
(MRS) 'DISGUSTED'
'SICKENED' (aka 'FORMER SPURS SUPPORTER')
'OUTRAGED' (née 'DOG LOVER')
'NOT AMUSED' (LORD)
'MILDLY AMUSED' (THE HONOURABLE MISS)
ALL THE LADS AT THE JOLLY WATCHMAKERS
Etc.

(1994)

What the mice foretell

The ancients tried to unriddle the secrets of the universe by an extraordinary variety of techniques, such as, according to Roget's Thesaurus, hieromancy and icthyomancy (examining the entrails of animals and fishes), austromancy and crithomancy (studying the winds and the dough of cakes), and myomancy (for those who preferred a little flutter on the mice).

These barbarous superstitions seem inconceivably remote from us today. Who can imagine any modern statesman resorting to crithomancy, and waiting, before he took action, to see exactly how the cookie crumbled? Or turning in his difficulties to austromancy, and not committing himself until he'd found out which way the wind was blowing?

In those far-off days they used to resolve their problems by balancing a hatchet (axinomancy), and by going round in circles (gyromancy). Picture President Johnson juggling with weapons in the face of a crisis! Or Mr Wilson gyromancing uncertainly about! The mere idea is enough to make one provide material for geloscopy, which is divination by the mode of laughing.

Nowadays we do it differently, as I can tell you from personal experience. We journalists are the real augurs and haruspices of the modern world, ready at all hours with prognostications and divinations at popular prices. We don't use mice or dough, I can tell you, and we shouldn't so much as glance at the intestines of a holy pig if you laid them out in front of us.

We rely on much more advanced systems, such as taximancy, shrdlumancy, and freudomancy. Thus, taximancy teaches us that the views of one taxi-driver picked off the rank at random to drive us from the airport are more significant than any systematic survey of opinion. Because, in sending us that particular taxi-driver with that particular set of opinions, the gods, or the Norns, or any rate the taxi-dispatchers, are clearly trying to get some message through to us.

According to freudomancy, moments of misunderstanding and error offer us flashes of illumination from the Collective Unconscious which are unobtainable through regular channels. Misprints, similarly, are more revealing than something printed correctly; instead of a communication from some mortal author, we are vouchsafed a direct message from Shrdlu, the dark but playful god who lurks at every compositor's fingertips. And in general, what almost happened, and what one for a moment thought someone was about to say, is more telling than what actually did happen or got said.

The theory is abstruse; the practice is entirely straight-forward. For instance, in a recent book about the situation the writer in America, among other places, A. Alvarez reports that he woke up as his plane approached New York just in time to hear the cabin loudspeaker say, 'This is John F. Kennedy.' In the moments before he realised that this was the new name of Idlewild airport, Mr Alvarez reaped a rich harvest of significant confusion – 'a sense of being put off-centre in a macabre way – a sense of the absurd,' which turned out after touchdown to pervade everything and everybody.

Mr Alvarez is almost parsimonious in the use he makes of this ripe misunderstanding. If it had happened to me, I'd have made it support a chapter at least, and I'd have dined out on it every night before publication date into the bargain.

What happened to Mr Alvarez after getting out of the aircraft I don't know, because all I've read of the book so far is the paragraph about John F. Kennedy, which was quoted in a review. Somehow it seemed quite significant enough on its own. (This is what the ancients called *stichomancy,* or divination by passages in books.) But here's how I'd have gone on, if I'd been doing the job:

' "Anything to declare?" asked the Customs man, and for a moment I had the wild feeling that I was expected to say something like "Only that we hold these truths to be self-evident, that all men are created equal . . ." I didn't say it, of course, but it was an eerie experience, and the feeling persisted for a long time afterwards that this sort of lip-service to tradition was almost mandatory in America.

'I'd scarcely got into the arrivals lounge before I was practically hit in the eye by the sight of a slot-machine with the legend "Gun 5 cents." In fact it said "*Gum* 5 cents," and the third leg of the m was simply hidden by the end of somebody's cigar. But I couldn't get over the feeling that it was in some way symptomatic of the violence always lurking just below the surface of American life, or that at any rate my reaction told me a great deal about the general jitteriness of people over there.

'What the driver of the airport bus thought about integration or violence or cultural pressures on the artist I don't know, because he said nothing at all throughout the trip, which with the best will in the world I couldn't help feeling suggested some profound fragmentation and failure of communication in American society.

'I walked from the town terminal to the cable office, and it was the little things I noticed most – the hardness and greyness of the pavement, a crumpled newspaper lying in a rubbish-bin, the folded raincoat over my arm. As far as the raincoat went, I felt I could be anywhere – Berlin 1932, Budapest 1956, Stockton-on-Tees 1965.

'I told the man at the cable office that I wanted to send this urgent news dispatch to London. For a moment I thought he was going to misunderstand me and assume I meant not London, England, but London, Ontario. He didn't; but for that split second I looked the grim old ghost of North American isolationism straight in the eye.

'(Next week: I see myself in the shaving-mirror at the Sherry-Netherland, and think for a moment it's Theodore Roosevelt.)'

(1965)

What the peepers see

A perpetual state of conflict and unrest exists between my eyes and the printed word. To be blunt, my eyes do not find words congenial co-workers in the business of communcation.

It's not the fault of the words, which are patient and long-suffering in the face of constant abuse. It's my eyes.

They won't settle down to do one job at a time; they're slapdash; they jump to conclusions; and they're highly counter-suggestible. Speaking for the management, I can tell you they're a right pair of layabouts.

They read MACMILLAN PUTS PARTY'S TRUST IN HOME as MACMILLAN PUT PARTLY TRUSSED IN HOME. With salacious agility they leap five paragraphs of life-enhancing descriptive prose to the erotic events they have miraculously detected at the bottom of the next page.

They read magazines backwards, jumping unsteadily back through the country notes and the annual reports of holding company holding companies, and give out exhausted long before they reach MIXED MANNING: A CAUTIOUS REASSESSMENT? at the front.

They're at their very worst with the eight daily newspapers that face them each morning. The rich profusion of sizes and styles and arrangements exhibited by the words in the newspapers completely demoralises them. They run hopelessly back and forth from one story to another like panic-stricken chickens. And yet they're so hidebound by restrictive practices that even at this juncture they refuse to see more than one size of type at a time – if they see the small headlines they don't see the large ones, and if they see the text they don't see the headlines at all.

Heavens, it makes me mad to think of all the time and ingenuity the printers and sub-editors have expended to make life easy for the readers' eyes – only to have un-grateful young peepers like mine pick and choose and complain. But isn't that the modern pupil all over? All they think of is eye, eye, eye.

With typical cowardly idleness they always start by picking on the smallest type at the bottom of the page, hoping no doubt that my hand will absent-mindedly turn the page over before they come up against anything their own size.

Short of pinning the newspaper to the wall, and slowly advancing from the other side of the room with my glasses off, reading it line by line like an oculist's chart, I suppose I'm condemned to go on starting the front page each morning with the *This Funny Old World* section at the bottom:

HIS PET ATE – TROUSERS

Harold Morbidly (47) went to work in his underpants after his pet hamster, Lulu, ate his trousers, Chingford, Essex, magistrates were told yesterday.

Discouraged by this inauspicious intelligence, my eyes labour slowly up from the bottom of the next column along.

Last night a man was helping the police in their inquiries.

'I tried to stop him,' said Mrs Sough, 'by running after him shouting "Help, police!"'

He grabbed the money from the till and ran out of the shop. Then he pulled out a gun and said, 'This is a stick-up.'

'So of course,' said Mrs Sough, 'I assumed he was a perfectly ordinary customer . . .'

It doesn't make any sense to me. Hey, just a moment – didn't I catch a glimpse of 'intimacy occurred' seven columns over to the left somewhere? Ah, here we are.

. . . An opportunity to show that the Prime Minister knew the North-East with considerable intimacy occurred when . . .

Oh. H'm. Where was I?

'The morals of young people today,' said Sir Harold Sidewinder . . .

That wasn't it, was it?

. . . are to be either scrapped or put into mothballs.

Nor that. Where the devil was it?

HEAVY LASSES KEEP GIANT COMPANY IN BED

No.

'The morals of young people . . .'

What? Heavy lasses do *what?* Where did I see that? Oh, HEAVY LOSSES KEEP GIANT COMPANY IN RED. Yes. Heavens, I'm bored. Must try and stagger a bit higher, though.

. . . wiped out. First reports put the number of dead and missing at . . .

Funny about those heavy lasses, I must say.

. . . when disaster . . . many thousands rendered homeless . . .

What was that rather amusing story about a hamster going into mothballs? Forgotten already. More or less squeezed this page dry, haven't I? Just glance at the main headline . . .

WAR DECLARED

. . . and I can turn over. Nothing in the damned paper, as usual.

I don't know what the solution is. Perhaps lead the page with HAMSTER INCIDENT SHOCK and make the tailpiece at the bottom:

Page One Fun

WELL, I DECLARE . . . !

'I declare war on Russia,' said Sir Alec Douglas-Home (60) opening a Staggered Hours exhibition yesterday. Experts combing the radio-active rubble of London last night believed that what Sir Alec really said was not 'Russia' but 'rush-hour.'

My eyes would get round it somehow, though. Probably start reading the *advertisements*.

(1963)

What the stars foretell

It's odd how the Guide Michelin has established itself in English mythology. Few British tourists, hammering across France with a carload of camping equipment and the last £10 traveller's cheque preserved next to their heart, can afford anything more than the most modest of restaurants. Yet each new edition of the Guide is scrutinised by British newspapers, as if it were 'Who's Who' or the Honours List, for new accessions to three-star status, or even more interesting, demotions therefrom. And when the proprietors of demoted three-star restaurants shoot themselves, that shows the French behaving in an even more amusingly French way still.

Like Inspector Maigret and the *police judiciaire,* the team of Michelin agents who eat their way so secretly, expertly, and high-mindedly around France have caught the English imagination. One day there will be an English television series featuring Patrick Wymark as *l'inspecteur* Finbec of the Service Michelin (the Ser' Mich', as they call it in the business), one of the dedicated, lonely men who drive the long straight roads of France in their dark Peugeots (disguised with Pirelli tyres), grimly hunting down over-cooked artichokes in small country towns filled with birdsong.

In the first instalment, Finbec has scarcely finished his *salade niçoise* in a little restaurant in Cahiers (Marne-et-Loire), when the *patronne* says that her husband is away, and that she has some *primeurs* of asparagus upstairs in her room . . .

*

I think it's a pity that the mythology of the red Michelin has eclipsed that of the other famous Michelin guides – the *guides verts.* The green guides are the regional touring ones, and marvellous guides they are, with intelligent information about industry, geology, and the events of the last war, as well as old churches.

The *guides verts* have their own system of star-grading, with which they classify the attractions of towns, villages, beauty spots, public monuments, and works of art. Three stars means 'worth a journey'; two stars – 'worth a detour'; one – interesting.' Then there are two lower categories, distinguished only by the size of the type-face on the maps – places which are 'to be seen if the occasion arises,' and 'reference points,' which aren't to be seen even if the occasion does arise, but merely used to find the way to more fortunate locations.

So presumably there is an even larger force of green Michelin inspectors driving the roads of France in their discreet Peugeots, anonymously assessing the merits of abbey, view, and public fountain. Inspectors in the *Mich' vert* division of the service rather look down on those in the *Mich' rouge,* I suspect. Something of the branch's traditions comes through in this quietly dramatic report sent back to head office by *l'inspecteur (vert)* Pondéré after his triennial inspection of Grince (Charente-et-Oise)***.

'The speciality of Grince is its *cathédrale gothique avec le beffroi à la mode de Rouen.* But when I arrived (at 4.30 p.m.) I was informed by a rather surly verger, wearing a cassock which was none too clean, that the visit to the belfry was off. So was the visit to the treasury, and I had to make do with a cold and under-lighted crypt.

'I hoped I might have better luck with the *bas-reliefs en marbre de St-Boisson,* but they turned out to be undergoing repair and half-hidden behind screens. I washed the *cathédrale* down with a promising-looking *Chateau de Montvizier* 1542, which turned out to be reasonably viewable, though somewhat lacking in body and mellowness.

'I rounded the occasion off by sampling Grince's much-praised *panorama du belvédère de St-Astuce sur la vallée de la Buze,* to which we awarded three stars in our last edition. I regret to report that I found a large cement factory floating in the middle of the view, which entirely destroyed my appetite for it.

'I recommend that Grince should be reclassified "to be seen if the occasion arises."'

When this alarming report reaches headquarters, of course, a gigantic intelligence operation is put into motion. A whole team of secret agents infiltrates Grince and the surrounding countryside to check Pondéré's assessment. Every aspect of the town's Principal Curiosities and Other Curiosities is probed and sifted.

And when the Awards Committee sits down to consider the case, the whole field of comparative beauty-spot aesthetics comes under review. Are Gothic cathedrals perhaps a somewhat overrated form of architectural expression altogether? On the other hand, does a cement factory really spoil the view? Isn't there a case for saying that a cement factory, and a landscape whitened by cement dust, is a more characteristic expression of the twentieth century than old-fashioned woods and cornfields?

And is the Finger of St-Bolophon, which wags at pilgrims from its reliquary in Grince Cathedral on the third Sunday of April, before the tourist season starts, really more delightful than the Bile of Ste-Théodosie at Le Hoquet, which liquefies on the second Sunday of August, when the season is at its height?

The whole subject is so complex, and the general principles so hotly disputed, that the Committee decides to leave Grince with one of its stars as a compromise. Even so, of course, when the new edition of the guide appears the

Mayor of Grince poisons himself and the Bishop flees to South America.

But, in the British papers, not a word.

(1967)

Whereas

(A) The Author of this Deed is at present seised in fee simple and in stupor tremens by the process of moving house.

(B) The Author is of sound mind SAVE THAT the Vendor of the first part and the Mortgagee of the second part and the Assignor of the third part and the Leaseholder of the fourth part and the Lessee of the fifth part and the Curtainor of the sixth part and the Carpetee of the seventh part and the Gasholder of the eighth part HAVE AGREED to cover all floors walls tables and other surfaces in the present residence of the Author with three coats of prime quality LEGAL DOCUMENTS.

(C) The aforementioned legal documents are close carpeted throughout with verbiage of a tasteful period character.

Provided that

A space shall be kept clear among the said verbiage to accommodate an Excise Stamp charged at NOT MORE than one third of the Government's current defence expenditure.

And wherethemore

(A) For a consideration the Solicitors of the aforementioned parties have agreed to join in these deeds SEEING THAT no aforementioned party would really go with a swing without them.

(B) Given the slightest additional consideration the Solicitors' Solicitors and the Solicitors' Solicitors' Solicitors would doubtless also join in both in fee simple and fee compound.

Provided that

The aforementioned partygiver (hereinafter called 'the Mortgaged Soul') shall not be responsible for maintaining more than half the country's legal profession at any one time.

And wherewithstanding

IN THE EVENT of a person being both Vendor of one property and Vendee of another it is required by Logic that the Market cannot be unfavourable to him in both capacities.

EXCEPT THAT in the case of the Author the Market shall be guaranteed to be permanently against him whether as Vendor Vendee or Vendsoever.

And whereasmuchas

(A) The Friends of the Author (hereinafter called Christopher and Lavinia Crumble) bought purchased or became seised of their demesne two years ago for the sum of ONE THOUSAND POUNDS (£1,000).

(B) The value of the said demesne THEREUPON without let or hindrance and without prejudice to the liberal reputation of the aforesaid Christopher and Lavinia Crumble rose to TEN THOUSAND POUNDS (£10,000).

(C) This being achieved in part by the application of two coats of pale mauve paint by the said Christopher Crumble and in part by the removal of all adjacent tenants of immoral or drunken habits or small means and their replacement by new tenants of immoral or drunken habits and more substantial means.

And wheremoresoever

Even those Friends of the Author known as Horace and Doris Morris ordinarily situate in the same boat as the Author and generally supposed by the Author to be at least as fee simple about these matters as himself have acquired a residence the size of a small cathedral for A SONG (1 Sng).

And wherewithas

(A) In contradistinction to the Morrises and Crumbles the Author of this Deed (or Doer or Deedee) shall entertain all reasonable certainty that he will hereinafter be known as the Deedled or Done.

(B) The Author shall hereupon feel himself personally responsible for the maintenance in good condition of the Property Market heretofore known as the Property Racket.

(C) The Author shall be absolutely entitled to feel ground floor flat by the whole business.

Now it is agreed

The Author shall have in perpetuity the peaceful enjoyment of the dirty end of the stick.

Now this deed

WITNESSETH as follows:

The Author solemnly covenants with himself that notwithstanding overcrowding dilapidation infestation sudden enrichment sudden impoverishment conjugal representations or the purchase by Horace and Doris Morris of a royal palace in good order for fifteen shillings and sixpence NOR EVEN WITHSTANDING unemployment need and hunger among the Legal Profession HE SHALL before he contemplates moving house again meditate deeply upon this document for three calendar months following the first full

moon after the penultimate Quarter Day of the next Leap
Year but one.

In witness whereof the party hereto sets hereunder his
exhausted hand.

(1963)

A wisp of azure

My Bank Holiday was sombrely illumined by Miss Freya
Stark's long essay in *The Times,* entitled 'The qualities
needed to escape from mediocrity.' Miss Stark's analysis
of the nation's situation is bold and outspoken: we're
decadent.

'The decadence is there,' she argues, 'and anyone can spot
it, from a lack of candour in public life to the fact that scarce
a clock in any London street now tells the time correctly –
from right and left in chaos to eccentricities of dress.'

A solidly documented case, certainly – the wrongness of
the clocks is a particularly damning piece of evidence. The
conclusion came as no surprise to me. So far as I know,
human society has been in a state of perpetual decadence
ever since writers first discovered how to spell the word, and
the chances that we might somehow have slipped into a state
of undecadence since the publication of the last indictment
seemed fairly slim, even before the Bank Holiday.

What strikes me most forcefully about Miss Stark's
arguments is the prose they're expressed in, which is
largely verse – a rare quality for prose to possess in this
decadent age, and one which the compositors at *The Times*
seem to have overlooked in laying the piece out.

Take the passage I quoted, 'The de/cadence/ is there,/ and
an/yone/ can spot it,' she starts off, in five iambs and an
amphibrach. The lack of candour in public life seems to

have defeated her powers of metrification, as well it might, but she comes back strongly, in iambs varied with the occasional amphibrach again, on the fact

> *That scarce a clock in any London street*
> *Now tells the time correctly –*
> *From right and left in chaos*
> *To eccentricities of dress.*

She concedes that many of these symptoms 'are straws/ that an/y wind/ might carry.' What forms and phenomena the children of a particular age deck themselves with, she admits, is

> *Like foam dissolving on waves that dupe themselves*
> *To stabilise the sands of time they cover.*

I'm not too happy about that anapaest at the third foot of the first pentameter, but Shakespeare wouldn't have bothered about the odd anapaest in blank verse, and anyway, in a decadent age like ours you must expect a little rough workmanship here and there. In any case, Miss Stark makes up for it handsomely by *rhyming* a couplet before the end of the paragraph:

> *Their fluid arabesque need not detain us,*
> *But rather that hidden force beneath it push-*
> *Ing it with sonorous monotony*
> *Ashore. What power lifts it with such pulsations,*
> *Such raising and lowering of nations.*
> *Which we call progress and decay?*

The question here is not rhetorical, for it turns out that the power which lifts the fluid arabesque, with such pulsations, and, indeed, such raising and lowering of nations, is (or are) two fallacies. There's nothing like a couple of fallacies if you've got an arabesque to lift.

The fallacies in question, which Miss Stark believes gained currency after the First World War, are that mediocrity can lead to, or substitute for, Excellence. Miss Stark does not totally dismiss mediocrity, in spite of its small 'm'; she calls it, among other things,

> *The golden mean, the weft and woof of habit,*
> *The vine and fig tree of Isaiah . . .*

But she prefers Excellence, with a capital 'E', which she describes as a 'sprite', and 'not a result, but an apparition.' She says it 'comes out of the deep well and is either reached by its own paths or not at all,' And she writes:

> *It is whatever life may mean*
> *Apart from daily living,*
> *A wisp of azure,*
> *A visitation to the mind or heart.*

The trouble is, apparently, that instead of lifting up our eyes to the hills and dreaming dreams, we rested on our oars in a victorious sunset. So now mediocrity 'creeps into our English garden, where Shakespeare is still not only read but enjoyed, by a simple act of carpentry, the setting-up of the bed of Procrustes.'

But what of the future? Miss Stark drops into tetra-meters:

> *It would be desperate to watch*
> *Our hemisphere rolling into night*
> *Without a certainty of dawn,*
> *And day will come, we may be sure . . .*

Yet not/ so safe/ly sure, she warns, that 'our own people will carry its banner.' It's all up to the young.

> *Youth must think hard, and may walk free.*
> *Its feet on a mediocre and*
> *Perhaps improving floor,*
> *But its head as high as may be in the clouds.*

A hopeful note to end her sombre tale. But yet it seems

to me that youth may fail, while keeping wrapped in cloud
his thoughtful head, that mediocre floor to safely tread.
And if the floor in mediocre manner his stumbling feet
should once betray, he might put out his hand and drop the
banner, with which he beckons on the approaching *day.*

If no day dawns, no *azure wisp* can light the clouds which
do the youthful face benight. Without a wisp, how can the
lad unscrew or otherwise the *carpentry* undo? But with
the carpentry still firmly screwed, he'll miss the private
path into the *well,* where not *results* but *apparitions* brood,
and where the *sprite* herself is known to dwell.

And if we haven't got the blasted sprite, we'll *never* get
those damned clocks running right.

(1967)

Word sanctuary

FROM LORD DISGUSTED

Sir, – I must crave your indulgence for addressing you
in this style. It is, I suppose, somewhat unusual in
conversation, but after all these years the epistolary form
is the one in which I feel myself most at home, even
chatting to a journalist like yourself whom I am entertaining to lunch.

I am surely not alone, Sir, in finding that while sticks
and stones may break my bones, words can give me
apoplexy. Unless I have been intolerably misinformed from
my childhood up, the English language, its vocabulary,
syntax, and spelling, were given us by God in their present
form as an uplifting discipline. Misspellings, split infinitives, and neologisms I take as calculated affronts to my
whole moral code.

As you know, I have devoted a considerable part of my

life to hunting them down and dragging them into the Letters to the Editor columns, manacled to the orotund ironies of my own entirely correct prose-style. It has not been an easy vocation; I have had to hold myself ready to be outraged at all hours. The high moral tone I have been able to enjoy, however, has not been entirely without its satisfactions. A little more roast beef?

But I digress. Neologisms, I find, are the outrages the most likely to provoke a rise in blood pressure. New words! What the devil do we want new words for? Illegitimately formed, as like as not, half Latin and half Greek, by some semi-literate scientist to denote some damned piece of modern nonsense the rest of us do not wish to know about. A lot of canting jargon! Is the language of Shakespeare and Milton not good enough for some twopenny little nuclear nobody to blow us all to Kingdom Come with?

Perhaps I should make it clear that I am myself an Arts man. To a scientist, I suppose, words are unimportant, merely adjuncts to blowing things up. But to me words are essential tools without which I could not write my Letters to the Editor. I may say that I think the scientists have an infernal impertinence in interfering with my work, and a diabolical arrogance in inventing new words, when I, the generally recognised guardian of the language, should not dream of altering it by a hair's breadth.

But the Beelzebub of neologisms, Sir, is the Americanism. Let me ask a plain question. Whose language is it? Ours or theirs? It makes me furious when I see our own language larded with words like 'editorialise' and 'hospitalise.' Cannot people say 'give as an opinion in an editorial' and 'cause to go to hospital'? Are they too lazy to say the extra syllables? Are they too sunk in moral torpor to work out the proper syntax?

And 'commuter'! Every time I hear the word 'commuter' I see a red haze of rage in front of my eyes. It is an entirely unnecessary outrage, since there is a perfectly good English expression: 'A man who lives in one place and works in another, and who travels back and forth between the two each day.' There is simply no need for a new word. A man who lives in one place and works in another, and who travels back and forth between the two each day, is simply a man who lives in one place and works in another, and who travels back and forth between the two each day – and that is all there is to say about it.

It might be asked – though so far as I know it never has been – what is wrong with incorrect English. Surely anyone who has ever learnt any moral standards at all knows in his heart that 'Don't mention it' is right and that 'You're welcome' is wrong. One should think of words as applicants for positions of sacred trust in one's employment. Naturally one inquires into their backgrounds, and if they turn out to be foreigners, like 'You're welcome,' or of questionably mixed stock, like 'telecast' (ugh!), then one naturally thinks twice about employing them.

At a time like this, when our country is being attacked on all sides, the correctness of our language is more important than ever. If we thought of ourselves as being at all times on parade, if we tightened up the nation's spelling, ruthlessly stamped out split infinitives and hanging participles, and prohibited the manufacture or import of any new word whatsoever, unless designed by a qualified man like myself with a proper classical education, we could soon show our detractors where we stood in the world.

If I had my way, our security organisations would be employed to examine the antecedents of every word and expression in the language. Sometimes perfectly innocent-looking phrases one uses oneself turn out to be quite unacceptable when one inquires into them. One of my colleagues pointed out in a Letter to the Editor recently that the expression 'Have you got a . . . ?' is being replaced by 'Do you have a . . . ?' – and that the latter, which one might in all innocence have entertained on one's own lips, is of American extraction! As soon as one knows, of course, one can hear just how morally objectionable it is. But if the public had not been warned, the lovely English word 'got' would have been quietly murdered.

But to come to the point, Sir. I trust you will join the organisation I am founding, the Council for the Preservation of Verbal England. I expect massive support from all the columnists, humourists, school teachers, and writers of Letters to the Editor who have already cared so much and so long. Help us to set an example to *hoi polloi* by returning to our *lares et penates* – a close *rapport* with the *ens per se* of the English language.

And so, unless you would like another cup of coffee, I remain, Sir,

Yours, etc.

Disgusted

(1963)

The words and the music

They keep playing *music* on Radio 3, have you noticed? I find it rather intrusive. You're just settling into a good long interview with someone, you don't know who, because you missed the beginning, but he seems to play the flügelhorn, and you're finding out a great deal about his childhood in Leicestershire, and his views on Penderecki and the shortcomings of flügelhorn teaching in England, when they suddenly break off to play some symphony or concerto.

They keep playing music in concert-halls, too, and I read somewhere recently that audiences there are also getting pretty sick of it. What people want, it's been discovered, is

not just musicians playing at them relentlessly, it's someone to introduce it all, some familiar personality who can
talk them through it.

No one, so far as I know, has yet suggested it in the opera-
house. But it would be the most natural thing in the world.
There tend to be a lot of low moments in operas after a
famous aria ends, when everyone takes a bit of a break.
The composer's thinking up some more tunes for the next
famous aria, the baritone's gone off to have a cup of tea, a
mezzo has come on, and is making small talk to the soprano
about offstage political developments and the unreliability
of the men in their lives, the orchestra's vamping till ready,
or even off the stand altogether while the harpsichordist
fills in until the next set.

Wouldn't it be much better if they cut all this, and
Michael Aspel or someone, possibly in a costume suitable to
the piece, came on and asked the soprano how things were
going in her career? Not in her career as betrayed queen or
consumptive courtesan, of which we know only depres-
singly too much already, but in her career as a soprano,
where things will certainly turn out to be going much
better.

'Lorraine,' he'd say, 'you've just had a rapturous reception for your wonderful *Non sporgersi*. This was obviously
something you've been working towards in your career for
some time.'

'Yes, Michael, I've been looking forward to it ever since
the overture. I really felt I was ready for it. Any earlier in
Act One and the chorus would still have been singing
Vietato l'ingresso. Any later and I should have run up
against Rodolfo doing his wonderful *Quanto costa*. And
everyone has been so tremendously supportive.'

'I couldn't belp noticing Sir Edward down there on the
rostrum, waving his arms about and really urging you to go
for it.'

'Yes, the conductor has always been a great influence on

me – particularly in deciding the right moment to attempt something new.'

'I believe your immediate plans include one more aria in Act One?'

'If I can fit it in, Michael. I do have a rather heavy schedule of interview work.'

'Yes, tell me something about that. Is the technique involved very different from singing?'

'Oh, it uses completely different physical apparatus. It puts a tremendous strain on the zygomaticus major and the orbicularis oris.'

'Which of course are the muscles you need for smiling.'

'And which tend as you know to remain underdeveloped and flabby in the opera repertoire. The strain on them can cause tension in the digastric and stylohyoid – which can in turn affect the chuckle.'

'You are of course known for the amazing sprizzatura of your chuckle. I remember your wonderfully rich, sustained chuckling in Act Three of *La Pastasciutta* in San Francisco, in that famous interview you did with KCFR. But you've had some trouble with your chuckle recently, haven't you?'

'I think it was just the strain of trying to keep up my singing as well as the interviewing. Sometimes the chuckle just wouldn't come.'

'There was one occasion at the Met, I believe . . . ?'

'Yes, when I broke down in the middle of an interview, and just started to sing uncontrollably. It was very embarrassing. But I went to a wonderful woman in New York who helped me to see that question and answer are really yin and yang – part of the natural harmony of the universe. I think now I'm interviewing better than ever.'

'You don't intend to give up singing altogether?'

'I hope not. But I can't help feeling that there's so much conflict in opera, so much aggression. Everyone gets tremendously emotional. It's not surprising they keep murdering each other. All they can think about is treachery and despair and death. Whereas now for instance, we're both able to keep perfectly calm. We can just stand here and have a nice friendly talk about really interesting things, such as my career, and we've both got a chance to show the nice side of our natures. A lot of the characters in opera are frankly not very nice.'

They're having such a nice friendly talk, in fact, that they forget about the audience completely. She pours him some Ribena from one of the golden jugs brought on for the great drinking song earlier in the act. They wander among the cardboard trees in the moonlight, and she asks him what he thinks she ought to do about Rodolfo. Should she wait until Act Three, then simply die of consumption and a broken heart? Or should she make a pre-emptive strike in Act Two, and have him murdered by hired assassins?

He says that if she and Rodolfo could just stop singing for a moment, and talk to each other quietly, the way he and she are doing now, they might be able to get their problems sorted out.

'You're right,' she murmurs. 'It's the singing – it's the music. It's got to go. Insightful relationships and coloratura just don't mix. I feel I've become a lot more mature about my work in the last few minutes.'

He is fascinated by all this, but he can't help noticing that they are being watched. There is a face just visible out there in the darkness somewhere, with an impatient expression on it. He can see a raised arm, holding some sort of weapon.

'The conductor?' she says. 'Let him wait. I'm tired of being told what to do by conductors. I'm tired of having all my thoughts and feelings laid down for me on staves, measured out by bar-lines. I've got past that stage of my career now.'

Well, they talk for a long time. They have come to share a vision. They want everyone in the world to be inter-viewed. Not just musicians, but industrialists, generals, postmen, train-drivers. Because if everyone would simply stop *doing* things all the time, if they could just sit down on the scenery and *talk* about it instead, then obviously there would be fewer wars, there'd be less pollution. Letters wouldn't get mis-delivered, trains wouldn't run into each other.

'And the most wonderful thing of all,' they cry out at last in unison, 'is that it would be so much cheaper!'

No one hears this bit, though, because the audience has long since taken their point, and they're all rather noisily interviewing each other.

(1994)

The world: week two

1 And on the morning of the eighth day God woke up, greatly refreshed by His rest. And He remembered His work, that He had finished on the sixth day, and that He had beheld, and that He had seen was very good.

2 And He looked at it again. And behold, it was not very good at all, it was very bad.

3 The winged fowl was flying above the earth in the open firmament of heaven, it was true, and the creeping thing was creeping upon the earth. But the creeping thing was creeping upon the earth in considerably fewer numbers than might have been expected, because, lo, the winged fowl was zooming down out of the firmament of heaven and eating the creeping thing.

4 Meanwhile the fowl of the air was getting eaten by the beast of the earth, and the beast of the earth was getting eaten by the fowl of the air; and some of the creeping things were creeping right off the earth, and installing themselves in various warm corners of the beasts and fowls, where *plainly* they had never been intended to be.

5 And He looked at man, and He got a worse shock still. He had granted man dominion over the fish of the sea, certainly – but dominion was one thing, and what man appeared to be doing to the fish population of the world's shallower seas was quite another. Nor could any reasonable person think that the concept of dominion was ever intended to include all the things that man was trying out on the fowl of the air and the cattle, which involved pieces of specially sharpened flint and captive bolt pistols. All right, a little latitude in the case of the creeping things might possibly be allowed, since no one had much sympathy for them, and they were behaving in such a pestilential fashion themselves. But this could not for a moment be said about the great whales, which were extremely lovable, and almost human, and bothering no one at all apart from some tiny organisms which God could not even remember figuring in the original list.

6 It was strange. God remembered being immensely pleased with man when He had created him. He remembered the good feeling He had had at the end of the sixth day. Now He could not remember for the life of Him what He had been so pleased about. He began to think that He should have stopped much sooner; possibly on the first day, as soon as He had done the light, which was a brilliant success, everyone said so.

7 Though it would have been a terrible shame if He had stopped before He had done the grass, and the herb yielding seed, and the tree yielding fruit. These had all got wonderful reviews, and the only trouble was that they were succumbing fast before the depredations of His subsequent efforts.

8 Oh, and the fourth day had been one of the great days. At the time it had seemed no different from all the others, but looking back He couldn't think how He had ever done anything as simple and daring as the two great lights that ruled the day and night, and the stars also. He hadn't

thought about them! He'd just done them! Now people were writing poems about them.

9 Though now apparently man was doing something rather nasty to one of the great lights, and getting extremely confused about the stars.

10 He felt rather like tearing the whole thing up and forgetting about it. Or perhaps if He redesigned some of the beasts a bit, and made them more herbivorous . . . Though then that would ruin the whole concept of the fruit and the herbs. It seemed crazy to throw away perfectly good fruit and herbs just to fix the problem with the lions and tigers.

11 And on the ninth day God began to get very depressed about how He had really been able to create things back then in the early days, when He had done the trees and the stars. Now, who knows, maybe He was finished. Maybe He would never be able to create anything ever again.

12 And God thought, It was taking that day off, that's when it all went wrong. I knew it was a mistake – I only did it because My Wife kept on about having a holiday. Though heaven knows, He *needed* a day off, He'd been working all the hours that He had made, for the entire week, and if you can't take an occasional day off then what's the *point* of it all?

13 Yes, now He came to think about it, what was the point of it all?

14 And God thought about how He should perhaps have created one of the other possible universes He had had in mind – for instance, the one that consisted of differently-shaped smells, or the one that was all in the subjunctive.

15 And on the ninth day God became so depressed about the whole thing that He showed it to His Wife, and asked her what *She* thought. He couldn't really *see* it any more, He explained – He'd been living with it for nine days, He was too close to it. He would really value Her opinion.

16 And His Wife said it was wonderful, and that She liked it, She genuinely did – She wasn't just trying to reassure Him. She thought that He had done something absolutely

unique. She really adored the beasts of the earth, especially the aardvark and the velociraptor.

17 And God said, yes, He quite liked the velociraptor, too. But how about the squid? She hadn't said anything about the squid. He had been trying to do something rather special when He had made the squid.

18 And His wife said, yes, She liked the squid, the squid was a wonderful creation, particularly fried in batter. But there was something that worried Her just a tiny bit.

19 And God said, Oh? What was that?

20 And She said that it was only a small thing, and perhaps She shouldn't mention it.

21 But God said, No, go on, be absolutely frank, I never mind constructive criticism.

22 And His Wife said, Well, She wasn't absolutely sure about the chihuahua.

23 And God opened His eyes very wide in absolute amazement and said, You're not sure about the *chihuahua?*

24 And She said, Well, not absolutely. And just possibly, if She was being completely honest, there was also something a bit funny about the jellyfish.

25 Whereupon God grew extremely wrath. He would have understood, He said, if She had had doubts about the funnel-web spider or the staphylococcus or man. He had grave doubts about the last two Himself. But the chihuahua and the jellyfish just happened to be the two best things in the whole of creation, the only things that He was entirely happy with, and if She couldn't see that then She would never understand anything about His work at all.

26 And God's Wife flounced out of the room, and there was silence in heaven for about the space of half an hour.

27 And on the twelfth day His Wife came back and said She was sorry, She realised He was under tremendous pressure, and if He was really worried about man, why didn't He try creating woman as well? A woman might have some sort of moderating and civilising influence. She

might help man get more in touch with his feelings, and talk about things.

28 And God said that this was quite frankly the most ridiculous idea He had heard in all His born days, of which, He added, He had had more than She had had hot dinners.

29 And She said, Well, it was just an idea.

30 And on the thirteenth day God created woman. It smacked to Him of compromise, and He wasn't very happy about it, but He had to admit He couldn't really think of anything better. Anyway, in the end You had to make compromises here and there, You had to be prepared to learn from practice and listen to other people's points of view, He saw that.

31 And on the fourteenth day God won the Yorkshire Post Universe of the Year Award, and He made an acceptance speech that got a few laughs, and His Wife wore her dark blue silk with the pearl choker, and behold, things didn't seem quite so bad after all.

(1994)

Your inattention, please

Now will you please ensure that your seat-belt is securely fastened, ready for take-off.

Your table should be folded away, with the seat-back upright and the arm-rest down. Your mind should be in the closed position to be adopted when routine safety announcements of this sort are made. Faces should be completely obscured by newspapers, or eyes securely shut. If you are still conscious, you may find the level, hypnotic tone of voice in which this announcement is being made helpful in securing complete inattention.

In the pocket in front of you you will find a card showing aircraft safety procedures. In the interest of your own peace of mind, please studiously ignore this. Any attempt to look at it may result in your appearing nervous or in-experienced to your fellow-passengers. We are mentioning it purely as a test to make sure that no one is listening.

The cabin attendants will now demonstrate the use of the aircraft's emergency oxygen masks and lifejackets. They are not trained in mime or the use of theatrical properties, and they find this performance profoundly embarrassing. It is important to them to know that no one is watching. Those of you who are unable to read, or who are afflicted by insomnia, may look out of the window.

If for any reason the cabin air-supply should fail, oxygen will be provided. Masks like this will appear automatically. We say 'like this', but what in fact these masks are like you have of course no idea. In the unlikely event of anyone looking up, and seeing the entire cabin staff transformed into grinning effigies of Prince Charles, please remain seated. Place the newspaper back in front of your face and try to breathe normally.

The action of pulling the mask to the face automatically opens the way to less inhibited behaviour. Please do not smoke when the masks are in use, as the lighted end of the cigarette may be forced up your nostril.

There are emergency exits on both sides of the aircraft. They are not being pointed out to you now, because they are clearly marked. It is true that the cabin attendants are swinging their arms forwards and sideways, but this is part of a simple programme of physical exercise intended to relieve stress caused by the frustration inherent in the nature of the work.

Additional lighting is provided on the arm of your seat and at floor level for the convenience of passengers who have sunk even deeper behind their newspapers at this time.

In the unlikely event of a landing on water, you will find that you have no idea where your life-jacket is stowed. If this should happen, remove outer clothing and prepare for immersion. Place your jacket carefully under the seat in front of you, check that your shirt is free from the waistband of the trousers or skirt, then pull it upwards over the head in one steady movement, like this.

It is particularly important that no one watches any part of what follows.

Release the catch at the waistband, pull down the fastener provided, and let the lower garments fall to the floor. Please ensure that they do not obstruct the emergency exits.

There is a whistle attached to your lifejacket for attracting attention, which attendants are holding close to their lips, but being very careful not actually to blow in case attention should indeed be attracted. In a real emergency this would of course be still under your seat with the lifejacket, and you may wish to try alternative methods of persuading people to look at you.

Your cabin attendants are now demonstrating the procedure for these. Ladies should undo the fastenings at the front of the upper undergarment as shown, and pass it backwards over the shoulders, like this.

Now peel any hosiery downwards, like this, followed by the lower undergarment, taking care to keep the pelvis rotating at the same time, as shown. Once off, the undergarments may if desired be passed around various parts of the body, like this, then tossed lightly into the faces of potential rescuers, who may be engrossed in the Financial Times at least as deeply as passengers are now.

If you are still wearing the masks at this time, you may wish to loosen your inhibitions even further, as attendants are now demonstrating.

If necessary, the pressure can be increased by applying the mouth to this mouthpiece, but gentlemen, no pipes or cigars, please. For your own safety and comfort, kindly do not inflame other passengers until you are outside the aircraft.

Thank you for your complete lack of attention. Now please allow cabin staff a few seconds to retrieve their clothes and retire to the galley areas to dress, then open your eyes, fold newspapers away, settle back in your seats and enjoy the flight.

(1994)

Your quick flip guide

The quickest and flippest guide to all the entertainment of history since the dawn of time! Glance at it here and thank God you missed it!

14 billion BC	**The Big Bang.** Would you believe a more mindless way of opening the schedules than *The Big Breakfast*? They must be desperate.
600,000 BC	**The Old Stone Age.** Carry On Chipping. And on. And on.

40,000 BC   **The *New* Stone Age.** It says here. You could have fooled us.

2500 BC   **The Pyramids.** Early undertakers' bills were shockers, too.

1220 BC   **The Ten Commandments.** They make 'em, you break 'em.

1200 BC   **The Holy Bible.** Something Old – something New – something borrowed – can it be true? Some enjoyably naff special effects, though, particularly with corpses coming back to life.

30 BC   **The Roman Empire.** Lashings of nosh and booze, and some great sex, if you don't mind sitting through all those battles first. Lions *v.* Christians makes a change from the UEFA Cup. (Some scenes may upset animal-lovers.)

AD 400   **The Dark Ages.** Just when you thought it was safe to wake up and take an interest again.

1066   **The Norman Conquest.** Ever wondered why so many of the nobs seem to have Frog names? No? Back to sleep again, then.

1337   **The Hundred Years War.** Creaking slasher featuring ex-pats *v.* colourful locals in well-loved holiday landscapes. And you thought *A Year in Provence* was long!

1347   **The Black Death.** Noir-ish but predictable medical nasty with rats and pustules.

1400   **The Renaissance.** The Italians may have lost at home to Croatia, but they invented art, wouldn't you know it?

1478   **The Spanish Inquisition.** Your one-stop action sudser – cops *and* firemen. Only here's the gizmo – the cops are all in drag and the firemen start the fires.

1508   **The Sistine Chapel.** Geniuses – who needs

'em? Fellow here who's *right* up the wall, not to mention across the ceiling. But watch out for God getting static electricity out of Melvyn Bragg.

1545 The Council of Trent. Predictable ecclesiastical romp. Could this be the original vicarage tea-party?

1564 William Shakespeare. So – whodunnit? Was it Will in the study with the quill? Or was it Francis in the backparlour with the bacon? Or was it the butler all the time, and who cares?

1600 The British Empire. Stiff upper lip, chaps. The natives are restive – and they still haven't invented air-conditioning. (Black and white.)

1618 The Thirty Years War. Another leisurely ramble round the usual trouble-spots.

1687 The Law of Gravitation. When apples keep falling mysteriously off the apple trees, people suspect a poltergeist is at work. But eccentric scientist Isaac Newton believes there may be a more rational explanation . . .

PICK OF THE PICK

1739 The War of Jenkin's Ear. A real find. A fast-paced little war made on a shoestring, with a totally fresh and original starting point, that had a big influence in its time on better-known productions such as the War of the Austrian Succession. Terrific performance by Jenkin himself as the gung-ho mariner, and the severed ear is genuinely creepy. Everyone knows the shlocky remake with Vincent Van Gogh, but this rare original has been strangely overlooked by historians. British history-making at its best.

1760   **The Industrial Revolution.** Slime 'n' grime and Trooble at t' Mill.

1769   **Napoleon Bonaparte.** This is the one about the Little Man with Big Ideas.

1776   **The United States.** Great blues, great burgers – pity about the Polish jokes.

1837   **The Victorian Age.** The costumes are naff and the sex is kinky. Worth a glance, though, for the wonderfully tacky lighting effects. All that smoke and fog may have brought life expectancy down to the level of a prawn sandwich, but they must have saved art directors a fortune in dry ice.

1859   **The Origin of Species.** Shock horror! The whole schedule turns out to consist of *Planet of the Apes!*

1899   **Sigmund Freud.** Sigmund is a nice Jewish boy in Johann Strauss's Vienna. But when he meets screwed-up Mr Rat Man, strange things begin to crawl out of the woodwork . . .

1905   **The Theory of Relativity.** Things a bit slow down your way? Nip off for a Weekend Break in a space-rocket – and they get slower still. Geddit? No, nor do we. But watch out for the wacky prof with the fright-wig and the spaniel eyes.

1914   **World War I.** Mud 'n' blud, but what it's all about no one knows.

1917   **Communism.** Well, it seemed like a good idea at the time.

1939   **World War II.** Entirely predictable routine spin-off with bigger bangs – plus Vera Lynn. (See Interview feature: Adolf Hitler – 'my dream bathroom', p.17.)

1969   **Moon landing.** One small step for them –

one large vodka for us, please.

1995 Meltdown. How predictable can you get?
The biggest switch-off since they canned the
Epilogue.

(1994)

Your shameful secret

A cold shock of apprehension ran through me when I saw
Ken Follett described in the *Guardian* as a luvvie.

Ken Follett? I know *actors* are luvvies, we all know that.
But Ken Follett's not an actor – he's a writer. So the disease
is spreading. Maybe *I'm* a luvvie. I've worked with actors,
shared toilet facilities with them, possibly drunk out of the
wrong cup of coffee in a rehearsal room . . .

But Ken Follett doesn't even write for the theatre. And
now I see that the term 'Luvvies for Labour' is being used
to apply to celebrities of all descriptions. So plainly the
problem is not being contained within the theatrical
community at all. Everyone is at risk. Maybe *you're* a
luvvie! Yes – you!

You laugh. But then you start to wonder . . . What's the
first symptom?

The first symptom is that you're sitting there in a reasonably warm room, with food on the table in front of you, and
a glass of wine, and you feel some faint spasm of sympathy
passing through you for some other group of human beings,
who as a result of their own fecklessness, or through the
operation of natural laws beyond your control, are not sitting in a reasonably warm room, with food and a glass of
wine in front of them.

The glass of wine in front of you is not claret, I assume –
I hope. Claret-drinkers are particularly at risk – were
known to be even before the luvvie virus was first identi-

fied. But you're sitting there with your glass of burgundy, say – burgundy is perfectly all right – when suddenly, out of nowhere, you hear this terrible . . . thing coming out of your mouth. This pious, sententious, canting, do-gooding, expression of hypocritical concern for someone not yourself.

How could it possibly have happened to you? You're not an actor! You haven't avoided all life's pitfalls, perhaps, but at least you've avoided that one. It's true you thought of taking it up when you were at school. And you could have done – everyone said you were a wonderful Bernardo in the school *Hamlet*. By now, if you hadn't exercised real self-discipline, you could easily have been sitting in the Groucho giving interviews about European monetary policy. But you steeled yourself. You turned your back on it. You didn't become a writer, either, though God knows you were tempted at times. You didn't even go into cultural administration or arts funding. Remember how you almost responded to that advertisement in the Careers pages? Forgotten yearnings come flooding back . . . But you didn't. And now, suddenly, out of nowhere . . . *this*.

Another terrible suspicion comes to you. Perhaps you are a member of *the chattering classes*! You cast your mind back. What have you been saying at dinner parties recently? Nothing, surely. You sat there, you ate your food, you drank your . . . well, it might have been claret – but claret on its own is all right. It's claret and concern for others which is such a deadly cocktail. And you certainly didn't express any concern for others, not in public, not at the dinner table. You smiled a little sardonically when other people spoke. And all right, you spoke, of course you spoke, you're only human – but you always practised safe speech. You talked about the kind of things that the non-chattering classes talk about. Schools, holidays. How you don't understand computers. The ridiculousness of luvvies and members of the chattering classes. But chatter? No one could call that chatter . . .

And then you remember ... it was late at night, you'd had quite a lot of the claret, and you dropped your guard a little. You were just fooling around, of course, it wasn't serious. It was something that the person sitting opposite you said. Something about luvvies or the chattering classes, perhaps. For some reason you felt you wanted to disagree. Some actors, you said, were perfectly decent people who knew their place. And if the chattering classes didn't chatter, then what would the non-chattering classes have to non-chatter about?

Maybe, you think, nobody else remembers – maybe they never even noticed. But *you* know it happened. *You* know that deep down you have these strange unacknowledged feelings. *You* know you were tipping claret down on top of them. And next time you go to a dinner-party you're going to be looking at everyone, thinking 'Does *he* know about me? Does *she* know?' And just as you think you're getting away with it once again you'll realise that there's something familiar about the person who's looking at you across the table, not saying anything, a little ironical smile playing about the lips ... Yes – it's someone who was present the night you committed your little indiscretion.

You try to keep calm, but you feel the panic rising within you. He *knows* – you know that from the little smile. Is he going to out you to the rest of the company? Is he going to ring you at work next day, as you sit among all your carefully-chosen, discreet, unforthcoming, intensely non-theatrical colleagues, and try to blackmail you?

Or worse, suggest meeting somewhere privately, just the two of you? Because you realise, from that little smile, that he is a secret luvvie himself – a closet member of the chattering classes. He'll take you to some special bar he knows, full of actors and people in leather jackets flaunting progressive opinions. He'll ply you with claret. You'll find yourself exchanging shy doubts about the enterprise culture and the sovereignty of Parliament ...

As you sit there at the dinner-table, the whole vertiginous downward spiral opens in front of you. You make a supreme effort to avoid your fate. You start to babble wildly about schools and holidays – the incomprehensibility of computers and Stephen Hawking – the difficulty of finding good servants – the prospects for the stag-hunting season . . .

Everyone gazes at you. They've never seen you like this before – so red in the face, so fearless of received opinion and political correctness, so profoundly unchattering. The man opposite goes on smiling his little smile, but now it simply drives you to bolder and bolder achievements. You denounce Europe – and Asia for good measure. You call for the return of the death penalty for trespassing and being foreign.

You begin to feel wildly exhilarated. You realise you're doing something you've never done before . . . Until suddenly it dawns on you what it is.

You're acting.

(1994)

A good stopping place

How on earth did I get into this situation?

I mean, at the start of another piece, which is appearing exactly a week after the last piece, which was exactly a week after the piece before it . . . How has this come about? I wrote a regular column when I was a young man for a number of years. Then I stopped. I stopped because I didn't want to grow old and find I was still at the start of another piece, which was appearing exactly a week after, etc. Now I've grown old and what do I find? I find I'm still at the start of another piece, which is appearing, etc.

Let me try and work out what happened. I had a little time in hand last year when I couldn't start any major new project, because I was waiting for directors for plays, and so on. So I wrote a short piece or two, to keep by me for a rainy day. What sort of rainy day? I don't know. Sometimes a piece is required. It's not a bad idea to have one in the store-cupboard, along with the two tins of sardines and the packet of dry biscuits that was best before April 1987.

Then I remembered a few more ideas I'd put by over the years, and I wrote a few more pieces. I think there were about eight of them. Eight seemed a good round number, not too few and not too many. I sent them off to the *Guardian*. I had not the faintest intention that this should be the start of any regular arrangement. This was a limited engagement, as they say in the theatre. Eight weeks only. Season must end on such-and-such a date due to prior commitments.

The articles started to appear. 'How do you like writing a column again?' people asked me, in the carefully pleasant tone of voice one might adopt if one was remarking to an alcoholic that he seemed to be holding a drink in his hand, in case he hadn't noticed himself. It wasn't a column, I explained. It was a series of articles, a limited engagement. They smiled. I was just going to have the odd drink and then stop again, was I? They'd heard that kind of story before.

And indeed, as the end of this limited season approached, to stop at that particular point began to seem a bit . . . *odd* . . . Eight didn't seem to be such a good number, now I'd got to it. Wouldn't it be more natural to stop after nine, or ten? Ten, yes. Ten was a good, natural, self-explanatory number. I could say to people – I could say to *myself*, Well, I'm just writing ten pieces . . . No, I couldn't. You can't just casually happen to do ten of something. What you *can* do – nonchalantly, who's counting? – is *a dozen*.

All right, so a dozen. But then to write exactly twelve pieces seems a penny-pinching, mean-spirited way of justifying talk of a dozen. Make it a baker's dozen. No, make it fourteen. Then I can talk about a dozen and have the private satisfaction of knowing that I'm generously understating it.

So, I'll stop after fourteen. But then fourteen . . . that's just about enough for people to have noticed they were under way. So they'll notice if there isn't a fifteenth. They'll think I've been fired. Caught stealing the petty cash. Drunk in charge of the fax machine.

Better hang on for a few more. Slip away after twenty, say. No surprise if I went after twenty. Everyone's on short contracts these days. No one's hanging around waiting for the pension and the chiming clock. Nothing has a permanent structure any more. Be a bit of a surprise if I stuck around *after* twenty, in fact. People might start thinking I'd got into a groove, couldn't think of anything else to do, was suffering from some form of neurotic compulsion.

Which *I* know is nonsense, of course. All the same, once you've got up into the twenties it is starting to look more and more like a regular column. The enterprise is acquiring a certain momentum of its own, a certain historical gravitas. Its beginnings are getting lost in the mists of time. There are several million people in the world who hadn't even been born when this thing started. It would have been all right if I'd stopped after eight, I see that now. Eight's nothing. But twenty . . . twenty-five – it's starting to be part of the great chain of being, a short but significant fibre in the ongoing texture of the universe. It's becoming an institution. It's like a chain letter, or the monarchy. Totally pointless, but to break the chain now seems somehow wilful, violent, unthinkable.

Isn't this how things start? Alcoholism, relationships – or indeed the monarchy. You have a few drinks with your friends when you're a young man. You go out with someone a couple of times. You crown two or three insignificant local kings. Then you find yourself in the pub fairly regularly . . . She comes round to your place, you go round to hers . . . The kings beget a few more kings . . .

And before you know what's happened the habit has taken over. One moment you're enjoying the odd Ethelred, one or two Edwys, everything very civilised and delightful – stop any time, no problem – you might put in a nice warlord as dictator instead, if you feel like it, or elect some Professor of Theology as president – and the next thing you know you've had eight Edwards, eight Henrys, four Georges, four Williams, not to mention two Elizabeths and a few odd Victorias and Matildas – in fact you've lost count – you're right out of control – and you *can't* stop now, not just before your third Charles . . . !

I don't want to be that sort of person. I want to be the sort of person who can take it or leave it. Come and go. Put things down, pick them up. Work one day, have fun the next. Enjoy a king or two, then switch perfectly happily to a General Secretary. Chuck the chain-letter in the waste-paper basket, let the funnel-web spider die out, avoid the cracks in seven paving stones and then cheerfully step on

the eighth . . . tenth . . . no, no . . . twelfth . . . fourteenth . . .
sixteenth . . . no, no, no! Nineteenth . . . twenty-first . . .
stop!

So I'm striking a blow for sanity and freedom. *Tout passe,*
tout casse, tout lasse. Before you're *lassé* and I'm *cassé,* I
passe. I'm stopping. Not after a hundred, or a hundred and
forty-four. Not in the year 2,000, or on my ninetieth birthday, or to celebrate the next coronation. After the however-
manyeth, on the wherever-we've-got-to-th of whichever
month it happens to be.

I've got a bottle of very expensive vintage champagne
that a friend gave me about twelve years ago. I've still got
it because I couldn't think of an occasion sufficiently
definitive to justify ending its venerable existence, and it
looked set to continue undrunk forever. But I'm going to
open it today, without any occasion for it at all, except
to celebrate a small victory of spontaneity over habit, of
reason over obsession, of stopping right here, bang in the
middle of

(1995)